RED MEN
REBORN

A SOCIAL HISTORY OF LIVERPOOL FOOTBALL CLUB

RED MEN
REBORN

From   To
**John   Jürgen
Houlding Klopp**

John Williams

First published by Pitch Publishing, 2022

Pitch Publishing
9 Donnington Park,
85 Birdham Road,
Chichester,
West Sussex,
PO20 7AJ
www.pitchpublishing.co.uk
info@pitchpublishing.co.uk

© 2022, John Williams

A CIP catalogue record is available for this book
from the British Library.

ISBN 978-1-80150-150-7

Typesetting and origination by Pitch Publishing
Printed and bound in Great Britain by TJ Books, Padstow

Contents

Dedication

For Alison F, a Red, and also for Ryan,
a young Kopite lost far too early, but
not forgotten.

For Sheila Spiers, who would have
celebrated the title in 2020 as wildly as
any great Liverpool fan.

We miss you all.

Introduction and Acknowledgements

THIS COMPLETELY revised version of the original *Red Men* took shape during the various lockdowns for the Covid-19 pandemic between 2020 and 2022. I want to thank all those who have been writing, texting and emailing me, waiting patiently for it to be born. I apologise for the delay. But I make no apologies for producing another substantial book: it is needed to tell a big story and I hope readers of the original text will find much that is rewarding in this very different version. The new ownership situation and the current era of the club under Jürgen Klopp, including the recent European and domestic successes, the ending of 30 years of league title drought in 2020 and the amazing campaign of 2021/22 certainly merit a new, up-to-date account of the Liverpool FC journey.

I wrote the original version of *Red Men* soon after the city of Liverpool had proved a spectacularly successful 2008 European Capital of Culture. At that time, this seemed to me to be a fine reason to publish a cultural history of Liverpool Football Club. I wrote then that there was no doubt that football is as much a feature of the cultural heritage and artistic landscape of the city of Liverpool as any film, theatre production, media installation or art exhibition. I still believe that today, perhaps even more so. The year 2010 when *Red Men* was published was also the very moment that Liverpool FC faced an ownership crisis that was resolved only in the High Court. There is a serious discussion to be had here, of course, about the global corporate ownership of great local communal sporting institutions, which I try briefly to address later in this book. The Liverpool club survived in 2010 and has since prospered in the hands of Fenway Sports Group (FSG) and its coach Jürgen Klopp.

However, in 2020, at the very moment that Liverpool FC were in sight of their first league title for 30 years, the entire world was engulfed in crisis as Covid-19 swept around the globe, ravaging families and neighbourhoods and closing down schools, stores, sports venues and football leagues. It even raised questions about if, and when, any of us might be able to attend a professional match again. Football eventually did return, of course, as it had done after two world wars. But initially it came back neutered, without fans. How its future might look then, nobody yet quite knew.

That Liverpool FC in 2022 under Jürgen Klopp are back among the game's elite once more, there is no question. In fact, it is of little surprise that so many commentators today talk about Klopp in the same way they once discussed the great Scottish manager at Anfield, Bill Shankly. Shanks took over an ailing Liverpool in December 1959, languishing in the Second Division of the Football League. Within five years he had revamped the whole idea of what a football manager can and should be in a city such as Liverpool. Shankly won league titles, European honours and the club's first FA Cup, in 1965, after 73 years of longing. He became a much-loved national public figure. Jürgen Klopp inherited a club in mid-table in the top flight and 25 years from its last English league title. In fewer than five years *he* had brought home the Champions League trophy, the FIFA World Club Cup and the Premier League title. He had also changed minds about emotional football management in an era largely dominated by more clinical Continental technocrats. The comparison with Shankly, therefore, is not entirely a specious one.

In this new book, covering mainly the club's post-war history, I look in detail again at Shankly and Paisley, Houllier and Benitez, but also at all four managers who sometimes toiled but also blossomed at Anfield since the original *Red Men* was published more than a decade ago. At that time, Liverpool FC was facing an existential threat, more than it did a possible resurrection. Much of the groundwork for the early part of this book, now covered much more briefly in Chapter One, was undertaken at the Liverpool Central Library by my researcher, David Gould, and I want to thank him again, and also the local staff in Liverpool, for looking after us so well during our many visits there between 2006 and 2008, as well as on my recent return.

My good friends and confidants, the late Andrew Ward, Stephen Hopkins, Neil Carter, Chris Gladman, Phil Breen, Riaz Rivat, Sylvia Williams and Alec McAulay, all read early versions of some of these chapters and offered useful comments and scholarly support. Riaz was trying to get the best out of Liverpool FC's Equality and Diversity Fan Forum. He deserves our support. We all look forward to seeing one day on stage Phil Breen's much-delayed play about the unimpeachable Bill Shankly. I also want to repeat here my thanks to the historian Stephen Done at Liverpool FC for offering many priceless correctives and pieces of sound guidance and advice on the early pre-Shankly period. For *Red Men*, Stephen allowed me to look at the surviving official Liverpool FC Minute Books (1914–1956), for which I remain hugely grateful.

Over the past ten years or so, countless websites and excellent fan podcasts have begun to challenge some published sources. Most recently, *The Anfield Wrap* podcasts have been provocative, informative and hugely enjoyable. Arnie Balderursson and Gudmundor Magnusson have done a great job of writing and data collection in *Liverpool: The Complete Record*. Vital, too, is the website lfchistory.net for providing important historical information about the club's past fixtures, journalistic reflections and Liverpool's past players and managers. Finally, John Belchem's edited collection of Liverpool life, *Liverpool 800: Culture, Character and History*, gave me plenty of general material to contemplate on history, culture and social change in the city.

After 1990 the Reds came close a few times to winning the league title again: 2002, 2009 and, of course, 2014. But I have had both to endure and enjoy the 5,000/1 triumph of so-called no-hopers Leicester City as they took the Premier League crown in 2016 in the most unexpected fashion. My stepdaughter Zelda and stepson Seb have always kept the Liverpool faith, joined recently by my youngest granddaughter, Clemency. I have had less success with Millie, Sasha and Esmée. Although I am originally from Bootle and remain an Anfield season ticket holder, I now live in Leicester and my close family today are mainly Leicester City fans, including my wife, Sylvia. My son-in-law Adam, however, is a devoted Coventry City fan. Our family events are infused with talk about the game. Because of Jürgen Klopp's brilliance between 2015 and 2022 and because of the skill and commitment of this latest outstanding crop of Liverpool players that he recruited to win the Premier League title in 2020, at least I can now finally look my wife and all my Leicester-based family squarely in the eye once more. Praise be.

Back in the 1980s, at the high point of Liverpool's successes, it was still difficult to envisage that the club record home crowd of 61,905, for an FA Cup tie versus Wolves in 1952 could ever be challenged. But in June 2021 FSG announced plans for the expansion of the Anfield Road end to bring the envisaged new stadium capacity back to 61,000. It confirmed a new 'golden age' for the English game and for Liverpool FC under Jürgen Klopp. (If only *access* to the stadium could also be improved, we car travellers could truly rejoice.) Finally, in 2021 as this new edition was being written, Liverpool FC's American owners announced themselves to be one of six English clubs set on forming a new European Super League (ESL) outside formal UEFA structures. This hush-hush news was eventually coughed up inexpertly, spreading anger and despair among the club's fans and supporters everywhere. It also raised some age-old questions for English football, about owner-accountability and financial versus sporting values. These debates continue to rage today, as American billionaires, Russian oligarchs and nation states have all acquired some of our historic sporting assets. I try to cover some of the key points in one of the closing chapters.

Inevitably, one wonders what Liverpool FC's past proprietors, including its visionary first owner, John Houlding, would have made of such shenanigans (Houlding may even have supported them). But where else can I begin this 130-year journey than the astonishing 2021/22 season, when Liverpool and Jürgen Klopp chased four trophies to the bitter end, played in all possible matches and appeared in an unprecedented three elite cup finals? It may yet be the greatest in the club's history. In Chapter 2 I briefly introduce you to Houlding's world and to characters and events that preceded Liverpool FC's modern transformation under Bill Shankly. For those interested in the club's early history, this earlier period is covered in much more detail in the original version of *Red Men*.

Finally, as always, I have tried to report on events covered in this book (not always successfully) critically and analytically, as a researcher might, and not simply with a supporter's blue-eyed gaze, although I was present as a fan at many of the major matches reported on here since 1977. My readers will review my judgement and indeed on how I may have further reflected on some of the positions I took in the first version of *Red Men*. Interpretations of history are moveable feasts. Needless to say, all the errors in the text – although only some of the insights – remain mine, and mine alone.

John Williams, June 2022

Chapter 1

The Impossible Quadruple

The extraordinary 2021/22 season
Liverpool's owners FSG are blessed with a boss
who loves his players and is reluctant to spend big
money. Jürgen Klopp also discovers the domestic
cup competitions at last but injuries and doubt
are never too far away. A familiar face turns
up across Stanley Park in 2021, although he is
not universally welcomed. A record win at Old
Trafford precedes a canter at Goodison and,
generally, there are goals galore, even if Liverpool's
game management sometimes falls short. The
Africa Cup of Nations (AFCON) proves no
problem and Wembley calls – three times. By the
middle of May 2022, Liverpool are still active in
all four competitions entered and face an old foe in
the Champions League final in Paris. What's not
to love?

'There is only one heroism in the world: to see
the world as it is, and to love it.'

Romain Rolland

True love's ways

After the fiasco of Liverpool owners FSG's involvement in the ESL's pre-emptive 'launch' in April 2021, matters of politics and football ownership – and much worse – would soon return to haunt us all in 2022. But there were also rather more rewarding things for Liverpool supporters to enjoy. The arrival of a superior *fussball* trainer from Germany in 2015 had not only promised to save the club from a playing crisis, but also from the moral sewer. He was not the club's American owners; Jürgen Klopp was nothing like them, in fact. But FSG knew full well Klopp's value to the Liverpool boardroom, not only as a truly great football coach but also as a vital public relations shield when things got difficult. It was a point that regularly shone through in Klopp's expressed public delight with his job and with his players. 'I loved them before, but I love them all over again.' This was a typical outpouring of emotion about his team from a jubilant, spectacles-free, Jürgen Klopp late in 2021, those remarkable new choppers of his gleaming in the Anfield floodlights. Klopp was luxuriating in a very inexperienced Liverpool 3, Leicester City 3 (Liverpool win 5-4 on penalties) result in the League Cup quarter-finals on the evening of 22 December. A very late Taki Minamino equaliser had saved the day. Liverpool would now face Arsenal in the semi-final.

And there was absolutely no artifice here. You can see just how much Klopp (and this Liverpool crowd) is thrilled by the final outcome, a now familiar show of youthful resolve in adversity under the German. He fills the frame with unadulterated joy, a different man from the coach who was so haunted by personal and professional demons as his Premier League champions had spectacularly capsized in empty stadiums in season 2020/21. This is exactly what Klopp likes best, of course; a come-from-behind, underdog victory against stronger (and more expensive) opponents, with Liverpool academy talent at the very heart of it. And what other elite football manager has ever delighted in talking openly about his men in quite this way? Not Paisley or

Kenny, certainly – not even Bill Shankly himself. Absolutely not Rafa, Alex Ferguson or Wenger. Did Brian Clough ever publicly emote like this? I think he once might have said how much he *loved* his favourite winger, John Robertson, but that's about as far as it went. Don Revie? Mourinho or Guardiola? A bit of expressive man love? I don't think so.

Jürgen Klopp obviously enjoys inhabiting the fans' world, because he relishes using fan idioms like this one, about *loving* his team. He still has a child-like fascination with the heroic nature of sport and for the collective passions for the game. In truth, he would rather be a fan than a coach. Soon after the Leicester win, Klopp tweeted: 'If I'd known how special this football club is, and how much we mean to each other, I'd have wanted to be here much earlier. This club is absolutely outstanding.' I ask you, what more can any coach say? And Klopp feels no need, as many other football bosses might, to remind you that he actually *runs* this whole enterprise: analyses every kick and tactical adjustment; recruits and inspires these global stars; gees up and protects the young Anfield wannabes. He is simply happy to be here, to have shared in this occasion and in other Liverpool triumphs with these players and these people, in this city and in this stadium. Even in a cup competition that he really has no great love for, Jürgen Klopp takes great care to mention in his post-match Leicester interviews every single young performer who has contributed something to this latest Liverpool memory. It is as if these players are his own sons – which, in many respects, they really are.

Klopp understands that the business side of football is necessary but, like us, he sees it mainly as an infringing blight on the sporting landscape. He visibly hated the ESL saga of 2021 and his club's role in it, but he also understands the importance of finishing in the Champions League spots, even when all seemed lost in 2021. Klopp has no love of spending large dollops of cash on established players, unless he has already raised the means elsewhere. FSG are routinely in his ear on this matter. Having just bought up the Pittsburgh Penguins ice hockey franchise, the value of the FSG empire late in 2021 had moved close to £8bn, more than one-third of which was now tied up in Liverpool Football Club. The Americans appreciated that Klopp had no time for high-priced celebrity stars, walking egos who might disrupt pay grades and profit, and poison the positive atmosphere in Liverpool training sessions and the dressing room. Even modest Brighton (and many other clubs) had spent more in net terms on transfer fees than Liverpool had in the past five seasons. In fact, Klopp enjoyed publicly chiding those journalists who insist at press conferences on asking searching questions about his relative lack of transfer activity. 'Who do *you* think I should buy?' he liked to retort. 'Who is better than what we already have?' Klopp welcomed, above all, the challenge of making stability, teamwork and collective resolve trump individualism and economic power. He and his staff have no interest in buying success. 'We have a good feeling here. We know what we have.' (His assistant Pep Lijnders often shouts *'Together!'* as the Liverpool players run on to the field.)

So, while many of his close rivals were busy spending heavily in 2021, Jürgen Klopp was focused on signing up Virgil van Dijk, Alisson Becker, Jordan Henderson, Andy Robertson, Fabinho and Trent Alexander-Arnold on contract extensions. Bobby Firmino, Sadio Mané, Mo Salah and a few others would require more work. Keep members of the core group tight was the message. The only new arrival at Anfield in the summer of 2021 was Ibrahima Konaté, an inexperienced but towering 22-year-old centre-back from RB Leipzig, for £36m. Here was another development project for the manager and his staff – and the new man needed some work.

Okay, unlike us fans, Jürgen Klopp could quite easily jump ship in a couple of years, so planning for the longer term by building up our talent stock may not exactly be the first thing on his mind. Why should he care? Instead, Klopp was twinkling in August 2021 about holding on to what he already had and the future promise of a kid, Harvey Elliott, who had barely played top-level football at all (he was soon a long-term injury absentee, kicked and damaged at Leeds). When asked if he expected talismanic striker Divock Origi to leave Anfield in the August transfer window, Klopp replied, smiling: '100 per cent!' In fact, Divock stayed, some said like a horse stuck on an escalator. But Origi had plenty of credit in the club's collective memory bank and he wanted to remain in this house, to share the same space, breathe the same air, as Jürgen Klopp (he would even score some crucial goals in the new campaign).

The Premier League outspent all of its European league rivals tenfold on transfers in the first post-Covid transfer window in the summer of 2021, but not Klopp or Liverpool FC. Not even with the AFCON championships due in Cameroon in January 2022, taking Salah, Mané and Keïta out of the club equation, mid-season. 'We hold our ground' was Klopp's message. This was also a risk, of course, relying on a smallish, ageing squad, some marginal subs and a largely untried group of academy kids. But the injured would soon be returning and the Liverpool manager had earned both our trust and affection, so his judgement was worth fans' support. After all, a bunch of reserves had seen off Leicester City's first team in the League Cup. At least until things started to go badly wrong, we believed in all of this – and in him.

Watching the defectives

A white stag is found wandering the mean streets of Bootle as the new football season kicks off. Naturally, the Merseyside police shoot it dead, no questions asked. Was this some sort of veiled warning? Payback perhaps for England's failings in the Euros in the summer of 2021 and the ugly racism that followed? Not for Jürgen Klopp. His sense of certainty and comfort in his own skin at Liverpool eclipsed England's problems and the troubled managerial situation at both of Liverpool's historic local rivals, Manchester United and Everton. For a few quid, a grifter sits outside Old Trafford today, happily photographing fans sitting alongside full-size replicas of the FA Cup, the Premier League and Champions League trophies. These tourists long for 1999 again, now only a distant dream. In 2021 their club is unsure whether Ronaldo's late goals or Pogba's occasional brilliance make up for this couple's gross lack of industry and general negative effect on the United coffers, match shape and team ethic. United manager Ole Gunnar Solskjaer is a nice guy but he is a coach little acquainted with the tactics board; a man hungrily waving a fork in a world full of soup. So, Liverpool's visit to Trafford Towers in late October promises possible early season reward. Which somewhat understates matters, because by half-time, in a packed and largely mournful tomb of a crumbling stadium, Liverpool are four goals to the good. The Manchester 'faithful' are already trudging to the exits, as if on an unannounced mass fire drill. United seem stuck between press and no-press, with their full-backs all at sea, Fred on no-talking terms with the ball, and Bruno Fernandes and Ronaldo beseeching the gods for help. Keïta, Trent and Mo all have unfettered access to United's chaotic left side. After just 50 minutes Salah has already claimed a hat-trick for 5-0, before a frazzled Paul Pogba is early bath-bound for an assault on Naby Lad. All of which leaves half-an-hour for Liverpool to play keep-ball against ten men, classily choosing humiliation over total annihilation. Klopp calls it an 'insane' result, one widely reported as if a national tragedy. It is also a record home defeat in this fixture, a quite glorious day destined to be recorded for posterity in song (and possibly expressive dance) in the diocese of Liverpool 4.

Across Stanley Park, meanwhile, at the People's Blue Republic, turmoil is the usual order of the day. Boutique Italian manager Carlo Ancelotti has decided that a spell back in the Spanish sun at Real Madrid is a much better option than eating bacon butties in the rain on County Road and coaching Tom Davies and his pals. Who could blame him? Against all good sense and decorum, it is Rafa Benitez who has been chosen to become the first manager to preside at *both* Merseyside clubs since William Barclay briefly did so way back in 1892. Naturally, not all Evertonians are happy with this outcome. With a weak squad, an ambitious owner, frustrated supporters and a grand new stadium planned for the Mersey dockside, here was a football job filled with both promise and jeopardy in almost equal measure. Seasoned Liverpool fans know enough about respecting Rafa to be assured that cold-eyed professionalism, rather than emotion or loyalty, always dictates his employment preferences and indeed his managerial style. What would Rafa have made of the reluctant Ray Kennedy as a prospective midfielder, for example? Could he have nurtured a late developer such as Roger Hunt to World Cup greatness and to become Elvis Costello's all-time Liverpool FC hero? Good questions.

Sir Roger has passed away, aged 83; Ray will soon follow at just 70, a double-winner at Arsenal and a goalscoring midfield glider and enforcer under Paisley from the mid-1970s. Both men were quality members of great Liverpool teams. Kennedy's physicality and languid movement in training reminded Bill Shankly of the boxer Rocky Marciano; Ray and Jimmy Case became chief dressing room pranksters under Paisley. For most of his life, Kennedy lived with the degenerative Parkinson's disease and later had to auction his medals and England caps to fund his own care. Sir Roger moved from World Cup hero back to his successful family haulage business on retirement, but even his heroic England team-mate Geoff Hurst ended up on the dole in the 1980s. Memories of these great Liverpool servants live on. Hunt got the late winner in a tight Anfield derby back in 1967 and ten years later Ray scored in the 3-0 FA Cup semi-final replay win against Everton, so both would have enjoyed this latest league encounter with the Blues under the Goodison lights in early December 2021. Rafa Benitez, not so much.

Following the mad public address sirens that traditionally start proceedings here, comes a brutal 4-1 neighbour's drubbing of a hapless Everton. The very first approving 'Rafa' chants heard at Goodison during this campaign actually come from the carnival that is soon aflame among the 2,902 Reds packed into the ancient Bullens Road stand. The Blue reply? *'Murderers!'*

Evertonians are not bad people, it is just that even in our low times we have had some glory and they have had precisely nothing. Which means self-loathing and some real hatred is on show tonight, on an evening punctuated by Liverpool excellence, missiles from the crowd, pitch invaders and a generally decadent sense of decay, anger and mutiny. A once great institution has gone to seed. As at Old Trafford, Mo Salah has his goals and with ten minutes left the home areas are near-deserted. The hosts on *Toffee TV* later look as if they are living a full-on mental breakdown in real time, describing their beloved Everton as 'a ramshackle mix of garbage, a rubbish football club' (don't hold back, guys). Jürgen Klopp later reflects with the press on the occasion, about learning to succeed in derby matches and about playing angry, but in a football way:

> PRESS: Why was this game such an important step up?
>
> JK: Look, the two derbies for us, against Everton and United, are big games. And you have to learn to keep yourself calm and together if you want to play your best football. I told the boys when I looked back at the derbies at Goodison there was not one game when I said, 'Wow, that was a great game, nearly perfect.' I wanted us today to be really mature and, yes, very aggressive, but in a football way. Angry as well, but in a football way. You can't counter-press without a bit of anger and a bit of greed. But there are moments when you just have to move and pass the ball, and for that you need a different mindset. That's what we had tonight.

The very presence and assurance of Jürgen Klopp at Anfield has helped prolong these calamities, of course, but even he finds it difficult to make reason out of the total mess and the toxic atmosphere across the park and the fact that his team has now ruined *both* United and Everton away from home within a matter of weeks. Surely, no Liverpool manager had ever completed this double in quite this extravagant way before? Both Solskjaer and Benitez would be gone in a matter of weeks, another first.

Europe calling – for Virgil and Trent

After a decent enough start in the Premier League, being drawn in the 'group of death' in the Champions League meant that Atlético Madrid, Inter Milan and FC Porto all lay in wait for Liverpool. Klopp smiles wryly; he already knows a key question in this campaign will be about the fitness of Virgil van Dijk. Is VVD the same imperious defender of 2018–2020, a man bored and disdainful of all opponents and totally secure? Or is this a reduced, post-injury, version of the Dutchman, a defender now playing too high and quietly afraid? Virgil himself seemed uncertain, not unreasonably asking for more time to get back to his maximum level. 'I'm not a robot,' he says, helpfully. A late developer, Van Dijk sees his delayed route to his summit role under Klopp as a 'perfect' journey: raised in Breda by a Dutch father and a Surinamese mother; rejected at the Willem II club while dishwashing twice a week; initially struggling at FC Groningen, despite cycling to work; acclimatising to Britain at Celtic Park with an added rehearsal in the Champions League; stepping up to a regular Premier League slot at Southampton under a demanding but compassionate Ronald Koeman; and then on to become the world's greatest central-defender at Liverpool FC under this Svengali, Klopp. Van Dijk had found his people and his purpose – his destiny. His manager was also willing to wait and pay a premium for Virgil because Klopp knew what he was getting. And Van Dijk's early assurance had allowed Liverpool to play what was effectively a front-foot 2-5-3 formation at home, routinely compressing space while overwhelming the opposition down the flanks. Right now, even if Virgil lacks the absolute certainty of his pomp, the ecosystem that is the Liverpool squad benefits from his calm squeezing of the game and his organisation of a near suicidally high defensive line. His serenity, pace and talent – and the new judgement lines of the video assistant referee (VAR) – all allow Klopp's men to live right on the edge of chaos.

A wild Champions League night in Madrid in October 2021 offers more clues about VVD's rehab. After 13 minutes Liverpool are already two goals to the good against Atlético, sailing home. Except this is Simeone's place of worship; absolutely nothing is given away here. Even before half-time it is 2-2, Naby Keïta defensively culpable but with Virgil, himself, seemingly ill at ease against Antoine Griezmann's movement and pace. Atlético 's second goal involves a simple right to left drift and reverse shot by the Frenchman, a move that the old VVD would lazily have countered without thinking. But here he seems unaware, on the half-turn, hesitant and lost. Worse, the Wanda Metropolitano is now rocking. Only Griezmann's second-half red card and Mario Hermoso's foolish off-the-ball lunge on Jota for a saving penalty, see Liverpool home. But not before some collective howling at the moon and general shithousery has demanded home redress. It is denied here by some unusually ballsy refereeing and Alisson Becker's heroics. By the end, Mo Salah has his by now statutory two goals and the Reds have their eighth successive three-goal away haul in all comps. Nine points are already banked in the *groupe de décè* vault (Klopp will end up with a record full house of 18). Mo Salah is on a scoring mission, a man with the grimiest of Cairo accents, the full Egyptian Robbie Fowler. A smiling Liverpool manager later calls this anarchic victory in Madrid 'three dirty points'. He enjoys a winning scrap. But he also knows that we may still need to talk about Virgil.

Without breaking the bank, in five years Klopp had developed a Liverpool squad filled with experienced world-class performers, but the German has a special soft spot for high-achieving local products, those kids he has watched, nurtured and honed into the Liverpool first team. His aspirant sons. For sheer god-gifted talent, every red shirt past and present is now routinely challenged by a young Scouser who was taunting Atlético. Trent Alexander-Arnold has been a Liverpool FC footballer from six years of age.

When he was four, Trent turned up to his local football hub and cried every weekend because the coach said he was too young to train. He did the drills at home instead; he was already driven. Like his exceptional full-back partner Andrew Robertson, Trent is a converted winger, a man given forward licence by Klopp mainly because of VVD's absolute security behind. I got my first close-up when Trent was just 18, playing for Liverpool's Under-23s on a breezy Monday afternoon in April 2017 at Holmes Park in the leafy Leicestershire countryside. Only a few hundred locals were present to see Joe Gomez, Curtis Jones, Harry Wilson, Neco Williams and others, but it was Trent who glowed. He had played a handful of first-team matches by then and already had the look of a classy, distracted slacker, a man waiting impatiently for his day. Just over three years later Trent had played in two Champions League finals, won one World Club Cup and a Premier League title, had played for his country, had his own street mural and was an acknowledged role model for Liverpool's black community and every snot-splashed kid in the red half of the city. (He had also taken the most famous corner kick in the history of world football.) From rural parkland to the very top of the pile in just three seasons. You might say Trent had arrived.

In early November 2021, facing Atlético in the group stage return fixture, it is Trent who kills the contest, delivering two daggers from Liverpool's right flank, first for Jota and then for Sadio Mané to drive home. Now sporting a jaunty Bob Marley mop, Trent looks so relaxed, one journalist remarks, that you half expect to see a surfboard tucked under his arm. He oozes calmness and class, a young man thriving under his German guide and the on-field tutelage of Van Dijk. He is a boy who, with his Anfield coaches, has uniquely reinvented the game at the very highest level, wearing a number 66 shirt and often dictating matters from the defensive right side. No kid in the city wanted to play right-back before this revelation – now they all do. His assist figures are scary. The young Scouser is even investing in a project to do more to help those young players rejected by clubs. In short, he is the complete package. But, right now, Klopp and his staff will need to scout and sign players from the city and further afield without the input of Michael Edwards, the much-praised recruitment and analytics guru, who is leaving Anfield after ten largely successful years. Edwards refuses to say who his favourite Reds signing has been in that time but concedes that his dog is called Bobby. Don't leave us hanging there, Michael.

Day-trippers, yeah

'When you are younger you manage with less baggage. You nearly don't give a fuck.' Wise words from David Moyes, talking freely late in 2021 as the returned and experienced boss at West Ham United. The Hammers under Moyes have actually found their feet again, even beginning to love the gauche London Stadium. They also have a talented first-team squad made up of brutal giants. So, West Ham 3, Liverpool 2 in the Premier League on 7 November is always a possibility if VAR is against you, attitudes are wrong and corners are defended as poorly as they are here by Alisson Becker and his mates. It is a first Liverpool loss in 26 matches but the manner of it is concerning. It even means that ambitious West Ham climb above Liverpool to third in the table. Alisson insists that Klopp recruits the Brazilian Claudio Taffarel to aid with Liverpool goalkeeper coaching. Let's hope the new man has an A* grade in dealing with crosses under pressure. We need him.

This defeat at West Ham is probably more of an unfortunate inconvenience than a full-on disaster for some people watching from the front sections of Kop blocks 106 and 107 at Anfield. It is here where many Liverpool day-trippers gather. They group fortnightly and anew in excited animation behind the official photographers and some of those fantastic Kop flag bearers ('Never Trust a Tory' has just arrived), and also the Kopite wheelchair warriors, who have served their time but now have to endure home matches from bunker level in the wind and rain, often under plastic sheets. One of Liverpool's deaf stewards, Steve, works these sections; he is brilliantly efficient with simple sign language and he always has a knowing smile. This is precisely the spot where many Kop-end Liverpool scorers end up celebrating, where diversity rules, merchandise bags overflow and half-and-half scarves appear. It is also where mobile phone cameras are at full pelt for selfies and those 'I was there for one day' precious memories of Anfield. It is all positivity and matchday spend, greedily banked by the club.

Drifting down pre-match from my own block 207 in mid-November, a young Glaswegian guy asks me to take his picture as the Liverpool squad warms up in front of us. As usual, Jürgen Klopp is carefully studying our opponents' pre-match routines from the centre spot. What can I say? I take the Scot's phone. Just yards from us, recent Liverpool 'legend' Stewart Downing is being interviewed pitchside for LFCTV. The very moderate Downing was actually in the last Reds XI to lose at home to today's opponents, Arsenal, back in 2012 under early Brendan Rodgers. This current Arsenal team is unbeaten in ten and a symphony commemorating the Gunners' title win at Anfield in 1989 is currently performing at the Barbican in London. These are all bad omens, of course. But recently the Londoners have hated it here, regularly taking a hiding. And so it unfolds today, another 4-0 surrender in front of the perpetually standing Kop. (Any chance of the occasional sit down, people? My legs ache.) As usual, Trent and Mo torture our visitors on the Liverpool right flank, complementing the intense counter-pressing led inside today by the Ox, Thiago and Mané. Diogo Jota makes hay again as Arsenal are swamped. Even Taki Minamino gets on the scoresheet as a late sub, joyfully mobbed by his pals right in front of Kop 106 and 107. The emotional reaction to this otherwise meaningless fourth goal shows just how much the Japanese is loved by his team-mates, by day-trippers, by Jürgen Klopp and by the entire LFC coaching staff, although this alone will not get him into the Liverpool first team.

By early December 2021, after a last-gasp Divock Origi winner at Wolves, Klopp's Liverpool had scored more league goals

(43) than any club in the top five European leagues. And yet, and yet, they are still looking up the table at Manchester City, with Chelsea lurking nearby. Each of these rivals had already stolen points from Anfield. Careless draws with Brighton and Brentford have caused Liverpool further damage. This season is set up for a grand struggle, for sure.

Covid in the house

Also in December a new super-infectious Covid variant, Omicron, had begun stalking Premier League and European fixtures. This is not season 2020/21 but matches are postponed and Bayern are already playing in an empty stadium in Munich. What carnage lies ahead in England? Here's the answer: Curtis Jones, Virgil and Fabinho all test positive. Alisson, Firmino, Matip and Trent will soon follow. Even Klopp and Pep Lijnders will eventually succumb. Call the health police! Stop the clocks! Jürgen is commended by journalists for *naming* the Liverpool players in the first infection round, and the German writes a strong and responsible pro-vaccination message in his match programme notes about 'following the experts'. But perhaps, despite his leadership, it is already too late. Are all of our infected men even double-jabbed? (False positives are rumoured.) Players in England are reportedly well behind the vaccination rates for footballers in Spain, Germany and Italy. Fans fare little better: few people in the Kop concourses tonight are wearing masks, even though they have been explicitly instructed to do so. We are not yet out of these Covid woods, not by a long way.

Our opponents tonight (16 December) are Arab-owned Newcastle United, who five years from now, it is said, will be up there in the European places, perhaps even contesting the title itself. Enough Saudi cash can collapse time. But here they are the usual pallid relegation fodder under new man Eddie Howe, and a depleted Liverpool do just about enough to scramble home. Trent hammers in a late one from distance to wake us Kopites up and confirm a 3-1 Thursday night win. (Let's be honest, there is nothing he can't do.) The club's hierarchy also announces today the historic formation of its new Supporters Board in the wake of publication of the national *Fan-Led Review of Football Governance* following the ESL debacle. The report calls for more supporter involvement and an independent regulator to ensure club licensing for greater financial sustainability. Good luck with that. But the *Spirit of Shankly* guys are all over this 'new direction' at Liverpool FC, so it could even get interesting soon. Meanwhile, we walk home past the giant girders sprouting up behind the Anfield Road stand for the latest ground extension. The industrialisation of elite football continues apace, with or without fans or its local communities.

Already well into his annual Christmas address to journalists about English football's unacceptably intense winter fixture congestion, for Jürgen Klopp, Spurs 2, Liverpool 2 in late-December 2021 is both a blast and a chaotic piece of sporting gibberish. Covid and other illness issues mean that Van Dijk is again missing and James Milner, the youthful Tyler Morton, and Naby Keïta are set up in a Frankenstein-like Liverpool midfield. This strange combination is never fully balanced nor in control in a high-paced, far-too-open contest. Morton is physically lost and Keïta is absolutely no help at all in this department. Milner toils; not even he can see off time. Klopp's famous 'rhythm' is sorely lacking here and Antonio Conte has already made a managerial impact at Spurs, filling the locals with both energy and belief. Andy Robertson, somehow, ends up with an assist, a goal and a red card. Later, Jürgen Klopp is justifiably incandescent about yet another dire refereeing/VAR performance; even Alan Shearer later on *Match of the Day* digs these guys out. A Covid postponement of the Anfield Boxing Day fixture with Leeds is soon secured but, with AFCON now looming, a hugely depressing Leicester City 1, Liverpool 0 post-Christmas let-down (the local idiots in absurd 'Feed the Scousers' form), follows on 28 December. Mo misses a penalty (we love Mo but I can tell you that all of us in the away end are secretly thinking: so near and yet so shit).

By now Manchester City are flying, eight points clear at the top, so winning at second-placed Chelsea in early January 2022 seems non-negotiable to sustain Liverpool's wilting 2021/22 title credentials. Covid-case Jürgen Klopp will be absent from the Bridge. Lucky man.

At 2-0 to the good in the first half hour (Mané and Salah), all seems perfectly scripted at Chelsea but, once again, the visitors are pulled back by half-time. A bad habit is forming. (Kovačić scores a goal here that he will never repeat in 100 years of trying.) Game management and the sort of defensive resilience that was second nature back in 2019/20 is now absent. Pep Lijnders highlights in TV interviews later what a 'thoroughly entertaining' 2-2 Premier League armchair spectacle this has been, as if this matters to us one iota. The current 11-point lead Guardiola and his petrodollar outfit has now established over skittish Liverpool (two points from three festive matches, three from four London visits) already seems improbable to breach. More salt in Liverpool wounds, City announce record revenues of £558m (up 17 per cent) for the Covid season, the highest in Europe. Their desert owners can do financial magic it seems. Even Klopp appears resigned, calling his rivals' current form 'ridiculous'. He knows that it may well take another 90-plus point haul to maintain this battle – and that his men may still end up short. It has not always been this hyper-competitive in the Premier League era; back in 1997 that coaching genius Alex Ferguson won the title for United with a frankly absurd 75 points. 'It's quite funny,' says Klopp, poking derision only at himself. 'I said it is impossible for anyone to play on both 26 and 28 of December, and then we lose to a team [Leicester] who played on both days!' Actually, it is not that funny at all. But it *is* typical Jürgen Klopp.

Thirty years ago, today

'Serbian cable-TV tycoon snaps up Southampton FC from Chinese in £100m deal.' Just another headline day in the 30th anniversary year of the global English Premier League. Closer to home, Covid, injuries and our men away in Africa on AFCON duty all mean that Jürgen Klopp and his staff face a serious striker deficit, probably for over a month. In fact, Liverpool may not even have fixtures at all for a while because, with both senior coaches now in Covid isolation and the Liverpool AXA training base closed, Carol the Liverpool tea lady may soon have to manage the Reds' first team. We did field the kids in the League Cup, remember, when Liverpool needed to, back in 2019. It may come to that again. As a result, League Cup semi-final first leg away action against Arsenal is deferred. Is there no end to this contagion – or to elite football's manipulation of it? And then this happened:

> *13 January 2022: rearranged League Cup semi-final first leg: Liverpool 0, ten-man Arsenal 0. (I really don't want to talk about it; you can't make me.)*
>
> *20 January 2022: League Cup semi-final second leg: Arsenal 0, Liverpool 2. (Arsenal had to come out to play and, when they did, Thiago, Trent and Jota (2) nailed them.)*

Already in a major domestic final and rising majestically out of this fog of illness and uncertainty, in the first six weeks of 2022 Jürgen Klopp's record after a flood of league and domestic cup fixtures, played mainly without our star Africans as starters, ends up reading: played seven, won six, drew one. This alchemy means that, even lacking his top forwards, the German has taken Liverpool to a League Cup Final (against Chelsea), progressed to the FA Cup fifth round (via Shrewsbury Town and Cardiff City) and, in second place, has even snatched back some ground on Manchester City in the Premier League. Diogo Jota stands at 14 Premier League goals, second nationally only to the indefatigable Mo. Goals against Liverpool have also started to dry up, as Virgil has continued to find his feet alongside the outstanding Joël Matip. It has not always been pretty but Klopp and his men have defied logic and are still alive in all four competitions entered.

Even the darkest ESL days for FSG of April 2021 might yet be forgiven – by some. How short fan memories can become when the game is this entrancing. Moreover, in a winter transfer window in which desperate Premier League outfits are seen to trash £300m on players on ridiculous salaries who have already failed elsewhere, Jürgen Klopp secures, instead, the wondrous Colombian winger, Luis Díaz from FC Porto, a fresh wind to add attacking pace and aggressive trickery to Liverpool's left side. With Harvey Elliott returning from injury at last, suddenly what felt like a depleted and ageing Liverpool squad has a youth injection and some very viable bench options. The impressive Díaz grew up in the impoverished Wayuu tribe of indigenous peoples in the small village of Barrancas (let me tell you a story of a poor boy, etc.). His arrival means new dynamism and hope abounds, just as a season of all possibilities is spreading before us and the San Siro is calling for a showdown with Inter Milan in the Champions League first leg round of the last-16. The ghost of Bill Shankly from 1965 still haunts these Italian parts.

Four routes to heaven – or hell

What exactly did Jürgen Klopp (and all of us) learn from Inter Milan 0, Liverpool 2? That this sort of top-end contest was a little too early, even for the precocious returning Harvey Elliott as a starter; that you can change the flow of a match, as Klopp did here, by using all five subs strategically, *if* you have a strong enough squad; that Ibrahima Konaté could yet prove to be the long-term answer to Liverpool's future defensive needs; that VVD is close to finding his very best form again; that Luis Díaz will soon be one of Liverpool's first-choice forward options; that attacking set pieces continue to be our friend; and that Klopp's team (secure at the back and two attempts on target, two goals) will rightfully be feared by every other club left in Europe.

A come-from-behind, heavily rotated 3-1 league home win against Norwich City on 19 February has Kop patrons around us in disproportionately mad delight at a Mo Salah special and a first Anfield goal for Luis Díaz, celebrated (of course) in front of Kop 106. We later get three fist-pumps from our jubilant coach. Why the carnival celebration for a scruffy win against these relegation certainties? Perhaps because we (or Jürgen) somehow anticipated that two hours later, as we are driving home, there will be news of unassailable Manchester City 2, Spurs 3, with Harry Kane reportedly pretty much unplayable at the Etihad. This minor earthquake means that a midweek Anfield win against struggling Leeds will further chisel the deficit at the top to a very plausible three points, when the gap had once been 14. All this becomes the focal point for some pre-Leeds, early evening red-hot soccer chat over a Shankly pie, mash and gravy in the marvellous community-run Homebaked Bakery behind the Kop on Oakfield Road, a regular pre-match haunt. It turns out to be great prep for Liverpool 6 (six!), Leeds United 0. Leeds fans may love their top man Bielsa but at this rate their favourites could easily be practising the Argentine's precious full-on philosophy back in the Championship (actually, Bielsa is sacked a few days later). Luis Díaz shines again and Matip and Virgil both score; a record 17 Liverpool players have now netted in all competitions. Klopp doubles his celebratory on-field fist pump action in front of us. Perhaps he really does know something.

Now, are you beginning to think what I am thinking? Because with every tantalising passing week, this Liverpool squad feels as if it could be on the very brink of greatness – or else possibly on the verge of total collapse. Nowhere in the world are people watching quite what we are seeing right here. Certainly not in Ukraine. Because the morning after the Leeds rout we are hit with news that beautiful Kiev (now Kyiv), the city where in 2018 we roamed among friendly locals in the spring afternoon sunshine before our first Champions League Final under Klopp, incredibly is now under Russian military attack. Newspapers carry pictures of local people huddled and sheltering for their lives in the same subway stations we once used to get to a football match. This is so very fucked up. In the least important detail of this criminal invasion, it is announced that the 2022 Champions League Final will now be hosted by Paris and not St Petersburg. The despot Putin has already had his own home World Cup four years ago, of course, courtesy of FIFA. And so the world turns.

27 February 2022: CARABAO (LEAGUE) CUP FINAL – LIVERPOOL 0, CHELSEA 0 (Liverpool win 11-10 on penalties)

I will tell you a secret: we meet up in a bijou Harrow-on-the-Hill restaurant-bar hours before the season's first grand occasion, the Carabao (League) Cup Final. Even theatre director and mad Liverpool fan Phil Breen is here. This is my 23rd major Liverpool final attended. Fellow fan John Spiers has 32. Phil has only one – but impressively it is in Yokohama. These domestic finals are still special, so a pre-match sit-down meal seems right, even for we mortals, the fans. And although this is posh-city, we are only a few short tube station stops away from the madness we know awaits us. Liverpool have not won a domestic cup since 2012 under Kenny but we can still remember what it feels like and the seasonal lift it can provide. Or what defeat can do to morale. For our opponents, the Moscow apologist and Chelsea owner, Roman Abramovich, has been forced rapidly to transfer his 'stewardship' to the club's charitable foundation to avoid losing his billions and inviting other Ukraine-related heat. Not that many Chelsea fans will care for a second today what kind of vile kleptocracy has been funding their dreams since 2003. Over almost 20 years Abramovich has pumped £1.5b into Chelsea to win trophies and he has been completely unaccountable. He never speaks publicly, and it was Abramovich who opened up English football to the stench of shady foreign money and the kind of financial doping that now so dominates the elite game and indeed much of our public life. The Chelsea man will soon be sanctioned by the UK Government as a Putin henchman and Russian undesirable, and he will have to leave Chelsea under licence, its assets frozen, and in debt.

Walking up Wembley Way these days is no longer about navigating a wasteland, as it was back in the 1980s. Today it is like wandering down a Hong Kong thoroughfare, all acid-coloured screen messages, flashy restaurants and regenerated high-rise apartments. But getting access to the national stadium for Liverpool fans is still reassuringly and depressingly old school and English: a disorganised scrum, with scallies adding to the pain by trying (and succeeding) to scam their way in. Wembley's young multicultural security staff look on, afraid and bemused. On the sticky-floored concourses inside, toilet provision may satisfy the National Football League (NFL) fixtures and rock concerts hosted here but it falls far short of what is needed for 30,000 tanked-up visiting football fans. It is a tawdry mess, to be honest. After the ritualistic expressions of support for the Ukraine people on the PA finally quieten, the kick-off is a blessed relief. It is Chelsea's corporate banner wavers, their plastic flags and dire songs about 'always the victims' and Steven Gerrard's mishaps, versus the Anfield anthems and the great organic home-made messages strewn extravagantly across the entire Liverpool end. So now excitement and anxiety can take over for a while from abuse and a general sense of discontent.

We take our seats to learn the bad news that Wembley Stadium now has its own DJ and that a tearful Thiago Alcantara has managed to crock himself in the warm-up (Bill Shankly would sell him instantly), so Naby Keïta starts. As does Caoimhín Kelleher in goal, the Liverpool manager's gift for a talented League Cup regular. Diogo Jota makes the bench. Later, Klopp says that there is still room for sentiment in football and that he is a human being as well as a manager (again, Bob Paisley and many other Liverpool bosses would challenge this kind of sophistry). The Londoners start well but Liverpool soon take over and Chelsea's glovesman, Edouard Mendy, makes an inspired double save from Keïta and then Mané. Luis Díaz is sparkling on Liverpool's left side in a match that is far too open; holding the irrepressible Colombian at bay is like trying to keep smoke behind a door. Mason Mount breaks the Liverpool defensive line from deep between Trent and Joël Matip and misses two clear chances; in fact, three times Chelsea will have the ball in Liverpool's net, all ruled offside. We consider this to be brilliant defensive organisation by VVD, a calculated VAR bonus. Kelleher is also standing up well to the test. Then, Liverpool do manage to 'score' in a dominant second half, a Matip header from a well-worked free kick. But even following mass crowd ecstasy, with all 22 players already lined up for the restart, our VAR man, Darren England, is scanning the tape looking for any possible reason he can find to rule it out. No player or spectator has seen any offence but Stuart Attwell, the Premier League's very worst referee in a highly competitive field, enthusiastically agrees that there has indeed been an infringement, albeit one committed in an entirely different postcode to Matip's header. Another perfectly good goal (and a wild celebration) is lost to football because of desperate officiating and VAR.

So, this has now evolved into possibly the highest quality 0-0 stalemate you will ever see. Multiple substitutions (Henderson and Mané visibly furious, Díaz simply exhausted) and extra time produces no goals. Would these foolish officials even *allow* one? We are into penalties. Mendy in the Chelsea goal has been virtually impassable today but Thomas Tuchel insists, nevertheless, on replacing him with Kepa Arrizabalaga. It is a pre-planned technocrat's gamble against an emotional rival who has already made his key goalkeeping decision. The penalties are played out in front of the foaming uncertainty that is the Liverpool end and we are sited almost directly behind the goal. The woman sitting next to me already has her head in her hands. To be honest, she has been like this for most of extra time, wishing the minutes away. I also feel quite sick right now but here, for the record, is how this psychodrama unfolds.

The 2022 Carabao Cup Final
– Penalty Shoot-Out

Milner: Kepa loiters on the penalty spot like a teenage groupie; referee Attwell pushes him back to his goal. Nerveless, Milly scores wide and low to Kepa's right. Impossible to block.

Alonso scores for Chelsea.

Fabinho: Again, Kepa tries to psyche out the taker, this time madly star-jumping on his line. He dives right. Cool Fab strokes a gentle Panenka down the middle. We collectively gasp.

Lukaku scores for Chelsea.

Virgil: Kepa offers the taker a huge gap to the keeper's left. Virgil scores high on the narrow side, to the keeper's right, then stares down Kepa with 'fuck you' indignation.

Havertz scores for Chelsea.

Trent: Bobbles the ball in hand, looking for a sweet spot. Lashes it just below where Virgil had pierced the net, Kepa helpless once more. Trent points to Kelleher, fist-pumps the crowd.

James scores for Chelsea.

Mo: Attwell again tells Kepa to retreat to his line. Mo whips his kick high to the keeper's left as Kepa dives right. He then laughs dismissively at the Chelsea man.

Jorginho scores for Chelsea.

Jota: Long run-up and, as is his way, simply bangs it hard and low down the middle. Risky perhaps, but Kepa dives right (of course he does).

Rüdiger scores for Chelsea.

Divock: Longish run, hits it low and left of centre. Kepa dives to his right, waggling his feet behind him. Origi looks to the skies with thanks.

Kanté scores for Chelsea.

Robbo: Seems gaunt and unusually nervous. Places it low to the keeper's right, while Kepa has long gone left. Wildly fist-pumps to the crowd, with obvious relief.

Werner scores for Chelsea.

Elliott: Looks even more like the kid he is, small and lonely. Puts it high to Kepa's right, keeper dives left. Harvey grabs for the badge and screams at the Liverpool fans.

Thiago Silva scores for Chelsea.

Konaté: Liverpool fans are now taut with worry. Fast run-up, hits it mid-height to the keeper's left. Kepa gets a hand on it, the single real chance of any save so far.

Chalobah scores for Chelsea.

Kelleher: Last man standing. Smashes it high to Kepa's right side, unstoppably so. Bye-bye; Chelsea keeper dives left. Kelleher does not even celebrate, but takes up his spot.

Kepa *misses* for Chelsea; launches it skywards.

FINAL: 11-10 Liverpool.

Nerves have been shredded. Within days, this faultless Liverpool's penalty roll will attract 5.3 million hits on Instagram. Kepa's Miss Universe girlfriend watches in the stands but even she can offer little comfort. By contrast, Caoimhín Kelleher, Liverpool's Mr Cool from County Cork, has made no shoot-out saves, has barely been close, but he scores the winning kick here. Klopp reveals later that Liverpool have been working with neuroscientists from Germany to build confidence and improve player accuracy from dead-ball situations, including penalties. Small margins. It is a long way indeed from 1984, when we watched in Rome as a reluctant Alan Kennedy closed his eyes and then apologetically chipped the winning European Cup Final kick into the back of Roma's net. Thirty-eight years later and everybody can breathe once more; even the distraught woman sitting next to me thinks it is safe enough at last to look up and smile. How much this matters.

Before us now the entire cavorting Liverpool party goes wild, with Dua Lipa's 'One Kiss' as our anthem. Football and music seem increasingly blended these days. A different dance track booms out as Jordan Henderson and his men finally lift the cup aloft on a balcony sited in outer space way up to our left. On the long climb to the summit a Scouse dad will ask Alisson Becker if his small son Beau can 'geg in' on the celebrations. Sure thing. This lucky Scouse kid, black eye and all, ends up holding the cup with the Liverpool team, being hugged between Klopp and Alisson, a very nice human touch (we can see none of this until later). John Henry is soon seen chatting with Jürgen Klopp on the pitch – about what? In the winning dressing room it is players and staff only for more alcohol-free tomfoolery, yet another major benefit of having a world-class Muslim core to your squad and a further key difference from the drunken post-match chaos of 1984.

Jürgen Klopp, so little acquainted with English finals and the sheer joy that they can bring, admits later that the day compares pretty well to the 2019 Champions League win in Madrid. He also says this is a trophy for the whole club to celebrate: up to a record 34 players have been involved in this ninth Liverpool League Cup-winning campaign, one that has connected the skinny under-18s wannabes and squad marginals to the first-team global stars. Our German coach is actually learning to love the English League Cup. And as the players and the club staff fly home with the trophy, the rest of us can shuffle off at last to join that giant, dishevelled people-snake that now slowly crawls its way up to Wembley Park tube station, en route to celebratory drinks back in Harrow. We are cold, utterly exhausted – wrecked, in fact – but happy. It has, as they say, been a very emotional day.

Paddy 'the Baddy' and 'Meatball' Molly

A run of four consecutive tests in four different competitions had now begun; rotation and adaptability will be Klopp's watchwords. After the drama of the League Cup, the Reds' reserves see off Norwich in the FA Cup at a sedated Anfield and then Liverpool 1, West Ham 0 in the Premier League, let's be honest, is a bit of a trial. Before the match we even manage to get upstairs in the Flattie (The Flatiron pub) and meet up with old friends Steve and Cath, Paul H, Nev, Dave Squibbs, Faith and Tom, JS, and David and his young son Benjamin, who is soon swigging enthusiastically at his dad's beer. Only Phil Breen, Moany Simon and ace LFC scribe Steve K are missing. The Flattie is packed, so Covid is obviously officially over here. Later, from our Kop seats, we can all see the giant inflated cat's head that appears in the main stand lower to greet West Ham's Kurt Zouma. The defender has stupidly kicked a pet moggy and then saw his even more idiotic brother film and post the act on-line. Rather than 'Attack! Attack! Attack!' The Kop is soon singing 'A Cat! A Cat! A Cat!' (we're only human). After Sadio Mané's first-half goal, this contest becomes a chore but Liverpool just about make it home. Stuck in our multi-competition football bubble, Jürgen Klopp can afford only to lose one match in this run – so, of course, he *does* lose it, 1-0 at home to Inter Milan in the Champions League second leg, with Mo Salah busily battering away at Inter's woodwork. Mo's bilious agent has recently sent laughing emojis to the Anfield board in response to its latest contract offer. A Twitter junkie reports that only 14 outfield players in the whole of Europe have played more top-level minutes this season than Mo, although he has not been firing since toiling for a terrible Egypt side at AFCON in January. We *do* need him to stay.

The admirable Norwegian FIFA delegate Ada Hegerberg, gives the FIFA Congress in Doha the heads-up on the appalling treatment of migrant workers and of human rights in World Cup hosts Qatar. She is a lone voice at the top table but more power to her elbow. And after Arsenal 0, Liverpool 2 (Diogo Jota in his pomp) in the Premier League on 16 March brings Liverpool to within a single point of Manchester City, not even Ada, or anyone at Anfield for that matter, is allowed to mention the 'Q' word. But every journalist and every supporter now talk about little else. This is not Qatar, of course, but Quadruple. Even the usually measured talking heads on *The Anfield Wrap* are hypnotised, because old-timers like us have never been quite this close to smelling a possible four-timer. Jürgen Klopp insists that it is 'crazy stuff', 'cannot be done', but nobody listens for once. His men seem mentally up for the challenge and the Liverpool defence around VVD has now sealed itself off against all comers. After the teams are paired in the FA Cup semi-finals but kept apart in the Champions League draw it becomes increasingly clear, too, that everything may yet come down to a series of showdowns against Manchester City in all remaining competitions: between Jürgen and Pep; Mo Salah and Cancelo; Virgil and De Bruyne; Alisson and Ederson. One club left standing. Everything in. True greatness beckons.

And perhaps greatness calls, too, for the UFC lightweight champion and rabid Liverpool fan, Paddy 'the Baddy' Pimplett and his fighting sidekick 'Meatball' Molly McCann. Scouser Paddy reveals that he wanted to urge his fans to sing 'Fuck the Tories!' after his latest win at the O2 in London (would anyone join in?). His choir-boy blonde DIY hairstyle, smiling clean looks and his avowed socialist principles make him the unlikeliest of all cage warriors. He resembles more the manic and vulnerable Jay in TV's *The Inbetweeners* than a ring killer. Paddy wants his next big fight to be staged at Anfield. He will need to stand in line because the Liverpool women's football team is also excelling, nailed on for promotion back into the Women's Super League (WSL) and for elite home field encounters next season. But Liverpool Women face a problem: Chelsea, Manchester City, Manchester United and Arsenal all lie in wait. These rivals are years ahead and much better resourced than we are. Meanwhile, in Spain the sublime FC Barcelona Women attract a world record crowd of over 91,000 for a Champions League match. The women's game has huge commercial potential but exactly how much Liverpool FC wants its women's side to prosper in the city and beyond depends entirely on what our business-headed American owners are willing to invest to help them succeed. No holding of breath is required.

April, come she will

The Liverpool men last faced eight April fixtures in the 2001 treble year. They played nine matches in April 1977 (no defeats) when chasing the league title, FA Cup and European Cup, and a ridiculous *ten* with a painfully small squad in 1965 under Bill Shankly, losing five, when Shanks fielded kids. No Liverpool outfield player has ever played more than the 67 starts made by Alan Hansen, Alan Kennedy and Sammy Lee in the treble season of 1983/84 under Joe Fagan. None ever will. Playing time is now measured by sports scientists in minutes, not matches; VVD has already clocked up a leading 3,450 outfield minutes for Liverpool. He could have ended up with a maximum of 54 club starts this season (although he will have strolled through at least half of these). He actually ends up with 50. After the latest international break, Klopp's men have probably *nine* matches heaving into view in April 2022. The nature of these contests in three different competitions suggests an entirely different kind of test:

April 2 – Watford (H); 5 – Benfica (A); 10 – Man City (A); 13 – Benfica (H); 16 – Man City (FA Cup semi-final, Wembley); 19 – Man United (H); 24 – Everton (H); Champions League semi-final first leg (TBC); 30 – Newcastle United (A).

Jürgen Klopp will undoubtedly blow a gasket (or two) somewhere in the middle of this crazy run. He soon complains, colourfully, that TV companies are effectively 'throwing a stick' between the legs of English clubs in Europe. He will need to decide when to rotate during this period – Watford? Benfica? Everton, perhaps? Newcastle away? Much will depend, of course, on what happens at the Etihad on 10 April. This D-Day meeting in the league will decide a lot. A win for City means that particular argument is lost. If Liverpool win, then who knows? Covid has finally got to me, so I will have to miss Watford. Trent, Díaz and Mané are all left out too. Diogo Jota scores once again.

Jota is a curious player. Technically, he is far from brilliant or graceful, and often he is not that much involved in open play. He can freely give possession away and seldom *passes* the ball into the net. At Molineux earlier in the season, under no pressure he inexplicably blasted his shot from six yards directly at Conor Coady standing on the Wolves goal line! He is a streaky striker, and yet Jota has a great work ethic and scores vital goals, as at Arsenal, and again here, a brilliant run and header from a Joe Gomez cross. 'He spoke it into existence,' says Gomez later, suddenly becoming a philosophy professor. For all his quirks, Jota has been another key Klopp signing. Mo Salah again has a frustrating afternoon, subbed just before a late Fabinho penalty settles this rather disjointed 2-0 win. The Brazilian takes the kick in Mo's absence – and looks better at it. No tectonic change is afoot, but one more league game is down.

SL Benfica is one of the great romantic European club names, twice winners of the European Cup in the early 1960s, but the commodification of football has plunged them down the game's international pecking order in the last 30 years. Today they are a feeder club for the European elite, so reaching the last eight of the Champions League is a major achievement for these 200/1 outsiders. This shows, as Liverpool boss the first leg of this quarter-final at the Estádio da Luz, with Luis Díaz outstanding throughout, sealing what seems like a decisive 3-1 win. Jürgen Klopp will now be able to rest key men for the return leg but he also has some unexpected selection teasers for the crucial Premier League weekend meeting at the Etihad. Surprisingly, he opts for Jota to start rather than the in-form Díaz or Bobby Firmino.

The pundits are now calling **Manchester City 2, Liverpool 2** the English *el clásico*. This moniker is a little lame but Klopp vs Pep is certainly a modern contest to rival Clough vs Paisley, Ferguson vs Wenger, or even Benitez vs Mourinho. Arguably, currently the two best club sides in Europe, these opponents have actually had a beef since 2014 and, right now, it is really only Liverpool under Klopp that prevents City from total domination of English football. Pep's innovation for this latest showdown is to play a much longer ball game, using Bernardo Silva from deep, with the exceptional De Bruyne in the pocket, while getting runners into the channels behind Liverpool's high line. Initially it works – Trent is caught napping by Jesus, and Fabinho seems utterly nonplussed by the chaos around him. That a nervous Liverpool reach half-time only 2-1 down (yet another goal for Jota) is something of a mystery; even Virgil looks edgy. But when Mané equalises seconds after the restart, for a while an away win even seems plausible. But City finish strongly, so a draw is about right in a high-quality contest. Pep remains just ahead of Klopp in league affairs but he knows that he can afford no slips.

Football managers – Klopp even more than most – typically insist that each match must take place on its own terms and deserves our total attention. But with so much at stake right now, this glut of fixtures surely has to be taken more in the round. Liverpool, in front of the Kop against Benfica on Wednesday, 14 April and two goals to the good, for example, is profoundly more inviting than Manchester City's horrible task away to Atlético, with wild skulduggery in the air and only one goal as a cushion (they survive, but only just). With that FA Cup semi-final clash with Pep's men upcoming on Saturday, Klopp seeks to gain maximum circumstantial advantage. Remarkably, little Villareal have dumped out Bayern, so seeing off Benfica means a club currently a distant seventh in La Liga would remain the last barrier to Klopp's progress to a third Champions League Final in five years. The route to Paris now seems invitingly (suspiciously?) tranquil.

The Liverpool coaching team makes an eye-catching seven changes for Benfica at Anfield, their thoughts firmly fixed on City. I am near halfway in the Kemlyn lower (the Kenny Dalglish Stand) for once. From here you can really absorb the physicality and pace of the match, marvel at the technical skills of everyone involved and map the incredible amount of ground covered by Díaz, Jota and Firmino. Watching from distance, players can sometimes seem like automatons or chess pieces. From here, the crowd shouters can even imagine that Joe Gomez and his mates actually hear their inane advice. And, of course, you do get to *sit down* for once among the scrubbed Merseyside middle classes and their kids, even if there is an annoyingly constant flow of up and down as punters deal with their various toilet ailments and the necessary fetching of pies, hotdogs and chips and gravy. You just have to live with it.

The polite collective bow that the Benfica players deliver to their noisy fans before kick-off tonight is symptomatic of what actually becomes a highly entertaining evening, one with little real edge or jeopardy for Liverpool. A dazzling new Kop song for Jürgen Klopp to the tune of the Beatles' 'I Feel Fine' echoes around us as the Reds slip easily into a 3-1 second-half lead (two for Bobby), and 6-2 on aggregate. Even the serenaded Klopp thinks this tie is over, but a VAR-enabled late surge from Benfica to 3-3, actually adds to the air of general satisfaction. Those travelling Benfica supporters can bask in the joy of an honourable draw at the world's most atmospheric football ground. They are probably still singing their anthems right now. For Liverpool, Tsimikas is aggressively impressive at left-back, while Joël Matip is the only outfield player to complete 180-plus minutes here and at the Etihad. What does it all mean, selection-wise, for the FA Cup? Kloppo, we can only assume, has a grand plan.

In Ukraine, the Gagarin Stadium of recent Europa League side FC Desna from Chernihiv, has been bombed to destruction by Putin. The club's playing staff has joined up to fight the Russians. 'We are normal people,' says Desna fan Oleg, 'but our normal lives have been taken away.' (Can this fucked up catastrophe ever really be unfucked?) Two million people have already left Kyiv. For us, 'normality' simply means our precious leader Virgil being wrapped up safely in the Liverpool dugout for Benfica at home, while City's Kevin De Bruyne has crocked an ankle during his club's night of madness in Madrid and is doubtful for Wembley. How little we have to trouble us compared to the lives of our footballing brothers elsewhere. In fact, Guardiola reports 71 separate 'treatments' needed for his players since Atlético – are they all in therapy?

I'm in love with him, and I feel fine

This time we catch the H17 bus from Harrow to Wembley Central to avoid most of the Wembley Park mayhem. It works an unexpected treat. Our match tickets are on the halfway line but high up in Block 552 and among some LFC tourists. The escalators are off, so the step climbing up to the Wembley summit is itself draining enough. Dads and even young sons around us are soon singing the 'Manchester is full of shit' garbage. We are forced to suck it up. Pep has made his own seven changes from the Madrid frontline, with the great De Bruyne only lurking on the bench for emergencies. City seem to have made clear their priorities, even fielding Zack Steffen in goal. They will pay a heavy price. By half-time in the spring sunshine, Liverpool, unimaginably, lead City 3-0: the brilliant Mané has two, including one from a suicidal goal-line dawdle by Steffen, while Konaté claims another scoring header from a Robertson corner. Keïta and Thiago are on easy street. City fight back late on to 3-2 but the victory is never in any real doubt and De Bruyne makes no show. Later, Jürgen will say that the first 45 minutes was Liverpool's best for the season but he knows that Pep (and Simeone) has helped deliver this Liverpool victory into the German's hands. Paris may yet be a very different kind of test.

Before the first-ever international match, in Scotland in 1872, the England players tuned up by smoking pipes and playing keepie-uppies. That would have worked for Liverpool on the evening of Tuesday, 19 April, because Manchester United are being walked, rather than run, under their interim German coach Ralf Rangnick. They have basically dissembled in the league but United still insist on attacking their opponents and not pressing in defence. Big mistake under the lights at Anfield. Thiago Alcantara, with Sadio Mané playing centrally and not far behind the Spaniard in quality, puts on a midfielder's school in destroying United. He gently hushes his opponents, warning that the grown-ups are now in the room. Paul Pogba, once heralded as a £90m future great, has had enough of all this shite after just six minutes, childishly limping away to many fraternal 'fuck offs' from the United throng. It eventually ends up a 4-0 home victory, with Mo Salah back in the goals, and a record 9-0 aggregate Liverpool win against United for the season. Thiago departs before the end with injured shorts (!) to a standing ovation – anything might happen in his universe right now. In post-match interviews the Spaniard later thanks his Liverpool 'strikers', but a smiling Mo gently corrects him: 'It's wingers.' He is right, of course: Klopp often plays three wingers up front these days, and few opponents can cope.

Next up at Anfield, on Sunday, 24 April, are neighbours Everton, the Blues suddenly in the bottom three. Manager Frank Lampard played in *that* cynical double-block Mourinho defensive masterclass at Anfield back in 2014, so he knows plenty about frustrating Liverpool and running down the clock. He tries it again here, a record low 17 per cent possession, with Brazilian midfielder Allan infamously completing just two passes in his 73 minutes on the pitch – both kick-offs. But with Richarlison and Gordon routinely breaking up play by succumbing to snipers' bullets everywhere, and the latter occasionally even evading Trent and troubling Joël Matip with his pace and bravery, for an hour it looks like this tactic could even work. Liverpool lack tempo and width, with Jota struggling on the left side and Keïta and Trent offering little on the right. Klopp turns to his bench, hoping that Origi, Díaz and Henderson can change the match. Of course they can.

You have to say that Evertonians must despise the mysterious, and often absent, Belgian just about as much as Liverpudlians seem to love him. Divock Origi is currently Klopp's sixth-choice forward but he has a peculiar taste for blue blood. 'A legend,' says his smiling coach later. 'Our best finisher, no doubt about it.'

Here, Origi and Mo first work together to set up Andy Robertson for a stooping back-post header. A calmer goalkeeper probably saves it, but Robbo's manic celebrations in front of Kop 106 and the rest of us tells you that he could not care less about Jordan Pickford's own personal psychosis. And then the audacious Luis Díaz terrifies Seamus Coleman before scissor-kicking a Henderson cross back for Divock to head home from under the bar in a way that, somehow, we all knew he would: 2-0. There is only enough time left for a pantomime ball flop from Alisson to satirise Everton's earlier time-wasting, raucously celebrated on the Kop, and for some of our blessed blue brethren to wreck the away end toilets before slithering home, mouthing their Hillsborough abuse. For our home delectation, Dua Lipa pipes up again on the public address, courtesy of George Sephton. Our pre-match Kiev songstress from 2018 has become this season's anthem maker. Journalist Jonathan Liew remarks later that 'Everton tried everything to derail Liverpool here, except play football.' About right.

Life After Life

Villarreal CF are the story of this season's Champions League, the romantic semi-final outlier in a sport increasingly dominated by dodgy nation states and suspect billionaire owners. 'El Submarino Amarillo' (Yellow Submarine) are a club locally funded by a ceramics manufacturer and based in a small town about an hour up the coast from Valencia. The press boys like the story that its entire population comfortably fits into Anfield. The club only gained promotion to La Liga as recently as 1998 but it is coached today by that wily European operator, Unai Emre, a man we know all too well from Basle in 2016. So, nothing will be taken for granted; Jürgen said so. But this turns out to be really a gentle stroll of a contest. Our guests come only to defend and, when Liverpool eventually take a 2-0 lead early in the second half, I swear Klopp is already thinking ahead to Liverpool's early Saturday Premier League appointment at Newcastle United. Villarreal barely get out of their own half, constantly hounded in possession by Fabinho and passed to a near standstill by Thiago. Any child from the Kop could have taken Alisson's place in the Liverpool goal, so underemployed is the Brazilian. So, this meeting has none of the verve of the Roma Champions League semi-final first leg of 2018, or the sheer joyful wildness of Barcelona in the second in 2019, but we will take it every time. Nothing to see here. Move on. A possible eight matches left.

The BBC is currently showing a dramatisation of Kate Atkinson's novel *Life After Life*. In it, a girl keeps on dying but is reborn to live again and again. Which sounds rather like Villarreal 2, Liverpool 3 in the second leg, because no team expires quite so emphatically as Liverpool do in the first half in Spain, only to revive so completely for another life in the second. At 2-0 down at half-time, Jürgen Klopp asks Peter Krawietz to find video of a decent passage of Liverpool play in the first 45 minutes for positive reinforcement. None can be found. On a tight, sodden surface and facing a full-pitch press and a committed home crowd, Liverpool concede early and Thiago and Keïta (surprisingly preferred to Henderson) can barely make a forward pass. The visiting full-backs are overloaded and frequently in trouble, while Diogo Jota, playing centrally, can do nothing to hold the ball high up the pitch. Fans in the home areas are visibly weeping with amazement at what they are experiencing. But after the break Villarreal seem to abandon everything that has worked for them so far. The swaggering Díaz replaces Jota to play wide left for Liverpool and suddenly the tables are turned. The visitors are now dominant, their hosts anxious and tiring, and three away goals result in a mad 12-minute period, led by Díaz.

Sometimes football simply defies logic; it is driven by emotion and forces beyond our understanding or control. 'These are the best times we are going to have as a team.' This is Trent talking to the press. He is still young but he knows just how special this current Liverpool group is, even when their general play has been more like a dog's dinner. No matter. Klopp and his men will move to Paris for yet another Champions League Final but it will not be to face Manchester City after all. The Mancunians are eliminated by another mercurial *Life After Life* late showing by Real Madrid at the Bernabéu. And, as in 2001 under Gérard Houllier, Liverpool will now play every possible fixture available to them in a single season. But more domestic trials await until we can think about Europe again. And even before all that, we must firstly listen to a dramatic and unexpectedly welcome message from off-stage.

Because, from nowhere, Mrs Klopp – Ulla – we are told has agreed to extend her family stay in the English north-west. So, with little warning, Jürgen Klopp and all his staff sign new contracts with FSG until the summer of 2026. Grown men weep in the street. Children are given snap school holidays. Netflix announces a ten-part dramatisation of the great man's life. Jamie Webster records a hip-hop version of 'I'm So Glad that Jürgen is a Red'. The BBC confirms Klopp as the new permanent chair of the comic TV news quiz show, *Have I Got News for You?* A statue and UN peace prize await the German (okay, maybe I exaggerate). 'I'm in love with *here*, and I feel fine,' says a smiling Klopp podcast. Last season's traumas seem completely banished – maybe that new supporters' love song about Jürgen has had its effect after all? Meanwhile, a Spanish guy called Pep from Manchester is reported to be ringing around seeking immediate psychiatric support. What a day!

The long road home

Back in the Premier League, the Saudi-backed Newcastle United have produced a string of home wins to banish relegation fears, a form team in the Premier League. But not even the Geordie fans can get in a bar much before a 12.30 scheduled lunchtime Saturday kick-off on 30 April, so the atmosphere (if not the plastic flag nation) is rather dialled down from what it can be here. A Klopp selection surprise, James Milner starts in midfield, with Joe Gomez in for Trent, and Mo Salah left moping on a stupendous-looking Liverpool bench. Without doubt, Milner is a remarkable man, a model professional. 'Nothing we achieved would have happened without Milly,' Klopp says later. On and off the pitch, and into his 20th season as an elite-level pro footballer, this 2015 free transfer has delivered hard work, quality and leadership throughout Klopp's reign and he has been a key figure for all Liverpool's young players. Even at 36 he gives a man-of-the-match performance in a leisurely single-goal Liverpool victory (Keïta), which is rather like watching a quack deliver chloroform to an unsuspecting patient. The life is simply squeezed out of Newcastle by 24 to 4 goal attempts. But in Yorkshire later, Manchester City flog a hapless Leeds so, again, nothing much changes. As in 2019, Liverpool and Klopp may simply run out of fixtures in the Premier League.

For the crucial Saturday night league visit of Tottenham to Anfield on 7 May, I chaperone Jessen Vencatachellum, a Mauritian academic and long-distance Reds fan. It is Jessen's first visit to the city, so in just a few days he takes in the club museum and stadium tour and all the local Beatles-related tourist stuff. His group also gets a pre-match outing from me to the Flattie and then the Homebaked Bakery for a little authentic local supporter colour. It doesn't help us (or him) much, because Antonio Conte brings a very physical and well-organised Spurs side to defend deep and then launch attacks at pace on the break. Both home full-backs look mentally tired, for once constantly making wrong choices in attack. And even Klopp is mystified at how they each end up (not) defending on the wrong side of the pitch in the second half, an exchange that leads directly to Son's well-crafted opening goal. Luis Díaz equalises, to wild delight on the Kop, but Liverpool make few chances in the last 20 minutes, even though a draw is absolutely *not* what is required right now.

Later, Klopp bad-mouths Spurs' limited approach, given the player quality they have, but Conte has now drawn twice with Liverpool this season and Spurs have beaten City home and away. He will not be apologising soon. Klopp also knows, deep down, that taking off Henderson and bringing on a listless Jota instead of Divock Origi pretty much sunk Liverpool's fading hopes. He needed to gamble. We, loyal supporters that we are, give our boys plenty of rousing and sympathetic applause to take home, but we all fear that these dropped points might finally be the end of matters in the league. After the weekend, City will be three points – and goal difference – clear.

Sadio Mané may well be Jürgen Klopp's favourite Liverpool player in a tough contest. As he hugs his prize forward, the manager often whispers into the ear of this proud man from the tiny Senegalese village of Bambali on the banks of the Casamance River that he is a 'beautiful machine'. Mané was Klopp's first major signing, and when Mo Salah arrived at Anfield in the summer of 2017, Sadio happily skipped from the right to the left flank of Liverpool's attack. Now Luis Díaz is here the Senegal man has been shunted to play more as a central striker. No problem. Mané's versatility, physicality, reliability and goal threat – especially in the air – all make him a modern, mobile number nine. He works non-stop, is super-brave and never misses through injury. He has been an adaptable pivot throughout Klopp's Liverpool project. And, just as it was in the title-winning season of 2019/20, Aston Villa 1, Liverpool 2 on 10 May includes a winning late header from Mané, this time stooping low to gently guide home a smart Díaz cross. All this follows a crazy opening six minutes in which Kostas Tsimikas, in for the rested Robbo, performs like a Sunday league hacker for Villa's lead, and then Joël Matip angrily prods in an equaliser from close range as if he fully expects that he will be off the team sheet for Saturday's FA Cup Final (he will be). Someone who will also definitely not be lining up against Chelsea is Fabinho, subbed here with hamstring trouble. Jürgen Klopp is downcast but he reports later that his Brazilian defensive midfield general is likely to be recovered for Paris.

It is astonishing even to see it written down on the page but here it is. I am writing this on 13 May 2022 – in just four matches and 15 days' time this incredible football trip will all be over. And this squad, possibly the club's greatest-ever group of Liverpool players, one honed and nurtured by its remarkable coach, has two more cup finals and two vital Premier League contests to face. Liverpool could still win all *four* major competitions entered, even from here. Wembley calls for the third time this season – it is Liverpool's 60th fixture of the season, 46 wins so far, including penalty shoot-outs. Phew! Now read on.

14 May 2022: FA CUP FINAL – LIVERPOOL 0, CHELSEA 0: (Liverpool win 6-5 on penalties)

Back in the pre-Sky 1980s, of course, the FA Cup Final was still a standalone, season-closing, destination event. A nationally televised cultural and citizens' royal occasion of real stature. It was a TV occasion to match the Grand National, the Wimbledon finals, the Open Golf championship and even the *Morecombe and Wise Christmas Show*. Today? Well, it has slipped down the pecking order somewhat, overtaken by Champions League qualification, relegation fears and Premier League excess. Money and the FA has almost scuppered it. *Almost.* Jürgen Klopp admits that there will be no extended player celebrations if Liverpool win the FA Cup – his club still has big matches to play. But there is nothing especially new here; it was the same for Bill Shankly in 1965 and for Bob Paisley in 1977.

But this great club has not won the FA Cup since Steven Gerrard's final in Cardiff in 2006. Just seven FA Cup wins to our name and none won at Wembley for 30 years. Even the great Bob Paisley never held the FA Cup as either manager or player. Only James Milner of the current Liverpool squad has an FA Cup winner's medal – as an unused sub. This trophy is still important to Reds fans; it took us 73 years of trying to win the damn thing after all. And our African and South American stars will all have seen some of the 'great' FA Cup finals at home, on TV. So, this really matters, both in the dressing room and in the stands. It is the 150th anniversary of the oldest of all football competitions in the world – it says so on our match tickets. I am not sure how much those ex-public schoolboys who, in the Freemason's Tavern in London established the FA Cup in 1871, would still approve of it today. Liverpool fans booing 'Abide with Me' and the national anthem, for example? 'There must be a good reason for it,' Jürgen Klopp will say later, our supportive Scouse leader to the last. And what would the founders have made of a pounding Pete Tong DJ set? Or shooting flames to welcome the teams? Vile abuse from Chelsea fans about the death of some of our fellow supporters? Or even endless queues for tinned lager, poured at near £8 a pop? A Wembley review on Tripadvisor later complained about 'terrible toilets' (they are) and: '£5.80 for a coke that had been dead longer than my granny.' I could go on.

Today we get through security okay and, blessed heart, the Wembley escalators are working. Our tickets are on the halfway line in a 'neutral' Block 552, but on row 40, the very last seats in the house. We can just about see the pitch in the distance, monitor the complete shape of the match and observe much of today's crowd. Just to our left lies Chelsea's hordes in their yellows and blues. They, and their half of the pitch, are bathed in spring sunshine. Everything else we can see is in shade. There are some 'tourists' in Block 552: people who are late for the kick-off and who waltz back into their seats after half-time on about the 60-minute mark. We just glare at them. Today I am with my mate 'Moany' Simon, a massive Reds fan, a season ticket holder with an encyclopaedic knowledge about the Liverpool teams of the 70s and 80s and especially about his club hero, Graeme Souness. Simon *really* loves this football club but he is also a man born with a residual pessimism burned into his very soul. He wants perfection, pointing out Liverpool players' failings in every iteration of the game. Today his main target is Trent's alleged lax positional defending (a specialist subject), and the 'weak' finishing of one Luis Díaz. Both are world-class footballers. Both, of course, will have quite outstanding matches today.

Game on

Neither Werner nor Havertz is available to Thomas Tuchel, so Chelsea start Lukaku up front and have the returning Kanté haunting the bench. ('70 per cent of the Earth is covered by water', say the T-shirts, 'the rest by N'Golo Kanté'. It could even be true.) The departing Christensen has asked to be left out – of an FA Cup Final squad? Graves are being turned in. For Liverpool, Fabinho is still absent and Firmino and Jota are omitted from the starting XI. We begin aggressively and well, Trent passing brilliantly and Díaz shocking Chalobah with his pace and direct running. Mendy saves in an early one-on-one. 'What a boy!' a beaming Jürgen Klopp will say later of Díaz. 'But he should have scored. He knows it.' Moany, for his part, just gives me one of his 'I told you so' looks. But Liverpool continue to make chances, and Thiago, Henderson, Mané and Trent are all prominent. This is even after Mo Salah retires with what looks like a minor first-half strain. Mo is still showing traces of those post-AFCON (possibly new contract) blues but we will need him firing for Paris. A spritely Jota comes on ... and misses an easy finish. 'Got to score those,' says Simon. You know he is right.

The second half is a little more even; Reece James, Pulisic and Alonso all become more threatening, but Alisson is there. Both Andy Robertson and man-of-the-match Díaz hit Chelsea posts late on. Until he is eventually replaced, the hulking presence of Lukaku is about as much use to our rivals as a concrete trampoline. Extra time has long seemed inevitable and both sides struggle in the heat in the additional period. But Firmino, Tsimikas and Milner all provide new energy (and penalty expertise). Matip comes on for Virgil, a mere precaution we are told later (it better be). Joël and Konaté work perfectly together and remain impregnable. The honest truth is that Liverpool deserve to win this match, certainly more than they did the Carabao Cup Final, but once more it ends nil-nil. So to penalties (again). No Wembley final goals in 240 minutes of trying this season. Our American cousins would surely eye-roll at the pointlessness of it all. But there *is* something new today. This time, the first kick in the shoot-out will be taken by Chelsea, and at the Chelsea end of the stadium. 'That's it,' mutters a downcast Moany. 'We're done for.'

Penalties

As we manage our nerves and the players congregate and refuel around the centre circle, right away we can see that Liverpool look better organised, well set. Klopp is talking individually and calmly to his agreed penalty takers. Thomas Tuchel, by contrast, seems to be working things out with his men on the pitch, in real time. But one Liverpool man, Sadio Mané, is soon alone with his thoughts and is pacing in small circles. 'He is getting chilled, in the zone,' says Simon, surprisingly assured. But Sadio looks troubled to me, anxious. He will be facing his national team goalkeeper Edouard Mendy in what turns out to be the crucial fifth spot. Sadio is concerned about the psychology of over-familiarity. Does he stick or twist? Even from Row 40, we can see that Mané seems to be talking to himself – or to his god. What we *don't* know yet is that Jürgen Klopp has already had a chat with Sadio and advised him to 'reverse' what he would normally do from the spot. This has clearly not calmed matters; Jürgen admits as much later. This Senegalese pair of Mendy and Mané *will* get to play out one of the key dramatic scenes of the 2022 FA Cup Final. Because, after Azpilicueta's solitary miss, and confident successes for James Milner, Thiago, Firmino and Trent, it is indeed Sadio in slot five. He has only to score past his mate Mendy to win the FA Cup for Liverpool.

Our hero's tortured walk to the penalty spot has the Liverpool end in bubbling raptures, a mix of anticipation and dread. Even the tourists nearby looked gripped. Around 75 per cent of all penalties are converted, but not always under these circumstances. And so it proves today. Mané clips his kick weakly to Mendy's left – AND IT IS *SAVED*! And now, of course, momentum swings violently back to Chelsea. Their fans are full of the joys of reprieve. They know it is their day after all and, just to prove it, their next man, Hakim Ziyech, scores emphatically. But so too does Diogo Jota, nervelessly. Ex-G will say that Jota's placement – high and to Mendy's left – has a 99 per cent predicted success rate. 100 per cent as it turns out.

He is unaware of it right now but Chelsea's talented Mason Mount is about to have *six* major Wembley final defeats chalked up against his young name. Because Alisson Becker brilliantly saves his spot kick, low and one-handed to the keeper's left. Which leaves the Liverpool dressing room funny man, our Scouser-Greek left-back Kostas Tsimikas, to walk the walk, either to the gallows or to glory. 'Fuck me!' says Moany. Tsimikas had been farting around pre-match and on the bench with Curtis Jones, but now he is ready. Have we found another unlikely left-back penalty hero, like Alan Kennedy back in 1984? Can lightning *really* strike twice? Mendy dives hard left, Tsimikas goes low and right – like Kennedy did – and then whirls in a tattooed wheel of triumph. The entire Liverpool party is suddenly sprinting in his wake. '*Yeeeees!*' bellows Simon, nearly strangling me. 'I told ya!' For us, the great unwashed, it is that familiar mix of wild abandon and relief.

As if suddenly part of a mass illusion, the entire Chelsea end to our left now vanishes, sucked out of Wembley in a couple of minutes. But, cruelly, their players must wait. Mané consoles Mendy. Hendo commiserates with his England buddies in yellow. The Liverpool end, meanwhile, is a mass of punching arms and red mist.

Simon and I even manage to get down to the scrum at the very front of Block 552 to see the cup raised by Jordan and his men in the Royal Box below. A young steward is also straining over the balcony with his mobile phone for a view. Like Superman, he tears open his top to reveal beneath his hi-vis jacket … a Liverpool T-shirt. Ring home: another major piece of silverware is heading north.

And after these global millionaire superstars have jigged about to Dua Lipa and tried on the FA Cup lid as a stupid hat – just as our underpaid local men did back in 1965 – Jürgen Klopp jokes about his damaging penalty advice to Sadio. And that he loves hugging Luis Díaz, even if neither man can yet understand a single word the other says. Klopp also name-checks again his German scientists for their spot-kick training, and teases Thiago Alcantara that he would have signed the Spaniard *much* earlier if he had known quite how good he was. Thiago replies, dryly, that his manager has taught him only one thing: running. And this time, Thiago insists, there *will* be some sponsors' ale drunk in the Liverpool dressing room. Mainly, it seems, by himself. Jordan Henderson, Liverpool's underrated Mr Reliable, has now lifted more major trophies (six) than any other Liverpool captain. Trent, for whom nothing is impossible, has already won every major club honour in the game at just 23 years of age. And Jürgen Klopp is the first Liverpool boss to capture *all* the major trophies. He is truly a force of nature. There is still time for Mo Salah to invite his friend, the incurable wheelchair-bound ex-Egyptian international player, Moamen Zakaria, to join in the Liverpool dressing room celebrations. They are not only great players these men, but good people.

The club gets to fly home with the cup – lucky ducks. For us, on the H17 back to Harrow-on-the-Hill, a young couple board with grandma and their five little kids. The children race to share the back seat area with our drained group of Liverpool supporters. These kids, full of vim, positively light up the bus. They are looking at their screens, pulling each others' clothes and jabbering away excitedly in a language none of us can understand. 'A nightmare,' says a good-natured Moany. They have no idea, or care, about the madness we have just experienced, and we know little about who *they* are, what they've been through, or indeed where they come from. But when we eventually wave our goodbyes, I even have a daft thought that one day, no matter all the crap they are likely to face, one of these great little kids might just discover our own religion (LFC) and be lucky enough to be able to share it with us. And at the end of it all, as we sip our celebratory drinks, a mellowed Simon agrees that it has been, without doubt, another near perfect day out with our wonderful football club. What else could make it even better? A City collapse; or a ticket for Paris perhaps?

Playing to the last – and for keeps

The issue of facing Southampton in the Premier League on Tuesday evening also comes up in the post-FA Cup Liverpool press conferences. Jürgen responds with near-hysterical laughter. 'How can you do that?' he asks of nobody in particular. 'Could we not at least play on Thursday?' To this there is no answer. And he will soon be aware that he will have to field a meaningful Liverpool team on the south coast, because on Sunday – and from 2-0 down to West Ham – Manchester City manage to eke out only a 2-2 draw at the London Stadium. Another Liverpool victory on Tuesday will thus reduce the Premier League gap to a single point for the final matchday. Jürgen Klopp will not discuss the fact, but you and I can whisper it here: that mad quadruple dream is still on.

But Klopp is willing to risk few of his 120-minute men at St Mary's, which means players we have not seen for a while come back into sharp focus. Cup hero, Taki Minamino, for example, may have thought this season's work was over but here he is in a Liverpool Premier League starting XI. In fact, there are *nine* changes from the Liverpool Wembley line-up. It is also a return for Harvey Elliott in midfield alongside Curtis Jones and Milner. Jota and Firmino join Taki up top. Despite going behind, this 2-1 Liverpool win (Taki and Joël Matip) should provoke wider concerns about the playing health at the top level because it is a comfortable night for these Liverpool reserves against a mid-table Premier League outfit. So, now we will have to fight it out in the Premier League to the bitter end.

Liverpool's last league match of 21/22 is Wolves at home, the quadruple dream somehow still alive. But how are we fans supposed to feel? City at home to Villa is a banker, surely, despite that recent blip at West Ham. 'Let's hope they are 3-0 up at half-time to erase the hope,' say some. And yet, we know that anything can happen under this sort of pressure. At Anfield, Liverpool concede early – the fifth time behind in the last six matches – Konaté caught under a goalkeeper's clearance, his first blot since Lisbon. But then Thiago cutely back-heels Mané into space to score. Soon after, another guttural roar starts to circulate from the Main Stand and around the Kop, which can only mean that 35 miles away Aston Villa have scored to lead at City. Half-time is abuzz with possibilities. And when our old boy Phil Coutinho miraculously scores a *second* goal for Villa, Anfield is now screaming hysterically at its team to do the same.

There is actually a period of just about six minutes – 'six minutes' is embedded deep in Liverpool's history – from roughly 4.20 until 4.26 on Saturday, 21 May, that Liverpool are favourites to win the 2022 Premier League title and possibly that quadruple too. Because now City need three goals to be sure of top spot and Liverpool require only one. But, playing without a handbrake or much guile, Klopp's men cannot find their way through Wolves' packed defence and, by the time they do so (a scrambled late finish by Mo Salah), crazily, Manchester City have scored those three goals they needed – and, yes, in just six minutes. The Kop is caught between celebrating Mo's winner and a gloomy realisation that it will still not be enough. The after-match Liverpool pitch parade now seems to involve the population of a small town, the players lost among kids, friends and various hangers-on, in dresses, suits or trackies. How must the Liverpool squad be feeling – 92 points and no title? Later, with me acting as a conflicted guest speaker at a fans' social event in the city organised by Reds, Wally and Karen, we collectively try to comprehend what we have just experienced – musing about how our gallant group of men have less than a week to recover for Paris. And that four will now, at the last, mean three.

28 May 2022, PARIS: UEFA CHAMPIONS LEAGUE FINAL: LIVERPOOL 0, REAL MADRID 1

In the first half against Wolves, it seemed apropos of nothing at all, Thiago had slammed the ball off the park and then morosely limped off after it, convinced that a muscular injury would rule him out of the Champions League Final. Like an itch that must be scratched, the conscious hours of most Liverpool fans are now spent on-line, monitoring the Spaniard's progress because, gamely, Jürgen Klopp is unwilling to rule out his key creative force in midfield from Paris. How else will Liverpool counter those cunning old heads of Modrić and Kroos at Real Madrid, men who have done so much to undo us in the past? We know the great hordes will travel to Paris – 60,000 estimated; let's just hope the local authorities have a cunning plan to cope with our many excesses. My sports academic colleague Patrick Mignon, with whom I stay in Paris, offers an early warning about steering clear of the Paris riot police. I intend to.

On the morning of this match, in a café in Place D'Italie in the south of the city, we meet a global grifter with one of those fake European Cups, so we have our pictures taken. He is off to Monaco the next day to scam punters at the Formula 1 Grand Prix. Nice work if you can get it. I have missed out in the various ballots, so young lad Mark and I urgently need to find match tickets. Using his phone, within seconds we are able to purchase two Cat 1 tickets on-line, face value a cool €690 each. Our safety check here is that they will appear on our mobiles and we must access the tickets via the official UEFA app. This is where the sporting underworld truly meets the overworld, a matter surely worthy of further investigation. I am not proud that we have to pay very well for this assurance but I need to be at this final settling of affairs. Why this murky world of illicit ticket transfer is relevant will soon become clear soon enough.

The Liverpool fan park at Cours de Vincennes is about 35 minutes away by RER from the stadium area and tens of thousands of Reds are already gathering around Metro station

Nation by late morning. There is little hope of getting near the bands on show but drinking has been well underway here for some time, with some local entrepreneurs fuelling the festivities with trucks filled with iced beer wheeled into the crowds. The statue at the Place de la Nation, 'The Triumph of the Republic', is already engulfed by Liverpool fans. The square is widely known for having had the most active guillotines during the French Revolution. Today it welcomes a familiar sun-drenched working people's festival, a carnival of laughter, corporeal pleasure and alcoholic excess. 'No one left behind' as one of the Liverpool banners on show here attests. It certainly feels like every male Reds fan under 50 worth his salt is here, with a smattering of veterans, women fans and kids. There is no trouble. A big screen will be available later in these parts for those without tickets but the temptation to slide along with the crowd will be too great for a few who have come this far. There is already some casual talk about 'taking a chance' at the ground. Most people are sympathetic. The Madrid fan zone, by way of contrast, caters for just 6,000 fans and is much closer to the Stade de France stadium.

We decide to get to Saint-Denis early, for around 6.15pm; the match is due to kick off at 9pm local time. We have no problems with ticket checks and easily walk through an underpass to the ground among a smattering of visitors. There are only a handful of Reds here at this time, mainly older men and families, people busy buying food, souvenirs and programmes outside this spaceship-looking venue. We see, as soon as we get inside to our Block U19 at about 6.45pm, that around half the Madrid fans have already arrived and are safely in their seats. Which, for some reason, feels disconcerting. Hardly any Reds fans are inside. Our tickets are in a 'neutral' area on the halfway line but high up in the third tier. Below, the world's TV media pundits are stretching and rehearsing. We even have time for a handshake and chat with Glen Hoddle and for a watery stadium beer. It feels bizarre to be on site quite so early but we will soon learn that we have missed chaos outside for pretty much all those Liverpool fans who arrived at the local RER station soon after we did. What exactly happened outside will eventually delay this global TV sports event for a highly embarrassing 36 minutes and provoke something of an international governmental stand-off.

Liverpool fans had started to arrive in numbers from around 6.15pm and clearly UEFA, local stewarding and the police had difficulty managing this influx of boisterous but well-behaved newcomers. With little signage, Reds fans took a different route to the stadium and early ticket checks were absent. The French authorities were also panicky about fake paper tickets and the possibility of determined and skilled bunkers-in. Moving from virtually no Liverpool fans present to a mass arrival – but still an early one by British standards – was quite beyond their planning and scope. There were too few ticket scanners and the process became more and more laborious, causing bottlenecks, frustration and alarm. The technology started to fail and even some genuine tickets began to test as fake, adding to the confusion.

Eventually, with the hosts by now in total disarray, gates at the Liverpool end were closed for a reset. Still no communication was offered and supporters were penned for lengthy periods in potentially dangerous conditions; tear gas and pepper spray were used arbitrarily by police on ordinary fans, the vast majority of whom had valid tickets. Even VIPs got caught up in the madness – Steve Rotherham, Liverpool's mayor, was robbed. Gangs of local lads now started to agitate the police, adding to the latter's anger and hostility. Despite more Spanish fans arriving earlier on organised trips, some of them also complained later about pickpockets and police violence. Local gangs would return after the match to mug some departing Liverpool and Madrid supporters. Most Madrid fans were using mobile phone tickets – why not Liverpool? The French authorities reported later that by the scheduled kick-off time 97 per cent of Real Madrid supporters were in place but only half the Liverpool fans. We could see this was true with our own eyes.

Organisers in France complained later that they had only three months to plan for this relocated event and the French interior minister Gérald Darmanin and sports minister Amélie Oudéa-Castéra both said that they 'regretted' how Liverpool supporters had been held, massed outside the stadium gates: 'We have nothing to be proud of about what happened on Saturday night,' admitted Darmanin. But initially he also insisted that there had been ticket fraud on 'an industrial scale', with up to 40,000 Liverpool supporters allegedly involved. This was pure fantasy, of course, a wild attempt to control the blame narrative that would emerge, inevitably focused on their own incompetence. A small minority of Liverpool fans may have turned up ticketless or with fake tickets and this blue riband fixture should always have been a 'red flag' from a Liverpool point of view. Paris is easily within reach and a cheap trip, and this match could well have proved to be the last of an historic quadruple triumph. Demand in England far outstripped legitimate ticket supply – it did so in my own case. Jürgen Klopp was later criticised for encouraging ticketless fans to travel to France but it was also clear that the French authorities have critical domestic problems in managing and policing football fans. Their own citizens are fearful of the police. In fact, the vast majority of Liverpool supporters without tickets watched the match peacefully on a big screen in the designated fan zone.

We could have a much wider discussion here, as some journalists later did, about the 'levers of power' that control the game in Europe and the blue-chip sponsors, corporates and oligarchs who now matter much more to UEFA than the supporters who attend its showpiece matches. The real embarrassment to UEFA was not the abuse of ordinary people in Paris but that there was global TV airtime to fill with no product to show. All this is painfully true. Despite all the new talk in football about fans as 'customers', their reward for spending hundreds of pounds (or more) on match tickets is often little more than shabby disrespect – or much worse. On this awful night in Paris, the hunger and need for the sport among loyal Liverpool supporters met the corrupt vagaries of the marketplace and the incompetent incapacity of UEFA and the French authorities to cope with the energy and desire of well-behaved British people for whom the term 'customer' barely even scratches the surface. Some ticket holders from Liverpool never even got inside the stadium. On the pitch, while all of this was still going on, the Liverpool players were completing a repeat on-field warm-up just to fill in the time. Who knows if, or how, the delay affected their performance? We do know that some players had friends and family members caught up in the dangerous chaos that was happening outside.

> ### Liverpool FC: FA Cup & Carabao Cup Winners Champions League finalists, 2021/22
> *Alisson (Kelleher)*
> *Alexander-Arnold Konaté (Matip) Van Dijk Robertson*
> *Henderson Fabinho Thiago (Keïta)*
> *Salah Mané Díaz (Jota)*

Thiago warms up with Liverpool coaches, separately from the rest of the first team, but he starts in what turns out to be a disappointing night all round. In front of an unsurprisingly subdued crowd, Liverpool begin well enough, but this is against a Madrid team that is happy to sit deep and counter-attack, thus casually subverting their own traditions. Courtois makes good saves from Salah and then Mané, but by now Modrić has started to impact the match and possession is evening out. Carvajal is physically dominating Luis Díaz. Real are denied a 'goal' from Benzema by a lengthy VAR intervention as half-time approaches.

Given that Liverpool's recent record in major finals over 90 minutes is actually a very poor one, the first goal here is likely to be especially crucial. Around the hour mark, it is Real Madrid who score it. Valverde gets free on the Liverpool left and there are enough red bodies there to block the shot or cross, but somehow his driven ball reaches right across to Vinicius Junior, who is free at the far post behind Alexander-Arnold. Alisson has no chance to make the save. And now Real try to run down the clock, with Courtois as their reliable defensive shield, again thwarting both Jota and Mané. Liverpool's players finally look tired – and who can blame them? It ends 1-0. The Belgian keeper will justifiably be pronounced man of the match, a player instrumental in completing Real Madrid's extraordinary sequence of escapology throughout the Champions League knockout stages. Klopp's team has had 24 shots to Madrid's four, but with no return. Not taking chances has become a familiar tale. For Liverpool FC and its fans there is only despair about what should have been a major sporting experience to treasure, but one that has instead been shattered by circumstances both on and off the field.

So, how to weigh up a season that promised so much, delivered remarkable victories and two domestic trophies, but could only produce runners-up plaudits in the two campaigns that really matter at this level. This is an outstanding Liverpool squad with a remarkable coach, for sure. But later, a reflective Klopp will remark, 'Second place? It is my middle name.' Harsh, perhaps, but maybe it also contains some difficult truths we need later to unpack. More broadly, how exactly did we get here? What follows covers the entire history of the club from its origins in 1892 to the current Jürgen Klopp era, narrated mainly through the prism of Liverpool team managers. In the final chapters I discuss the wider impact of Klopp on Liverpool in some detail and return to the debate about where this exceptional current squad of Liverpool players, and its inspirational manager, figure in the wider history of this great football club.

Chapter 2

Before Bill Shankly

Some deep history of Liverpool Football Club
*In the spring of 1892, 'King John' Houlding heaves
Everton FC out of their Anfield home and establishes
Liverpool FC, made up largely of Scots. Local rivalry
is keen. Tom Watson, English football's first great
team manager, arrives to win two league titles, in
1901 and 1906. His team is led by the legendary Alex
Raisbeck and the city of Liverpool is briefly the centre
of the football world. More league titles follow, in
1922 and 1923, with iconic Irish goalkeeper Elisha
Scott a firm Kop favourite. In a unique early move
at internationalisation, Liverpool raid white South
Africa but then fall into long-term decline. There are
only two Liverpool FA Cup finals to show before
the 1960s, both losses. The winter of 1946/47 is a
vicious one, necessitating summer football. Albert
Stubbins, Bob Paisley and Billy Liddell eventually
get their post-war league title reward – in sweltering
June. Chairman Billy O'Connell grabs the league
championship trophy only just in time. But then
Liverpool FC slump and are relegated, before being
bushwhacked by little Worcester City in the FA Cup
in 1959. Time for a major change.*

In the beginning: one seed two clubs

As every amateur football historian on Merseyside knows, it was Everton Football Club that first played at Anfield when the world's first professional Football League, made up of 12 northern and Midlands clubs, was launched in 1888. A local brewer and prominent Conservative politician, John Houlding, sat on the Everton board as chairman, often uneasy among his Liberal, teetotaller colleagues. Houlding had negotiated the deal and acted as representative tenant when Everton FC moved to their new stadium at Oakfield Road in Anfield. He rented the venue to the club he served. Everton players would get changed and drink afterwards in the Sandon Hotel, a pub owned and named by Houlding after a local Tory grandee. The pub still stands today and it hosts Liverpool supporters and corporate guests before matches.

After a struggling start, in 1891 Everton won their first Football League championship and with it the newly purchased league title trophy, attracting average crowds of just over 10,000, the largest in the league. Everton's board, led by George Mahon, a Methodist and an accountant, asked for a long-term lease to Anfield, which John Houlding refused. Instead, he raised the rent.

The anti-Houlding lobby at Everton disliked 'King John's' commercial tone and his Tory politics and they now began looking to establish their own limited liability company so that they could purchase land for a new stadium. They even thought they had already seen a suitable site, some wasteland just the other side of Stanley Park at Mere Green Field. It would later be known, of course, as Goodison Park. On 26 March 1892 the *Liverpool Review* carried a spoof account of the critical special general meeting (which was officially closed to the press) that finally ejected Houlding and his followers from the Everton club. The whole sorry affair took just over an hour. When ale had been supped and the dust had finally settled on what had been a poisonous dispute, John Houlding claimed that it was not his business plans for Everton but the 'teetotal fanaticism' of his political opponents that had forced these actions and produced the split. In truth, it was probably a bit of both.

'King John' then set up the Liverpool Football Club and Athletic Grounds Company Limited at Anfield, thus establishing a completely new venture, to be run by a board full of Tory freemasons and Orangemen who were already entrenched in local civic organisations. The embryonic Liverpool Football Club was born into a city with the keenest possible local rivals any sporting club could wish for: an outfit across the park whose owners positively disdained Liverpool FC's commercial hierarchy and its politics and who were now digging the foundations of a new stadium in a field just about a mile away. With a few Everton renegades in tow, including Everton team manager/trainer William Barclay, John Houlding had the basis for the administration of an entirely new football club and some time to sort things out while his new asset found its feet in the regional Lancashire League. Everton would block Liverpool's initial applications to join the Football League. He needed some star players and his Irish associate and club secretary, John McKenna, went to Scotland to find them, home of the early football 'professors'.

Having finally been accepted into the Second Division of the Football League in 1893, Liverpool strengthened for the winter challenges that lay ahead. For the first and only time in its history, the club would finish a season unbeaten in the Football League. Not even Shankly, Bob Paisley or Jürgen Klopp could achieve this feat. But it was the appointment, on 1 August 1896, of ex-Sunderland man Tom Watson, the prototype of the modern football manager, that would make Liverpool FC a market leader and a national force. Under his leadership, league titles followed, in 1901 and 1906, for a team graced by the forwards Sam Raybould and Joe Hewitt, but captained and inspired by the quite brilliant Scottish centre-half, Alex Raisbeck.

> ## Liverpool FC: League Champions, 1900/01
>
> *Perkins*
> *Robertson (J) Dunlop*
> *Wilson Raisbeck Goldie*
> *Cox Walker Raybould Satterthwaite Robertson (T)*

In 1901, with Everton FA Cup winners, the city of Liverpool had justifiable claims to be considered the first football capital of the world. Raisbeck's speed, aggression and precision in the tackle and in defensive recovery were legendary in the crucial centre-half pivot role for Liverpool. Pickford's *Association Football* published in 1908 describes Raisbeck as an 'intelligent automaton'. Behind his captain, what Tom Watson uniquely provided at Anfield was not only positive direction and cohesion in both team and financial affairs, but also a considerable flair for public relations and the constructive use (read manipulation) of the popular press, especially important as the professional game continued to grow, both in its reach and status. Working together, the pair – Watson and Raisbeck – were irresistible off and on the pitch. John Houlding, meanwhile, the great self-promoter, used his Liverpool FC role to work on his business networks and drum up support for his local political ambitions. As it turned out, he had little time left.

The passing of 'King John'

John Houlding died in 1902, and on 22 February 1905 a public meeting was held at the Carlton Hall on Eberle Street to finally start to plan the post-Houlding era for the Liverpool club. Chairman Edwin Berry told the meeting that the club had £700 in the bank and was financially stable, but also that: 'In name it [LFC] was a limited company, but practically it was a one-man show.' Out of 3,000 existing Liverpool shares the Houlding family held 2,000. This needed to change. The club's debt to the late John Houlding was £10,000, with a further £5,000 bank overdraft guaranteed by the Houlding family. William Houlding had approached the board, said Berry, to put the club 'on a more popular basis, so that it would really belong to the people'. William had agreed to give up the 2,000 family shares and to wipe out the debt, if the club agreed to relieve him of the bank loan guarantee. Other existing shareholders, it was reported, had also agreed to give up 50 per cent of the money they held in the company. It was a new beginning; a share issue was agreed for 1906 of 15,000 shares at £1 each and, supposedly, a more 'popular control' of the club with much more public accountability would be the result. It never worked out quite like that. Part of this new ownership structure was focused on the first remodelling of the Anfield stadium, which took place in 1906 after Liverpool's second league title had been secured.

The influence and popularity of professional football expanded at an astonishing rate in British cities in the new century – the 'football fever' – so new club owners sought ways of increasing stadium capacity, improving customer comfort, but also of maximising returns on their investment. The brilliant young Scottish engineer Archibald Leitch was a revolutionary figure in stadium design, a young man now determined to use new advances in technology and materials to build a bigger and better Anfield. This included large exit gates on all four sides, a raised pitch (by five feet) and an extended 'elevated terrace consisting of 132 tiers of steps, which will afford space for something like 20,000 spectators'. Only the Anfield Road end would survive unaltered. The original plans, laid out in June 1906, had also included a roof over the terraced 'Spion Kop', newly named as such by the sports editor of the *Liverpool Echo*, Ernest Edwards. But this cover would not be added until 1928 and then by a different architect, local man Joseph Cabre Watson. The topmast of SS *Great Eastern* was incorporated into the footprint of the new stadium and it remains proudly outside the Kop to this day. The jewel of the Leitch plan, however, was to resite the then current main stand (opened in 1894) to the Kemlyn Road side of the ground and replace it with a completely new structure, a gable front combining a seated area with a standing paddock. It was Leitch's first football stand made in reinforced concrete and was lauded by building design experts for its 'elastic strength' and 'durability'. It was probably the first of its kind anywhere in Britain. The curved gable of the new main stand would be the characteristic Leitch signature for Anfield until it was replaced by a much more functional (and ugly) flat-roofed unit in 1970.

Liverpool FC: League Champions 1905/06

Hardy

West Dunlop

Parry Raisbeck Bradley

Goddard Robinson Hewitt Raybould Cox

The great Sam Hardy in goal, and Sam Raybould and Raisbeck further forward, helped secure another title for Liverpool, but soon the new 1906 league champions had begun to look increasingly uncertain. In September 1907 the *Liverpool Echo* noted Alex Raisbeck's absence from the Liverpool line-up once more 'as one never likes to even contemplate what might happen in his absence'. This was no serious injury: Raisbeck was suffering from a rather strong dose of diarrhoea. But he would play only 23 league fixtures, for two goals, in 1907/08. Indeed, the years leading up to the First World War were very disappointing ones for Tom Watson and Liverpool FC. League finishes of 13th, 17th, 12th, 16th, and then 14th in 1914/15, were hardly what the Anfield board and the Liverpool public had hoped for, and now expected. After a controversial semi-final defeat in 1899, neither had there been any lengthy FA Cup runs for Liverpool to offer to their supporters as compensation for lack of success in the league. Securing the FA Cup would become the aim of all Liverpool managers until the mid-1960s.

But change was in the air. In September 1910, Bolton-born right-back and future Liverpool and England captain, Ephraim

Longworth, made his debut for Liverpool, the first of 490 near-exemplary appearances for the club, both in peacetime and during war. On 31 May 1912 the *Evening Express* reported that a Bootle-born full-back or wing-half, Walter Wadsworth, had also signed professionally, having 'last season assisted Ormskirk with distinction'. The fearless 'Big Waddy' would prove a crucial figure and fierce local leader in the dual championship-winning Liverpool team of the 1920s. Scottish left-sided defender and dead-ball specialist Donald MacKinlay signed in 1910 from a local club in Glasgow, an inspired Watson discovery, a man who went on to give Liverpool 19 years of near-unblemished service. Along with Longworth and Wadsworth, MacKinlay became the club's new defensive shield in the early inter-war years. Finally, on New Year's Day 1913, the brusque and brilliant teenage Irishman, Elisha Scott, made his debut in the Liverpool goal. Newcastle United instantly offered Liverpool £1,000 for the young keeper but it was turned down. In goal, at least, the Reds' future could reliably take care of itself.

However, there was trouble ahead. Two years later, on a rain-soaked Manchester afternoon on 2 April 1915, some Liverpool players, incontrovertibly, were involved in a match-fixing scandal, a sensational 2-0 defeat at Manchester United that saved the latter from the drop. The ensuing FA inquiry resulted in four Liverpool players being suspended. But the war and the expansion of the First Division from 20 to 22 clubs meant United escaped the relegation places after all. The suspensions for the Liverpool players involved were eventually lifted soon after the end of hostilities. But it was an early stain.

The intense solidarity

Liverpool FC finally reached the FA Cup Final in 1914, playing Burnley, a khaki affair staged on the very cusp of the First World War. It was the first final attended by the king, a sign of the game's growing respectability and national status. But it was a 1-0 defeat for Liverpool and, in its shadow, on 5 May 1915, the much-loved 'Owd Tom' Watson died suddenly at 56 years, of pneumonia and pleurisy. His death came barely a week after he had been attending a South Liverpool vs Liverpool match, where he had complained to friends about 'feeling odd'. What had made Watson so unique in the early professional game in England was his huge network of trusted contacts in football, which aided his famed 'talent tracing'. As one newspaper put it, 'Tom, as a manager, must have had the record for signing on men he had never seen.' Watson also had an assured capacity to bend the press and the Liverpool board to his will. 'Bee', the *Liverpool Echo* football columnist of the time, recalled that Watson had insisted to him that newspapers should always 'encourage' football and that the Liverpool man had argued that it was sometimes difficult to convince journalists that the game was not 'the blackguardly thing some supposedly good folk believed it to be'. Not much changes. At his funeral at the Anfield cemetery, paid for by the club, hundreds of supporters and celebrities from the English and Scottish football world turned out to pay their respects, including all the Liverpool club directors. There were over 100 wreaths at the funeral, which 'represented all the leading football associations'. Seven former Liverpool players, including Alex Raisbeck and goalkeeper Ted Doig, and also the great Liverpool trainer, William Connell, acted as pall bearers. The sport – and the city of Liverpool – agreed that it had lost one of its early greats

After the war, the moustachioed, pipe-smoking ex-referee David Ashworth was appointed Liverpool secretary/manager, a man recruited from Stockport County for what would prove to be a memorable 1921/22 season. On 21 August 1921 the Liverpool minute books reported: 'It was decided that the duties of the manager be to have the full charge of all players and trainers on the books of the club and that all matters appertaining to the players be under his control.' Here was a clear statement of managerial status and duties, but one that stopped short of the key issue: *selecting* the Liverpool team. Indeed, nothing much would change on this account until the appointment almost 40 years later of Bill Shankly. Nevertheless, this 'new' Liverpool built around Scott, Longworth and MacKinlay in defence, Wadsworth, the skilful Tommy Bromilow and the fearsome Scot Jock McNab in the middle of the pitch, and the bow-legged and left-footed Harry 'Smiler' Chambers up front, won two consecutive league titles, in 1921/22 and 1922/23. The obvious strengths here were the solidity and security of the Liverpool back three, the sheer power and consistency of the half-backs, the trickery and work ethic of the wide players, plus Bromilow's organisation, intellect and creativity in the centre, and the goals of the willing Chambers. Elisha Scott was, unquestionably, the greatest goalkeeper of his day, probably the best of all keepers before the Second World War. He was a perfectionist, routinely berating his defenders for their failings, especially if they allowed the rival who became his nemesis, Everton's Dixie Dean, any meaningful advantage.

Because of family illness, David Ashworth left his job halfway through the second title season and when Liverpool organised an event to celebrate the 1923 title win his successor, the modest ex-Liverpool player Matt McQueen, absented himself so that he would not receive the secretary/manager's medal that was really not of his deserving. McQueen had tinkered admirably little with the winning formula he had been bequeathed and he was mainly directed in his management duties by the Liverpool board. Walter Wadsworth, with an eloquent little speech in his best Bootle accent, presented the Liverpool backs and former captain and current captain, Longworth and MacKinlay, with a miniature cup on behalf of the players and staff as a tribute to their service, leadership and sheer playing quality. It was a touching moment and typical of the respect with which players in the 1920's Liverpool squad held each other. The club got permission from the Football League to give presents to the players to the value of £25 each – about three weeks' wages.

Liverpool FC: League Champions, 1921/22 & 1922/3

Scott
Longworth (Lucas) MacKinlay
McNab W. Wadsworth Bromilow
Lacey Forshaw Johnson (Lewis) Chambers Hopkin

Chambers had contributed 22 league goals in 39 appearances and Dick Forshaw 19 in 42, but it was in conceding only 31 times in 42 fixtures and losing only once at home that the title was retained by Liverpool. 'There were mounted police outside to ensure there was no Wembley nonsense' said a scathing *Liverpool Echo* in its conclusion to the day's events. The newspaper was reflecting, of course, on the chaotic inaugural 'white horse' Wembley FA Cup Final of 1923. Altogether, the *Echo* agreed 'it was a memorable day in the history of the club'. Consecutive league championships – it sounded wonderful. Where next for Liverpool – and indeed for English football? Change, as always, was lurking just around the corner.

They shall be our teachers

How did the Liverpool board try to bolster the club after those league title triumphs of the early 1920s? A new strategy was born. On 1 October 1924, Liverpool turned out a strong mix of first-teamers and reserves to play a touring amateur representative team from white South Africa. On paper, it looked like a gentle training exercise; it was anything but. Liverpool lost 5-2 in a blistering exhibition of technique and movement, 'one of the most enjoyable games ever witnessed on the ground'. The *Daily Post* saw the drubbing as 'A lesson for English players', an exciting alternative to dominant British approaches, which still required that the ball be passed slowly within the team and then to the wingers, who tried to outwit the opposing half-back before crossing. The South Africans played a much more direct and artful game, one sprinkled with the 'back heel touch', and an approach of 'simple methods of passing and by the upwards pass'. For 'Bee' in the *Liverpool Echo*, the South Africans were nothing less than a revelation: 'We must learn our lesson afresh,' he advised. 'They shall be our teachers.'

In what was a revolutionary move for its time, Liverpool made an early batch of 'foreign' South African signings in the 1920s and early 1930s, which was actually a decent piece of business for the club. The big and powerful, if rather ungainly, Gordon Hodgson (241 goals in 377 appearances) was to become the main forward spark for Liverpool and the club's regular top scorer for much of the next decade. Hodgson was joined at Anfield, in 1933, by Berry ('Nivvy') Nieuwenhuys, a tall, loping right-winger with deceptive pace and a fierce right-foot shot, who made 257 Liverpool appearances over 14 years, including 15 in the 1946/47 championship season. Goalkeeper Arthur Riley from Boksburg, a pragmatic, brave and reliable number one, was signed as cover and the long-term replacement for the ageing Elisha Scott. These were turbulent years of transition for Liverpool FC, with the unfortunate Riley often facing a barrage from the opposition. In November 1934 Liverpool lost 8-0 to bottom club Huddersfield Town when, reportedly, 'Riley kept the game from a cricket score.' This era was clearly a time for forwards and for goals – and no goalkeeper was entirely safe from its effects. When Liverpool were humiliated 9-2 by Newcastle United on New Year's Day in 1934, it was the ailing hero Elisha Scott who was in goal.

In fact, as Liverpool struggled in the late 1920s and into the 1930s under secretary George Patterson, the aura around the club's remaining great individual talent, their Irish goalkeeper 'Leesh', continued to grow stronger, even when most of the 93 league goals conceded by Liverpool in 1931/32 were actually put past the great man. This mythologising accelerated as Scott's duels with Everton's Bill 'Dixie' Dean offered an alternative focus for a generation of Liverpool supporters who were now pretty much starved of FA Cup and league championship success. These two great rivals were made for each other and they were undoubtedly good for football business in the city at a time when, frankly, Liverpool FC were labouring to be even vaguely competitive with the near neighbours.

Even so, derby matches did not always go Everton's way – a 7-4 home thrashing at Anfield in February 1933 was probably the Reds' highlight of this entire period, still the highest Liverpool goal tally against Everton and the highest aggregate score in any Merseyside derby. Although he said later that he rarely saluted the men in the Kop, Scott, very willingly and very publicly, *communed* with the Liverpool supporters behind him, said the *Liverpool Echo*: 'They have heard him; he holds conference with them; he chats and back-chats; they hear his opinion about positions and positional play. He was built in with the Kop!' Scott was often most furious with the unfortunate Liverpool defender, Jimmy 'Parson' Jackson, a former Clyde shipyard worker, a church elder and devout Christian, a more than unusual footballer who had studied Greek and philosophy at Cambridge University and would be ordained as a presbyterian minister in 1933. Jackson's chief crime was that he was usually the man who had allowed Bill 'Dixie' Dean to humiliate Elisha in front of his own people.

After much public debate and angst in 1934 about Liverpool possibly selling the by now creaky 40-year-old Scott – perhaps even to Everton – the Irishman eventually returned, instead, to Belfast after 21 years of exemplary club service. Because he was injured, Elisha missed the season's closing fixture, at Anfield against Manchester City on 2 May 1934, but a microphone was set up in the Main Stand for him to deliver his public goodbyes. It was a poor crowd of below 20,000, the stadium barely even one-third full. Was this even an early protest from Liverpool supporters against the board? The Liverpool chairman Walter Cartwright, another from the Liverpool 'family' of administrators who was followed into the role later by his son, Harold, in the late 1960s, told those present that the club would honour the full share of Scott's accrued benefit and that 'Scott has taken the view that football is a young man's game, and it was his own desire to make room for a younger man.' The Kop then howled its unhappiness when a young supporter broke the spell by running on to the pitch to get a better view of matters. The intensely private and obviously emotional Scott spoke briefly in his distinctive Belfast growl: 'We have always been the best of friends and shall always remain so,' he said. 'I have finished with English association football. Last, but not least, my friends of the Kop. I cannot thank them sufficiently; they have inspired me. God bless you all.' A generation of Liverpool fans had grown up alongside this stooped, wiry figure guarding the Liverpool goal in front of them, risking life and limb and zig-zagging with the ball in hands bawling, 'All clear!' And now that it was all over, many hardened working men were in tears; it was, indeed, the end of an era. The brilliant Elisha Scott was never forgotten by those Liverpool supporters who had shared two decades of their winter Saturday afternoons with Scott from the Kop. He had success as a manager at Belfast Celtic and there was even talk of Liverpool's directors travelling later to Ireland to try to recruit 'Leesh' as the club's secretary manager. But it never happened.

A new start

On 14 July 1936, the Liverpool board finally advertised for a new football secretary manager, a man who might better understand the emerging modern game. Fifty-two applications were received. The club recruited, from Southampton, George Kay on £600 p.a. and a £250 bonus for finishing first or second in the league. They had some ambition. The Liverpool board even resolved to build a manager's office for the first time, erected by Tyson and Co. in 1936 for £63. The Manchester-born Kay certainly knew the game and he was sympathetic to players, even if it was difficult to describe him as a 'tracksuit' manager. Kay insisted on wearing a collar and tie always, in order to identify with the board and club officials above him, rather than with the dressing room below. But he was a good talker and motivator and he could get close to professional players. A young Matt Busby, for example, was greatly influenced by Kay and the way he managed to treat his players at Liverpool with both loyalty and consideration, compared to the brutality of the regime Busby had experienced at Manchester City. Busby also saw how the pressures of the job eventually got to Kay, who was often seen on the trainer's bench, according to the *Echo*, 'shouting, beseeching – wringing his hands, holding his head in apparent anguish, and making an excellent attempt to head and kick every ball in the match'.

George Kay at least had more to say than others before him over Liverpool's transfers and selections and his team's tactics on the pitch, and perhaps he also, initially, had a little more luck than some recent Liverpool managers had. Because it was Kay who was sitting in the manager's chair at Anfield in the summer of 1938 when the club made its best signing for almost 30 years – and for no fee. A slight, 16-year-old winger called Liddell scrawled his signature on the dotted line as an amateur. On 17 March 1939, Billy signed professional forms on £3 a week for the Liverpool 'A' team. Here was a future Reds star to take over the mantle from Raisbeck, Longworth and the recently departed Elisha Scott. The son of a Scottish miner, Billy Liddell had played both rugby and football at school and he had considered careers in both the ministry and in accounting, while playing soccer for Lochgelly Violet for 2s 6d expenses. When Partick Thistle fatally hesitated over taking Liddell on to the club's staff, it was Matt Busby who rang George Kay suggesting that Liverpool 'take a look at the boy'.

Despite this crucial signing, George Kay would have his work cut out finding success at Anfield. Liverpool's form continued to oscillate alarmingly. Bizarrely, the Reds began their FA Cup campaign of 1938 in highly irregular red and white hoops against Crystal Palace and, in February of that year, after yet another FA Cup capitulation, this time at home to Huddersfield Town, the *Evening Express* reported on innovative plans among a group of revolutionary supporters who wanted public feedback on an idea for the formation of a Liverpool Football Supporters' Club. Meanwhile, Fred 'Bullet' Rogers, a tidy, blond, Cheshire-born centre-half or right-half, played 30 times in the final pre-war season of 1938/39, with young Jackie Balmer and the increasingly impressive Matt Busby being the two ever-presents in the Liverpool team.

On 6 May 1939, the 'international situation', as the impending war was now euphemistically described in the British press, would not, said the *Echo*, interfere with Liverpool's post-season plans to tour Sweden. But the Liverpool club became the first in Britain to announce that all its players, plus the manager George Kay and assistant secretary Jack Rouse, were to join the Territorial Army as a unit: 'A grand example to the remainder of the football world.' These seemed like strangely mixed messages from Anfield as the country now prepared for war. The band struck 'Auld Acquaintance' on 6 May 1939 as Manchester United and Liverpool players left the field after the final league match of 'intense dullness', according to the *Daily Post*, with Everton anointed 1939 league champions for what would turn out to be the whole of the war period. Of course, at this precise moment no one could quite say exactly when the world's oldest football league might restart. Or, indeed, exactly *which* Liverpool football club it would be that arose again from the ashes of conflict.

Amazingly, Anfield avoided suffering major war damage, although the strategically important city of Liverpool suffered substantially in the Blitz. Much of the national focus on the bravery of the British people, however, ignored Liverpool and other provincial cities and honed in, instead, on London, a subject of considerable Merseyside resentment. However, many Liverpudlians responded to the privations of war with typical innovation and energetic creativity. Almost anything – including, it was rumoured, Spitfire parts – could be found offered for sale in pubs in the city and, as the war and its misery progressed, it became clear, as Jack Rollins in *Soccer at War* put it: 'The whole of Liverpool was beginning to feed and clothe itself on the black market.' Tragically, the stylish Reds full-back Tom Cooper lost his life on 25 June 1940 when his motorcycle was in a head-on collision with a bus near Aldeburgh. He was the sole Liverpool FC fatality during the conflict. Only Crystal Palace and Wolves contributed more than the 76 players in total from Liverpool FC who gave wartime service.

Football was also important in raising the national spirits, especially after the initial shock of the conflict slowly began to diminish. A letter to the *Evening Express* on 4 January 1940 commented, for example, that wartime regional football in Liverpool was 'spirited and skilful to a high degree' and that 'football is a valuable asset to the home front and deserves the support of all lovers of our characteristically British game'. Of course, football would also help to keep local and national spirits up during the terrible Covid-19 pandemic some 80 years later, not least in Liverpool. A survey by Mass Observation in 1940 found that 65 per cent of pre-war football supporters were not attending matches because of a variety of wartime reasons, but by 1945 the sport's followers were beginning to flood back to matches, in Liverpool and elsewhere around the country. A new football dawn was coming for both the city and for the British people.

At last, the 1947 show

The powerful and speedy red-haired 27-year-old Geordie centre-forward Albert Stubbins, a former shipyard draughtsman born in Wallsend, had had a good sporting war – 29 wartime hat-tricks, and five-goal hauls on another five occasions. This man could score goals for fun. Stubbins was powerful, fiercely quick, but also 'dainty', unpredictable and exciting, hardly attributes that had characterised pre-war Liverpool centre-forwards. But Stubbins had no real intention of leaving his native Newcastle United. In fact, he had grand plans to open a retirement business there and his family was well settled in the north-east. That is until *both* of the top Merseyside clubs came up with a record offer for him of £12,500 in September 1946, the sort of cash the Toon could not refuse. Stubbins, famously, was watching a film in the Northumberland Street News Theatre when a message flashed across the screen that he was to report to St James' Park right away. He loped off in his size 11s to find that United had already accepted the offer. All Stubbins was required to do was to decide *which* Merseyside club to join.

On the face of it, this selection might have seemed fairly obvious. Everton, after all, were the reigning league champions and had won the FA Cup in recent memory. All Liverpool's league successes were more than 20 years ago and the Anfield men had *never* won the FA Cup, the focal point at the Newcastle club. But because he had made no plans to move, and he had had little time to think, and perhaps because he feared causing offence by being seen consciously to make a choice, Stubbins tossed a coin to decide which club to speak to first. It came down in Liverpool's favour. It was the most important coin toss in the club's history – at least, that is, until its European escapades began in the 1960s. The silver-tongued Liverpool chairman Billy McConnell probably helped convince Stubbins to come to Anfield by offering him a club house – much sought after following the war – but also with assurances about a column for the *Echo* and that he could spend time in Newcastle to look after his business interests (there would be ructions about all this in time). For now, at least, Liverpool FC had paid out big money and it had its goalscoring centre-forward at last. Stubbins never did speak to Everton.

Liverpool manager George Kay was able to take his squad to the USA in the summer of 1946 for some good food and intense training in a pre-season tour designed to recover the squad and avoid the privations of rationing. Back in England, meanwhile, in early March 1946, 33 people were crushed and killed at Burnden Park, Bolton, in the type of stadium disaster that had actually threatened throughout the entire history of the English game. Admirably, the Liverpool press called for instant change: a new licensing regime for sports grounds; capacities of sports stadiums to be assessed, section by section; and for ticket-only matches to be introduced. As the *Evening Express* aptly put it on 11 March 1946, even after six years of daily sacrifice in war 'the thought that men and women should be suffocated and trampled to death in the atmosphere of sport is distressing beyond words'. Throughout the late 1940s and into the 1950s, however, there would be a succession of 'near misses' at Anfield and elsewhere, when sometimes hundreds of people were injured on the terraces or were forced to leave the stadium – sometimes well before kick-off – because of the risk of excessive crushing. It was a warning.

Liverpool began the first full post-war league season of 1946/47 slowly but steadily, and without the prodigy Billy Liddell, who was still with the RAF. A last-minute winning goal by the little used ex-local amateur, 31-year-old Len Carney, claimed both points at Sheffield United. But a confidence-draining home loss to Middlesbrough followed, with defender Lawrie Hughes scoring a classic own-goal header. The new post-war impatience of football supporters was already apparent as the local press reported 'a hurriedly called meeting of Liverpool fans … assembled outside the club's offices … with the object of calling upon the directors to make quick team changes'.

It was the Anfield clash with a strong Chelsea team on 7 September that showed the real potential of this new Liverpool team. It ended as a 7-4 home win but, as the *Evening Express* reported, there could have been many, many more goals for Liverpool, who led 6-0 on 50 minutes, and whose forwards 'made the Chelsea defence look absolutely inept on occasion'. Liddell (2), Balmer and Fagan (2) all scored, as did Bill Jones, a long-serving 'play anywhere' squad man who appeared twice for England and got two goals here as a forward. He would move back into a more defensive role later in this campaign. Jones also proved his intelligence and adaptability when he returned to work for the club in the 1960s, this time as a scout.

The *Evening Express* complained in January 1947 that three key Liverpool players – Billy Liddell, Cyril Sidlow (still not demobilised either) and Lol Hughes – were effectively still part-timers and that this had affected the Reds' early season cohesion. Better was to come at Bolton, with Liddell back and Albert

Stubbins on debut in a 3-1 win. 'This is the best forward line I have ever played in,' said the grateful new Liverpool centre-forward to the club's blushing chairman Billy McConnell. 'I am only sorry I could not give you more than one goal.' Scoring on debut and still apologising? It was music to any director's ear. And it was also exactly the type of goal the club had signed Albert Stubbins to score: a header-on from Nieuwenhuys, with the new centre-forward latching on to it and shrugging off two defenders before driving the ball right-footed past Wanderers' keeper, Stan Hanson.

If Stubbins was to deliver some of the extra goals that Liverpool needed – eventually he would score 83 in 178 matches for the club – it was the presbyterian, Billy Liddell, who provided the essential speed, guile and bite down the left side that marked out this first post-war Liverpool team as exceptional. On occasion, the 24-four-year-old Scot was simply unplayable – although Everton were alert to his tricks for the Anfield 0-0 derby meeting on 21 September. With Phil Taylor playing 'delicious football' in the middle of the field, Liverpool chairman McConnell said that he thought it was the best local derby match he had seen for some time, although most supporters present saw it differently.

Albert finds his scoring boots

Albert Stubbins – all £12,500 of him – had still not scored at Anfield, so the winning goal he produced against relegation-bound Brentford on 26 October 1946 was a relief as well as a guarantee of two hard-won points. Billy Liddell sped up the Liverpool left and crossed low to Stubbins, who beat the stubborn Brentford goalkeeper Crozier low down in the left-hand corner after 50 minutes. The Liverpool man was given a 'tumultuous cheer' by the locals. But although the Reds were supported by 'trainloads of fans, including a contingent of schoolboys', next up at Blackburn Rovers they had to settle for a goalless draw in east Lancashire. Billy Liddell was at last playing for the club again as a civilian. Liverpool now lay in third place, two points behind early leaders Blackpool. Manager George Kay, a thinker and a boss who cared about the wellbeing of his players, announced that he would be taking his squad to Buxton around the fixture with Derby County on 16 November for some country air and relaxation. This was designed 'to help tone them up for the hectic holiday rush and the FA Cup ties ahead'. It was good management and a sensible strategy in a long season. It would also pay handsome dividends.

The experienced Jackie Balmer sometimes lacked the commitment and confidence that a full England international cap might have brought, so George Kay and the players made him Liverpool's captain for the home match against Portsmouth. More good management, and it worked. The inside-forward would stay captain and he scored a hat-trick in a 3-0 win, then set off on an astonishing record league run of scoring ten goals in three matches, while also scoring in six consecutive league fixtures. At Derby, on 16 November, he got all four in a 4-1 win, including 'one of the best goals he is ever likely to get' according to the *Liverpool Echo*, drifting to the right past four defenders and then cutting back his shot into the left-hand corner. Harry Eastham did a 'Matthews trick' in dribbling to make the fourth so adeptly that another Balmer hat-trick in the 4-2 home win over Arsenal on 23 November was no longer a surprise. Perhaps these were the early signs of a new approach to playing league football, one more directed at winning matches come what may rather than just entertaining the crowd. Post-war supporters certainly seemed more demanding, quicker to condemn. But Liverpool followers could say they had both good football and points: 27 goals in ten matches, seven wins, no losses, 17 points and top of the table.

The Liverpool team that played Wolves at Anfield on 7 December was the standard one in a very loose version of the W-M formation, with Harley and Fagan both injured. With the exception of the versatile Bill Jones – who would fill in brilliantly later for both Lol Hughes and Barney Ramsden – and also the fading Berry Nieuwenhuys, this was, broadly speaking, the team that would win the 1946/47 league championship for

Liverpool. It was a highly competent one, rather than a truly great one, but lit up by Balmer and Stubbins and especially by Billy Liddell on the left. There was no one of the quality of Alex Raisbeck or Elisha Scott here, nor defenders to match Dunlop, Longworth or MacKinlay from earlier Liverpool eras. There was no star wing-half or inside-forward schemer of the Tommy Bromilow type from the early 1920s either. Neither Balmer nor Done were really classic inside-forwards in the W-M tradition. Phil Taylor certainly had a touch of class at half-back, and Bob Paisley did have something of the tenacity of Bill Goldie about him from the 1901 team, or even the bite of a Jock McNab from 1922/23. These two, Taylor and Paisley, complemented each other well.

Some of this relative weakness was about to be highlighted at Anfield because, frankly, this Wolves encounter was a horror show: a home thrashing by your closest rivals in front of 52,512 people, most of whom had expected something quite different. It was the sort of 5-1 home defeat, in fact, that had manager George Kay tossing and turning in his bed, looking too hard and too long for solutions, damaging his brittle health. Liverpool crumpled to a team for whom forwards Pye and Hancocks were constant threats to a nervous home defence. Hughes and Sidlow were on different wavelengths for once, as long balls straight up the middle accounted for goals three and four for Westcott. Mullen scored a fifth, after a slip by the Liverpool centre-half, who had a truly miserable day. A late Jack Balmer penalty was all the deflated Reds could manage in reply.

The roots of the Reds' recent problems were clear enough. The young defender Lol Hughes had begun to lose his nerve and Jack Balmer had gone off the boil. Fagan and Cyril Done were missing through injury and Billy Liddell had lost some vim over the holidays. The half-backs were struggling to compensate. Were Liverpool already tired, despite all that rest and early good food in the USA? At Leeds United, where the ball dragged in the snow and there were drifts on the wings on a near-unplayable pitch,

Willie Fagan was back and created a goal for Stubbins, the one Liverpool man who had kept on scoring during this crisis, even though the local press now saw him as 'more a creator of chances than a taker'. But an equaliser from Grainger 'sent the 25,000 spectators joyful, as if it had been a cup final goal'. No matter, red-headed Albert delivered again on 85 minutes and Liverpool were back on the league rails.

But was there no ridding of this awful weather? The winter of 1947 was as severe as anyone could remember and some clubs resorted to using former prisoners of war to help clear snow from their pitches. Liverpool beat Derby County at home 1-0 with a welcome goal from a limping Jack Balmer in frosty conditions in the fifth round of the FA Cup. For the first time, a standing area of Anfield, the paddock, was made all-ticket for this match, after a belated safety campaign launched by the local press. The same tactic might soon be tried for Liverpool's younger fans, it seemed: 'The club asks the lads of the boys' pen to keep their orange peel to themselves,' warned the *Evening Express* on 7 February, 'or else other arrangements will be made for boys in future.' Some threat, for what was a newly opened area for juniors on the Kop. Only the one-inch cushion of snow hiding an iron-hard Anfield pitch allowed Liverpool 5, Grimsby Town 0 to take place in the league on 12 February. No snowballs were reported. Two hard-fought 2-1 Liverpool wins followed in the league – against Blackburn Rovers at home and in desperate, blizzard conditions at Portsmouth away – which meant Liverpool had clawed their way back up to second place in the table with 11 matches still to go.

A possible double?

Was the league and FA Cup double on? Potential league champions Liverpool FC were drawn against Second Division Burnley in the 1947 FA Cup semi-final – but lost the plot after a replay. Before that there was important league business to attend to, with a brutal three fixtures in four days over Easter. Paisley (ankle), Jones (groin), Liddell (thigh), Stubbins (leg bruising) and Harley (thigh) were all doubtful for the visit to Preston. Fortunately, Lawrie Hughes was back from injury, and army man, the Scot Tom McLeod, made his debut at centre-forward in a much-changed Liverpool team that dogged it out for what would prove to be a crucial 0-0 draw. Next day, against Blackpool at Anfield, George Kay made *nine* changes – Rafa Benitez did not invent rotation. But despite leading 2-0, Liverpool eventually went down to the odd goal in five and fell five points behind Blackpool and four adrift of Wolves, with only eight league matches left.

The Reds were now a 100/1 shot for the title, according to the *Daily Post*. It looked like the end of the league challenge. But against Preston at home on 8 April they dug into their reserves and won 3-0. A certain Bill Shankly missed a penalty for Preston after Liverpool captain Jackie Balmer tipped off Minshull that the kick would go to the goalkeeper's left – it did. Liverpool ground out a 2-1 league win at Aston Villa, with goals from Willie Fagan and the 25-year-old, ex-Prescott Cables right-winger Bill Watkinson, who would replace the injured Cyril Done in the last six league matches of the season. Results had favoured Liverpool in the league, so when Albert Stubbins scored the single goal from a Liddell cross to beat the blue-shirted Manchester United at Anfield on 3 May, local press headlines predictably declared, 'Stubbins' Goal Worth 4 Points.' For the *Liverpool Echo* 'there was more than a shade of spike and spirit' about this contest. The league table now read:

	Pld	Pts
Wolves	37	53
Man United	39	51
Stoke City	37	50
Liverpool	38	50

A Stubbins hat-trick in a 3-1 win followed at FA Cup winners Charlton Athletic, thus keeping Liverpool in the hunt. Painfully, two female Dagenham Pipers paraded the FA Cup before the start at the Valley, so that the Liverpool players and supporters could take a jaundiced look at what had already been lost. Liverpool was now left with two tricky away fixtures to complete their season, at Arsenal and Wolves. Bob Paisley would miss both with a knee ligament strain. The Reds were now level with Stoke City on 53 points and just one point behind Wolves and Manchester United. Any one of these four clubs could still win the title. Liverpool's brave 2-1 win at Arsenal ensured the trip to Molyneux would at least be meaningful. Liverpool were now two points ahead of Stoke, one ahead of Wolves and United.

George Kay – who, incredibly, missed some closing Reds matches to scout players elsewhere – had moved Jones forward to replace Fagan in the last ten minutes at Highbury and two Liverpool goals resulted. It was a master stroke. But with Stoke City having two matches left and a superior goal difference to Liverpool's – and not due to complete fixtures until 14 June – even a Liverpool win at Wolves on 31 May could not yet decide matters. On 2 June, in 'blistering heat' during the week of the Epsom Derby, the *Daily Post* commented, not unreasonably, that 'football in June seems out of place' (wait until 2020!) The *Liverpool Echo* reported: 'The Reds produced speed, stamina and classic football to sweep Wolves off their pedestal at Molyneux.' In 91 degrees in the shade, with the officials refereeing in white tops, no blazers, and soft shoes, Wolves 'had four scoring chances to Liverpool's one'. But it was a 'picture goal' by Jackie Balmer, and a brilliant dash half the length of the field by Albert Stubbins for the second that won the day in a gutsy 2-1 Liverpool victory. Today, an opposition coach would berate his players for not fouling Stubbins, but this was a different age. A tearful Stan Cullis was inconsolable later but there could be no Liverpool celebrations yet. A summer victory by an in-form Stoke City at Bramall Lane in two weeks' time would still scupper everything. After all their hard work – seven wins and one draw in the last eight league matches, five of them away from home – Liverpool FC could win the 1947 Football League title only by waiting.

There were no Anfield officials in Sheffield on 14 June 1947 to ensure fair play. After all, Liverpool were playing a weather-delayed and locally important Liverpool Senior Cup Final against Everton at Anfield on the same summer evening. One unidentified Reds player reportedly had to be smuggled into Anfield to avoid the police, who had questions to ask him about alleged tax evasion. In Sheffield it was a story highly typical of the English game and the resolute British football professional. Sheffield United had nothing to play for, save for pride and a £2 bonus, and yet they battled like demons in a deluge that threatened to swamp the pitch. Stoke City, searching for their first-ever league title, simply could not cope with the pressure on a shifting, unstable surface. Their hopes, according to the *Stoke Evening Sentinel* on 16th June, 'crashed on the rock-like defence of Sheffield United'. The news of Stoke's eventual 2-1 defeat was greeted with scenes of extraordinary joy back at Anfield, where supporters watching the Reds destroying Everton invaded the pitch in wild celebration. Sir Francis Joseph, president of Stoke City, said later that it might be strange to some people abroad that a country in crisis, so short of coal and short of production, should focus so intently nevertheless on a *mere* football match. But this devotion to sport was essential, he said, to the British character. 'Had not [Francis] Drake completed his game of bowls with the sails of the Armada in sight, before setting off to rout the Spanish?' No hyperbole here.

To commemorate this dramatic title win, the Easton Press published a pamphlet, *The Sport's Spectator's Story of Liverpool Football Club*, for 1s 6d. As a tilt at the club's history so far and a summary of the current players' strengths, this publication had its moments – and its faults. It noted that others had described this 1947 Liverpool as the 'Crazy Gang' – an inconsistent mix of the very good and the very bad. Albert Stubbins was described as being 'very tall, very gentle', Bob Paisley as having a 'riotous tackle' and Willie Fagan as having 'a nonchalance that makes his work stand out'. Bill Jones, it argued, 'could be the best back in the world'. A touch of English hubris perhaps? It had certainly proved an extraordinary season, the final poignant act of which was for the ailing Billy McConnell to leave the Radium Institute, where he had been a cancer patient for five weeks, to collect the championship trophy from the offices of the Football League. It was a lifelong dream to hold this title for his club. Liverpool FC cancelled a proposed 400-people championship celebration dinner scheduled for 8 August, because on 7 August 1947 the former butcher's boy and Liverpool supporter and director since 1929, died, aged just 59. Several thousand people attended McConnell's funeral at the Anfield cemetery, where he would join Tom Watson and many other Liverpool greats in eternal rest. He had done his duty for his club and for his people – the Liverpool supporters.

Liverpool FC: League Champions, 1946/47

Sidlow

Lambert Jones (Ramsden)

Taylor Hughes Paisley

Balmer Fagan (Done)

Nieuwenhuys (Eastham) Stubbins Liddell

When fellow Reds director and ex-chairman Walter Cartwright died in October 1947 after 27 years' service, the cover of the much-reduced Liverpool match programme was printed in black as a mark of respect. Now a new generation would have to pick up the Anfield reins to face the challenges that surely lay ahead.

Liverpool's bleak 1950s

Liverpool FC struggled in the years after their 1947 league triumph. One reason why was that the club and Albert Stubbins soon fell out. Stubbins wanted to live and train in Gateshead and, not unreasonably, the Liverpool board argued that this was not a great way to maintain squad cohesion. Stubbins soon disappeared from the Liverpool first team. A bright spot in a generally gloomy period was Liverpool's second FA Cup Final appearance, against

Arsenal in 1950, having disposed of Everton at Maine Road in the semi-final. *Off* the pitch in Manchester things were tense, even in this so-called 'golden age' of generally good behaviour among English football spectators. Outside Maine Road, it was reported to be a very 'lively' afternoon. A letter in the *Liverpool Echo* from 'Fairplay' of Kenyon Road, Liverpool, for example, was from a man who said that he was no 'crank' and that he enjoyed himself 'among the lads of the Kop' as well as 'under the clock at Goodison'. It described the kind of eventful trip to Maine Road that could have occurred at any time over the 30 or more years that followed: 'I was ashamed of being a native of Liverpool,' he said, reporting on fights, stealing and obscene language among the visitors. 'I do hope those folk who are going to Wembley behave in a reasonable manner,' he pleaded. Away from such supporter escapades, incredibly the Liverpool board agreed to make special pre-Wembley training arrangements available at the club for the Arsenal captain, the local man Joe Mercer, as a personal courtesy. Liverpool simply insisted that Mercer train in the afternoon and they even provided the Arsenal half-back with a goalkeeper for shooting practice and a player in the outfield to aid with his ball work. Helping your cup final opponents? These were very different times, indeed.

Famously, Bob Paisley was left out of the 1950 Liverpool cup final team, but it was no real surprise locally. Bill Jones was a more mobile and certainly more flexible half-back at that stage than Paisley. Manager George Kay was taken ill before the final and turned up at Wembley pasty-faced and drawn, on what should have been one of the greatest days in his managerial career. Sadly, Liverpool's arrangements for the final were shambolic. The club was forced to buy *blue* hooped socks as part of their Wembley change strip, and then the hotel they had chosen to stay in before the final was overbooked. Trainer Albert Shelley and inside-forward Kevin Baron found themselves bumped on to camp beds in the hotel ballroom. Baron would therefore play in the biggest match of his young life having slept the night before in a put-up bed, alongside the club trainer. It seemed more like Sunday league chaos rather than well-planned preparations for an historic Liverpool FA Cup Final appearance. Unsurprisingly, Liverpool were bullied to defeat in the final, so a man who by now knew Anfield and its coaching staff very well would visit the Royal Box to pick up the 1950 FA Cup. But Joe Mercer's shirt was a plastered and sweated golden yellow, rather than the white one carrying the rain-splattered Liver bird.

George Kay resigned on health grounds soon after the final and he died on 19 April 1954, as the club he loved was also ailing. There was little side or polish to Kay, a man who was a good friend to his players and a very human confidant almost as much as a boss. He was someone who found it painful to make hard but necessary decisions about their futures. Worst of all, every important football match for Liverpool was a test of nerves for their manager. Kay would frequently start matches relatively detached in the stands but then end up on the touchline, pacing out meaningless yardage, making every tackle or pass and wringing his hands with tension.

Out of more than 40 applicants, in March 1951 Liverpool appointed the ex-Charlton Athletic forward Don Welsh to the manager's role. Welsh was in charge at lowly Brighton & Hove Albion, without exactly pulling up any trees, but he had also played for Liverpool as a guest player during the war, so the Liverpool board knew and trusted him. He was young enough (just 40) to offer a good link between the boardroom and the Liverpool players, and he was seen as a tracksuit moderniser, but not one who was too headstrong or who had too many of his own ideas. And, best of all for these cautious, pecuniary Liverpool directors, he was cheap.

T.V. Williams, who had joined the Liverpool board in 1948, was at least a man with a little more vision than other Liverpool directors, and it was he who decided that the club now needed its own training ground away from Anfield, so he orchestrated the purchase of land in West Derby for the purpose, bought from a local school. But beyond building a new boundary wall, the Liverpool board was unwilling to spend much cash on the new facilities at Melwood. Williams was also the key figure in appointing Bob Paisley as second-team trainer and budding physiotherapist when the rugged wing-half retired at the end of the relegation season in 1954. Bob Paisley could instinctively judge a footballer's body as easily as many working-class men from Durham could weigh up racing animals, dogs, horses or pigeons. It proved a very useful skill to have.

In 1954, with just nine wins from 42 fixtures, Liverpool went down to the Second Division for the first time since the 1890s, just as neighbours Everton were on the up escalator and moving back out of the second rank. But things got even worse than this: a record 9-1 league defeat, by Birmingham City at St Andrews on 11 December 1954. The explanation offered – although it seems grossly unprofessional – was that Liverpool staff had misread the wet but frost-bound Birmingham pitch, so players wore the wrong boots in the Midlands, struggling for balance. Nothing at all was said about the *scale* of the defeat in the Liverpool minute books, or the need to change selection policy. Indeed, the same team was picked for the next match, a 4-1 loss to Doncaster Rovers. Perhaps the Birmingham defeat never really happened?

The Liverpool board seemed completely unwilling to invest what it would cost to get the club promoted and home crowds slumped, occasionally below 30,000. In May 1956 the inevitable finally happened. The *Liverpool Echo* reported that Don Welsh had resigned, noting: 'During his period at Anfield he has not had a free hand with the selection of the team and this, no doubt, is one of the reasons for his recent unhappiness with the club.' Welsh had no more to offer. 'As everybody knows,' he told the local press, 'the team selection at Liverpool has always been a board affair and there we have not always regarded things in the same light.' Welsh's replacement indicated that little would actually change. Phil Taylor was a well-liked ex-player for Liverpool who was now a coach at the club. But the board even described his appointment as that of a mere 'liaison man' in the dressing room. Taylor became the acting Liverpool manager on a wage of £18 per week – a saving of £12 a week on Welsh. The club's board, it was announced, reserved the power to have 'the final say in all matters of importance affecting the success and wellbeing of the club'. It was a sorry case of back to the future.

A run of eight straight league wins in December 1958 and January 1959 under Taylor actually carried Liverpool up the Second Division table to second place and it might even have saved the beleaguered Liverpool manager his job, if it were not for the events of 15 January 1959, the most notorious in the club's inauspicious FA Cup history. The desperate weather at the time saw Liverpool appoint the tough Scot Reuben Bennett as the club's new chief coach. The board had actually wanted to give Bill Nicholson the job, but he had already accepted the team manager's post at Spurs. Who knows what might have happened next. Bennett was claimed to be the best coach in Scotland. He was certainly a fearsome one. He had been a sergeant major and PT instructor during the war, a goalkeeper with Hull City, Queen of the South and Dundee until 1950, then trained and managed at Ayr United. Deciding that management was not his bag, Bennett had returned to coaching at Motherwell and Third Lanark, before throwing in his lot with Liverpool. He would be a key influence at the club for the next 30 years. But right now, on a horrible, ice-rutted pitch in the west of England in January 1959, Liverpool lost catastrophically to Worcester City, 2-1 in the FA Cup. It would prove the final death knell for Phil Taylor and would provoke the eventual arrival, later that year, of Liverpool's first manager who had any real character and independence, probably since Tom Watson back in 1896. Beware, the coming of the man from Glenbuck. The modern game was finally arriving at Anfield.

Chapter 3

'Among Folks of My Own Kind'

Bill Shankly and the new Liverpool

Billy Liddell and Phil Taylor bow out, as a Scottish whirlwind arrives to spark the Anfield boot room. A future World Cup winner is picked up from local football. The Liverpool FC board opens the cheque book at last. Anfield is scrubbed down – by the new football management team. The Saint comes marching in, alongside a Scottish colossus. Promotion follows, out of the depths of the Second Division: a new dawn has broken over Oakfield Road. Meanwhile, Merseyside becomes the epicentre of global youth culture and the boot room forms. Bill Shankly pilots his team to their first league title for 17 years. The Kop gets its own psychoanalysis by the BBC.

The end for 'nice Phil'

After ending up fourth in the Second Division table in 1959, following a poor start to the new campaign two letters to the *Liverpool Echo* on 28 October summed up local feelings about Liverpool FC. A Mr K. Dickenson from Belper Street, Liverpool 19 worried that: 'The blunders made by the board in the past have put the team in a dangerous position. A drop to the Third Division is a real possibility. We followers of Liverpool have never had it so bad.' A Mr G. Unwin of Kingathorne Road, Liverpool 24 agreed, saying that, 'Never in the history of the club have their local supporters' spirits and enthusiasm been at such a low ebb. We see no optimism or hope for the future in the present team.' This was bleak stuff indeed, even compared to the darkest Liverpool years of the 1930s and early 1950s. By November 1959, Liverpool had won only six out of 17 league matches. In the Empire Theatre in the city, comedian Arthur Askey described his new show in November 1959 as 'this indescribable and varied act'. It could easily be applied to the manager's job at Anfield. Change had to come.

On 18 November 1959 the *Liverpool Echo* announced what many people had anticipated since the appointment of Reuben Bennett: that Phil Taylor had resigned as the manager of Liverpool Football Club. But this seemed like a strange time to leave his post, especially since cultish Everton striker Dave Hickson had recently signed for the club and a young Roger Hunt had been plucked by chance from local football. Taylor informed the local press that it was the strain of the job that had finally told on him, that he was 'very tired at times' and that 'I have never tried to cause anyone any trouble, and I must say few have caused me concern'. It was the usual, apologetic tone from a nice man who had been uncomplaining but who had never been given the full power of his own office.

The Liverpool board announced that they would be interviewing candidates for the job but Huddersfield's Bill Shankly was already the man they had in mind. Shankly had first been contacted about the manager's job by the Anfield board back in 1951 but he would not accept the Liverpool directors picking the team, so was summarily rejected as a candidate. The club's board was wary of Bill Shankly's independence and charisma but the Scot was also developing the sort of managerial reputation it liked: a man known for capably running and reviving football clubs on a shoestring budget. They took the plunge.

The man from 'Monkey Row'

Right from the start Bill Shankly's brand of exuberant west of Scotland popular socialism and ambition clashed with the rather penny-pinching, cautious individualism of the English Conservatives in the Liverpool boardroom. But the new manager actually liked the current Liverpool club chairman, T.V. Williams, and rather than seek out early confrontation Shankly simply sought to establish a very different identity for himself to the 'employee' or even 'servant' tags that had been hung like millstones round the necks of Kay, Welsh and Taylor and many before them. For one thing, Shankly chose to have no contract for his £2,500 p.a. position, saying confidently, 'If I cannot do the job, it is up to the people who employ me to do as they wish.' For another, Shankly wanted the freedom to manage, precisely the arrangement denied to the men who had gone before him. The Liverpool board swallowed hard – and accepted. Shankly sought to establish a sense of personal ownership of the Liverpool project, mainly in two ways: first, through his sheer devotion to the club, its supporters and to the sport – few men *lived* football as Bill Shankly did. And, second, by his very practical determination to improve the basic infrastructure of his workplace: the Anfield stadium and the Liverpool training ground. When Shankly filled in forms at hotels and elsewhere that asked for details of his place of residence, he often wrote in the space provided: 'Anfield'. It felt like he lived inside the football stadium he had now adopted as his own.

Shankly was, in fact, from 'Monkey Row', a group of streets in the tiny mining village of Glenbuck in the Ayrshire coalfields, a place renowned for producing the sort of Scottish 'professors' who had confounded early England international football teams. Shankly was one of ten children, including five brothers, born into poverty and all of whom played professionally. Poaching and guddling (catching fish with one's hands) was required even to survive in Glenbuck, but it was escaping the privations of the pit that made professional football such an essential ambition for local men. 'Wullie' Shankly liked a bet but he was a teetotaller who never smoked, rare among working men at the time. Nevertheless, his core values and native socialist beliefs around community and belonging were all rooted in sport and life in Glenbuck. When he later signed players for Liverpool, Shankly's core concern was always whether the new man truly *loved* the game, had the same natural enthusiasm for football as he and the men from Glenbuck did. Because of the intervention of war, he won but five full Scotland caps and Shankly knew the strengths, as well as the vagaries, of his fellow countrymen: 'If you've got three Scots in your side,' he said later, 'you've got a chance of winning something. If you've got any more, then you're in trouble.' This wisdom generally stood him in good stead at Anfield.

Shankly soon started to attend to the Liverpool stadium as if it was his own home. He got the Liverpool directors to pay for a pipeline to ensure all the toilets in the ground could be properly flushed – what privations fans in the 1950s had to endure – and he had the apprentices and the Liverpool ground staff busy painting walls, staircases and crush barriers. He and Bob Paisley were often discovered by the Liverpool directors – he probably engineered the meetings – late at night inside Anfield painting the toilets or the ground's endless passageways. Paisley even built the dugouts at Liverpool when the traditional box for the brass band sited under the main stand was no longer needed. All this was part of the informal contract Shankly felt he had made with the working people of the city: to provide regular stadium upgrades and something they could be proud of on the field. He also tried to keep his bargain with local people by *involving* them more inside the club; by rebuilding the strong bond that used to exist between the club staff and local supporters when Tom Watson or Elisha Scott had been powerful local characters in the city. In many ways, Shankly's presence and style began to epitomise the sort of intimacy that Scott himself had once engendered with Kopites.

Although the *Liverpool Echo* initially described him, insanely, as 'not a man with the gift of the gab', Shankly actually communicated his enthusiasm and commitment very well to a local Liverpool press starved of decent copy during the troubled recent club regimes. He also wanted to establish a more grounded link between players and 'ordinary' people in the city, something challenged by the lifting of the maximum wage in 1961. This was one of the reasons why he invited in local workers – including Liverpool's dustbin men – to play football matches against his young apprentices. This was more than simple match practice. The message here was that no one should be outside the scope of the club and that no player should ever get beyond his station in relation to the working people who funded their careers. 'I knew that, by and large, the people who produced that [Kop] roar were men just like myself who lived for the game of football and to whom football was their abiding passion,' Shankly said later. 'I knew that no matter what trials lay ahead I would be at home among folks of my own kind.'

Bill Shankly used to tell his hard men at Liverpool, his leaders on the pitch, 'Don't take any shit from anyone,' and he warned the Scots who came to the club never to soften up and never to lose their working-class Scottish accents. He wanted his imports to be proud and impervious to temptation in a city fast reawakening with the hum of pop culture and youth consumption. Shankly was also suspicious of the 'modern' coaching regimes then being established at the FA in the wake of the country's international failings. Simple formulae – talent plus practice – were what really mattered to Shankly: pass to the nearest red shirt; pass and move for the next pass. This might sound like typical mulish British opposition to modernisation but the Scot was no simple traditionalist, no blind flag-waver for the British way above all others. As the *Liverpool Echo* put it on 15 December 1959, Bill Shankly's approach would be a real eye-opener to those Liverpool supporters who had been raised on an outmoded and now mundane diet of rough-and-ready British playing styles:

> Shankly is a disciple of the game as played by the continentals. The man out of possession, he believes,

is just as important as the man with the ball at his feet. Continental football is not the lazy man's way of playing soccer. Shankly will aim at incisive forward moves by which continentals streak through a defence, when it is closed up by British standards. He will make his players learn to kill the ball and move it all in the same action, even when it is hit at them hard and maybe awkwardly; he will make them practice complete mastery of the ball; he will ensure that whatever else they may not learn, it won't be the fundamentals of good soccer.

Shankly developed new Melwood training regimes, approaches which prioritised much more ball work, the playing of small-sided matches and five-a-sides, and the use of wooden training boards to build up control, passing and shooting accuracy, and stamina. He looked great in a suit but, at Melwood, Bill was a tracksuit manager, always desperate to get out of the office and on to the training field with his men. New signings enjoyed the constant work with the ball but they were also astonished at the fitness levels demanded under the Liverpool coaching staff. 'No team will field fitter men,' promised Shankly. 'They will all go flat out for 90 minutes.' They always did, shades of Jürgen Klopp. Bill Shankly's first competitive match in charge was at home to Cardiff City on 19 December 1959 and 27,291 came to see it, a spluttering 4-0 defeat. Liverpool were tenth, exactly the position Klopp would inherit at the higher level 56 years later. A 3-0 loss at Charlton followed immediately, but then Shankly found his feet, with six wins and two draws from the next eight league fixtures. A poor run in March 1960 killed off any improbable promotion ambitions, including a 4-4 draw with Aston Villa after Liverpool had led by four goals – that fitness problem again.

Billy Liddell and a changing game
Although intrigued by Shankly, the *Liverpool Echo* now began to report on the sadness of seeing a wonderful club servant, Billy Liddell, 'once the lion of Anfield … left out in the cold so often

as a player whose active days are numbered'. It was almost as if the great man Liddell had to sign off the desperate 1950s before the new era for the club could begin in the breathless 1960s. The end of the great Liverpool hero, Liddell – a man whose 22-year Liverpool career since 1938 had produced one trophy, modest wages and, later, a two-days-training-a-week regime to fit in with his accountancy work – corresponded almost exactly with the 1960's consumer boom, the rise of televised sport in Britain, the lifting of the maximum wage and the emergence of some football players as authentic sex symbols and televised national celebrities. Liddell's last Liverpool match came barely a couple of years before the debut of George Best at Manchester United, but the two men looked – and were – decades apart in terms of their respective styles, symbolic power and their attitudes to sport and life. The world was changing. The FA even sanctioned Sunday league football in 1960 and the Football League Cup was added to the professional roster in England in the same year. In 1960, too, the city of Liverpool was announced as one of the hosts for the 1966 World Cup finals. In the Liverpool press, meanwhile, flashy advertising for home goods and services – cars, televisions, twin-tub washing machines, bank loans, hi-fidelity music systems, 'luxury' underwear – now challenged regular news stories for space. In November 1960 the first bona fide pop acts started playing at a then little-known Liverpool nightclub, the Cavern. American-style skyscraper blocks even started to appear on Merseyside and more were planned. This was the modern world.

By April 1960 Bill Shankly was ready to start experimenting with some of the young talent he was unearthing at the club. Locally born left-back Gerry Byrne, transfer-listed and unwanted under Phil Taylor, was now in the Liverpool first team under Shankly, heading for league and FA Cup winner medals and eventually a place in the 1966 England World Cup squad. So, too, was the 18-year-old right-winger Ian Callaghan from Caryl Gardens in the city, who was en route to a never-to-be-beaten record 857 appearances for the club. Callaghan played brilliantly and received a standing ovation on his debut in April 1960, a 4-0 Anfield walloping of Bristol Rovers. Shankly's bond with Callaghan was especially true: he had visited Cally's parents in Toxteth to get permission to sign him on professional forms for Liverpool. 'He is everything good that a man can be,' Shankly said later. 'He listened to the gospel ... the gospel of dedication and enthusiasm.' In June, Shankly managed to wring a record £13,000 out of the Anfield board to buy Kevin Lewis, a 19-year-old right-sided goalscoring winger/forward from Sheffield United, and then in August 1960 he brought in Gordon Milne, another record £16,000 man, a polished but tough little right-half, who joined from Preston North End. Shankly had been a neighbour of the Milnes, a feted football family, and he had watched this kid grow up like himself to become a 'right-living, right-thinking boy. He neither smokes nor drinks'. Another disciple.

Here, already, were the beginnings of the new Liverpool. Suddenly, the 1960 Liverpool AGM looked interesting and Bill Shankly 'played a blinder' according to the *Liverpool Echo*. The new manager said he felt that he had the full support of the board and that 'a new chapter had begun at Anfield'. He called on supporters and shareholders alike to 'forget the past ... all the hard-luck stories. I am sure success will come much sooner than some people anticipate'. No Liverpool manager had ever spoken in public quite like this, at least not since Tom Watson before the First World War. There was hearty applause at the boldness and style of the manager's delivery. Here was a Liverpool boss, at last, who was hugely enthusiastic and definitively his own man. Maybe this was real change after all? Even the Reds' supporters had a voice of sorts now at the Liverpool high table. A man called Solly Isenwater spoke from the floor for the newly formed Liverpool Shareholders Association, although he raised only minor issues: ticket prices for OAPs, and had Liverpool, by any chance, bought a loan copy of the film of Real Madrid's 7-3 destruction of Eintracht Frankfurt in the 1960 European Cup Final? It was hardly the *Spirit of Shankly*, but it was a start.

To puncture this excitement just a little, Liverpool reported a loss of £4,918 due to a fall in attendances connected to poor form but also to rising home leisure, car ownership and increased televised sport. Football was now an uncertain part of the new 'entertainment' business and there had even been early talk in football circles in 1960 of a possible British 'Super League', while television coverage of floodlit English and European football was now a very live and present issue. Liverpool's average home gate, at 30,269, had actually held up pretty well for a club in the Second Division in the light of all this flux and change. In the relegation season of 1953/54, First Division home gates at Anfield had averaged some 40,488, which meant a 25 per cent fall in home crowds over six years.

English football, generally, had been losing supporters year on year but everyone at Anfield knew that a promotion campaign and a return to the First Division would bring the crowds back. Maybe this garrulous young Scot, a man who liked boxing, hard-men American cinema heroes, and family holidays watching reserve-team football, really could perform the football oracle. But it would not happen right away. Billy Liddell's final competitive match for Liverpool was at centre-forward in a 1-0 home defeat against Southampton on 31 August 1960. The new manager admired Liddell as a great professional and Scottish international and he was not beyond a touch of sentiment in deserving cases. But without Liddell, who would now offer Liverpool a creative spark? When a labouring Reds beat Scunthorpe at home 3-2 in September, it was, for the *Liverpool Echo*, a 'lifeless, uninspiring, untidy display' and there was slow handclapping on the Kop. A crowd of 38,789 then turned out on a filthy Liverpool night to salute Liddell in his testimonial match, launched by a magnificent 16-page *Liverpool Echo* souvenir in which Danny Blanchflower described the Scot as 'a wonderful, stirring, awesome force, liable to erupt at any moment'. It felt like the club would never see his like again, and yet the young Ian Callaghan (and others) would eventually comfortably beat Liddell's Liverpool appearance record of 534 starts.

With Billy celebrated but now gone, after a poor start in the league in 1960 Liverpool went on a 14-match unbeaten run to take them up to second place by Christmas, behind Sheffield United, until a 1-0 defeat at Rotherham on 27 December broke the spell, with police climbing into the crowd at the end of the match, according to local press reports, 'to deal with a fight between rival supporters'. When Liverpool lost 4-3 at home to Middlesbrough on New Year's Eve, a brilliant Brian Clough scoring twice, police ended up patrolling the goal areas after the visiting goalkeeper Appleby had been struck in the face by a coin thrown from the crowd. Liverpool's crowd problems, routinely visible in the Second Division years, clearly had not disappeared. The Reds finished third again in 1960/61 but things were finally taking shape. Gerry Byrne, Lewis and Hunt were all now established in the first XI and Milne and Callaghan were gradually being eased into first-team duties. Veterans Bert Slater, in goal, and Dick White, at centre-half, both played 42 matches, and John Molyneux played 39 at right-back, but 58 goals conceded were too many advantages lost for the liking of Liverpool's coaches. Bill Shankly and his staff had much work still to do to get this squad into the sort of shape he wanted.

On board a powerful new racing car

'In my opinion, Liverpool can, and will be, one of the leading 12 clubs in the country.' This was Bill Shankly talking at the end of 1960 at the Liverpool FC AGM. What was he thinking? Liverpool had not even regularly finished in the top half of the First Division since the early 1930s. But these words, quietly spoken in that characteristic west of Scotland growl, offered something of a release from the icy wastes of barren decades. Local people were starting to believe in Bill Shankly and he fed on their energy and hope. So, too, did club captain Ronnie Moran, to whom Shankly had cleverly written a long letter explaining his expansive approach to management before even coming to Anfield. Liverpool FC had been conservative, unimaginative and rigid, both on and off the pitch for too long, with a team poorly led, cheaply recruited and badly selected by the club's directors. Training facilities at Liverpool were abject. The contrast with dashing and successful Manchester United, where its brilliant, recovering young manager Matt Busby had already been in charge for more than a decade, was stark. Liverpool FC's playing staff were shamed by their shambolic facilities and the club's holed and ragged austerity training kit. The new Melwood coaching team – Reuben Bennett as head coach, ex-player Bob Paisley as first-team trainer and physio, and Joe Fagan as reserves trainer – was hardnosed, but it was also young and dynamic and full of imaginative work and new ideas. It just needed a whirlwind, a catalyst like Bill Shankly, to galvanise and release them from the clutches of the inert Liverpool board. Now things could really change.

Rueben Bennett was the fitness man; he pounded out merciless laps at Melwood with the players, building up their reserves of strength and mocking the freezing-cold weather by rubbing blood injuries with a Brillo pad. Joe Fagan was recommended to Liverpool by Harry Catterick, then manager at Rochdale. Bill Shankly had once tried to sign Joe as a player, for Grimsby Town. Fagan was kindly, a good listener and a man to reason with, a conduit to reassure first-team players who had been dropped or injured. But he also had a very sharp football brain and was a good coach; he pushed his best reserves up the Anfield supply chain. When Fagan moved to first-team sponge man duties under Bill Shankly, his job was also to have a subtle word on the pitch about decisions to get into the referee's head and try to secure a better deal for his team. But Bob Paisley was later proven to be the key backroom character here. Bob had grown up at Anfield, of course, and was someone who had studied physiotherapy towards the end of his playing career. The Liverpool directors got Bob informal access into Merseyside hospitals so that he could study the mechanics of the human body close up. He was one of the few trainers in the Football League in the 1950s to have any kind of medical knowledge or training, a major step up from trainer Albert Shelley's random cursing and cold-water bucket treatments. Paisley even managed later to get the club to buy some of the latest heat and sonic equipment for the treatment of muscle injuries. It was a little like bringing the vestiges of science to bear on otherwise primitive communities. The first of these machines was known enigmatically at Anfield simply as 'The Electric'. Many injured players were reluctant to try it out and Paisley had requests to trial it on the pets of dog walkers passing by Anfield.

In fact, Bob became very well known among the players for his intuitive capacity to diagnose injuries from simply watching them stand or walk, as he would sum up the runners in the paddock for the 5.15 race at nearby Haydock Park. Great footballers implicitly trusted their bodies and their careers to him, and Liverpool developed a deserved reputation as a club whose players simply did not get injured – or at least hid their injuries and fears well. Paisley often slipped the young Ian Callaghan and Tommy Smith a slug of Scotch before matches; Bob had been given sherry and eggs as a Durham schoolboy. Paisley was no great talker or motivator – Shankly did all that stuff. And he was no trusted counsellor for the players; this was Joe Fagan's job. But he did have the task of keeping the impact of the local nightlife on Liverpool's players in check, a generally uneven contest. But, most of all, Bob was a dispassionate and astute assessor of footballers, focusing on their mental and physical make-up equally, making sure that Liverpool recruited men who were competitive, courageous winners, as well as having a physique to match the brutal task of playing in high-tempo, intensive British football matches.

This kind of collective backroom expertise and mentality – the core of the famous Liverpool 'boot room', of course – was a more than useful legacy for the relatively inexperienced Bill Shankly to inherit. He had to concede that Tom Williams and his boardroom colleagues had at least chosen the club's backroom staff incredibly well, even if the Liverpool board was often weak at selecting and signing players. Gone now, too, were the rag-arsed training outfits. Were these professional footballers or tramps?

'Every phase and detail was planned,' said Shankly of Melwood training, 'so we could move swiftly from one function to another.' After about a year spent eyeing things up, checking on all the club's players and facilities, 'everything changed', said the young Roger Hunt. 'Suddenly, everyone seemed to be walking about with a new sense of purpose.' New winger Alan A'Court noticed that 'in no time at all, both Anfield and Melwood were buzzing with an electric atmosphere. It was rather as if you were on board a powerful new racing car and he had just switched on the engine'. Gone was the disorganisation and easy-going atmosphere at some Liverpool training sessions. Notes were taken and kept on the effectiveness of different routines, and players were graded and trained in groups because, as Shankly put it, 'Different players require different exercises and quantity of training.'

No eating facilities were built at Melwood because Shankly wanted his players to cool down on the coach journey back to Anfield before they ate. These daily coach trips also helped to generate banter and bolster team spirit. This was mainly informal but actually very advanced football thinking in England for the time, the sort of detailed preparation designed, in Shankly's words, 'to size up the requirements of individuals to reach and retain peak fitness'. Today it has become second nature. On the pitch, the Shankly emphasis was on organised fluidity within a team structure: being constantly available for the next pass and having the highest possible levels of fitness. Shankly was not interested at all in set pieces, he thought they were static and unpredictable, too dependent on luck and players' instincts. So, Liverpool never practised them. When the first team did try out something for free kicks in a match situation it invariably ended up in chaos.

Shankly was keen on psychology and tactics but not on how FA coaches taught mental preparation and the new theories of the game and its systems. He barely lasted a couple of sessions on FA coaching courses at Lilleshall, hating the new technocratic language of football of 'overlapping full-backs' and the 'penetrative through-ball'. Magnetic discs representing opponents would be theatrically swept off a metal pitch board in team meetings at Melwood, the Scot showing his frustration that he could find nothing positive at all to say about these pitiful Liverpool rivals, or that he was wasting his time even trying. His own team talks he attributed to what he had taken from his early coal-mining experiences, where he learned that brashness or humour could relax working men for the physical and stressful task at hand.

Many players in the Liverpool dressing room came from similar northern manual working-class roots to his own. A typical pre-match 'tactical' session at Liverpool evoked the comradeship and co-democracy of the recent past: that football matches were peacetime battles to be won by shows of determination, fortitude and brave hearts. Toughness was central to all this. Weak or uncommitted opponents typically had 'a heart as big as a caraway seed'. Whenever his own football hard men were growing cocky or showing weakness, Shankly would simply throw photographs of real-life American gangsters on to the dressing room table saying that *these* guys had it really tough; they could be shot for making mistakes. There was little room here for overcomplicated tactics or any consciously planned strategy, beyond pass and move at pace. Shankly told the *Liverpool Echo* in 1962: 'It is not my function to stand in front of a blackboard haranguing the lads. A tactical session is more like a good discussion group in the Forces, with me as the officer leading it … I start the ball rolling, but anybody who has anything to say knows that he is expected to say it.'

The Second World War and its impact on physical education lingered long as a contributing – sometimes disabling – feature of coaching in the British game. Most young footballers still had to complete their two years in the forces before they could commit themselves entirely to their professional clubs. And who could say what the game might look like when war memories eventually faded? Within four years Liverpool FC under Shankly would be travelling to Iceland to begin a rollicking adventure with Europe's football elite that would last for decades. It would, in time, bring back six European Cups and various other European and world baubles to Anfield. Few people in the early 1960s – except perhaps Bill Shankly himself – could have predicted that. But first the new manager would have to convince the frugal Liverpool board to start spending big money. As it turned out, he would receive help to deal with this once intractable problem from a rather unexpected source.

The money game

Bill Shankly and his staff now set themselves the urgent task of dragging the Reds out of the Second Division, and the Liverpool board, kicking and screaming, out of its transfer fee torpor. Littlewoods Pools man and Eccles-born Blues supporter, John Moores, had taken over as chairman at stumbling Everton in 1960 on the back of a promise to pump cash into the Goodison club. Moores was true to his word; Everton won their first post-war league title in 1963, mainly on the back of the new chairman's free spending. But the Moores family also held shares in Liverpool FC and John Moores was a card-playing bridge partner of the Reds chairman T.V. Williams. Moores gently chided Williams about Liverpool's parsimonious transfer spending. A stronger Liverpool would stir up local interest in football.

John Moores decided to place his own nominee, Eric Sawyer, on the Liverpool board. The shrewd Sawyer was in charge of accounts at Littlewoods and became the finance director at Liverpool in 1961, with a mandate from Moores to try to loosen up the Anfield purse strings. Moores wanted to see *both* of the major clubs on Merseyside become successful and competitive; after all, the turnstiles at Rangers and Celtic and at City and United in Manchester rattled best when bitter local rivals were successful at the same time. With attendances falling, having Liverpool FC near-dormant in the Second Division was simply bad for local football business on Merseyside. Something had to change.

The modern Liverpool FC transfer revolution finally began in the spring of 1961. Before the transfer deadline Liverpool had offered £40,000 to Middlesbrough to sign their star centre-forward Brian Clough. But the bid was again rejected; Clough would move to Sunderland. Frustrated, Bill Shankly then spotted a small item in the Scottish sports press early in May 1961. Motherwell's young Scottish international Ian St John was being made available for transfer. He blinked. St John was a clever, deep-lying centre-forward who positively bristled with intelligence, youthful aggression and energy. Shankly had been tracking him for close on two years. The Motherwell forward might even be a *better* fit than Brian Clough – *and* he was a Scot. But signing Ian St John would cost. Shankly collected director Sid Reakes and chairman Tom Williams to check that his club was in big spending mode. He wanted no sticking points. The trio then drove in Reakes' Rolls-Royce to watch St John play against Hamilton Academical that same evening, sweeping into Fir Park like land-grabbers. At half-time the clubs' respective directors went into negotiations and just after midnight a deal was struck. Ian St John and his wife Betsy, meanwhile, sat outside the boardroom whispering, like nervous patients in a surgery waiting room. After the signing, the couple were driven directly to Merseyside and shown a club house under construction in 'salubrious' Maghull, north of Liverpool, where they might live in comfort with their new baby. The St Johns had been living in a pokey flat in Motherwell and the £1,000 signing-on bonus Liverpool had promised would buy a new Vauxhall car and some furniture. The Anfield board had finally learned to bend its own rules a little.

Although a full international, St John was still playing part-time football in Scotland but he knew and admired Reuben Bennett from his Motherwell days, so joining Liverpool with Shankly in charge seemed something like a home from home to the young Scot. This signing signalled a sea change in Liverpool's post-war fortunes and particularly the club's future intent. Above all, the brash, young Ian St John symbolised the arrival of the 1960s at Anfield. He had the swagger and confidence to challenge authority and the irreverent youthful style that underpinned wider social changes in Britain, including a wonderful surge of working-class musical cultural creativity in the city. On the pitch, St John produced real verve and invention – and the sheer devil that had been missing from the Liverpool team for a decade or more. Off it, he was at the head of many of the illicit adventures involving the club's players in the new fleshpots and nightclubs at home and abroad. Bob Paisley would soon be on his case. St John now would be better paid at Liverpool but not on the rates reported elsewhere in the early 1960s. Bill Shankly wanted all his players to be locked on to the same basic wage structure in order to maintain common purpose and a sense of natural justice – it was his nod to the strong belief that 'team spirit was a form of socialism'. Ensuring all players were on controlled, level wages with bonuses was also a way of keeping costs down, of course, and of making more money available for the manager to spend on transfers.

'Boy, what a ride!' the USA spaceman Alan Shepard told the world's press in front-page headlines in the week Ian St John signed. It could easily have been Bill Shankly enthusing to his new signing and his prospective Kop worshippers about the glorious Liverpool future he was planning. Shankly had more than doubled the club's previous transfer record. On 8 May 1961 Liverpool faced First Division thoroughbreds Everton in a locally prestigious Liverpool Senior Cup Final and Ian St John made his debut before a crowd of 51,669. The new Liverpool man was up against Brian Labone, a player fast emerging as one of England's toughest and best young centre-halves. St John confused and then terrorised Labone, completing a last-minute hat-trick in a hugely promising 4-3 Liverpool defeat.

Shankly at least now had something positive to take to the 1961 Liverpool AGM, where he blamed the accumulated tension of seven years of trying for the latest Liverpool promotion failure. But he also argued that the memory of his new man's debut was 'a tonic'. Shankly sparkled; he knew promotion was now in reach. Nevertheless, the members of the Liverpool Supporters' Association present at the AGM were reported to display an unusual 'underlying annoyance', arguing that the Liverpool board had, as normal, acted too little, too late, and that it should be condemned for this latest promotion failure. For once, the usually unflappable Tom Williams lost his temper. He rose to his feet and bellowed 'rubbish!', claiming that the Anfield directors had travelled hundreds of miles in the season to look for new players. He was agitated and angry, having laid out a cool £37,500 for a new centre-forward. A Mr Adler then jumped up from the floor and shouted that this was no way for the chair to talk to the club's shareholders and he called for a shock vote of no confidence in Williams. This was real drama, for once. Meanwhile, Bill Shankly looked on, both intrigued and impressed: these supporters had guts as well as loyalty. It was the first real sign of a direct challenge to the Liverpool board but Adler could get no seconder for his motion. The meeting eventually calmed down, with Williams, Reakes and Clifford Hill all being re-elected, unopposed. The storm had quickly blown over but it was probably the most exciting – and the most disharmonious – Liverpool FC AGM in the entire history of the club as a limited company so far. At last something compelling and challenging seemed to be brewing in Liverpool 4. Bill Shankly was at the heart of it.

Slaughterman five – for promotion

Shankly now had the front end and the middle of his new team pretty much sorted out. Ian St John would be the perfect foil for the young Roger Hunt, a man to link up defence and attack, and Callaghan and Milne would add dynamism wide and in midfield. But the Liverpool defence still lacked a pivot and a leader, a real physical presence. Shankly had tried, illegally, to tap up Leicester City's Scottish captain Frank McLintock for the role, even dragging him out of that club's banquet on the night Leicester lost to Spurs in the 1961 FA Cup Final. McLintock declined, joining

Arsenal instead. Bill Shankly typically rubbished the Scot for his audacity – and stupidity. He turned his attention to Scotland once more, carrying with him Eric Sawyer's best wishes and the once little-seen cheque book of Liverpool FC.

Ron Yeats was from Aberdeen but he was a Glasgow Rangers fan. In junior football at 14 years of age he had been converted from left wing-half to centre-half and the growth spurt that followed confirmed him as a traditional left-sided defensive stopper. Yeats happily worked on shifts as a slaughterman from 15 years of age, enjoying the toughness and the camaraderie of the job – it certainly paid more than part-time professional football. When he signed for Dundee United in 1957, Yeats typically went to work at 2.30am on Saturday mornings, clocked off at 11am, grabbed a few hours' sleep and then played football. After just 28 United appearances, Yeats went on to do two years National Service in the Royal Army Service Corps, including captaining the British Army football team in a match against Liverpool.

Bill Shankly took note. But he and his directors were greeted at Dundee with what he later called an 'arctic reception'. They persisted, but Yeats knew nothing about Second Division Liverpool, or their slightly deranged Scottish manager – he hoped to sign for Manchester United or another 'big' club. His bosses at Dundee United had always been rather shabby and insecure figures, cast only just above the shop floor of the Tannadice Park dressing room. By contrast, Liverpool's Bill Shankly had the glossy, almost corporate or film star air of a man really going places. Here was a character who had smile appeal, backed up by his red ties specially made for him in Germany. Shankly made a big first impression on Ron Yeats when they met:

> I always remember this: he was a lovely dresser: lovely suit and tie, and white, white teeth. That really impressed me. And then he's walking round me, I can hear him at the back of me and he says: 'Jesus Christ, son, you must be about seven feet tall!' And when he comes back to the front, I said: 'No, I'm

only six foot two,' and he said: 'That's near enough fucking seven foot to me!' I thought, there and then, I *like* this man.

Yeats signed for around £20,000. Now Shankly had his new side – Byrne, Milne, St John, Hunt, Callaghan and Yeats were the core – and he was almost completely in charge of selecting it. Liverpool's directors would decide, from now on, about the stadium and the club's finances, but not the players or the team set-up. There would be no more weekly submissions of the manager's proposed line-up for board approval and late changes. The average age of the Reds' first-team squad had also been reduced, radically, from that under Phil Taylor in 1959 – Byrne, Yeats, Milne, Hunt, St John, Lewis and Callaghan were all in their early twenties or younger. In the Liverpool reserves, the names of Lawrence, Lawler, Arrowsmith, Gordon Wallace and Tommy Smith were already showing. These were talented and hungry young men, players with enough skill and toughness to challenge their elders. A combination of shrewd purchases, the fruits of the club's youth policy and a lucky break in spotting Roger Hunt in local non-league football, had produced a team and a club that no longer looked at home in the Second Division of the Football League.

The truth of it was that, in season 1961/62, Liverpool simply *ruined* the opposition in the English second tier; it was a profoundly unfair contest, almost embarrassingly easy right from the start. After a crushing 3-0 defeat of fancied Sunderland in August 1961 the local press reported that 'football was reborn at Anfield last night' and ran headlines praising 'Liverpool's finest team for many years'. A 5-0 pounding of Leeds United followed, with a first Roger Hunt hat-trick, some 71 matches into his Liverpool career. Hunt would score three more league hat-tricks in that season alone; the signing of Ian St John had released Hunt to ransack defences. The Merseyside press agreed that the presence of Ron Yeats had also 'bolstered the defence almost beyond belief' and that St John was 'an artist ... full of ambition'. In honour of their new Scottish forward, the Kop had begun to sing its first real modern song in anger: 'When the Saint Goes Marching In', further adapted later to 'When the Reds Go Marching In.'

By the end of November 1961 there were only two Liverpool league defeats to report. No club would win at Anfield during the season and only three took league points there. Liverpool were now unbeaten in the league at home since 31 December 1960, making Anfield a real fortress. Even the club's reserve and B teams were unbeaten at home. That important link with fans was also reviving. A supporter, John Spiers, remembers first-teamer Tommy Leishman finishing training around this time before having a kick-about with locals on Stanley Park.

The Reds were already clear, destined for promotion, but Shankly wanted more. In March 1962 both Everton and Liverpool bought new Lancashire-based goalkeepers in the same breath, Liverpool signing Jim Furnell from Burnley for £18,000 and Everton splashing out even bigger money on the erratic but entertaining Gordon West from Blackpool. Bert Slater had conceded only 27 goals in 29 league matches but Shankly had decided, ruthlessly, that his keeper was just too small to really dominate his penalty area and Furnell went straight into the Liverpool first team. With Ian Callaghan now in for Kevin Lewis on the right wing and Ronnie Moran filling in for Dick White at full-back (Gerry Byrne had moved across to left-back), the 'new' Liverpool was in full bloom, a group of players who would not only win promotion as champions but could actually achieve something in the First Division. And then – who knows?

Liverpool FC: Second Division Champions, 1961/62

Furnell
Byrne Yeats Moran (White)
Milne Leishman
St John Melia
A'Court Hunt Callaghan (Lewis)

With seven matches left, five points clear and with one game in hand over nearest chasers, Leyton Orient, it looked like a clear run-in would be a formality. Roger Hunt had already smashed Gordon Hodgson's 36-goal club league scoring record in a season – he would eventually end up with 41 league goals in just 41 appearances – and he had scored on his full England debut, against Austria. Ian St John contributed 18 goals. Later, 'Sir' Roger was presented with (and he valued) a canteen of cutlery, by the Liverpool Supporters' Club for his achievements. Another age. But real life then took a hand – as it would much more severely, again, in 2020. A deadly smallpox outbreak in South Wales meant that Liverpool's fixture at Swansea in early April was postponed. This medical scare meant that promotion was finally clinched only on 21 April 1962 in a constant downpour against Southampton at Anfield, with two goals from the returning Kevin Lewis, filling in for the suspended Ian St John. The Saint had typically sneaked into the ground to watch proceedings, even though the FA had banned him from Anfield.

There were still five league fixtures left, including the entire Easter programme, but Liverpool's promotion had been an open secret almost since the early exchanges. They ended up eight points clear of Orient and, tantalisingly, on 99 league goals scored. The Southampton players gallantly made a rather sodden and bedraggled guard of honour for Liverpool as the teams left the field, and one soaked pitch invader plonked a kiss and a red-and-white hat on a bemused Ron Yeats's head. Tom Williams and Bill Shankly both tried to make speeches from the Main Stand but the Liverpool PA system was so poor, and the supporters so excited, that no one could hear them. The team went and got showered while the Kop repeatedly chanted 'We want the Reds!'

The players now attempted a lap of honour in mufti but it lasted about 20 yards before they were mobbed and forced back into the players' tunnel. The fans had to feast, instead, on dressing room photographs in the next day's newspapers, showing the team and staff drinking champagne together out of crockery mugs – a nice touch this one, the sporting artisans getting just a little taste of the high life. At the front of the shot a proud, teetotal Bill Shankly was beaming. Ron Yeats later described it as 'the best season I had at Liverpool football club'. When the Second Division trophy was finally presented later at Anfield, in the crowd was a list of past Reds greats, including Fred Hopkin, Eph Longworth, Bill Jones and Jim McDougall. Six-year-old Reds mascot Leslie McCann was also excited and present, as he had been at all Liverpool's matches, home and away, that season. But pride of place here went to the 80-year-old Joe Hewitt, a man who had served the Liverpool club for more than 60 years as player and club worker, including 164 starts, 74 goals and a league title in 1906. As Ron Yeats held the trophy aloft, Joe had a discernible tear in his eye as his hand grasped something in his pocket that day: it was his own Football League championship medal. The message from Bill Shankly for old Joe and for his current team was that there would be no more Liverpool gloom with the club stuck in the second rank of the English game. All that darkness was over. Anfield had sleepwalked into a dreadful slump, led largely by its own complacent directors. It had taken a stimulus from local rivals Everton to refloat the Liverpool boat, but now the Reds had an inspiring young manager for whom nothing seemed out of reach. 'A trip to Wembley' hazarded Leslie Edwards in the *Liverpool Echo*. 'That is the next mission, I would think, on Shankly's list of priorities.' It would take the new boss three more years to achieve that elusive Liverpool FA Cup target – and we all know that a lot can happen in football in three years.

Moving on up

With promotion assured and Bill Shankly acting as both bold figurehead and chief club cheerleader, Liverpool's average league crowds had jumped in 1961/62 to 39,237, just below Everton's First Division seasonal average of 41,432. These were Liverpool's best crowd figures since 1953/54, the club's last season in the First Division. But the general trend in football attendances in England was still decidedly downwards. A Football League survey in April 1962 identified some interconnected themes of rising incomes and growing consumer choice for the young in accounting for the relative decline of active football club support. The report highlighted greater prosperity but also uncomfortable league grounds and defensive football, as well as pressures from women for their husbands and boyfriends to spend more time with them and their children on Saturdays, as the key reasons for falling attendances. Pop music also offered a new leisure outlet for young men and women away from their parents, an option that had very different things to offer from standing, exposed, on open football terraces, often in the rain. The game needed to modernise to keep pace with change. A local fan, Joan Kennedy of Anzio Road, Huyton resented what seemed to be the underlying assumption here: that women had no place at football in Liverpool, or elsewhere. She wrote angrily to the *Liverpool Echo* on the matter on 27 April 1962, criticising the sport for its chauvinist attitudes:

> Women don't like to be left out, as they feel they are when their husbands and boyfriends go off alone or with their pals to football matches. Why not encourage the girls and women to go along and watch, instead of discouraging them? Girls can be just as enthusiastic as men about football.

In June 1962 the *Liverpool Echo* even reported on a possible new local enlightenment on the football and gender front: 'It seems there is sufficient interest to form a Liverpool ladies football team in the city.' But it was another false dawn. Women's football was slowly stirring but it would take another 30 years for the English football establishment to begin to take the role of women in the game seriously, either as players or spectators. A series of official reports on restructuring men's football in England in the 1960s was summarily rejected by the heads-in-the-sand Football League. The English game would continue to plough along its traditional furrow, even as crowds continued to tumble.

At the celebratory Liverpool AGM in 1962, chairman Tom Williams warned the club's occasionally disorderly young male supporters about their behaviour, saying, 'Do not let yourself be carried away by the excitement of the moment.' He might have better addressed his remarks to his perpetually excitable Scottish manager. An iridescent Bill Shankly sparkled with a story about the 'cauldron' Anfield had now become and how he had recently been paid a wonderful touchline compliment by a visiting manager. This rival boss, reported Shankly, was calm 'almost to the point of contrition' in contrast to Shankly's own touchline animation. The Scot paused for maximum effect now, eyeing up his entranced Liverpool AGM audience. The visiting coach had looked up the touchline and nodded toward the Kop before growling to the agitated Shankly, 'You're worse than those people on the terraces.' The Liverpool boss beamed with pride at the memory of the moment, as his audience laughed approvingly. The Scot, as he liked to say, was among his own people. But the Liverpool board was not yet completely cowed by their young manager. They moved the winger Johnny Morrissey on to neighbours Everton for a £10,000 fee in August 1962 – and to a league title, of course – behind Bill Shankly's back. The Scot was furious at the sale and he had to be persuaded not to walk out on the spot. The Liverpool directors finally agreed to do no more deals without the manager's approval, and there were no other major board-induced arrivals or departures at Anfield as the Reds prepared for their return to the top level.

To rise to the new challenge, in came a silky, left-sided wing-half from Glasgow Rangers for £20,000. Willie Stevenson was an exceptional passer, if a reluctant tackler, a man who was just about holding up the progress of the great Jim Baxter at Ibrox, so he was keen on joining the Liverpool project. 'Willie Stevo' did not lack in confidence, a man with more than a touch of the grand stylist about him, preferring cognac and expensive suits to beer and the knitwear favoured by the 'peasants' in the Liverpool squad. When Peter Thompson arrived to play on the Liverpool left, Stevenson told him, 'Just stay out on the wing and I'll supply you with everything. In fact, I'll make you an international, if you're good enough.' The caustic, often belligerent, Liverpool dressing room banter of the modern period had already begun.

Stevenson's arrival on Merseyside coincided with the promotion of the Lancastrian-Scotsman goalkeeper Tommy Lawrence to replace Jim Furnell. The stocky Lawrence hardly matched the photofit of a modern keeper, even in the 1960s – he was neither especially tall, nor particularly agile. He was known affectionately by Liverpool fans as 'the flying pig'. But he was brave, solid and reliable and he also had some of Elisha Scott's hyper-alert reading of the game. Lawrence was quickly off his line whenever he spotted danger, confidently sweeping up anything that got behind his defenders, even straying out of his penalty area to deal with local alarms. Much of this was new. Indeed, like many keepers today, Lawrence could use his feet as ably as most outfield players could, and he helped to revolutionise the traditional goalkeeping role because of the way he knitted his job in with those men in his back line.

These new recruits, Lawrence and Stevenson, made an almost immediate difference to Liverpool's results, a nine-match winning league streak in the higher level in November 1962, conceding only five goals in the process. Bill Shankly was in ebullient mood, telling the national press that his attacking Liverpool side 'might do even better if so many of their opponents were not obsessed with negative soccer'.

This winning league run was ended by bogey side Leicester City on 2 March. Leicester also later saw off the Reds in the FA Cup semi-finals at Hillsborough in 1963 and were described by football historian Percy Young as having played 'the most imaginative football seen in a cup tie for years'. Imaginatively dull, perhaps, as Liverpool had more than 30 attempts on Leicester's goal, compared to City's three. For Shankly it was a match that echoed the one-sided 1947 semi-final Liverpool defeat to Burnley, and it only confirmed his fears about being caught on the break by defensive opponents. In the league, meanwhile, champions-elect Everton also shut up shop in a 0-0 draw at Anfield in April, as Liverpool had even briefly threatened a title challenge, following a 5-2 Easter thumping of Spurs, only to be crushed 7-2 by the same opponents three days later in London. A slippery Jimmy Greaves scored four times. This collapse prompted the Liverpool-born teenager Tommy Smith to confront Shankly to ask why he was still out of the Liverpool first team, a reasonable question. But he would need to wait for an answer. The result also seemed to sap Liverpool's resolve and they rapidly slipped out of contention, with only one win secured in the last nine league matches.

As the league season dribbled away, Bill Shankly experimented with a robust Manchester-born forward, the extravagantly quiffed Alf Arrowsmith, who scored goals and promised to do much more at Anfield, before injury would cut him down. However, a 5-1 win versus Birmingham City early in May 1963 finally gave a certain Tommy Smith his chance. Smith had captained Liverpool in the FA Youth Cup Final and he was an England youth international, very much a sign of things to come. But the emerging new Liverpool star for the future was actually a tall, young, technically gifted centre-half and ex-England schoolboy captain. Chris Lawler was one of 15 children, including 11 boys, all Liverpudlians. His father had told young Chris to spend one day training with Everton, just to get a free pair of Adidas boots. Smart move. Bill Shankly shifted the near wordless Lawler from the ground staff to training at Melwood soon after, before his first Liverpool match, deputising for Ron Yeats against West Brom in March 1963. Matt Busby was interested in signing both Lawler and Tommy Smith but Bill Shankly knew better. It would take the youth system at the Liverpool club another 50-plus years to produce a local attacking right-back as good as this one. Fans who were old enough could readily bracket Lawler and the precocious Trent Alexander-Arnold in the same sentence.

In August 1963 the Liverpool board sanctioned a £37,000 bid for Preston's outrageously talented left-winger Peter Thompson.

Shankly had actually wanted to sign the Yorkshireman Mike O'Grady, from Huddersfield Town, so fortune played its capricious hand here when the Yorkshire club refused to sanction the deal. The dashing Thompson thrilled his manager, who saw him as a modern, if occasionally over-elaborate, version of his beloved Tom Finney. The Liverpool crowd of the 1960s also fell in love with Thompson's trickery and his sinewy runs and crosses. He was the perfect foil for the more direct and hard-working Ian Callaghan on the Liverpool right side. What a pair of wide players this was: 'Cally' could run night and day, while 'Thommo' drifted elegantly past hypnotised defenders. With Alf Arrowsmith available to cover for injury in the forward positions and Phil Ferns and the ghostly Lawler ready to do the same defensively, Shankly knew that, if he could steer clear of injuries, this basic 14-man squad was even capable of challenging for the league title in 1964. He was right.

Shankly also now had the appropriate setting for title success because, in the summer of 1963, the old stand along the Kemlyn Road side of the Anfield ground had been demolished to be replaced by a cantilevered new structure seating 6,700 spectators at the substantial cost of £350,000. Popular local demand insisted it be called the Billy Liddell Stand but this was rejected by the board on the basis that it raised the status of players – mere employees – too highly. Talk was now ongoing in the Liverpool council chambers about developing a new 3,500-space football car park on the shrubbery area of Stanley Park, sited between the city's two football stadiums. It was the age of the car. But even this new modern version of Anfield had only 11,000 seats in a 54,000 capacity (compared to Everton's 18,000 in 73,000). The changes also annoyed those Anfield supporters who had enjoyed the fun of changing terrace ends at half-time. They signalled, nevertheless, that Liverpool FC were going places and moving, at last, into the era of more modern and more diverse spectator provision.

The Football League title, 17 years on

In August 1963 Bill Shankly finally signed a contract at Liverpool for the first time; the deal was for five years. He told the *Daily Post*, 'I suppose it is the modern trend to have agreements such as this, and I have simply fallen into line.' Ambitious Nottingham Forest had been making overtures to Shankly, so the Liverpool board wanted some assurances. The move also offered some general stability to the club as well as more security to the Liverpool manager and players. Shankly had begun to identify strongly with the Liverpool people – and they with him. He was made for the new TV age of football. The Liverpool and Everton football clubs were both riding high after some years in the wilderness and the city's pop music success had brought the world's media to Merseyside. With a new Labour government forming and headed by the Huyton MP, Harold Wilson, it felt as if the city was at the very epicentre of a radical shift in generational and class change and was *the* key place for popular culture in Britain, perhaps the world.

This dynamic version of the city of Liverpool was very different to the rather austere provincial backwater it had appeared to be just a decade earlier. Bill Shankly was, of course, a Labour man – he conducted a famous TV interview with Wilson – but he was no great lover of formal politics, glamour or pop music. Instead, the Scot preferred working a crowd, a quiet game of cards or else listening to ballads by Jim Reeves, Tom Jones or Ray Charles, to suffering the racket produced by Liverpool's new pop groups. But Shankly also recognised and enjoyed the energy of the city and its people and the public focus they now attracted. His players regularly mixed socially with local celebrities and some of them had begun to exude some of the latter's youthful self-confidence.

Bill Shankly was actually well attuned to the demands of this emerging, comedic local 'performance culture' in the city. He was, after all, something of a comic performer himself. It was no surprise to him that the BBC's first match on its new

Saturday night BBC2 TV football highlights show, *Match of the Day* on 22 August 1964, would be screened from the home of the First Division champions Liverpool (or 'Beatleville' for Kenneth Wolstenholme). Where else? Only 75,000 armchair viewers watched as the Reds team defeated Arsenal 3-2, but it was a start. The club's younger fans were soon singing Beatles, Cilla and Gerry and the Pacemakers pop songs on the Kop – BBC documentary coverage followed – thus defining the new links between the three key modern cultural domains of the moment: youth, football, and popular music. Shankly had no great desire at all, of course, to produce a self-consciously 'glamorous' team. Manchester United, along the East Lancs Road, with Denis Law and the teenage George Best already in bloom, were dominating the national press in the razzle-dazzle stakes. Shankly was more than happy at hard-working Anfield; why leave this city stage and this young team when everyone else seemed so desperate to move to the city of Liverpool? So, Bill Shankly signed his new contract and he was well prepared for his assault on the league title.

Using Bill Shankly's preferred 'Tomlinson T' orange ball at Anfield, the Football League championship win of 1963/64 was eventually almost as definitive, almost as predictable as the Second Division triumph had proved to be for Liverpool in 1962. But it did not start that way, not even close. Has any other title-winning team begun their season of triumph by losing its first three home matches, as happened here? Shankly even called in a psychoanalyst to help his players and he drily assured the Liverpool board that he was sure that his team would win at least *one* game at home. Already, the disgruntled newly seated fans in the Kemlyn Road were leaving early, thus establishing a tradition in the process. Liverpool had managed to win at Blackburn, first up, provoking a celebratory pitch invasion, and they also eventually thrashed Wolves 6-0 to break the home losing streak, but by the time champions Everton visited Anfield on 28 September 1963 the Reds had accumulated just nine points from nine league matches. Jimmy Melia was the fans' chief whipping boy but two Ian Callaghan goals were enough to see off the champions from Goodison and to kick-start the Anfield club's season with a run of five straight wins. It was Liverpool's first league victory against Everton since 1950. Not that Leicester City could be shaken off that easily – another 1-0 home defeat followed to the East Midlanders, which produced booing and missile-throwing at Leicester players and the reported abuse of some visiting fans outside Anfield.

Hooliganism was just starting to take a real hold in England, forcing neighbours Everton to introduce curved areas behind each goal end at Goodison to control those fans pelting opposing keepers. Football Special trains would soon be banned from Lime Street because of the damage caused on them. This would mean an 11.30pm Friday departure for any Merseyside-based fan travelling by coach for a Saturday south coast fixture. Meanwhile, a further string of league wins, and a 6-1 Boxing Day home trouncing of Stoke City (who were minus the injured 48-year-old Stanley Matthews) revived Liverpool's title hopes. The new Kemlyn Road season ticket holders in the pitchside rows were still not happy, however; they told the *Liverpool Echo* that getting rained on and having patrolling police officers obstruct their view of the last ten minutes of every home match was not ideal. Perhaps it was why they were leaving so early?

However, the atmosphere at the 1-0 Liverpool home win vs Manchester United on 23 November 1963 was decidedly muted in all areas. US President John F. Kennedy had been assassinated the day before and the city of Liverpool has strong Irish-American connections (something similar would occur in 2001 at Anfield, after the 9/11 assault). After 19 matches the Reds were top, ahead of Blackburn Rovers and Spurs by one point, but a home defeat to Rovers in December saw the Reds slip back to fourth. Liverpool would eventually lose 11 league matches in the season but drew only five, thus stacking up 57 points, a Premier League equivalent today of 83 points. After another strong league run in January, losing the derby return to Everton 3-1 in February seemed like a painful blip rather than a defining moment. So, by the time Liverpool lined up against Second Division strugglers Swansea Town at home in the sixth round of the FA Cup on 29 February 1964, having already dumped out Derby County and (with difficulty) Port Vale, before seeing off Arsenal 1-0 at Highbury in the fifth round – Ron Yeats and Joe Baker both sent off for a bout of the Henry Coopers – it even felt, once again, like a possible Liverpool league and cup double.

It was distracted thinking. This fixture is lodged in the brain of every Liverpool fan of a certain vintage who saw it. Swansea's goalkeeper, Noel Dwyer, had an inspired match – and bucketfuls of luck. When he dived the wrong way under the Liverpool siege, the ball simply hit his legs, or else struck the post or the bar. Liverpool conceded two early goals, got one back through Thompson, but when Ronnie Moran stepped up to take a Liverpool penalty kick it was almost ordained that he would miss. And he did, his fourth failure of the season. Liverpool could do little else to try to avoid the 2-1 defeat, echoes of the Worcester City disgrace in 1959. But at least it meant that the league title could be the sole focus now.

The 1964 First Division title was decided, as many had been before, during the crowded Easter programme, after Everton had briefly moved to the top of the table. In nine days, between 27 March and 4 April 1964, Liverpool defeated title challengers Spurs twice, bogey team Leicester City at Filbert Street, and eventual league runners-up Manchester United 3-0 at Anfield, scoring 11 goals in this critical period and conceding only two. Roger Hunt scored a brilliant hat-trick at White Hart Lane in a 3-1 win, and his combination with the burly Arrowsmith, while Ian St John played in the withdrawn Jimmy Melia role, had given Liverpool an attacking edge they had previously lacked. No one could match this burst of points-collecting. As Everton crumbled, a comprehensive repeat 3-1 Liverpool defeat of Spurs at Anfield – with fans queueing from 8am for their places – and a 3-0 win away at Burnley on 14 April 1964 (two goals for Arrowsmith), set up the home match against Arsenal as a potential title decider, even with three fixtures still outstanding.

Everton were also hit, right now, by Sunday press revelations of the Tony Kay match-fixing bribery scandal. It had been a poor week for the Blue half of the city, just made much worse. Right after their win at Burnley, Liverpool signed Phil Chisnall from Manchester United for £25,000, thus providing a football quiz query for the ages about players moving directly between these two north-west rivals. Chisnall was the last, and he would play only a handful of times for Liverpool, spending most of his professional career at lowly Southend United. But it was a sign that, even on the verge of a title, Bill Shankly was already making plans for the future.

Liverpool FC: League Champions, 1963/64

Lawrence

Byrne (Ferns) Yeats Moran

Milne Stevenson

Hunt St John

Callaghan Arrowsmith (Melia) Thompson

Roger Hunt had an ankle injury but he kept the worst of it from his manager and played in what turned out to be the season's deciding fixture. Fans camped outside Anfield overnight and chaos ensued the next day in the surrounding streets as the pay-at-the-gate turnstiles opened. On the pitch, had George Eastham scored a penalty – a brilliant Lawrence save – to equalise St John's early goal, the result might even have been different. But Liverpool stormed away instead, Peter Thompson scoring two goals in a 5-0 rout. The game was reduced to exhibition football by the end. This relaxed finale allowed the Kop to go through its complete repertoire of triumphant songs for the BBC TV boffins present. The home squad returned after the final whistle with a makeshift papier mâché red-and-white trophy for a lap of honour after a run of seven straight wins. Shankly refused to join them, saying, 'The pitch is for the players,' but he was there with his men in the directors' box as the champagne (and tears) flowed. It echoed, of course, some of the emotion on show for the departure of Elisha Scott, exactly 30 years earlier.

Roger Hunt and Ian St John between them had scored 52 of Liverpool's 92 goals, but perhaps the key to this success had been moving Jimmy Melia on and playing St John in a more withdrawn role, thus allowing Alf Arrowsmith to play alongside Hunt. Few teams could cope with this attacking formation. After Arsenal, Liverpool lost two and drew one of the 'dead' fixtures they had left – the club's players have never shied away from celebrations – so their final points tally of 57 was four points clear of Manchester United. The margin could have been much greater. Before this title win, Liverpool FC had won one major trophy in 41 years, so this was a moment of significant change. It was recognised in distant Robben Island where the apartheid prisoner Nelson Mandela, in the early stages of a 27-year sentence, raised a faint smile; he was, of course, a Liverpool FC and Bill Shankly fan.

Chapter 4

A Brave New World

The FA Cup, Europe and Bill Shankly's Gap Years

The red-and-whites become the all-reds. Seventy-three years of waiting is finally over and Gerry Byrne becomes one of the game's great FA Cup heroes. The Liverpool adventure in Europe begins but a trap is set as 'the wizard' casts his evil spell in Milan. A good man is lost at Liverpool FC, while Bill Shankly has a seven-year furlough. Shankly finally has to ditch his loved ones. He builds his second great Liverpool around three brilliant Englishmen. There are triumphs in Europe but not the trophy Shankly really wants. A shock retirement beckons.

Welcome to Europe

Liverpool now had a new chairman to support or frustrate Bill Shankly – probably both – as Tom Williams finally stood down in 1964, moving to a new role as club president. The new chair, Sid Reakes, a haulage businessman from St Helens, had joined the board back in June 1955. The deputy chair was Harold Cartwright, a local manager for the Royal Liverpool Friendly Society and a self-designated 'lifelong follower' of the club. His father, the late, Walter Cartwright, was a former chairman and Harold would become chair in 1967. At Anfield, like at many English clubs at this time, everything changed behind the scenes but it also pretty much remained the same. Directors and chairmen were not expected to fund success. With cash flow always an issue, the Liverpool board agreed to a gruelling ten-match, money-making post-season tour to the USA and Canada, thus denying this small squad meaningful rest after their heroic exploits. The players, of course, saw it as a bonus; sports science was the future, and tiredness and fatigue were barely discussed inside the game at this time. It was simply assumed that top players could churn out repeat performances, irrespective of the mental and physical stresses of playing top-level sport week in, week out.

It would certainly have its impact here. With these new ideas, new men at the helm, an exhausting tour in the players' legs, but without the stricken Alf Arrowsmith, unsurprisingly Liverpool struggled badly to defend their hard-won league title: eight defeats in the first 15 league matches in 1964/65 and only four victories told the story. New versatility signing Geoff Strong from Arsenal, for around £40,000, struggled to make an early impact. Included in this sequence was a humiliating 4-0 home reverse to Everton. The visitors' Mother Noblett, the Toffee Lady, had been sprayed with rubbish and orange peel on her pre-match parade before the Kop, and Everton fully took their revenge.

Suffering, it would take the Reds until January 1965 to secure a place even in the top ten league positions. This had been quite a slide, but retaining the league title in the intensely competitive period between 1959 and 1975 would prove impossible for any club. Moreover, this Liverpool team had risen to the top very quickly and, frankly, Shankly's main focus was now elsewhere – on the Continent and in the FA Cup, to be precise. The Reds were late into Europe compared to some of their main English rivals and it was difficult to balance priorities at home and abroad, even though the first Liverpool European adventure began with an early season 5-0 European Cup win in Iceland, part of an 11-1 aggregate walkover against little KR Reykjavík that was completed in September. It was a relaxed way to get your feet under the European table.

A much stiffer task came against the Belgian champions Anderlecht, who included in their number the prodigious inside-forward Paul van Himst, arguably Europe's best young player. Back home, Van Himst was wittily nicknamed *Polle Gazon* (Paul Lawn) because of how frequently he was fouled to ground. This Anderlecht team was essentially the Belgium national team performing in club colours. Before the home leg, Shankly came up with not one, but *two*, innovations. First, that Liverpool would wear an all-red strip for Europe from now on, ditching their white shorts and red-and-white socks. Psychologists have long argued that the colour red offers a positive advantage to its wearers. Why not *all* red? The players liked it, so Liverpool would also play in all-red in the 1965 FA Cup run and eventually for all fixtures. Second, Shankly wanted to get his tough young defensive tyro Tommy Smith into the Liverpool team, perhaps to shadow the dangerous Van Himst. The Belgian might yet find that he had earned that nickname of his.

The number 10 shirt was available and Shankly wanted to try Smith in the new defensive position he had discussed with his staff, alongside Ron Yeats, even if the shirt numbers looked a little strange in defence (they should see them now!). Tommy Smith had lost his dad as a teenager, so the Liverpool coaches became acting father figures to this abrasive, local young man. His approach to the game, as one journalist astutely put it, 'involved marrying skill with terror'. From now on Smith would be firmly in the Liverpool first team and he was already acting like a veteran as Liverpool's league form picked up. But Manchester United and Leeds were stretching away at the top, so the cup competitions at home and abroad became the key targets for the Reds in 1965.

West Bromwich Albion away in the third round of the FA Cup was a tough enough assignment without Ron Yeats picking up the ball in the penalty area after he heard a crowd whistle, only to see the referee pointing to the spot for handball. Bobby

Cram missed the kick, sparking Liverpool to a 2-1 win. The Reds were even luckier at home in round four against bottom of the Fourth Division Stockport County, grinding out a horrible 1-1 draw, courtesy only of a last-second goal-line clearance by Gerry Byrne. Almost uniquely, Shankly had missed the match as he was on a European Cup spying mission in Germany; when a customs officer told him the score on his return to England the Scot assumed the official was mad. Paisley and Shankly now came up with some 'magic' footwear for the replay, which was fought out on a frozen and rutted pitch. These rubber-soled, cleated boots (possibly picked up while the boss was abroad in Germany) allowed Roger Hunt to score two goals to see Liverpool through. Ian Callaghan was the unlikely hero at Bolton Wanderers in round five, with a late *headed* winner in a very hard-fought 1-0 victory. Only really dedicated Reds could recall Cally heading goals for Liverpool. The FA Cup was within sniffing range once more, but how often had this been said about Liverpool in the previous 70-odd years?

As this domestic cup run unfolded, Liverpool also now faced the Germans from FC Cologne in Europe. In two classic meetings, the Reds held their opponents scoreless in West Germany in early February and then had to wait until 17 March for the return – a severe Liverpool blizzard, after the crowd were already inside Anfield, postponed the proposed earlier meeting. A full five weeks after the first leg, Liverpool could not break through the German international keeper Toni Schumacher and his defenders in another 0-0 stalemate. A third match at the 'neutral' Feyenoord Stadion in Rotterdam in front of almost 48,000, mainly locals, saw Liverpool take a 2-0 first-half lead before the Germans replied with two goals of their own. Extra time produced no more returns. UEFA preferred the toss of a disk over *any* kind of test of football acumen to resolve this epic contest. It seemed like a farce, a gross dereliction of duty, but the clubs were stuck with it. As had happened before the 1950 FA Cup Final, the first toss here, agonisingly, came up stuck in the mud and indecisive. But it was Liverpool who eventually 'won' through. As the players celebrated, Bill Shankly shook his head and walked quietly over to the Cologne bench to commiserate with his counterpart Georg Knöpfle. He told the opposing coaches that this was no way to decide such a tight and evenly balanced European Cup tie played over a 42-day period, and that there was no real honour for his own club in moving forward in such an unsatisfactory fashion. Inter Milan now lay waiting in the European Cup semi-final.

But Liverpool were also still alive in the FA Cup, having held old adversaries Leicester City at Filbert Street in round six and winning through at Anfield with a lone Roger Hunt goal. All this meant that, three days after playing an emotionally and physically draining match, including extra time, in the European Cup in the Netherlands, Liverpool now faced a young and talented Chelsea FC in the FA Cup semi-final at a muddy Villa Park. The London club was managed by the flamboyant Tommy Docherty, another potential headache. Docherty had definitely alarmed the Liverpool management in Rotterdam by inviting Ron Yeats and Ian St John for a few late-night beers in the Chelsea man's Dutch hotel room right after the Cologne match. Enraged, Shankly and Reuben Bennett managed to track the meeting down and ordered the Liverpool men back to the official party, before laying into the Doc. Docherty, supposedly, had access to spare FA Cup Final tickets, gold dust for players. But drinking abroad with the opposing manager a few days before an FA Cup semi-final and being offered cup final tickets by him? Well, the press would have a field day today, and you could see their point.

After flying directly to their Birmingham base and ordering a couple of days of almost complete rest, Shankly inspired his players at Villa Park by producing in the Liverpool dressing room a copy of Chelsea's presumptuous FA Cup Final brochure (he might even have printed it himself). In any case, with experienced warriors such as Eddie McCreadie and Ron 'Chopper' Harris in the Chelsea ranks, and Tommy Smith and Gerry Byrne lining up for Liverpool, this was never likely to be a quiet or a restrained affair. After a little over an hour of sparring, stopping a few inches short of out-and-out violence, one of the few real creatives in the match, Peter Thompson, made the decisive play. Willie Stevenson and Thompson had their usual grinding relationship on Liverpool's left side, Stevo wanting more help defensively and Thommo chiding Stevenson for lacking the pace to offer more support in attack. They were constantly at each other's throats. Shanks loved Thompson but even he criticised the winger occasionally for not getting the ball into the box early enough. And what about coming inside and shooting for goal now and again? Thompson had a decent shot in both feet but he seemed so consumed with humiliating his full-back and dancing down the line that he seldom went for goal himself. But today he did so, cutting inside for once and firing high past a startled Peter Bonetti. The Red half of Villa Park, still steaming from the rain and the heat generated by thousands of alcohol-enhanced bodies, erupted. When Ian St John cleverly 'bought' a penalty from the furious Ron Harris on 79 minutes, the only other surprise was that it was Willie Stevenson who silently grabbed the ball and took the kick, a moment of supreme confidence and willingness to take responsibility. Liverpool FC were through to only their third FA Cup Final in 73 years of waiting.

Gerry Byrne's FA Cup Final

Liverpool now stumbled to the end of their league programme, with four consecutive defeats in April and just one goal scored. Gordon Milne, crucially, picked up an injury that would rule him out of the rest of the campaign. In the club's last league fixture, at already-relegated Wolves (Liverpool won 3-1), Wallasey-born forward John Sealey played and scored in his only-ever appearance for the club in an unrecognisable Reds team that also included one-match-wonders defender Tom Lowry and England schoolboy international wing-half Alan Hignett. (Another Alan Hignett had also played just one match for the club back in 1907/08.) It was one of the very few occasions that Bill Shankly ever rested or rotated players in an era when the FA came down hard on clubs that failed to field their strongest team in all fixtures. He had some cause: Liverpool had played an extraordinary and unprecedented ten league matches in April 1965, including three in four days. The Reds eventually finished an exhausted seventh in the league, with 15 defeats, a country mile behind champions Manchester United and second-placed Leeds United.

It was Leeds they now faced in the FA Cup Final. By 1965 the city of Liverpool's brief but ecstatic reign as world 'Beat City' was already flagging; pop music little touched Bill Shankly in any case. But, as a sign of the national affection for him, the Scot was featured on BBC radio's *Desert Island Discs* in the week of the final and he chose an eclectic mix of old favourites, sentimental ballads from the 1950s and before, and some Scottish standards. *The Life of Robert Burns* was his patriotic book choice and his luxury was a football, what else? It was great build-up work. The players listened to the show on the coach en route to the stadium, groaning, but they also loved it, especially as 'You'll Never Walk Alone' played last. A second bus followed behind the first, just in case the Reds' vehicle broke down. Typical belt-and-braces thinking.

In the 1960s, the FA Cup Final remained a very special national event, the country coming together to celebrate and sign off the domestic football season. Every fan watched it – it was the only club football available live on TV – with fans of the finalists consumed by the endless pre-match build-up and the ritual dressing of houses with home-made rosettes and favours and souvenir full-colour pictures from the local press stuck to front windows. By stocking up with beer and drawing the curtains in mid-afternoon to lock out the world for a few hours, fanatics, supporters and their families could collectively climb into the football bubble and see their team perform for once, if only on a tiny black-and-white TV screen.

Officially, only 12,000 Liverpool supporters had tickets for the final; the club's average home attendance in 1964/65 was over 41,000. In short, fans were still generally treated dismally by the administrators of the sport, mere terrace fodder. Before the match, local entertainer Frankie Vaughan and comedian Jimmy Tarbuck were invited into the Liverpool dressing room to keep the players relaxed. The Liverpool fans, according to the sniffy *Guardian* newspaper, produced 'barbaric songs from Merseyside which drowned the organised community singing'. A new Kop favourite here was, 'Ey aye addio, we've come to see the Queen'. Captain Ron Yeats was very confident that Liverpool would win; he had spent weeks practising what he was going to say as Her Majesty handed over the cup. Shankly gave the players a rousing pre-match speech about being 'willing to die' for the supporters, perhaps sensing some understandable tiredness in the ranks. But, frankly, the 1965 FA Cup Final was pretty unremarkable – Frank McGee for the *Daily Mirror* called it 'a morass of mediocrity' – except, of course, for the historic result.

Leeds United was a club on the rise, a tough, talented and cynical team under manager Don Revie, a unit orchestrated by Collins, Bremner and Giles in midfield and held together at the back by Jack Charlton and Norman Hunter, an almost mirror-match for Yeats and Tommy Smith for Liverpool. Maybe the two teams just cancelled each other out at Wembley. Neither club had yet won the FA Cup, meaning additional pressure, and Liverpool's recent programme had been torrid. Ron Yeats called it later 'a bloody awful game'. Both teams certainly played cautiously, in Liverpool's case a little more justifiably because after just three minutes full-back Gerry Byrne broke a collarbone in a collision with the hard, little Bobby Collins. Injury jinxes were not unusual at Wembley and with no substitutes the stricken team invariably ended up defeated. This fact was not lost on Bill Shankly, or his staff. The obvious thing – the compassionate and the *losing* thing to do now – was to bring the defender off, or else visibly strap him up and move him to the touchline for nuisance value only.

But Byrne was teak tough and he could still run reasonably freely, albeit slightly holding his arm across his chest. Johnny Giles was no conventional right-winger and Shankly reasoned, drawing on an example from his own playing days with Andy Beattie, that if Byrne soldiered on in defence sheltered by the best player on the field, Willie Stevenson, then Don Revie and the Leeds players might not even notice his weakness. And so it was.

Liverpool FC: FA Cup winners, 1 May 1965 (vs Leeds United)

Lawrence

Lawler Smith Yeats Byrne

Strong Stevenson

Callaghan Hunt St John Thompson

None of the other Liverpool players knew about the severity of the injury until half-time. No TV commentator noticed it at all. Reuben Bennett spent the whole match with eyes glued on Byrne, alongside a nervously chain-smoking Joe Fagan on the Liverpool bench. Bennett and Gordon Milne sheltered from the rain by draping training tops over their heads like a couple of troubled nuns. They need not have worried as Don Revie missed their concern and made no attempt to play on the damaged Liverpool left side. In a very tight contest, it was the sheer bravery of Gerry Byrne that probably won the first FA Cup for Liverpool. Bill Shankly certainly thought so: he said later that the man who was all but transferred out of Anfield in the late 1950s 'should have had all the medals to himself'.

After a dull, goalless 90 minutes, fittingly it was the overlapping, injured Byrne who got to the Leeds byline to pull a low cross back early in extra time for a stooping Roger Hunt to head in. When Billy Bremner equalised, this was not in the script, but back came Liverpool, Callaghan sprinting down the right this time to cross for St John to head in spectacularly. The winners' interviews and photographs later captured English football in its timeless, traditional working-class guise and yet already in transition. The Liverpool players, still in their red shirts, dutifully filled the FA Cup with milk as part of some sponsor's agreement, while a hollow-cheeked Geoff Strong slyly cupped a dressing room cigarette. Bill Shankly reflected later on the press accounts and the public perceptions of this Liverpool team and how his men were still undervalued, regarded in some quarters as merely functional:

> Our players worked for each other, not for individual honours, and by working unselfishly they still won the glory of being selected for international matches. Everyone at the ground worked for a common cause. The manager trusted the players and the players trusted the manager.

There was Shankly's native socialism, once again, and it reached downwards for its inspiration into the club's loyal supporters. The celebrations in Liverpool when the FA Cup was finally brought back to Anfield dwarfed anything seen in the history of the club – or of any English football club. Some 250,000 people turned out to cheer and sing Beatles songs and 'You'll Never Walk Alone' as their heroes paraded the FA Cup. The trophy had only once been seen inside Anfield and that was more than 50 years ago, brought there by Burnley in 1914 for a charity match after Liverpool had lost to the east Lancashire club in the final. But now it was Liverpool's to parade and keep for a year, by right. And all those great players from the past who had tried so hard to bring the FA Cup back to the city for Liverpool – Raisbeck, Raybould and Cox from the early 1900s; Longworth, MacKinlay and Bill Lacey from 1914; Scott, Bromilow and Chambers from the 1920s; Liddell, Stubbins and Phil Taylor from 1950 – they were all equally honoured now. After so many ifs and buts and near misses, after so many hard-luck stories and broken promises, and after so much bitter disappointment, Liverpool Football Club under their great Scottish leader had finally won the FA Cup.

Compromised in Milan

And maybe the Liverpool story of 1965 should have ended right there, with the passion and jubilation of the club's first FA Cup win. It would have made a natural and wonderful conclusion to an epic journey, one spanning almost three-quarters of a century. But there was still a place in the European Cup Final to play for, starting with a home semi-final first leg against Internazionale of Milan. It had been a busy few days, perhaps especially for Chris Lawler – he got married in the short gap between these two matches, rushing from the wedding reception to join his colleagues in their European training camp in Blackpool. Sadly, this Inter tie left a sour taste after the glories of Wembley and the joy of those wedding vows. Inter were managed by the Argentine Helenio Herrera, *Il mago* (the wizard), the man who claimed to have invented the modern version of the defensive sweeper system, *catenaccio*. Herrera was something of a shadowy figure from the very start: he had allegedly changed the date on his birth certificate in Buenos Aires. A natural authoritarian, Herrera insisted on controlling everything a football manager could possibly control, including, ideally, the match officials. He was accused by some Italian players of wanting to run their entire lives and of experimenting with pills with his junior squads. It was suggested in Italy and elsewhere that Hererra habitually rigged big matches, including a European Cup semi-final against Borussia Dortmund in 1964. He was certainly as much of a cod psychologist as Bill Shankly was; Shanks called his opponent 'a remarkable little fellow, a cut-throat man who wanted to win'. He underestimated the South American.

At Anfield on Wednesday, 4 May 1965, Bill Shankly cleverly insisted that Inter should take the field first, which they did to a monumental howl of such volume and vehemence from the Kop that it almost blew the visitors back inside the Main Stand. Shankly also instructed his wounded warriors, Milne and Byrne (the latter wearing a sling), to parade the newly won FA Cup around the ground to further stoke up the crowd. Liverpool emerged into this swirling torrent of emotion and they tore into their opponents, the Italians struggling against their energy and pace. Roger Hunt scored an early stunning volley from Callaghan's cross but Mazzola equalised after ten minutes, following a slip by Yeats. And yet Inter seemed troubled by Liverpool's incessant attacking frenzy, at a pace they had never faced in Italy. The second Liverpool goal, from Ian Callaghan, even came from a complex set-piece move the Reds had actually practised that morning in training at Melwood. When St John scored Liverpool's third, Bill Shankly was convinced he had a decisive lead to take to Italy. Herrera said magnanimously later that his Inter team had been beaten before but had never been so comprehensively *defeated* as they had on this evening. Shankly could see that his rival was shaken; he may even cheekily have asked Herrera for tips on Liverpool's likely final opponents, the Portuguese men from Benfica. Sympathetic Italian journalists smiled at the craic but they remained unconvinced. Even if Liverpool could outplay Inter again, they warned the Liverpool camp, 'You will never be allowed to win.' Of course, they were right.

Near Lake Como, on the night before the second leg a week later, the Liverpool players were kept awake in their hotel by false alarms, church bells and rowdy locals – of course they were. But it was on the field, in front of 76,000 witnesses, where things seriously began to fall apart, after the Italian press had urged local fans to make as much noise as possible 'to better the Beatles'. Inter's lazy midfield genius Mario Corso started things rolling by scoring directly from a controversial free kick after just eight minutes, which was signalled by the referee, Ortiz de Mendibil, as *indirect*. It was the start the Italians needed and the one Liverpool had feared the most. Within a minute Liverpool's entire night's work – and more – at Anfield had been wiped away, after Joaquin Peiro illegally stole the ball out of Tommy Lawrence's hands as the goalkeeper prepared to kick it downfield, to score the second. This was a circus goal, a type not even allowed in park football. Incredibly, the Spanish referee allowed both goals to stand. The

Liverpool team was shattered, bowed, by this injustice. Giacinto Fachetti's third goal in the second half was a brilliant irrelevance.

Referee De Mendibil was later implicated in a European-wide match-fixing scandal reported in the *Sunday Times* in 1974 but Inter escaped punishment or even any serious investigation of this tie. As Italian journalists had known it would be, the outcome of this match had been shaped by Herrera's darkest desires, which was an affront to Bill Shankly and his innate sense of competitive fairness. The Liverpool manager was as desperate as anyone to win football matches, but not like this. The Scot would have his future European successes with Liverpool but to his considerable frustration he would never win the European Cup – or ever come quite this close again. Instead, his great friends Jock Stein at Celtic (1967) and Matt Busby at Manchester United (1968) would first secure these greatest British honours in Europe. As Shankly's ambitions receded on this front, so his desire to manage Liverpool FC was also compromised. Although it seemed unimaginable at the time, the boot room apprentice Bob Paisley would rule European club football in the grainy technicolour of the late 1970s and early 1980s more decisively than Bill Shankly had been able to shape the British and European game in the black-and-white days of the 1960s. But for Bob to step up, Bill Shankly would eventually have to stand aside.

Lost and fatally adrift

On 24 April 1962, spoiling somewhat Liverpool's Second Division promotion party, thieves on Merseyside had returned to check out a familiar target. Safe-blowers stole £4,000 of match takings from a safe situated in the Anfield offices of the then-Liverpool FC club secretary, Jimmy McInnes. These persistent crooks had finally got a decent result out of Liverpool, and the conscientious McInnes felt the loss personally, as if somehow it was his direct responsibility. It was typical of the man. The diminutive Scot, nicknamed 'Soapy', had played 51 times at left-half for Liverpool after signing from Third Lanark in March

1938. In line with the club's 'family' policy of recruiting ex-players on to the staff, McInnes had joined the administrative team at Anfield after the war. He would have seen, first-hand, the chaos around the distribution of FA Cup Final tickets in 1950 and the madness for the final league match in 1964. He had been club secretary since 1955 but had since witnessed his responsibilities grow considerably. McInnes was generally an undemonstrative man, a university graduate who dealt with his duties quietly but efficiently, although he did not suffer fools gladly. He would summarily end difficult telephone conversations in his office by angrily slamming down the receiver. By the spring of 1965, office pressures at Anfield had already become acute. Liverpool had reached the European Cup semi-final for the first time and played in the FA Cup Final within a matter of days, so the demands on ticketing and other connected matters in these pre-computer days would have been off the scale, beyond anything the club had previously dealt with. The daily pressures behind the scenes were intense.

The precise circumstances of what happened next are unclear, beyond the fact that McInnes and his small staff were stretched enormously by Liverpool's sudden, extraordinary success. This is what everyone in the club had been striving for since the war but it was the backroom staff who typically bore the brunt of supporters' anxieties, expectations, complaints and demands in these times of plenty. Stress was inevitable but mainly unseen by fans, and the club was unlikely to have taken on additional senior staff to cope. Bill Shankly knew Jimmy McInnes well, describing him as 'honest and he was also quick-tempered. Sometimes he could be rude to people – some of them needed it, and he was right – but he would be gentlemanly with people he respected'. What we do know is that on 5 May 1965, one day after Liverpool had hosted Inter Milan, a distressed and exhausted Jimmy McInnes walked into the silent darkness at the back of the Spion Kop and under a turnstile roof he hanged himself. He was just 52 years of age. The Liverpool Supporters' Club secretary, Arthur Mercer, told the press about McInnes: 'He was a great guy to us. He must have been working under a terrific pressure during these last few months.' It was, to put it glibly, a very tragic and unintended outcome of an unprecedented period of Liverpool success.

Bill Shankly's gap years

Winning the FA Cup in 1965 was the end of a grand quest at Liverpool Football Club, a moment of closure on a fabulous story that had started with William Barclay, John Houlding and his assistant John McKenna when they had established the club out of their struggle with the Everton board back in 1892. Winning the cup had become the club's obsession. The early 1960s also signalled the start of the modern history of Liverpool FC, the precursor to a period of near constant success in the 1970s and 1980s, which is still unique in the history of the English game. Seventy-three years without winning a senior cup tournament was followed by a period of 17 years when the club routinely claimed knockout silverware. The Liverpool club, arguably, now had the best manager and the smartest backroom staff in English football. It also had a seasoned, if small, group of players who were talented and still ambitious, a stadium that was both feared and respected at home and abroad, and supporters who were known around Europe for both their knowledge and their passion.

By now the great Liverpool Kop, imbued with local pop culture, had become a celebrated national institution. The writer Arthur Hopcraft described the Kop brilliantly and affectionately in 1968 in *The Football Man* as a 'soft-sided crane grab' that dangled its members for minutes on end, a 'monstrous, odorous national pet' that would be a cruel act of denial to kill off. Despite the changes wrought by youth culture and new supporter styles, the Kop was essentially still the great bubbling terrace that had bonded with those great Liverpool players of the past, including Elisha Scott. It had another 26 memorable years left to breathe its friendly fire as a standing conference on Liverpool's performance, their opponents and the work of hesitant match officials.

Meanwhile, the Kop's spiritual leader Bill Shankly was to add another FA Cup and two more league titles to his personal Liverpool roster, as well as continuing to blaze the club's early trail in Europe. But from now on his progress would be more uneven. In England in the World Cup year of 1966, when Brazilians, Hungarians, Koreans, Russians and West Germans all came to play football in the city, Shankly's own team stormed, virtually unopposed, to another league championship. There were no new major signings but World Cup man Roger Hunt was the undoubted star, 30 league goals to his name. Nine players played 40 league matches or more. It was resilience, cohesiveness and defensive solidity that really pulled this team through, with only injuries to right-half Gordon Milne threatening the Reds' shape and serene progress to a six-point final margin over Leeds United. Either Bob Paisley's intuitive physiotherapy knowledge, or fear of his fiendish electric machines, was keeping Liverpool players out of the treatment room. In the 1966 European Cup Winners' Cup, Liverpool overcame the Italians from Juventus, then Standard Liège and Honvéd, before a drink-fuelled semi-final night had Scottish fans in drunken disorder in the Anfield Road end as their Celtic team were dismissed by a 2-1 aggregate scoreline. Whisky bottles were liberally strewn on the sacred turf in the wildest night seen in the ground for over 50 years. The Reds would now face the West Germans from Borussia Dortmund in the final, at what turned out to be a less than half-filled Hampden Park.

This rather unloved European tournament would become the only notable competition entered by the modern Liverpool club, at home or abroad, that it failed to win at some stage. Dortmund were formidable opponents in 1966, no doubt about it. The German team contained a core of players who would face England in the World Cup Final in three months' time. One of them, the dynamic blonde forward Sigi Held, scored the opening goal on a quite filthy Glasgow night, from a long ball and against the run of play. The Liverpool equaliser, scored by a struggling Roger Hunt, came from a cross after Peter Thompson had seemingly run the ball over the byline. Hundreds of Liverpool fans invaded the pitch in celebration. But, unfazed by this setback or the intrusion, the Germans would not be denied and, in extra time, Libuda floated a brilliant 35–yard lob over the stranded Tommy Lawrence to win the trophy for the men from the Ruhr. Shankly reacted bitterly and ungraciously, claiming that injuries to Hunt and Smith had stalled the Reds, before complaining, 'We were beaten by a team of frightened men. They had no real attacking plan but they won, and I am quite sincere when I say they are the worst team we met in the competition this season.' This defeat in the club's first European final seemed like a blip but instead it announced a mini-drought for the boot room boss; no Liverpool trophy followed for seven long years.

What happened to the Liverpool machine, to Shankly's indomitable trailblazing? Several factors probably combined here. First, both major Manchester clubs, and also Leeds United, had noticeably upped their game in the late 1960s (United with that European Cup win in 1968). Everton and Arsenal also had spells of real excellence, which brought league titles to both and even a double for the Londoners. Arsenal had beaten a transitional Liverpool team in the final in 1971 to win the FA Cup part of that deal. In short, the English First Division was highly competitive once more. Second, Roger Hunt's bountiful partnership with Ian St John was slowing and Liverpool's goals began to dry up as a result. Most clubs would struggle to replace this sort of quality and the sheer quantity of goals they produced, and Liverpool were no exception. Hunt's desire, work rate and deadly quality were hard to replicate. Third, some of the players brought in by Shankly and his contacts to score goals and freshen up his team were simply sub-standard.

Ex-Red, Geoff Twentyman (and his distinctive trilby hat), returned to Anfield in 1967 as the club's chief scout and it took him time to hit his straps. After the original spending binge sanctioned by chairman T.V. Williams in the late 1950s, Shankly knew that he would have to shop around for young talent once more: 'Liverpool, successful by the cheapest possible way,' as he put it. It seemed like risking a return to the old unsuccessful strategies of the recent past. Local journalist Simon Hughes later wrote a book based on Twentyman's scouting diaries, which listed the key things the Liverpool man looked out for in prospective players. The first was a 'clean kick'. As Twentyman put it, 'I've never looked twice at any prospect who couldn't kick the ball properly.' Good advice. Next was passing ability, followed by pace and attitude, and then craft and brains. All this, and you had the complete package. His first recommendation to Shankly to address the Anfield goals problem was the free-scoring forward Francis Lee at Bolton Wanderers. But Lee would inspire Manchester City to European and Football League titles instead, while Liverpool struggled. Bobby Graham, Tony Hateley, Alun Evans, Jack Whitham and Phil Boersma were all tried up front but none were from the very top drawer (or even close) and all failed to reignite Liverpool. There were also growing signs of the wider vulnerabilities that would soon become serious problems for Shankly and his staff.

A famous early example was the 5-1 away leg defeat to Ajax of Amsterdam in the European Cup in December 1966, the Dutch club taking a four-goal lead before half-time in the legendary *mistwedstrijd* (fog game). It was not Tommy Lawrence's, nor Liverpool's, finest hour. Shankly blustered about a 'comeback' on a clear night at Anfield but two goals from a young Johan Cruyff had a strange-looking Liverpool (playing in yellow) struggling even to achieve a 2-2 draw at home. Ajax had still been a mainly part-time club as recently as 1965 but Cruyff had been coached there from five years of age. No English club could make such an attachment. Defeating those studious young European coaches, such as Rinus Michels and his 'total football' ethos, was not going to be easy. The big news story of the night, however, was the 200 people injured on the Kop as a haze produced by heat and rain-soaked fans had supporters at the rear pressing on those in front for a better view. 'Absolute bedlam' according to the

St John's Ambulance people on the spot, as grown men cried and dozens of fans were stretchered away, although secretary Peter Robinson for the club reassured that it had 'all happened before' at big matches. It was another missed warning. On the field, meanwhile, Shankly would make no meaningful impact in Europe for the next six years, while Ajax would go on to contest four consecutive European Cup finals between 1969 and 1973, winning three of them.

The final reason for this Liverpool mini 'black hole' was undoubtedly the manager's excessive loyalty to his players. Shankly found it hard to discard the men who had given him so much. His signature names of the late 1950s/early 1960s – St John, Yeats, Thompson, Lawrence and Hunt – were all still around the Liverpool first team as the club prepared to move into the 1970s. A famous turning point of sorts came on 21 February 1970 when Liverpool lost 1-0 at lowly Second Division Watford on a muddied heap in the sixth round of the FA Cup. With Everton flying in the league, Shankly had targeted winning the FA Cup to get his team moving once more, but with this loss he finally ran out of patience and love for some of his favourites. Lawrence, Yeats and St John were all dropped for the home defeat to Derby County; Hunt had already been discarded. Ian St John took his exclusion especially badly. His manager had been unable to face probably his favourite player with the news that his time at Anfield was finally coming to a close. It was Joe Fagan who had to pick up the pieces here, mollify those men who Shankly had finally cut loose with no backward glance. The Saint knew that he was on his way out for sure when Liverpool's assistant secretary Bill Barlow doled out a scraggy club turkey to him at Christmas, gleefully telling the Scot that the plumper birds were being saved for 'first-teamers only'. St John left to play in South Africa, spitting feathers. The family football club finally showed that it was able to deal ruthlessly with those who had once been its nearest and dearest but who were now simply not up to scratch.

Rebuilding with Scunthorpe's finest

Bill Shankly now set about building his second dominant Liverpool team. In came the talented but impetuous 20-year-old Larry Lloyd to replace Ron Yeats. Roger Hunt noted astutely that Lloyd's willingness to bring the ball forward on his strong left foot added to the confidence and forward momentum of this new Liverpool, especially in Europe. Alec Lindsay, a left full-back from Bury, a deceptively talented but ungainly ex-pig farmer, displaced Geoff Strong, and Alun Evans, an inconsistent 19-year-old striker from Wolves with a look of a gaunt missing blonde Beatle, replaced Hunt for a gambler's record £100,000 fee for a teenager. Bill Shankly fed Evans chicken and chips on the day he signed and the new man was placed in digs with Emlyn Hughes and Peter Wall, on the third floor of a doctor's surgery. Evans was viciously attacked in a nightclub in December 1969 and required 70 stitches to his face, after which he found it hard to recover his confidence, although he scored a hat-trick in the Inter-Cities Fairs Cup against Bayern Munich in March 1971.

The awkward but effective Welsh lighthouse and cod poet John Toshack also joined, from Cardiff City, for a very tidy £111,000 in November 1970 and he went on to form vital scoring partnerships for Liverpool over the next eight years. Steve Heighway and Brian Hall both signed up, unusually two amateur forwards and university graduates, each of whom had initial problems convincing hard men like Tommy Smith that they cared just as much about winning professional football matches as he and all Liverpool supporters did. Steve Heighway was bright, coltish, long-striding and direct; Hall was earnest, hard-working and combative. Both impressed and would also offer Liverpool valuable service after their successful playing careers were over. The latter inadvertently entertained the Liverpool dressing room and his manager by turning up for his first training session at Melwood wearing the bus conductor's outfit he wore while earning some extra cash as a student, working on the Lancashire buses.

English football dressing rooms at this time were not really places for cerebral exchanges, and soon after these 'intellectual' arrivals, a scrawny and dodgy-permed young, hyper-competitive Kirkby kid with sparrow's legs started to claim a place in and around the Liverpool defence. Phil Thompson would become a key figure in the new era, a modern, ultra-moaning, version of Tommy Smith. A European Cup defeat to a cultured, quick-passing Red Star Belgrade in November 1973 finally convinced the Liverpool coaching staff that the days of the stopper British-style centre-half were now over. Larry Lloyd had been the bridge. Footballing central-defenders, men who could read the game keep the ball and pass it, would now be required in the modern era, especially to progress in elite European club competitions.

Surprisingly, perhaps, the Liverpool manager's only real concession to his beloved Scotland during this period of rapid change was the recruitment in July 1972 from Nottingham Forest of the high-stepping midfielder Peter Cormack, a man who briefly added class and goals to this department – and also a Scottish voice to the Liverpool dressing room. Cormack bravely (if foolishly) stepped in at Melwood one morning when Tommy Smith and new man Lloyd were locking horns in a typical training session ritual designed to test the balls of the new recruit. Predictably, it was the intervening Scot who came out worst.

After so little change for a decade, all these men would now play their part in a re-engineered Liverpool but Bill Shankly constructed his new vision around three other key signings, all of them Englishmen, all of them outstanding bargains. The Liverpool scouting network really earned its corn here. Barrow-born left-sided defender or midfielder, Emlyn Hughes, first attracted the attention of the Liverpool scouts in Blackpool's reserve team. Bill Shankly was especially impressed by the physical presence, sheer competitiveness and the cold-eyed nerve of the youngster. He even offered £25,000 for Hughes straight after his Blackpool first-team debut, but in March 1967 he agreed to pay £65,000 for the teenager. Initially, Hughes replaced

Willie Stevenson on the left side of Liverpool's midfield and his leadership, confidence, boyish enthusiasm and immense power made him an instant crowd favourite at Anfield – and eventually a truly great Liverpool player.

With this 'Crazy Horse' on board, Shankly's Liverpool would finally win the league title again, in 1973 (the first of four at Liverpool for Hughes), beating Arsenal and Leeds United to the punch. They also won the UEFA Cup in the same year, the first time in the club's history that two major trophies had been claimed in the same season. Hughes was later successfully converted to centre-back to counter the pace and cleverness of European forwards. Under Bob Paisley, he won three more league titles, the UEFA Cup again in 1976, and consecutive European Cups, in 1977 and 1978. For all his great qualities, the effervescent 'Yosser' could also show just too much brass neck on occasions for the barrack room Liverpool squad. He thought a lot of himself in a team with plenty of competing talents and some powerful egos. The self-promoting Hughes eventually urged Bill Shankly to replace the then-Reds captain Tommy Smith with someone younger; the doting Shanks took note. So, in 1974 it was Emlyn Hughes, not the loyal and abrasive Smith, who hoisted the FA Cup for Liverpool after the 3-0 Wembley rout of Newcastle United. It was Bill Shankly's last great Liverpool FC occasion and Smith never forgave the manager, or Hughes, for this act of personal treachery. The two players now refused to talk on the field, with Hughes asking centre-half Larry Lloyd to 'tell that fat bastard to pass the ball'. Smith could also be heard under his breath congratulating any opponent who had managed to lamp his braggart defender colleague. The message here was that great teams seldom get along in *all* departments.

Skegness-born 18-year-old goalkeeper Ray Clemence was bought by Shankly just after Hughes arrived, from Scunthorpe United for a paltry fee of around £18,000 in June 1967. Clemence was unsure about playing in Liverpool's reserves but Shankly told the young keeper that Tommy Lawrence was an elderly 30 years of age and on his way out of Anfield (Lawrence was actually 27 and in his prime for a goalkeeper). In fact, the new man would have to wait two-and-a-half years to make his Liverpool senior debut, after the Watford FA Cup debacle. There was no discussion at all about salary when Clemence agreed to sign; Shanks simply told him he would be 'well looked after', playing for the greatest football club in the world.

Clemence was agile and supple but not huge for a goalkeeper, under six feet tall and under 13 stone, but he was an excellent decision-maker and a good and very vocal defensive organiser. He was a man, like Elisha Scott, who demanded excellence from his back-four colleagues. His concentration levels were immense, something vitally important when the Liverpool goalkeeper had to stay in the game, as Paisley insisted, even when he was getting little real match action. His sweeping behind the back line (he played ruggedly out of goal in Melwood five-a-sides) and his distribution from both hand and foot were first class and he hardly seemed to make any mistakes or get injured. For 11 Liverpool seasons, from August 1970 until May 1981, Ray Clemence missed only six league matches and he ended up with 665 major domestic and European appearances for the club, joint sixth on the all-time list with Emlyn Hughes. In 1978/79, he helped achieve the greatest defensive record in 42-match Football League history, conceding just 16 league goals, and only four of them at Anfield. Clemence was also a positive character in the Reds' dressing room, a very upbeat and intelligent influence, the attributes of a future England goalkeeping coach. He said he left Liverpool after sitting in the dressing room and 'feeling empty' after the 1981 European Cup win in Paris. The arrival at Anfield for £250,000 of the precocious 23-year-old Bruce Grobbelaar may also have been a factor.

The third key Shankly signing for this period was, of course, the forward Kevin Keegan. This future international and honed national sporting product – a precursor of the Michael Owen England era – also came in from lowly Scunthorpe United, in

May 1971, for a fee of around £33,000. The Liverpool manager later described the deal, proudly, as 'robbery without violence'. Keegan was recommended to Shankly by his old mentor Andy Beattie, who was bemused that no other club had even registered an interest in him. Absurdly, some good judges thought Keegan lacked courage. As soon as Bob Paisley saw him, he told Shanks to start preparing to woo this new talent. As other suitors eventually stirred, Keegan signed just as Liverpool were about to lose the 1971 FA Cup Final to Arsenal. The new recruit went with the Liverpool party to Wembley and he was personally devastated by the defeat. Fagan, Paisley and Shankly raised their collective eyebrows; this was already some commitment from this kid to the Liverpool cause. Not that the new signing made a big splash in negotiating personal terms – Keegan's first Liverpool wages were little better than those he had been on at Scunthorpe. Bill Shankly had given Keegan the 'move to a big club like Liverpool and the money will follow' speech he had worked on with Ray Clemence, and the youngster had lapped it up. But this was no deception on the Liverpool manager's part, no politician's spin or wind-up. Shankly passionately believed that his younger players should properly appreciate their rise up the ranks. He wanted to know that they were playing from the heart for Liverpool Football Club, not for their pay cheques. He need have no fears about Keegan. The two men actually became very close, Shankly as a kind of mentor to this rapidly uncoiling ball of football energy, as he had once been to the young Tommy Smith.

After a poor league show from Liverpool in 1970/71, Shankly promoted Keegan directly into the first team in August 1971. A raw recruit from the English Fourth Division being thrown in without any of the detailed Anfield grooming and reserve-team apprenticeship looked like desperation, and the manager certainly needed a boost. Keegan did not disappoint. Again, like the later Michael Owen, his work rate and sheer naïve exuberance seemed to unhinge even experienced First Division defenders and he simply never gave up. He teamed up instantly with the tall

Welshman John Toshack in a 4-4-2 formation that was to become the attacking fulcrum of the Liverpool team for the next six years, first under Shankly and then Bob Paisley. This pair replaced, at last, the successful Hunt and St John forward partnership of the 1960s. Keegan starred in the club's second FA Cup win in 1974 and in Liverpool's first European Cup triumph under Bob Paisley in Rome in 1977. He also became one of the first players in the modern period to have an agent and the first to leave the Liverpool club to develop his career abroad, in Hamburg. It was a very early marker of the approaching era of players as free agents, brands and celebrities, and of where the European trade for elite footballers would eventually end up.

Too long gone

With these key signings in place and with Bill Shankly apparently rejuvenated and marked for an extended stay and for more trophies at Liverpool, new man John Smith (as chairman) and Peter Robinson (now as all-seeing club secretary) gradually became the driving boardroom and administrative forces around the Liverpool club for the 1970s and beyond. Smith had taken over from Eric Roberts in 1973. Roberts had recently retired from his position as an executive with Barker and Dobson, the sweet manufacturers. He told the 1973 Liverpool AGM that he had hoped to continue as the club's chairman but, because he was relocating some distance away, he felt unable to carry out the duties of the office (he was only moving to the Isle of Man!). He told the men responsible for recruiting players to Liverpool's senior sides – Tom Saunders, Ronnie Moran and Geoff Twentyman:

> If you feel it necessary to introduce new youngsters and you lose a game and maybe a championship, it is not the end of the world. Your principal task is to teach, coach and train the youngsters to ensure a steady supply of material, some of which may one day find its way into the Liverpool league side, and maybe into the international sides.

It was a nice touch but everybody knew that this was so much directors' flannel. Liverpool FC wanted and expected success right now. For 17 years, between 1973 and 1990, Liverpool's 'dapper businessman chairman' Smith, a brewery sales director and deputy chairman of an electronics firm and also chairman of the Sports Council between 1985 and 1989, would continue to run the club as the traditional Liverpool 'family' concern, but also as much more of a tight and cohesive administrative and business unit. Gone for good (or so we thought) was the era of lack of leadership and focus, but also the endless chairman re-elections of the 1950s. Smith and his board, with Peter Robinson close at hand, had a wider vision and they worked hard on raising the necessary cash for player recruitment to try to keep the club among Europe's elite. No director invested their own cash into Liverpool. They also worked on the basic modernisation of the Liverpool stadium. The new Main Stand, now seating 8,600 and with 2,150 standing in the paddock below, and also a modern floodlighting system, was officially opened in March 1973 during the club's eighth league championship-winning season. Only Lawler, Callaghan and a fading Peter Thompson now remained from the 1960's Shankly team.

All seemed set fair for the next great Liverpool advance and it duly came with the league title secured in 1973 and the club's first European trophy won, the newly named UEFA Cup. A novelty here was playing an English club in European competition, Spurs, in the semi-final, with the first leg at home. Liverpool squeezed through on away goals after a 2-2 aggregate scoreline, and so played Borussia Mönchengladbach in their second European final, but over two legs, a topsy-turvy affair. Inspired by a John Toshack and Kevin Keegan heading combo, Liverpool demolished the West Germans 3-0 in the first leg at Anfield. Uniquely, this was after a first attempt at the home leg was abandoned after a few minutes because of a torrential rainstorm. It led Shankly to change his original selection and bring in Toshack for Brian Hall to terrorise the German defence in the air the next evening. We

Kopites who came back to see the second attempt paid a princely 10p for the privilege, in a prime example of how even the greatest of managers can get their selection wrong in the most important fixtures – and still somehow win.

Liverpool FC: League Champions & UEFA Cup Winners, 1972/73

Clemence
Lawler Smith Lloyd Lindsay
Callaghan Cormack (Hall) Hughes Heighway
Keegan Toshack (Boersma)

A brilliant late penalty saved by Ray Clemence from Heynckes – he counted it his most important save ever made for the club – proved crucial here, because Liverpool were truly outclassed and pummelled in the return leg. Heynckes scored twice in Germany in a brutal first half. Shankly's men only just held on to this 'winning' scoreline. The Scot had told his defenders at the interval to get ten yards further forward and that the Germans would run out of steam. It worked; they did. The on-pitch presentation turned into a farce because of travelling Liverpool pitch invaders, and an unimpressed Tommy Smith struggled to get back to the dressing rooms with the UEFA Cup intact. But Bill Shankly had his European silverware at last – and he promised another assault, next season, on the European Cup.

The old, unseeded knockout format for the European Cup, mourned even now by some, was something of a lottery in the 1970s. Perhaps this was one if its attractions? The competition involved only league champions and could offer smooth passage to the later stages against lesser lights, or else a nightmare prospect before you even got started. Drawing Eastern Europeans in early rounds was especially hard to read; they could be magicians or pretenders. In October and November 1973 Liverpool's second round opponents, Red Star Belgrade, were little known to the Liverpool staff but they were Slavs, so their technical expertise was beyond question. But under coach Miljan Miljanić could they match the heart, speed and physicality of the English game? In Yugoslavia, Liverpool were taught a footballing lesson but escaped with a 2-1 defeat, so there was still hope. Back at Anfield, however, their opponents showed both backbone and skill. Kevin Keegan said it was 'the best game of football I have ever played in'. What he meant was that Red Star *embarrassed* Liverpool, cutting through the home midfield and defence at will, with the kind of vision, mobility and speed seldom seen in the English game. Chris Lawler scored in both legs but it was way below what was needed. The Belgrade club also won at Anfield, showing, with a late Janković free kick, just how the future would demand much more expertise in shaping the ball and working up free-kick routines. Liverpool FC – and the English game – was well behind in both skill sets.

This result and performance seemed to confirm that Liverpool were actually further away from Shankly's European dream, some eight years after falling to Inter Milan. First Ajax and now this, outcoached and outfought again. This may well have been the moment when the Scot decided, finally, that he would have to go, even though his 'bombshell' resignation announcement came almost eight months later, on 12 July 1974. Perhaps this Red Star lesson explains it. Shankly was only 61 years of age when he retired, not old at all for a football manager. His new team, playing a flexible 4-4-2, had finished second in the league to Leeds United (no disgrace there) and, inspired by Keegan, it had clinically dismantled Malcolm Macdonald's Newcastle United in the 1974 FA Cup Final, playing just the brand of superior British football he had always preached: passing, movement and power combined. An ebullient and twinkling Shankly had even poked gentle fun at opposing manager, Joe Harvey, live on BBC television before the match. A Liverpool supporter later took to the Wembley pitch to kiss Shankly's feet. Why throw all this away, when so many of the new players he had recruited and developed – Hughes, Keegan, Clemence, Phil Thompson, Hall and Heighway among them – were still so young and hungry? There are so many theories about his Liverpool departure but very few clear answers. Perhaps Shankly's despair about ever winning the European Cup, as his friends Jock Stein and Matt Busby had already done, should be right at the top of that list?

Bill Shankly had certainly dragged Liverpool Football Club into the modern era. He was television-ready and he had established the right of the club's manager to work without undue interference from the Liverpool board. His identity was now interwoven with that of the club and he had just won the FA Cup with some elan. So, his resignation story hit very hard in the city, so much so that people on the street either refused to believe it or simply cried or gawped at the news; they just could not take it in. Others thought he must have died. Shankly had long become part of the city's mythology, he meant so much more to local citizens than a mere football manager could. His values and principles extended well beyond the dressing room and it is not too much to suggest that Shankly had become something of a modern local exemplar of a kind of lived socialism. Many ordinary people had memories of him in this respect: Shanks seeking out unemployed supporters outside grounds where Liverpool were playing to offer match tickets; paying the train fares to away matches of down-at-heel Reds fans; attending, unannounced, the funerals of committed Liverpool supporters who he barely knew; or even helping to carry the weekday shopping of elderly people in West Derby Village. Shankly could also turn up unannounced at supporters' birthday parties or social events on Saturday evenings with one proviso only: that he had to be home in time to watch *Match of the Day* on TV. These were no simple urban myths and nor was this an ordinary modern football boss. When he told his players that he was going to retire, his captain Emlyn Hughes openly sobbed – much, of course, to Tommy Smith's disgust.

It is also true that Bill Shankly was something of an end-of-season serial resigner, depressed by impending inactivity and seemingly needing confirmation that he was still valued and wanted at the club for another season (traces of Steven Gerrard here). Until now, the club's directors and staff had always easily talked him out of leaving in this annual ritual. But by now, too, his backroom staff at Anfield had developed in stature – the famed Liverpool coaches had European experience and a collective voice that was separate and different from Shankly's own. Liverpool's directors never ventured into the deeply masculine boot room sanctuary of the club's coaches, with its brown ale, kit hampers for seats and its 'glamour' calendars. But they knew enough. If the man from Glenbuck really *did* want to go this time, then it was not quite the disaster it may once have seemed. His assistant Bob Paisley could conceivably step up, ably supported by a coterie of hardened professionals, which now included the fearsome Ronnie Moran on the Reds' coaching staff. And not everyone in the Liverpool boardroom always appreciated their manager's open disdain for the doings of football club directors. Not that the Liverpool board *wanted* him to go. Or, indeed, that loyalty or familiarity counted for much here; Peter Robinson intimated soon after Shankly had left the club that if Bob Paisley and his men failed to win a trophy, or to keep Liverpool in football's elite group in his first season, the club would very probably be looking for a new manager again. This, after all was said and done, was business.

The originals: John Houlding (centre) and the first men of Liverpool Football Club, 1892/93

Tom Watson, football's first team manager

Alex Raisbeck, Liverpool's first great captain

Liverpool, first league title winners 1901 and 1906. Dynamic blond leader Alex Raisbeck is in the centre of the middle row

Ephraim Longworth, king of full-backs

Elisha Scott, prince of goalkeepers

1947 title hero (and rebel) Albert Stubbins

Liverpool fans and Wembley comforts, FA Cup Final 1950

The great Anfield servant Billy Liddell, netting against Blackburn Rovers, 1957

A stylish new force arrives from Monkey Row

Shankly, Paisley and Joe Fagan plotting somebody's downfall

Get set: Shankly sees future World Cup man Roger Hunt and colleagues through their Melwood paces, 1961

Liverpool's first FA Cup win, 1965, toasted with milk and a fag. The long wait was over

The high life. Peter Thompson and friends join the used car business, 1967

Bill Shankly addresses his new Liverpool in 1972

Kevin Keegan, the new Kop hero of the 1970s

Bob Paisley studying form

Paisley and Joe Fagan 'entertain' the press in the Liverpool Boot Room

Hunks, Ray Kennedy, Kevin Keegan and super-sub David Fairclough drink to seeing off Saint-Etienne in the European Cup quarter-final, March 1977

Terry McDermott scores Liverpool's first goal in Rome, 1977 European Cup Final

These cool cats retain the European Cup in 1978, with scorer Kenny Dalglish triumphant

Chapter 5

The Blessed Boot Room

From Shankly to Bob Paisley and Joe Fagan –
in one difficult step

Bill Shankly retires on a high – but by accident.
Liverpool FC struggle with the process. Bob Paisley
starts his era slowly but then takes off. Nobody
has much idea what he is talking about. Three
great Scots for Liverpool define the English and
European game for much of the next decade. Titles
and cups at Anfield become routine, at home and
abroad. Paisley does in Europe what was beyond
even Bill Shankly – three times. Only the FA Cup
escapes Paisley's grasp. Howard Gayle briefly makes
history but then is gone. Joe Fagan inherits the
Liverpool managerial mantle and does the treble.
But there is trouble brewing on the Continent.

Bob Paisley's Liverpool: 'No bed of roses'

By now, Bill Shankly had courted the media spotlight at Liverpool
for 15 years and the intense pressure of constantly performing had
begun to tell. He once described football management as 'a soul-
destroying job' and rightly rated the most important quality of a
manager as being 'the natural ability to pick a player'. The lack

of it would unseat many pretenders who followed him. He was no simple romantic. 'Managing a football club is like drowning,' he once told Tommy Smith. 'Sublimely peaceful and pleasant once the struggle is over.' David Peace's book about Shankly, *Red or Dead*, captures well the exhausting, dull repetition of the seasons and the toll it took. Liverpool's manager knew that his utter devotion to the game had been especially hard on his family, particularly his long-suffering wife, Nessie. All those away trips and wearisome scouting nights away from his own bed. But he was clearly deeply uneasy about his decision to retire, almost as soon as his resignation letter was reluctantly accepted by the Liverpool board.

Often, a difficult life-changing choice, once taken, produces a sense of profound relief, a weight lifted from one's shoulders. But here there was only confusion and regret. Worse, Shankly looked as though he missed football and his day-to-day involvement at the club right from the very moment that he had left it. Had he acted on a whim, or for effect, expecting the Liverpool directors to do even more than usual to try to keep him? Had he wanted to see a public uprising, the people of the city demanding that he take charge again? He needed only to ask. He later wrote: 'It was never my intention to have a complete break with Liverpool.' But, surely, he understood that no new manager could have survived easily at Anfield with the ghost of Bill Shankly loitering in the background? And there seemed little realistic prospect of the Glenbuck socialist taking his place upstairs on the still very Conservative Liverpool board. That would certainly have been a major recipe for disaster.

For good or ill, a terrifying decision had now been made and there was no going back. Although Liverpool FC owed a huge debt to Bill Shankly, the club also now had to get behind the reluctant new manager, Bob Paisley. Not even Shankly could be allowed to haunt the Reds' training ground: it had to be all or nothing. All of this undoubtedly caused misunderstanding, unhappiness and tension. There were accusations that Liverpool

FC had dealt badly with their greatest modern leader. Shankly himself soon seemed bitter and resentful about his own decision; he clearly *did* feel somewhat rejected by his old club. He even suggested that *Everton* Football Club was warmer towards him than had been the Anfield hierarchy. Evertonians certainly enjoyed propagating the myth later that the Liverpool club and its supporters had somehow 'forgotten' Shankly's contribution (they ought to check out the Kop today and search for similar Harry Catterick or Howard Kendall flags at Goodison Park). The truth was much more banal than this. Liverpool had not pushed Bill Shankly out but, once his decision had been confirmed, the matter had simply been dealt with as ruthlessly and as professionally as the club dealt with footballers who wanted a move, or men who had passed their peak of usefulness to the club. It might have seemed callous but, as always in football, the future was all that mattered now.

Partly because of this sadness, shock and uncertainty, plus his own misgivings, Bob Paisley began his managerial regime as probably the most hesitant Liverpool incumbent since George Patterson had been pressed to take temporary charge back in the 1930s. The selection of Paisley as Shankly's successor was both inspired and unusual in the English game. Assistants did not naturally become managers, especially perhaps in the aftermath of so much recent success. Paisley told his players, 'I don't particularly want the job, but someone's got to do it.' It was hardly Churchillian-style rhetoric, no rallying call to arms. But then Bob was no public orator; he led by example and by sound decision-making rather than by fine words or native psychology, as Bill Shankly once did. In fact, Paisley hated the media and the public speaking side of the job, calling on Tom Saunders for help and support in this respect. Few players or journalists could understand Bob's north-east mutterings anyway, about 'doins' and 'what's its' and 'jag down there'. But the players respected him and trusted that Paisley would not change what already worked. 'Bob was great at not giving players problems,' as Alan Kennedy later put it, rather backhandedly. In other words, he kept things simple and he trusted key members of his team to make good decisions.

And plenty of things were in Bob Paisley's favour. He knew the club and its staff inside out and the players and coaches were all behind him, even if some national sportswriters had early doubts. Most football managers take over a club because the playing side is in a mess. Nothing could have been further from the truth here: Liverpool were riding high with a good young core of British players, including plenty of on-field leaders. In fact, the previous regime had just added to it by buying the disillusioned forward Ray Kennedy from Arsenal for £180,000, a player Paisley later converted into a graceful and imposing goalscoring left-sided midfielder, although a man who would ultimately be dogged by demons and illness. In short, Bill Shankly had left Liverpool Football Club in pretty fine fettle.

Paisley also made some astute decisions and early signings of his own, informed by Geoff Twentyman and the Liverpool scouts. Building on 4-4-2 rather than Shankly's early 4-3-3 meant that he needed more attacking threat from wide and deep. In October 1974 he recruited a versatile, authentically two-footed attacking defender from Northampton Town, Phil Neal, for £66,000, initially to replace Alec Lindsay on the left, but eventually to substitute for the veteran Chris Lawler on the right. It was a bargain price for Neal's versatility, defensive assurance and forward threat, not to mention his resilience. A raw young leg-biting Welshman, Jocy Jones, would come in a year later from Wrexham, briefly to hold sway on Liverpool's left side. Paisley's view here was that Jones was limited but he was a combative and mobile on-field presence and also a positive dressing room voice. The 23-year-old Neal was different: Twentyman thought that he was like a top golfer, a man able to chip, drive and weight a ball perfectly, and on both flanks. Neal proved simply to be the most consistent and reliable outfield player in Liverpool's history. In ten seasons – 420 league matches – between August 1975 and May 1985 he missed precisely *one* match for Liverpool, as a result of a freakish injury incurred at Old Trafford in September 1983. Neal is the only Liverpool player to win four European Cups and he played in five finals, while also winning eight league championship medals. He became the ever-present right-sided defensive pick of the Bob Paisley era, a priceless team man and without doubt one of the club's greatest-ever servants.

Although Paisley tried hard to keep him, out went Larry Lloyd, angry and rebellious about being ditched by Shankly for the 1974 FA Cup Final, to be replaced permanently by a more versatile ball-playing midfielder-cum-defender, local boy Phil Thompson. Paisley, like Shankly, was influenced here by European setbacks and his knowledge about where the Continental game was headed; it was not down the route of traditional British centre-halves. In, too, came Terry McDermott, a natural mimic, comedian and an ex-pat from Kirkby, a Duracell midfielder who had somehow ended up at Bury and then became stranded in the north-east, at Newcastle United. Many thought that Paisley had wrongly spent £175,000 on Terry Mac in November 1974, especially when the Scouser initially struggled to get into Liverpool's first team. But the new man later came to the fore with his ceaseless running and excellent goals record; and all this with a 'reluctant' attitude to training and some weirdly obtuse matchday preparations. Terry Mac liked a drink – many of the Liverpool squad did – he ate all the wrong things and he also enjoyed watching the horse racing in the players' lounge until 2.40pm on matchdays, before dragging on his kit and tumbling out on to the pitch like any Sunday league footballer might. The Liverpool coaching staff accepted his idiosyncrasies as long as he continued to produce where it mattered, on the pitch. For six great seasons, he did.

Paisley and his boot room men, ex-reserve-team player Roy Evans, Bennett, Fagan and Moran, would now spend a year settling into the new regime and, despite Peter Robinson's warning, they were allowed their time. Paisley was smart enough to know that he had to change his own role. 'I was the one who told them their faults,' he told the *Liverpool Echo*, 'but perhaps I'll have to switch it a bit more to the ego-building side and get someone else to be the hard man.' He would always have Ronnie Moran for that. Paisley's start was explosive enough. In a highly competitive 1974 Charity Shield curtain-raiser against the Brian Clough-managed Leeds United, Kevin Keegan somehow managed to get himself sent off after being blatantly punched, first by Johnny Giles and then by the also dismissed Billy Bremner. These were the first British players ever to be sent off at Wembley and much media hand-wringing ensued. Suspensions inevitably followed but Bob simply blanked out the media storm.

There would be no trophies for Paisley and his staff in this first season; far too many league matches were drawn and a late Máté goal for Ferencváros in Europe was enough to end hopes there. But second place in the league in 1974/75 was just enough to keep the Liverpool board off his case. The Liverpool directors (for once) knew what they were doing. The title returned to Anfield in 1975/76, a mainly functional Liverpool just pipping Queens Park Rangers, who had beaten the Reds in the season's opener. Paisley's plan was to make his version of Liverpool harder to beat, more cautious and often happy to settle for a point – 14 draws, especially away from home – rather than risk losing everything. But 4-0 wins away at both Spurs and West Ham showed what was possible when the handbrake was off. Returning, too, was the UEFA Cup. Liverpool dismissed Real Sociedad and saw off Dynamo Dresden in earlier rounds, before squeezing past FC Barcelona on a 2-1 aggregate in the semi-final. A 1-0 victory in Spain, courtesy of a John Toshack goal, would be emblematic of a proud Liverpool record established at the Camp Nou, only shattered in 2019 by a certain Lionel Messi. These positive results in Europe led to a meeting with Club Brugge KV in a hard-fought UEFA Cup Final in April and May 1976.

The two-legged format rather denied the final a real sense of occasion but it did mean home crowds could be a factor in the outcome. Ray Kennedy was now adding his class and goals to boost the Toshack and Keegan forward pairing. A tough-tackling young Scouser midfielder, Jimmy Case, had also been signed from South Liverpool and was making waves among Liverpool's opposition – and sometimes in local bars and clubs with his chief partner-in-crime, the unpredictable Ray Kennedy. From non-league local football directly into the hothouse of the First Division was still a player pathway in the 1970s. A flame-haired, often unreadable local attacker, David Fairclough, was also trying to force his way past Keegan and Toshack into the Liverpool first team. He would more usually make an impact as a substitute against tired legs.

The first leg of the 1976 UEFA Cup Final is sometimes missed off that lengthy list of great Anfield European nights but it surely belongs there. Liverpool were out of sorts and 2-0 down after 12 minutes. By half-time they were apparently out of the contest. Unusually, Paisley made a change at the interval, taking off the ineffective Toshack and bringing on the more abrasive and hard-working Jimmy Case down Liverpool's right side. Bob was actually no great fan of the big-man-up-front strategy against improving foreign opposition. The Belgians immediately looked alarmed. A three-goal burst in five minutes around the hour mark, with Case and Ray Kennedy at the heart of it all, turned this contest around as the Kop bayed its support. Kevin Keegan scored the third goal from the spot. To back up this ultimately decisive comeback, a clever free kick by Keegan produced the vital equaliser in the return leg in Belgium. The 1-1 draw in Bruges gave the Bob Paisley managerial regime its first European trophy. Maybe the Melwood coaching staff were learning from the Continent, after all, about the importance of devising inventive dead-ball situations?

Liverpool FC: League Champions & UEFA Cup winners, 1975/76

Clemence
Neal Thompson Hughes Smith (Jones)
Heighway Case (Hall) Callaghan Kennedy
Keegan Toshack

The critical moment in the league title campaign fell between the UEFA Cup Final legs, a chaotic, late win at Wolves in a dangerously overcrowded Molyneux, with the away dressing room invaded by friendly visiting fans. Liverpool, needing just a point, fell behind to a Steve Kindon goal on 13 minutes and it took another hour to retrieve the situation. Substitute David Fairclough changed the direction of the contest, with Keegan, Toshack and Ray Kennedy all scoring to wrap up a 3-1 win. Liverpool supporters were virtually on the pitch around the goal, like a crowd from the 19th century, as Kennedy's shot struck home. The invasion that followed the final whistle was an unthreatening human flood, with Wolves cruelly relegated. The Liverpool players had been desperate to show that 'Wee Uncle Bob' had what it took to follow Shankly, while Paisley himself was relieved more than excited. Characteristically, he pointed to a defeat at Ipswich in September, after which he had 'read the riot act', as the key turning point. He also admitted that being the Liverpool manager 'was no bed of roses' and that handling personal problems with players – including telling them when and why they were left out – was the most difficult part of the job. He usually avoided it like the plague.

The Guardian was unimpressed by his team, commenting that 'Liverpool will not be the most popular champions to represent England in Europe next season' because of their reputation for 'machine-like dourness'. They lacked, it went on, the 'sophisticated skills' of Queens Park Rangers or the 'youthful buoyancy' of Manchester United under Tommy Docherty. But this Liverpool side had a strong team ethic, good organisation and also patience, all vital ingredients of any worthy league title-winning team with European ambitions. Bob Paisley could now sign his own Anfield contract.

Of his new men, David Fairclough's chances of making a real splash at Anfield faded when the hard-working David Johnson was brought in from Ipswich Town in August 1976. It was also a stark warning for John Toshack about a probable change in direction. With Ray Clemence securely in goal and Emlyn Hughes now partnering Phil Thompson or Tommy Smith in the middle of a more mobile Liverpool defence, Jones and Neal at full-back and Case, Kennedy and Terry McDermott beginning to become the favoured personnel in midfield alongside the evergreen Ian Callaghan – an astonishing survivor from 1960 – the real Bob Paisley's Liverpool began to take some recognisable shape in the new league season. Except, that is, his star forward Kevin Keegan announced, before it had even begun, that this would be his last dance at Anfield. Keegan was determined to escape Britain's punitive tax regime but at least the Liverpool scouts had time to plan for a tax-paying replacement.

The university flyer Heighway, or new man Johnson, increasingly accompanied Keegan up front in the 1976/77 title season. Unbeaten at home but only five wins away from Anfield told a tale of local dependability and a lack of real adventure and assurance on the road. The outstanding blip here was a famously inexplicable 5-1 defeat away to Aston Villa in December 1976 – also the half-time score. Paisley was simply speechless at such defensive ineptitude, while the normally calm Joe Fagan hammered everyone at the interval. Nevertheless, in just three years and with all his misgivings and uncertainties, Bob Paisley had quietly built on the Bill Shankly legacy to produce a new and consistently solid team, if one that perhaps needed just a little more invention, imagination and freedom to play. He had also set his sights on doing what even his great mentor had been cheated out of doing by Inter Milan in 1965, winning the European Cup.

We're on our way to Roma

The path for Liverpool to the 1977 European Cup Final may look simple enough compared to today's testing marathon: Crusaders and then Trabzonspor (generally said by the players to be the worst venue anywhere in Europe) were comfortably put to the sword. But the campaign really took off in the quarter-finals, against the French champions Saint-Étienne, who had been mugged in the 1976 final by Bayern Munich. This was a real test. After losing 1-0 in France, in front of the loudest crowd Phil Thompson had ever heard, Liverpool faced an uphill task at Anfield when Bathenay equalised Kevin Keegan's cross-cum-early goal with an unstoppable long-range drive. Now two goals were needed, a situation calling out for heroes. Ray Kennedy had already scored a second goal for Liverpool in a pulsating match of high quality played out in a frenzied atmosphere, before substitute David Fairclough was summoned, once again, to replace the ineffective Toshack. Liverpool players marvelled at how 'lucky' the Bionic Carrot was to be able to score goals from the substitute's bench but Fairclough was less sure. He hated the 'super-sub' tag – he wanted to start in the team. Now put clear on the left of the French defence by Ray Kennedy, he accelerated and scored the crucial goal with six minutes remaining. The home crowd went wild. It was a coming of age for Paisley in *the* major European competition, a memorable occasion, but also a real signal of intent. His was now an experienced and hardened European unit, authentic contenders for the top European club title for the first time since 1965.

FC Zürich were casually brushed aside 6-1 in the semi-final but before the final in Rome against familiar foes Borussia Mönchengladbach could even be contemplated there was another league title to deliver. Three nervy draws in May (was it tiredness or just boredom?) closed the final gap ahead of second-placed Manchester City to just one point. Liverpool also survived into the FA Cup Final, via a hugely lucky drawn semi-final with Everton at Maine Road, before demolishing the Blues 3-0 in the replay. This meant that, four days before playing the biggest match in the entire history of the club, league champions Liverpool would meet Manchester United at Wembley in the small matter of the FA Cup Final. There had been no season for any English club quite like this one and none to test the marital status, pockets and employment record of the club's mainly working-class supporters in quite this fashion (it would happen again, of course, in 2001 and in 2022). Plenty of Liverpudlians set off to Wembley in 1977 and then carried on heading south to Italy; why bother driving back north? Even the Liverpool treble seasons that would follow in 1984 and 2001 lacked some of the intensity of this climax. Who could catch their breath?

Emlyn Hughes reasoned that Liverpool would either win both finals or neither, so this was not a good start, because the elusive treble proved just too much for his men. Paisley left out Ian Callaghan for Johnson to try to win the FA Cup on the day to avoid further fixture congestion – does this sound familiar? But then, inexplicably, he left Fairclough off the single substitute bench, if Johnson failed to deliver. He regretted both decisions later. In a scrappy match, United were often reduced to hitting long balls, but prevailed anyway with two deflected and fortuitous second-half goals to Jimmy Case's quality strike. Ray Clemence was so upset by his own role in United's first goal that he disappeared immediately down the tunnel after sullenly grabbing his medal. So now the Reds had to lift themselves in just a few days for their European Cup Final chance at last. It proved to be an unforgettable occasion, the greatest night so far in the 85-year history of the club.

Liverpool FC: European Cup winners, 25 May 1977, Rome (vs Borussia Mönchengladbach)

Clemence
Neal Smith Hughes Jones
Callaghan Case McDermott Kennedy
Keegan Heighway

The 1977 European Cup Final is probably mostly recalled by TV viewers for a sea of daft red-and-white checked flags in the Liverpool end behind a yawning running track, and for Kevin Keegan's signature 90-minute wrestling contest with the West German international defender Berti Vogts. Paisley left out David Johnson after his poor FA Cup Final showing, so Keegan would lead the line in his last match for Liverpool, and he was kicked from pillar to post for his trouble. He never stopped running or showing for the ball. Liverpool scored first through McDermott, but the Dane Simonsen equalised soon after half-time. Another final hero, Tommy Smith, had been on loan to Tampa Bay Rowdies in the summer of 1976 and was seemingly on his way out of Anfield, an escape at last from Emlyn Hughes. But an injury to Phil Thompson in March 1977 had offered a way back and Smith took it. This was his 638th and last appearance for the club, one marked by a bullet-headed near-post second Liverpool goal from a Heighway corner. It was Smith's only goal of the season; he was meant to glance the delivery across goal for someone arriving at the far post. Phil Neal's nerveless late penalty, after yet another foul on Keegan by Vogts, finally settled the 3-1 win. The right-back was no major Anfield leader or strategist but his consistency and excellence produced 23 major trophies in his 11 years at the club.

For those of us who were there in Rome this was more than a great contest won, a European club peak finally climbed. It was also a near-mythical cultural and community experience for the people of the city, one to far surpass the supporter flows from Liverpool to London for domestic cup finals that would become all too common, post-1965. Growing numbers of Liverpool fans had now travelled with the club around Europe but this was the first epic European exodus for a mass of Liverpool supporters – an estimated 25,000 travelled to Rome, using every conceivable route, every form of transport, every possible excuse for missing work and every feasible means of raising cash for the trip. Certainly, Merseyside pawnbrokers and moneylenders were in even better fettle than usual for a few weeks in May 1977.

These supporters were not particularly sophisticated and experienced adventurers. Nor were they members of the sort of well-padded, mixed-sex groups of global tourists that later supplemented hardcore male support for the Reds at major finals abroad, including to Kiev in 2018 and Madrid in 2019. They were, instead, pioneers; a pasty white-faced crowd of mainly working men, pretty much all of them from the city. Most afforded this arduous journey about the level of preparation and respect typically demanded for an overnight stop in southern England. Plenty of people from Liverpool (including the author) made a gruelling five-day round trip by coach to be there, with no overnight stops. Casualties were simply dumped off to hospitals en route. Other, younger scallies set out for this adventure in vans and by train, with only doctored railcards, the clothes on their back, a little (British) cash in their pocket, a plastic bag full of sandwiches and, as some fans put it, possibly an apple (a desperate nod here to the importance of dental hygiene). Most of these supporters got to Rome and into the Stadio Olimpico and had the time of their lives in the process. But some arrived only to slump in the city, or fall right outside the ground the worse for drink, ticketless or simply exhausted and confused by the whole process of making it to this distant, glorious place. In other words, it was a quite *fantastic* Liverpool affair. The anthem for this great trek was more lyrical and inventive even than the 1965 Liverpool FA Cup Final songs and those chants that had so charmed the British media in earlier periods of the football fever. To the tune of 'Arrivederci Roma' the following rang out from every bus, boat, plane and van that carried Reds fans southwards across Europe in May 1977:

> We're on our way to Roma, on the 25th of May.
> All the Kopites will be singing.
> Vatican bells they will be ringing.
> Liverpool songs we will be singing.
> When we win the European Cup.

Bob Paisley had now done the seemingly impossible: he had bettered the great Bill Shankly by winning the champions cup of Europe. He looked for the comfort of his slippers after the extraordinary official club celebrations in Rome had involved invading Reds supporters and the players locked together. These groups were still broadly drawn from the same stock, drank (and got drunk) in the same pubs, had pretty much similar lifestyles and diets in the 1970s. Footballers had not yet moved into the preparation regimes and the wage brackets that later had them sealed off behind tinted-windowed cars the size of small armoured trucks.

But this was also the period for the emergence of new terrace rivalries about clothes and attitude in English football support, initially spilling out of the north-west. Suddenly, the act of wearing sports clothing and trainers in the city was no longer just about leisure. These new outfits were all signs of class distinction: about 'hardness', style, capacious consumption, club loyalty in following the Reds to far-flung locales and bringing parts of the world back to the great seaport of Liverpool in time-honoured fashion. Eventually, discussions of the nuances of supporter style would make the pages of street-level music and football fanzines in Liverpool – Pete Hooton's *The End* was positively forensic in sniffing out terrace fakers and Merseyside woollybacks. It was the time of the casuals and the well-turned-out mob and, for eight years at least, this sort of performative fan culture at British football was hugely enjoyable, frequently anarchic and occasionally dangerous and violent for those involved. But after Brussels in 1985 when Liverpool played in their fifth, disastrous, European Cup Final, the whole business of travelling support for football abroad necessarily became something quite different. In fact, for a while it would disappear entirely for all club fans from England.

The time of the Scots

With the club's first European Cup now safely on Bob Paisley's mantelpiece, Kevin Keegan, as agreed, immediately left for Germany for a hefty £500,000 fee. Some Liverpool fans had given Keegan stick at matches for advertising his move in advance but Paisley barely hesitated at the loss. Bill Shankly had built his first great Reds team around three Scots: Yeats, St John and Stevenson, and his second around three key Englishmen. Now the Liverpool transfer committee of Paisley, Tom Saunders, John Smith and Peter Robinson looked to the far north again to construct a new, post-Keegan, Liverpool. They returned with three brilliant, highly intelligent and hungry Scottish players, a crafty balance to complement Paisley's native, intuitive football brain. These were men who would rule the Liverpool dressing room for a decade, run his team on the field when tactical adjustments were needed and also lead from the front if the Reds needed to scrap it out. It would be pretty much the last time a top English club would drain Scotland for some of the world's best footballers, because the talent pool north of the border would now start to dry up in the face of cultural change and global competition, as Continental clubs became less fazed in the 1990s by the sheer physicality of the British. So, these were the last knockings of the great 'Scottish professors' at Liverpool, a tradition that had stretched back over a century and that had been so central in establishing John Houlding's new professional club back in 1892. From 2017 Andy Robertson would once again revive the Scottish influence at Anfield, and with some success.

A rather gawky young Scottish midfielder had attended trials at Liverpool as a 15-year-old in the summer of 1970. He was rejected. The young Alan Hansen's laid-back attitude and lack of physicality and pace had underwhelmed the Liverpool coaches, showing just how capricious the process of finding real football talent can be. The Scot was much smarter than most young players (and probably than the club's coaches) and he was not even sure that he wanted to *be* a professional footballer at all. He was well educated and enjoyed golf more than football. He had other options. Nevertheless, in December 1973 Hansen signed professional forms for Partick Thistle and, as he grew taller, his manager Bertie Auld began to insist that he was actually a centre-back, the responsibility of which Hansen hated. The young Scot kept on pushing up from the back into midfield at Partick, and it was this combination of positional dexterity, defensive assurance and ball-playing invention that eventually attracted interest from south of the border. Most club scouts still thought that the Scot was slow and too relaxed and weak to deal with bruising English forwards. But Paisley and his coaches now wanted defenders who could survive at home but also flourish in Europe, where opposing forwards needed to be outwitted more than bludgeoned into submission. Not that Geoff Twentyman was overly impressed with Hansen initially: 'Gives the impression,' he wrote in his scouting diaries, 'that if faced with quick forwards would struggle.'

Nevertheless, in May 1977 Liverpool wisely invested £100,000 in the 21-year-old. Hansen filled out physically and became stronger mentally. In his defensive ability, intelligent game reading and comfort on the ball, he was arguably the best defender the club had recruited in 70 years. Until Virgil van Dijk arrived at Anfield in 2018, he had few other competitors. Hansen played 620 times for Liverpool, strolling to a first European Cup winner's medal at Wembley in 1978 and then replacing Emlyn Hughes for good in the Liverpool team in the 1978/79 season. His calm, unflustered defending and forward prompting meant that for the next 11 years, if he was fit (and often when he was not), Hansen was in the Liverpool team, no question. He was also part of the on-pitch Scottish brains trust that effectively ran each section of the successful Liverpool team under Bob Paisley and his Melwood coaches.

In the midfield department, the Scot who now ruled matters for Paisley was a haughty natural leader, a brutal football aristocrat and a superb technician. Graeme Souness was signed from Middlesbrough for £352,000 in January 1978. The Edinburgh-born Souness had a very flaky disciplinary record as a youngster; he had trouble controlling his natural aggression and his overwhelming cockiness. But under Paisley and his coaches he managed to rein things in, combining some of Ian St John's irreverent brio and cleverness and Emlyn Hughes's self-belief, with the uncompromising toughness of the soon-to-depart Tommy Smith. He forged these potentially toxic qualities into a stocky frame that lacked a bit of pace but wanted little for a winner's mentality and skill and that exuded an utter ruthlessness.

Politically, Souness represented the antithesis of Bill Shankly's native socialism – the idealism of the 1960s would soon give way to the greed and selfishness of the 1980s in Britain. The Liverpool midfield man certainly had a taste for money, champagne and beautiful women more than for the collectivism and home comforts of the Scottish west coast man Shankly. But *on* the pitch and at the training ground, the two football fanatics would have made a great partnership. As it turned out, Souness became an unlikely chief confidante of the rather more reserved Bob Paisley. Souness openly mocked lesser rival players and he soon assumed Tommy Smith's alpha-male role of testing out new Liverpool recruits on the Melwood training ground. His demanding standards could also be cruelly punishing in match situations: he taunted left-back Alan Kennedy for his lack of style and precision.

Souness's leadership, his passing and his imperious game management were his real strengths. But right up there was also his cynical determination to get the job done for his club, when others might waver. He would do most things to win, including famously in a tight European Cup home semi-final first leg against the dangerous Dinamo Bucharest in April 1984, assaulting the Romanian captain Movila off the ball, breaking his jaw. In the second leg, even the local police seemed to be up for revenge but the unflustered Souness was quite beyond intimidation and he fearlessly governed the match as boots flew. Liverpool won the match 2-1 and the tie 3-1 on aggregate. This sort of trial by fire he relished and it was good preparation for the 1984 final in Rome, where the home club were Liverpool's opponents. Fittingly, the Liverpool captain who lifted the trophy that night was a jauntily moustachioed and beaming Graeme Souness, a man peerlessly leading his club past all comers once more. Always ambitious and hungry for new experiences – and for big paydays – the Scot left for Italy soon after, but he would return later to Anfield as manager, in much more difficult times.

Up front, the final, brilliant, Scot of the Paisley era was someone many good judges argue is the club's greatest-ever servant. He certainly rivals Alex Raisbeck, Elisha Scott, Billy Liddell and Steven Gerrard for that title. After initial resistance from Jock Stein, the 26-year-old Glasgow-born striker Kenny Dalglish left Celtic for Liverpool in August 1977 for a record fee between British clubs of £440,000. Dalglish had already won four Scottish League titles and four Scottish Cups, a fact often forgotten amid the flurry of titles he won at Liverpool as both player and manager. His departure from Scotland and his successes at Anfield helped forge powerful links between the Liverpool and Celtic clubs, connections movingly visible after the Hillsborough disaster in 1989.

Like Alan Hansen, Dalglish had once been a teenage trialist at Anfield (in August 1966) but his shyness, unremarkable stature and lack of basic speed all counted against him. By the time he returned 11 years later to fill Kevin Keegan's number seven shirt, Dalglish had developed into the complete European forward. He was collected and deadly in front of goal, yet unmatched in his selfless work around the pitch for his team-mates. His ego-free passing and his determination to keep the ball and play the game simply was straight from the Shankly and Paisley playbook. His will to win was enormous. All this meant that Dalglish had more self-confidence than Hansen but he lacked some of the taunting bravado and disrespect for opponents of Souness. When Bob Paisley had looked at his most vulnerable as the Liverpool boss – when his touchstone forward Kevin Keegan left for Germany – Bob signed an even *better* player than Bill Shankly's adopted forward son. Was this good fortune, or simply great football management? Perhaps common interests simply coincided.

Whatever the answer, at Liverpool Kenny Dalglish improved more modest players simply by bringing them into the game and flooding them with confidence. Dalglish was also a magnificent reader of the game, near flawless in his capacity to hold the ball up, using his fantastic balance, awareness and lower body strength. Wise coaches spotted a real asset here; the Scot had a low centre of gravity – a 'big arse' – and he used it astutely to make both time and space. He could then concentrate on threading through exquisitely weighted and sublimely timed passes to his strike partners, later the nerveless Welshman Ian Rush. There was no greater sight for the club's supporters than the way this private man's boyish, blonde features lit up with unconstrained delight after he had scored or helped fashion a Liverpool goal during his 515 outings for the club. And there would be plenty of occasions to admire that smile. Moreover, when Liverpool FC were at their lowest ebb in 1985, banned from European club football and with its supporters unfairly reviled around Europe, it was Dalglish who stepped up as player-manager to secure the club's only league and FA Cup double. He also offered incredible dignity and leadership in 1989 when the Hillsborough tragedy struck. Along with a very select group of others – John Houlding and John McKenna, Tom Watson, George Kay, Bill Shankly, Bob Paisley, John Smith and Peter Robinson, and now Jürgen Klopp – Kenny Dalglish has claims to be remembered among the greatest architects of the Liverpool club tradition, both off and on the pitch. He is one of the modern proselytisers of the Liverpool Way and its mythology. In 2022 he is still a welcome fixture in and around Anfield on matchdays. He is simply 'Kenny', a truly great Liverpool football man.

Once these key signings were in place in the late 1970s, the merciless Liverpool dressing room banter and vaunted team spirit was orchestrated by these unimpeachable Scottish lairds. They were brutal in their put-downs and had some willing followers: Liverpool-born Jimmy Case and Terry McDermott, Kirkby-born defender Phil Thompson and Northumbria's Ray Kennedy were all talented and fearless competitors, crucial ingredients in the subtle chemistry necessary to produce another great Liverpool team. Bob Paisley and his new men retained the European Cup in 1978, defeating Benfica, and Gladbach once more, en route to seeing off an ultra-defensive Club Brugge KV in the final at Wembley, with Dalglish scoring a delightful winning goal.

At home, only the Shankly-lite young manager at Nottingham Forest, Brian Clough, routinely got the better of Bob and Liverpool. The European Cup holders were soon out of the competition in September 1978, mugged in the first round by Clough and his English champions, who were on their own way to two European Cup wins. Forest also drew twice in the league with Liverpool and beat the Reds controversially in the 1978 League Cup Final replay (Clough and his world-class winger John Robertson were becoming pests). Nevertheless, this new Paisley team produced the best defensive performance by a top club in 42-match Football League history, giving it a claim to be one of Liverpool's greatest-ever teams. In 1978/79 Liverpool won the league title at a canter, scoring 85 goals (36 from midfield) and conceding only 16, winning 30 matches. Included here was an early 7-0 virtuoso Anfield thrashing of a Spurs team containing two recent Argentine World Cup winners, Ardiles and Villa.

Liverpool FC: League Champions, 1978/79

Clemence

Neal Thompson Hansen A. Kennedy

Case McDermott Souness R. Kennedy

Dalglish Heighway (Johnson)

Apart from Ray Clemence in goal and Steve Heighway occasionally in attack, this was now, definitively, Bob Paisley's team, a powerhouse 4-4-2, completely revamped in five years from the one he had inherited from Bill Shankly. Four players – Clemence, Neal, Ray Kennedy and Dalglish – played all 42 league matches in 1978/79. Souness missed just one. Another title followed in 1979/80, with 11 players starting 37 or more league matches in a season that stretched to 60 fixtures. These levels of consistent appearances and avoidance of the treatment room during this period were truly astonishing, although the European Cup could still prove tricky work, even with close to a full squad. A meeting with Dinamo Tbilisi in front of 90,000 in the pouring rain in the Lenin Stadium in Georgia in the first round in October 1979 certainly qualifies. It raised all of Bob Paisley's prejudices about winter travel abroad in Eastern Europe, as hundreds of locals disturbed the peace in the early hours around the Liverpool hotel the night before. Later, banks of photographers and police behind Ray Clemence's goal in the second half surged on to the pitch to celebrate each Tbilisi goal. This was a testing and friendless place to play top-level football. Liverpool were rinsed 3-0 by the talented Georgians, meaning a 2-1 home victory in the first leg had been some way below par. However, Liverpool rather limped over the line to another league title in 1980, Johnson and Dalglish contributing 50 goals in all competitions, but also lost out to Arsenal after three replays in an epic FA Cup semi-final. Despite the successes, it was clear that forward back-up was urgently needed to compensate for David Johnson's growing failings.

When the nerdy Welsh teenager, Ian Rush, arrived from lowly Chester in 1980 for a record £300,000 fee, it initially appeared like a serious gamble. The badly dressed and gauche Rush failed to fit in at Anfield; he struggled to score in the reserves and was soon the butt of the savage Liverpool dressing room piss-takes from the resident Scottish-player mafia. He looked like (and was) a hick from the North Wales sticks. Rush soon wanted to leave Anfield and ditch these bastard big-heads from over the border who were running the first team and its social and drinking cultures, while also ruining his life. Even Bob Paisley began to doubt the Welshman's mental strength. But once Rush got settled and started to shoot back at these Scottish comedians, it positively rained goals for him at Liverpool, with Dalglish as the main provider.

Rush looked ungainly, but his pace, movement and clinical finishing were breathtaking, and he was also now a willing member of the Reds' off-field social club. When Liverpool played an evening fixture at Middlesbrough in May 1982, another league championship already won, most of the players, led by Graeme Souness, had been out celebrating in a local pub on the afternoon *before* the match – a weary 0-0 draw. With these two men in harness up front, a recent Anfield two-step striking tradition was continued – Hunt and St John in the 1960s, Keegan and Toshack in the early 1970s, and now Dalglish and Rush in the 1980s. Liverpool seemed as unstoppable in the new decade as they had been for much of the 1960s and the late 1970s. But although success on the field would continue, things off it would not be quite so simple.

Just following Bob

To prepare for the new decade, wider structural changes were afoot at Anfield. The economics of the sport were already changing in a way that made it impossible to fund European and domestic success largely on the basis of income from normal football activities. In 1980 the Main Stand paddock at Anfield was seated and, in 1982, seats were also installed in the home area of the Anfield Road end, thus reducing ground capacity to 45,600 but offering scope to raise more admissions and refreshments cash. But there was still little provision at Anfield for corporate customers – now standard at the larger European clubs. As stadium guru Simon Inglis pointed out, Anfield was lagging behind other leading clubs in terms of executive boxes and it was still often too small to cope with more affluent demand. A more visionary and expansive club board might have remedied this situation during the good times but Liverpool was in a positive cycle of playing success and, understandably, the board wanted to invest its limited resources on the pitch. Talk of attracting more 'business' fans simply riled Liverpool's supporters as an affront to the club's established traditions and its relationship with its core customers, the working people in the city. Why change tack now when things were going so well?

In the longer term, of course, this lack of investment in the commercial infrastructure of the club would prove to be a critical mistake. Not that Anfield stood still on the commercial side. In July 1979 Liverpool became the first major British football club to attract shirt sponsorship, a £100,000 deal with the Japanese electronics firm, Hitachi, the sixth-largest manufacturing company in the world. While still a player, Bob Paisley had predicted that footballers would eventually become 'human advertising hoardings' and earn huge salaries – although the latter was still some way off. Liverpool certainly needed this new source of cash. The club's turnover in 1978/79 was a paltry £2.4m, with profits a miserly £71,000, an accounting situation that Reds chairman John Smith described as 'absurd'. Merchandise sales were minimal. A local journalist reported around this time that Liverpool FC were 'virtually bankrupt'. As a result, the first-team squad was regularly dragged abroad to play money-raising friendly matches, even in the middle of a taxing set of league fixtures.

Smith had some tough messages to get across about the strange finances of the club and the game at large: 'While we are very successful in football terms,' he told the *Liverpool Echo* in 1978, 'in economic terms we are broke. Clubs like Liverpool cannot exist on the money coming through the turnstiles alone. Costs are going up all the time. Wages are high – and rightly so – and we have to use every avenue to increase our income.' Football League Secretary, Alan Hardaker, warned that English football, at the turn of a new decade, was in danger of 'bleeding to death'. The sport would have to change to survive was the message here, while Liverpool FC's main concern – and certainly that of the supporters – was that everything should remain exactly the same.

With little Sammy Lee now a first-team regular but Ian Rush not yet established, an unusually poor league campaign in 1980/81 – only 51 points gained from 42 matches – briefly threatened the Paisley project. David Johnson's goals were drying up (McDermott was top scorer) and 12 draws away from Anfield suggested a lack of forward thrust and a will to gamble. The season was saved, nevertheless, by a League Cup Final replay win over Second Division West Ham at Villa Park and another European Cup success in a forgettable final against a tepid Real Madrid in Paris. A much-weakened Liverpool team had heroically squeezed past Bayern Munich in the semi-finals, Howard Gayle to the fore, but this European final showpiece was a very poor contest, settled by a single goal from Alan Kennedy, of all people. In typical style, the club's players left the official celebrations early and hauled the trophy around the Paris nightspots for more drink-fuelled fun.

Some of the club's supporters were also on a mission. They were greeted by water cannon and riot police and a few did not exactly cover themselves in glory, ignoring bar bills, raiding local stores and stealing tickets from alarmed Spaniards, as well as from local touts. It was an early and serious warning to UEFA about the importance of planning and security that was mainly ignored. Things were going seriously wrong on the Continent concerning visits from English fans, but because there were few serious casualties and no mass brawling inside the stadium – at least not involving Liverpool supporters – few people in the VIP zones worried about the messages of the growing risk at these elite events.

For Liverpool's first league title success under the new three points for a win arrangements, in 1981/82, the South African-born eccentric Zimbabwe goalkeeper, Bruce Grobbelaar, replaced the departed Ray Clemence in Liverpool's goal, thus reviving memories of the club's South African recruitment polices of the 1920s and 1930s. Grobbelaar started like a drunken flapper but he would eventually play 628 times for the club, barely missing through injury. Between them, Clemence and Grobbelaar played almost 1,300 matches for Liverpool during some of the peak years of success. Later Grobbelaar was the focus of a major match-fixing accusation that never really went away.

Craig Johnston, a perky, if rather unconventional South African-born winger raised in Australia, also arrived in 1981, from Middlesbrough for £650,000. Paisley almost moved him on right away, so unconventional and resistant was Johnston to joining the prevailing Melwood dressing room culture. The Australian even wanted his own high-energy pre-match food rather than the garbage the rest were being served. But Johnston eventually settled and he was a prodigious worker helping his club lift five First Division titles in the 1980s. He also starred in the Liverpool European Cup-winning team of 1984. Always with a wider vision than the game alone, Johnston retired from football at just 27 years of age to turn his inquiring mind to matters other than playing sport. Both of these international players from so-called 'lesser' football nations arrived with Liverpool trawling in domestic league and European titles, while now also dominating the domestic League Cup competition. Spurs were the latest extra-time victims in the latter in 1982, undone in the final moments by a typical late Liverpool revival at Wembley.

But not everything was so rosy. Bill Shankly died of a heart attack in September 1981, producing an outpouring of local and international grief but also reigniting all those stories about his alleged maltreatment by the club. 'I still go to the matches, of course,' he had said in 1974. 'I sit in the stand. I would have loved to have been invited to away matches, but I waited and waited until I became tired of waiting.' Maybe the Liverpool board could have been more responsive back then. But most commentators simply recalled the enormous impact Shankly had made on setting the base for continuous Liverpool success. 'His motivation could move mountains,' said Ron Yeats.

It might yet have been needed again, because the 1982 league title was far from assured after a 3-1 defeat against Manchester City on a terrible Anfield pitch on Boxing Day 1981. It left the Kop in near revolt, one fan felling City keeper Joe Corrigan with a carefully aimed bottle. The press was all over this story and hard on Paisley's new signings, describing both Johnston and

Grobbelaar as 'hopelessly raw'. With Liverpool languishing in 12th place and 18 points off the pace deep into the campaign, they were pretty much written off. Captain Phil Thompson looked spooked by his goalkeeper's uncertainty. His leadership role moved to Graeme Souness after the City collapse and a dressing room shouting match with the Anfield coaching staff. A 4-0 FA Cup trouncing of Swansea City followed and a run of much improved league form, including a closing 15-match unbeaten run, produced yet another title triumph. Thompson and Grobbelaar both found their form, Ian Rush mustered 30 goals in all competitions and Souness simply dared anyone else to fail. This revival was not the result of great coaching or new tactics, just professional pride and a native understanding from Paisley, Fagan and Moran of how this group of talented, aggressive young men best worked together as a team. All the club had to do now was to get some new kit, or at least turn the heat down on the Anfield washing machines. Otherwise, the listing of the official Liverpool first-team club colours would soon need adjusting: to red with *pink* trim.

Bob Paisley announced in August 1982 that the next would be his last season in charge. Only the FA Cup had escaped him. Astonishingly, Paisley lost only once in the 11 visits he made to Wembley as a manager – the 1977 FA Cup Final. He had also presided over a then record sequence of home matches without defeat in all competitions, 85 between January 1978 and January 1981. He had made Anfield a fortress and had surpassed the achievements even of the great Bill Shankly in terms of trophies, although Shankly had built the entire club from Second Division obscurity. There would be no knighthoods for either man, as there would later be for others when English football had become a more pacified, gentrified and politically more acceptable product.

Paisley's player recruitment – save perhaps for the £450,000 wasted on Middlesbrough's David Hodgson in the summer of 1982 – had been exceptionally good. Liverpool players later highlighted a key secret of the winning mentality of the teams

Bob built. Basically, it was about not overcomplicating things and always having real leaders and winners in the dressing room. Talking of the 1982 League Cup Final defeat of Tottenham, for example, Ronnie Whelan pointed out that it was clear that Spurs had a more creative midfield than Liverpool, so it was privately agreed *by the players* that these dangerous opponents had to be 'discouraged' before Liverpool could take control. If a Liverpool player got booked, another man would step up the physical stuff to avoid a damaging sending-off. 'Like a wolf pack smelling blood,' was how Craig Johnston described it. This Liverpool team had talent but it also had pragmatism and an unshakably deep mean streak.

This general pattern of astute player recruitment coupled with managerial ruthlessness helps explain why Liverpool were so successful in the decade between 1974 and 1984. Two versatile defenders – the silky smooth and calming Mark Lawrenson signed from Brighton for £900,000 in August 1981, and Steve Nicol, a supremely consistent all-round recruit from Ayr United, arrived in the same year to add to Liverpool's combined rearguard strength. The teak-tough shy young Irish midfielder, Ronnie Whelan, had stepped up from Joe Fagan's reserves, alongside the bustling and determined Sammy Lee. But there was no massive money hike here for most players. Whelan revealed later that if the club wanted to keep a player, his wages could be doubled every few years but from a low base. Additional financial rewards came from appearances, points accumulated and the size of Anfield crowds. Few players at this time fully understood the formula, or their own market value, and fewer still talked to each other about wages or had anything in the way of financial advice. Agents were little in evidence. Whelan played, briefly, in the Premier League era but even here his wages could be as little as £2,000 a week. Nevertheless, he was winning and collecting trophies, so why worry that the finance cards remained so firmly in the club's hands?

In Bob Paisley's final season, with Ray Kennedy and David Johnson now out of the picture, Liverpool won the league title by 11 clear points. It was becoming too easy. This could even have been a 100-point season but the players took their foot off the gas and secured only two points from their last seven league fixtures, the title already assured. Ian Rush scored a record four goals at Goodison Park in a 5-0 humiliation for the Blues, which also meant the flourishing for 40 years of his own Anfield song. The Liverpool players were uninterested in breaking records, only winning trophies, and there was always drinking to do around the city's bars once the serious business was concluded (they were champions of celebrating, too).

Bob Paisley, of course, was furious with the 'unprofessionalism' of the late collapse. When he finally left this club that he had served so loyally since before the war, citing family matters and health concerns, Paisley showed none of Shankly's anxiety or regret. He simply returned to his carpet slippers and TV horse racing in his modest Liverpool home. Bob had no airs or graces and few ambitions beyond serving the club and its followers. Under him, Liverpool were league title holders and League Cup winners once again, beating Manchester United 2-1 in the latest Wembley final. Much of his managerial success was actually about *not* tinkering, not overthinking things. Later bosses might have learned something. Reduced to mere statistics, Bob Paisley's record in major competitions over his nine years as Liverpool manager still looks outrageous today. It comprises:

- Three European Cups
- Six Football League titles
- One UEFA Cup
- Three League Cups

Paisley was definitively old school. Save for consulting with his captain Graeme Souness, he barely had a meaningful conversation with any of his key players during his entire time as the Liverpool boss. He hated, especially, those difficult exchanges with players he had been forced to leave out. But, as the more garrulous Bill Shankly had done nine years before, Bob handed something impressive and stable on to his immediate successor. European Cups, as well as League Cup and league doubles, achieved in both 1982 and 1983, had begun to seem like par for the course for Liverpool under Paisley – routine rewards. But home league crowds at Anfield in the 1980s had perhaps begun to reflect the club's instrumental play and its easy superiority, as well as hard times on Merseyside. League gates under 30,000 were starting to appear for the repeat champions around this time. Not everything was well. Nevertheless, Paisley said later about his work with Bill Shankly and Liverpool: 'Bill built the house and I put the roof on it.' It was a pretty good analogy – and it was a very sturdy roof.

Troubling times, home and abroad

Of course, it was Joe Fagan, born in north Liverpool, who took over from Paisley; why stop a ticking clock? As it had been so often for Paisley – deceptively so, perhaps – it seemed the new Liverpool manager simply had to select his best 11 men, week in, week out in the 1983/84 season, and then sit back and let them play. Continuity was always the Liverpool watchword: the Riley family, groundsmen Arthur and his father Bert, had been tending the Anfield turf since 1908. One family, three-quarters of a century of dedication at the same club. At 62, Joe Fagan was perhaps a little old to be a debutant manager but he knew that to invite in a younger 'outsider' could threaten the jobs of himself and all the men in the Liverpool boot room. Nor did the players want change. The strong support for Joe from Graeme Souness was especially vital here. Souey did not need a new, challenging voice in the manager's seat – and in his own ear. What might happen to the players' power and their drinking school?

Joe Fagan certainly seemed at home and he was relaxed and at ease in his new role, although it was unclear to him at the start what, exactly, the manager's job at Anfield actually entailed. Why the need for a collar and tie? Often, beyond team selection issues, it was the senior players who seemed to be organising things for themselves, with the coaching staff overseeing their preparation and regal progress. Joe was twinkly and he entertained the press – this was his main job.

This slowly transforming Liverpool team was both experienced but also hungry for more success. The first signing on Fagan's watch was centre-back Gary Gillespie, from Coventry City, although the new man confessed he had no idea who Joe was. Gillespie played no league matches for the senior team in his first season, nor did a fast-fading Phil Thompson play for Joe Fagan. A burly, hard-working forward, Michael Robinson, incoming from Brighton, got more play, but he was an average talent who later excelled in TV coverage of football in Spain. Robinson was left-thinking, he dressed well, read books and browsed the serious press. But he was also a word-sharp and did his job, so the Liverpool dressing room shop stewards embraced him, nevertheless.

And what a first season it was for both Robinson and Fagan: a European Cup win in Rome, the first Merseyside Wembley final in the 1984 League Cup – although it would take a Maine Road replay and a Graeme Souness goal to see off Everton in contests that most people outside the city thought tedious – and another Liverpool league title. In short, an unprecedented *three* major trophies in one season. Seven players would miss just two league fixtures between them in 1983/84. Four boasted the maximum 67 starts in all competitions, the most of any player in this period. But it was Ian Rush who was now the Liverpool touchstone, scoring a ridiculous 47 times in 65 appearances and beginning to draw attention from all around Europe. The club's next-highest scorers were stuck on 12. This may not have exactly been the most competitive of Football League seasons – Southampton finished second – and Liverpool still struggled to perform away from home. In fact, in early December they were humiliated 4-0 at lowly Coventry City in the league, a performance described as 'pathetic' by Fagan. A teacup-throwing post mortem followed. Liverpool lost again in the FA Cup, to Second Division Brighton, so no change there. But three trophies! Could it possibly get any better at Anfield? As it turned out, the answer would be emphatically 'no': not for the city of Liverpool; not for Liverpool Football Club; and certainly not for Joe Fagan and English football.

With a neo-liberal Thatcher government now in power, stressing the bleak doctrine of market forces, and with the port of Liverpool long past its once global influence and jobs, the city of Liverpool and its people struggled for a foothold in the new world order. But having experienced the good times in the 1960s, the new generation of resourceful and expectant young people in the city were in no mood now to accept the 'no future' mantra played back to them from London in the 1970s and 1980s. With racism now official government policy, some rebelled on the streets, as in Toxteth in 1981, while others did so via the politics of Militant, which took a divisive hold inside the Liverpool City Council. Many more took the more creative culture and music route, by forming pop and rock bands and living off grants or on the dole, their way of sampling the good life. Others still decided to have their own adventures by setting off to see the world by following Liverpool FC across Europe and living off the land to fund their trips.

Alan Bleasdale's darkly humorous TV series *Scully* in 1984 showcased members of the Liverpool team, especially Kenny Dalglish. It had, as its central theme, the view that only football could offer an escape route for workless young men in the city. But taking the European football fan traveller 'solution' to this rejection and inertia came with some wider costs. These included the petty (and some more serious) thieving and the 'free' train travel often involved in these outings; the occasional disorder and fighting that took place; and the counterfeiting and the 'bunking in' that sometimes threatened fan safety inside grounds on European trips. In fact, it was becoming clearer all the time that ambitious young working-class men from *all* ethnic backgrounds in Liverpool expected rather more excitement and more opportunity in their lives than what was currently on offer from the powers that be in London. They were going to take them if and when they arose.

The Liverpool forward, locally born Howard Gayle, had actually become the first black man to play for the club in 1981, just the *99* years on from Liverpool FC's formation by John Houlding. *White* South Africans had been Liverpool's historic and main concession to ethnic integration so far. On a Paisley hunch about 'fielding the unknown', Gayle had been selected and had performed exceptionally well in a depleted Liverpool team that survived the European Cup semi-final away leg against Bayern Munich. While a young Sammy Lee was instructed to man-mark Paul Breitner – an unprecedented, last-minute decision from his manager – it was Gayle who had stretched and confused the experienced Bayern defence in a famous qualifying 1-1 draw. Was this the long-awaited breakthrough, the vital new connection between the club and the city's long-estranged black communities that would open up some of the old boundaries? Not so fast. In fact, Gayle struggled for form and would make only five first-team appearances in the nine years he was registered with Liverpool, being constantly sent out on loan. He was also frustrated by the prevailing racist banter and the culture of the club, and by Paisley and the Liverpool staff and players underplaying the prejudice he faced or the importance of this courageous black Scouser's ethnic background. Tommy Smith gave him a really hard time. Gayle said later:

> I first became aware of intolerant attitudes at Melwood through people who didn't realise I was close by and within earshot. Unacceptable phrases were used. It would happen in the canteen at Anfield. It would happen on the bus en route to training or games. Such language was delivered in jest. But I was not laughing.

While the urbane John Barnes would later simply brush off these tasteless dressing room jokes, in Gayle's eyes the club seemed determined to make invisible, or to disparage, his proud local heritage. Unlike Barnes, he had battled racism all his young life, but the Liverpool coaches only wanted to talk football and they let their players have their dressing room mockery. It was an old Merseyside story of prejudice, exclusion and division, albeit in new sporting clothes. Sadly, the club's one authentic black Scouser was no longer in the Liverpool first-team picture (or anywhere near it) as Joe Fagan prepared for his first European Cup Final as Liverpool manager in 1984. Nor were poverty, unemployment or government prejudice issues on the football field. Having seen off Spanish champions Athletic Bilbao in a very tight affair – Joe Fagan thought a 0-0 home draw would prove enough, and it did – and Dinamo Bucharest in that frenzied and violent atmosphere in the Romanian capital, Liverpool were assured and confident about the final, even though the opposition in a bouncing ground full of Italians, were local favourites AS Roma.

Life in Rome proved deeply troubling for we travelling Liverpool fans – the locals were dangerously hostile. And this match proved to be a stifling, tactical affair, the Italians seemingly nervous and inexperienced in front of their own supporters on such a major European football occasion. Not that the Liverpool players were especially well prepared either. Joe Fagan and Tom Saunders had watched Roma play but, as Graeme Souness later confirmed, the players were shown no video material, were given no instruction on their rival's formation, or on the standard Roma set pieces. Better not clutter the team with too much talk about the opposition. This was all too familiar territory to Chris Lawler, now part of the Anfield coaching team.

In the pre-match press conferences, the super-relaxed Fagan was also happy to feed local rumours that Liverpool were, indeed, complacent. But it was AS Roma who had never won the European Cup, and it showed. Famously, the visitors' exuberant singing of a Chris Rea song in the tunnel before the match seemed to have a surprisingly demoralising effect on the home team. A tense 1-1 draw was the outcome, Liverpool taking the lead through Phil Neal before comfortably holding on for extra time and a penalty shoot-out after an equaliser from Pruzzo. In fact, Roma had looked far more fearful of losing rather than striving to win. Joe Fagan and his staff had done surprisingly little work for this particular outcome, although it must have looked like a distinct possibility. He probably thought, as many coaches in England did at the time, that penalty shoot-outs were little more than a lottery and were barely worth practising for. In the few brief sessions that he had organised in training, no Liverpool players took penalties seriously and most had missed the target. Now everything rested on the penalty spot. 'Every player, I can tell you, was nervous, petrified,' was how Alan Kennedy remembered it. And he should know.

Liverpool FC: European Cup winners, 30 May 1984 (vs AS Roma)

Grobbelaar
Neal Hansen Lawrenson A. Kennedy
Johnston Souness Lee Whelan
Rush (Robinson) Dalglish (Nicol)

Joe Fagan selected his five penalty takers in real time on the pitch from those who showed willing or were simply too slow to scurry away. His chief shop steward, Graeme Souness, was the man to decide the order. But young substitute Steve Nicol said he felt confident and simply grabbed the ball and strode off to take Liverpool's first penalty. He missed it, spectacularly so. No problem, the experienced Neal, Souness and Rush all scored for Liverpool, while Grobbelaar's strange wobbly-legged and 'eating the net' antics induced two nervy Italian misses. Grobbelaar celebrated wildly as if the cup was already won, but one Liverpool taker was left. 'Oh no,' Grobbelaar said, in passing Liverpool's last man standing. 'I didn't realise it would be fucking you to take this!' Alan Kennedy had scored in League Cup finals and in open play in Paris to win the 1981 trophy for his club, but the left-back could barely have expected a repeat showing tonight. He said later that he had been quietly praying: 'Don't let it fucking come down to me. I would rather, honestly, that they'd [Roma] win the fucking cup as long as I didn't have to take one.' Back on the halfway line, Kennedy had forced himself to study where all the previous kicks had been aimed, but now, jelly-legged, he could remember precisely nothing about what he had been so closely observing only a few minutes before. So, he closed his eyes, shot low to his left-hand corner ... and to his grateful amazement the Roma goalkeeper Tancredi dived the *opposite* way.

In this punishing season an astonishing seven Liverpool outfield players had started more than 60 matches for Fagan. Team 'selection' seemed to be a misnomer. The players' night's work in Rome was now over, save, of course, for the partying. But for many of the Liverpool supporters in the city things would take an alarming turn. Italian gangs lay in wait in the dark parklands and on the Tiber Bridge outside the Stadio Olimpico, with the Rome police typically inert and inept. The Italian way in these matters is to attack the legs and buttocks of rivals with blades and to throw bottles and bricks indiscriminately. It was a dangerous chicken run, a horrible gauntlet that ensnared the streetwise, as well as the inexperienced, and included those willing and able to fight back. The hospital cases that resulted – remarkably no visiting fan was killed – meant that there would probably be a bounty to be paid the next time Liverpool FC met Italians in Europe. So, when the Reds reached the European Cup Final again in 1985 in Brussels, this time against the northern Italians from Juventus, it was clear that for this event to go off smoothly and safely it would require a well-appointed stadium, strong and efficient policing, excellent UEFA organisation and a sensible approach from *all* of the club's supporters. Sadly – and fatally – it turned out that plenty was badly lacking in all of these departments. Liverpool's great 20-year run in Europe since the 1964/65 season was about to come to an abrupt and unimaginable end.

Chapter 6

Into the Darkness

Heysel, Hillsborough and into recovery

Jan Mølby signals the new international invasion and Everton FC start to get tasty. Liverpool, their fans and the sport's authorities disgrace themselves in Brussels. Kenny Dalglish steps up in hard times for English football's first player-manager domestic double. Ian Rush settles the inaugural Merseyside FA Cup Final. John Barnes arrives to challenge local racism and light up Anfield but brutal Wimbledon thwart another potential double. Terrible Hillsborough losses produce decades of brave campaigning and also transforms the game. Arsenal steal the 1989 title before the Kop, and Kenny finally feels the strain.

Sliding into chaos

In the depths of a national economic depression that was impacting especially harshly on Merseyside, the Liverpool Football Club project was also perceptively starting to slide in 1985. The great enforcer Souness, at 31, had left for cash-rich Italy (an 'absolute doddle for a midfielder' he reported later) and Kenny Dalglish was slowing in his brilliant service for the club as a player. Ian Rush would soon leave for an unfulfilling brief stay at Juventus. The replacements signed by Fagan for these three giants were simply not of similar stature – who could be? Paul Walsh, unusually for Liverpool a southerner, was an average forward signed from Luton Town, a man who flitted in and out of matches and had little of Dalglish's assurance, guile and intelligence. John Wark, a loping goalscoring Scottish midfielder from Ipswich Town, had something of the Ray Kennedy about him, without ever reaching those classy heights, and Kevin MacDonald, another Scot and a left-sided ball carrier bought from Leicester City, was a one-paced workhorse who showed occasionally flashes of something close to what was required. Alan Hansen did not rate him and injury would blight his Anfield prospects.

The only really exciting capture here was a Dane, Jan Mølby, an Ajax graduate who joined in 1984 and stayed for 260 starts and a then record 12 years as an overseas player at one club in England. Foreign players were still something of a novelty in the English game, and big Jan was something else again. He had actually agreed to sign for Sheffield Wednesday but Tom Saunders hijacked the deal, inviting him instead for a ten-day trial at Melwood. Although nobody at Liverpool had ever watched him play, this audition was enough for a three-year contract. Mølby, a central midfielder, had mobility problems from the outset – he would fit perfectly into the Liverpool dressing room drinking club – but no one could doubt his exquisite touch, exemplary technique and luscious passing ability. His weight of pass was near faultless but his actual weight was a real problem. Mølby was astounded at how little Liverpool worked in training on combinations and tactics: 'You're on yer own here, mate,' John Wark had told him before his debut. Mølby asked the coaches at Melwood how he should play to fit into the Liverpool system. They looked at him blankly and shrugged, saying, 'Fuck off! Just do what you did at Ajax.' Mølby had much of what Graeme Souness had in his locker except, crucially, real athleticism and that unquenchable Scottish desire and willingness to turn to strategic violence whenever it was needed. The Dane had real quality but he never completely managed a potentially anarchic English football match quite as Souness once did.

Liverpool were easily eclipsed in the league in 1984/85 by a rising Everton under Howard Kendall and starring the Reds reject, Kevin Sheedy. It was hard to take. Liverpool also lost in a replay to Manchester United after an utterly poisonous atmosphere in an FA Cup semi-final in April 1985. The English game was by now run through with a nasty strain of hooliganism but a really spectacular darkness was revealing itself here, as rival supporters exchanged obscenities and missiles and fought running battles outside Goodison Park, where Liverpool had clung on against a superior United. Few Reds supporters present could remember quite this level of bile and disorder, even at this increasingly combustible contest.

Thankfully, the rounds of the European Cup in 1984/85 had produced relatively little of this sort of frenzied hatred (or competition) as Liverpool sauntered through to yet another final, dispensing with opponents from Poland, Portugal, Austria and Greece on the way. This was really not Europe's elite; the Greeks from Panathinaikos were operating way above their pay grade when casually dismissed by a 5-0 aggregate scoreline in the semi-finals. But the formidable Italian champions Juventus now lay waiting in the final, in the Heysel Stadium in Brussels. The bare details of what happened next are these. Juventus fans, mainly from Belgium, had bought tickets to a supposedly 'neutral' terrace Sector Z, next to an area that was housing Liverpool fans and separated from them only by what looked like a chicken wire fence and a handful of police. Some anger about the treatment of Reds fans in Rome the previous year might have fed resentment before the first missiles were exchanged. Liverpool fans then began dissembling the fence that divided these sections. This was followed, from around 7.20pm, by a minor 'charge' towards the Italians through the, by now, ragged fences. Police seemed mainly absent.

The Italian supporters in Sector Z – many of them 'family' fans – now panicked and rushed to their right towards an exit, away from the red invasion and trouble. Expressed in banal terms, the whole thing was an enactment of typical English territorial posturing at football grounds from about ten years before. But here local policing was inept and the mass movement in a confined space of terrified Italians caused a wall at the side of the terrace to collapse under the weight of their alarm. In all, 39 supporters were crushed or suffocated to death, 32 of them Italian, but only two from the city of Turin itself. The Liverpool players were sheltered away in their dressing room, only yards away from this unfolding horror. But they had heard the terrible rumble of the collapsing wall and the screams of panic outside. Alan Kennedy, not in the Liverpool playing squad, was now charged with going out to see what had happened and relaying news back to the team. He saw lifeless bodies and very angry and distressed Italians; he feared for his own safety. A few players – Bruce Grobbelaar among them – expressly did not want to play but, in the end, they all had to do their own job. The Liverpool supporters in the crowd had seen the disturbances and the kick-off delay told them something pretty extreme had happened, but many had no idea that people had been killed. Television viewers knew much more.

Amazingly, the match eventually took place – 'for safety reasons' – kicking off at 9.40pm British time. The Belgian police feared anger and frustration would turn to more violence between the rival fans if the match was abandoned. Television executives knew about the fatalities, so the TV coverage continued in a near-funereal atmosphere. After Juventus eventually scored the winning penalty, the Italian internationals Paulo Rossi and Marco Tardelli blamed the 'confusion and chaos' of the evening for the Italians' misguidedly joyous response. It was Juve's first European Cup win, achieved in the worst possible circumstances. After the trophy was presented in the privacy of the Juventus changing room, the players even came out to do a lap of honour, and fans in Turin marked the win into the early hours of the morning.

Back in Liverpool, chairman John Smith and others questioned who was *really* involved in the trouble. No convincing evidence ever emerged that there was some kind of alien right-wing infiltration of the Liverpool contingent and no case was made along these lines by the official inquiry that followed. It seemed, instead, that a relatively minor instance of drunken hooliganism (by English standards at least) had been allowed to escalate out of control in a stadium, and with a police force that was simply not up to the task. But at home the British press turned on the city of Liverpool and on the English game with a barely concealed mixture of venom and glee. Hooliganism in the 1980s was not a Liverpool FC problem, it was an *English*, and increasingly a European, problem. Twenty-seven supporters were arrested (60 per cent from Liverpool) and eventually held on manslaughter charges. After a trial in Belgium in 1989, 14 Liverpool followers were given three-year convictions for involuntary manslaughter. Most of them were from the city. UEFA Secretary-General Hans Bangerter was found guilty of negligence. Gendarme captain Johan Mahieu and the secretary of the Belgian FA, Albert Roosens, were charged with manslaughter and 'massacre' and each given six-month suspended sentences. The Belgian government collapsed in July 1985 when the interior minister refused to resign over the affair.

All English clubs were now banned from European competition for an indeterminate period – including the 1985 league champions, Everton. The English game was in shame. But perhaps what was *really* shameful here was the treatment of the Heysel dead and their families. Neither Juventus nor Liverpool seemed to want to focus on their needs or their memory. Most of the dead did not live in Turin, so mourning and solidarity there was distressingly limited. Juventus immediately displayed the European Cup, despite relatives of the dead saying that the trophy was stained with blood. Liverpool FC seemed unable or unwilling to take at least some responsibility for the disaster, and there were no proper memorials set up at either of the club stadiums. Nor was there serious discussion about compensation, or even expressed public regret for what had happened. Only when Liverpool finally played Juventus again in the European Cup in 2005 was culpability publicly acknowledged on Merseyside. Juve ultras at the match at Anfield, unsurprisingly, turned their backs on the Kop's well-meaning but belated mosaic of apology. Here was some closure of sorts on what had been a highly damaging and disreputable episode in the Liverpool club's history.

King Kenny steps up

As the recession kicked in hard on Merseyside in the 1980s and the reputation for hooliganism stalked the English game, so football attendances in the city and elsewhere continued to fall. Once mighty Everton had attracted average league gates below 20,000 in 1983/84, while treble-winning Liverpool could barely manage 32,000 for some league matches. In Liverpool's case, at least, reduced crowds was probably partly down to ennui; fans had become a little blasé about winning titles and cups. Who was to challenge Liverpool's domestic dominance? In fact, in the aftermath of Heysel the club's attendances actually *improved* in 1985/86, even as they fell elsewhere across England. Some Reds supporters certainly stopped attending because of their revulsion at what had happened in Brussels but it was also as if many local people had invested in another struggle. They were determined to get behind the embattled club and city once again and to reaffirm its traditionally positive bonds with the communities of Merseyside. A group of local fans under Liverpool man Rogan Taylor also started a new national supporter body in the city, the Football Supporters Association, to give fans a stronger collective voice in the sport and to raise the public profile of non-hooligan fans. It was the start of the fight back on the terraces and in the stands against the hooligans, the tabloid press and the European and English football establishments.

As Liverpool FC tried to rebuild *on* the pitch in these near-impossibly difficult circumstances, bravely and with great dignity,

Kenny Dalglish took over as planned, although as player-manager. What a workload, and in a moment like this! He leaned on Bob Paisley for advice and on the much-mythologised Liverpool boot room for his philosophy: 'Give the opposition very little and get as much out of them as you can.' Dalglish turned to the Joe Fagan signing, Jan Mølby, as the player he might shape his new team around. The rotund Mølby was hardly built for the typical high-tempo exchanges of the English game even in the 1980s, but what he lacked in mobility he more than made up for in technique. His penalty taking was also near faultless. Dalglish brought in the hard-tackling midfield Scouser, Steve McMahon (from Aston Villa), to offer balance and support for Mølby, and he played Kevin MacDonald and Ronnie Whelan ('a great player' for that harshest of judges, Graeme Souness) in Liverpool's midfield. A one-paced but reliable Irishman, Jim Beglin, had also replaced Alan Kennedy at left-back by this time, and the gangly Gary Gillespie was finally getting some game time.

The veteran Alan Hansen, for one, was highly sceptical about the group; he thought this lot was miles off being a league title outfit. It lacked leadership, depth and some quality. But sport is both unpredictable and emotional; it sometimes defies careful analysis. After a slow start and a mid-season blip, including a 2-0 loss at Everton, Liverpool then set off on a run that produced 35 points from the last 36 on offer. Rush and Mølby (mainly with penalties) topped the scorers' list. But fittingly it was Dalglish himself who scored the volleyed goal at a windswept Stamford Bridge to win the 1986 league title. Runners-up Everton, that club's best team for 20 years, vowed revenge. And they would have their chance.

Some kindly FA Cup draws meant Liverpool could eventually see off a stubborn Southampton in extra time in the semi-final at White Hart Lane, which meant a memorable and emotional first all-Merseyside FA Cup Final in 1986, some 94 years in its gestation. Reportedly, 5,000 fans turned up without tickets and some certainly tried desperate tactics to get inside. It was not a good look after Brussels. Everton were probably slight favourites and they looked it after 40-goal Gary Lineker outpaced Hansen to give the Blues a deserved first-half lead. Hansen was stressed for pace for much of the first hour when Everton were on top, while Jim Beglin and Bruce Grobbelaar visibly squabbled. But a Jan Mølby-inspired Liverpool rally, with two goals in six second-half minutes, eventually led to a 3-1 Liverpool win. Everton's (and everybody's) bogeyman, Ian Rush, scored twice to seal his club's first league and FA Cup double. Liverpool had hung on for dear life early in the second half but, once Rush had scored, the Everton players told him later, they had feared the worst. *The Guardian* wisely reported that 'behind that six minutes lay more than 25 years of continuous organisation and patient team-building'. Experience tells.

I was near the Royal Box to see Alan Hansen lift the cup for his club just days after Alex Ferguson had left him out of the Scotland World Cup squad. Like in 1906, *both* teams featured on the street parade that followed but Peter Reid had no time for a loser's tour, and with a merry 'fuck this!' he got off the Everton bus halfway round to go to the pub. 'Where I looked for a reason for success,' said the FA Cup's first-ever winning player-manager, 'I seemed to find it.' It had been a hugely resourceful response from Dalglish and his team on the pitch to desperate adversity, fan indiscipline and public shaming off it. As the *Liverpool Echo* put it, 'Twelve months after the tragedy at the Heysel stadium, our two great teams put the smile back on English football and showed the rest of Europe how to celebrate victory – and accept defeat.' Well said.

Liverpool FC: League Champions and FA Cup winners, 10 May 1986 (vs Everton)

Grobbelaar
Nicol Hansen Lawrenson Beglin
Johnston Mølby Whelan McMahon (MacDonald)
Dalglish (Walsh) Rush

Gillespie, the ex-Oxford United midfielder Ray Houghton, full-back Barry Venison, recruited from Sunderland, and the Scouse striker John Aldridge, would now all figure strongly in the 'new' Liverpool that was being reconfigured by Kenny Dalglish. Aldridge, especially, was delighted by the Liverpool drinking club but he was also a first-class finisher, a man who had fought his way up the football food chain back to his hometown club. His challenge was that he would be replacing a goal machine in Ian Rush. In the League Cup Final of 1987 something extraordinary happened, because Ian Rush scored and Liverpool *lost*, 2-1 to Arsenal. This run of Rush goals and no defeats had lasted 145 matches; it was clearly time for the Welshman to take a furlough – at Juventus – and to give Aldridge his chance.

However, the key new Dalglish recruits at this time were undoubtedly the England international forwards, John Barnes and Peter Beardsley. The arrival of the middle-class Jamaican-born Barnes, from Watford in June 1987, the first regular black first-teamer at the club, stirred predictable emotions – and some racist hostility – in the city. But his attacking play was sublime, quelling the idiots at Anfield and even some in opposing crowds. Barnes said that his father, an officer in the Jamaican army, was his key influence by instilling discipline and putting a football in his crib when he was an infant. A taxi driver saw Barnes playing as a teenager for Sudbury Court in Hertfordshire in 1981 and recommended him to Watford FC, then managed by Graham Taylor. By 1983 Barnes had even dragged Watford to second place – behind Liverpool – in the First Division. Taylor gave Sudbury Court a set of shirts and shorts in recompense. It was hardly generous because, six years after leaving his local junior club, Barnes was sold to Liverpool for a record £900,000.

Kenny Dalglish said that he had signed *two* players in the British Jamaican: a winger and a centre-forward. Barnes had the strength, touch and pace to defeat almost all defences, allied to a powerful left-foot shot and wonderful crossing ability. He was the most direct and effective goalscoring wide player at Liverpool since Billy Liddell, and he became almost as popular with the club's supporters. Barnes's fame and respect only increased in the red half of Merseyside when he was caught on camera flicking a banana off the field at Goodison Park during a losing 1987 League Cup tie. His talent and commitment were exceptional and his eventual general acceptance and celebration at Anfield signalled some progress, at least, in terms of the historic racial exclusions and prejudices at the club and in the city. Howard Gayle, of course, might well beg to differ.

By contrast, Peter Beardsley's north-east English qualities were rather more prosaic but no less effective than those of Barnes, at least on those occasions when he found his form. Beardsley lacked the reliable technique and strength of Barnes but he was boyishly enthusiastic, inventive and hard-working almost in equal measure. Together, he and Barnes, allied to the unerring finishing of Aldridge, energised a new attacking Liverpool.

Meanwhile, more local quality was already in the Melwood pipeline in the mid-1980s. A six-year-old Huyton kid was present for his first Anfield match in November 1986 when Jan Mølby completed a unique hat-trick of penalties in a League Cup win over Coventry City. The young Steven Gerrard might also have pointed to a record 10-0 Anfield defeat of Fulham in the League Cup in September of that year. But, for now, Everton under Howard Kendall reigned supreme as league champions in 1986/87 and the signing by Liverpool of Nigel Spackman in the same year for £400,000 may have served as an early warning sign about declining incoming player quality.

An impressive 87 goals resulted in the new 40-match league format for Liverpool in 1987/88 (in the following season it would be down to 38 matches), including five in a famous rout of close rivals Nottingham Forest in April 1988. Was this, as some claimed, the most complete league performance by any club at home since the war? Praise indeed, even if it was probably a little overplayed. But the overall Liverpool showing that season was exceptional. After starting with three consecutive away matches because of a sewer collapse on the Kop, Liverpool cantered to the title in 1988, with 90 points and only two defeats. Being banned from Europe helped but this was clearly an outstanding Liverpool group, even when measured by its highest recent standards. John Aldridge scored 26 league goals, with Barnes and Beardsley mesmeric in turn. Lacking any European diversions only seemed to make these Reds more ruthless at home.

But another domestic league and FA Cup double was stymied at the last by a deeply unsettling outcome in the 1988 FA Cup Final. After beating Nottingham Forest in the semi-final at Hillsborough, a brutal Wimbledon team (and bad luck) intimidated Liverpool to a shock 1-0 defeat at Wembley. Wimbledon used an old Liverpool trick of pre-match tunnel noise but it was routine violence and fouling, lax refereeing and the double marking of John Barnes that hurt more. Also, Aldridge concocted the first missed penalty at any FA Cup Final, with defender Andy Thorn standing directly behind him, bellowing, 'Miss! Miss! Miss!' That old master of planned psychological and physical violence, Graeme Souness, was probably growling displeasure and contempt somewhere at this sorry Wembley capitulation of the club at which he had once ruled, unopposed. As it turned out, this was also an early warning for Liverpool FC of imminent danger ahead.

Hillsborough, 15 April 1989

In the following season, Arsenal dramatically wrenched the league title from Liverpool on goal difference in the last minute of the final league fixture, at Anfield on 26 May 1989. That is the simple story, the barest of facts, a win still celebrated in north London. However, the Liverpool team (and its supporters) had reason to be emotionally and physically drained, as this was the club's eighth match in 23 days, including another Merseyside FA Cup Final. Television had dictated that this title 'play-off' match be moved to be the season's last fixture, a decision that infuriated Kenny Dalglish. It was, by any measure, a ridiculous and punitive programme, but placed in its context it was even more cruel than this. This was the latest finish to a Football League season since Liverpool had snatched the title ahead of Stoke City back in June 1947. Only the 2020 Covid-19 finish would be later than that one. But the weather in 1989 had been fine and there was no global pandemic to contend with. The reason for the delay, of course, was another terrible disaster involving Liverpool FC, this time at the Hillsborough stadium in Sheffield. There, the neglect and mismanagement of the South Yorkshire police caused the unlawful killing of (eventually) 97 Liverpool supporters on 15 April 1989, near the start of another FA Cup semi-final meeting with Nottingham Forest. As a result, the club and the city were thrown into a vortex of mourning and a forced defence of their own victimised supporters.

The police in Sheffield failed to monitor the Liverpool crowds effectively both inside and outside the ground. Some Liverpool supporters had been delayed arriving because of roadworks on the M62 motorway, and the Leppings Lane end of the ground had too few turnstiles to properly process fans in time. The police responded to dangerous overcrowding outside by opening an exit Gate C to allow supporters entry, but they then failed to direct arriving Liverpool fans to less crowded pens. As a result, supporters walked into already overcrowded penned terraces behind the goal where the deadly crushing took place. The police now failed again. The match was halted by referee Ray Lewis at 3.06pm but the police responded too slowly to obvious signs of distress among fans trapped in overcrowded pens sited beneath the police control box, with perimeter gates that would not open under crowd pressure (we could see all of this developing from our own seats in the North Stand). Desperately escaping supporters were even returned to the killing pens because police initially interpreted their panic and suffering as a pitch invasion, the result of hooliganism. In the confusion, only one of the 44 ambulances that responded to the disaster call was later allowed by the police into the stadium. Its crew was overwhelmed by the sheer number of Liverpool supporters requiring urgent treatment on the pitch. The police then compounded even all these gross errors by their later disgusting treatment of bereaved families and their attempts to smear Liverpool supporters via a cover-up promoted in national press stories, led by *The Sun* newspaper.

I was working for the Football Trust on this day and I had to take various luminaries around the site of the disaster. Liverpool supporters around us were already contesting the police account that fans had forced open Gate C. Historically, as we have seen, English clubs had long displayed too little care in the treatment of football fans. Football grounds were badly designed, essentially dangerous places that were poorly regulated, and it was only good fortune and the care that supporters showed for each other that had prevented similar disasters after the 1946 tragedy at Burnden Park. Britain in the 1980s was a harsher social and economic climate altogether, and football crowds were more volatile, less consensual and perhaps less caring. The Sheffield ground was argued to be one of England's best-appointed stadiums, mainly because of the way it was designed to deal with hooliganism. The English game had gone down a fatal route and was in danger of treating *all* of its customers as a potential threat. Here was the result. As the city of Liverpool mourned its huge loss and responded angrily to suggestions that its people, rather than the public authorities, were once more at fault, the Anfield stadium soon became a vast shrine, displaying flowers and mementos in memory of the dead. I took my ageing father there to pay our own respects, a highly emotional affair.

The Liverpool players and officials, particularly Kenny Dalglish and his family, now undertook the draining responsibility of attending funerals of Liverpool supporters, sometimes more than one on the same day. The FA discussed abandoning the FA Cup for that season, and the Football League also considered halting the season. This might have been the most sensitive response given the scale of the disaster. But followers of the clubs involved and even some bereaved families seemed to want the competitions to continue. So, after almost three weeks of playing inaction, taken up mainly with grieving and showing appropriate respect for the dead, and amid febrile public debate about where responsibility for the disaster really lay, the Liverpool team played out an emotional match at Glasgow Celtic and then a colourless 0-0 league draw at Everton on 3 May 1989 to restart their campaign. Local followers of the two clubs – some of whom had become rather distanced after the impact of Heysel – were now more united in a communal reassertion of their common bond as Merseysiders. Liverpool then completed their league fixtures, winning the next four matches to set up that title finale. They also defeated Forest 3-1 in the replayed FA Cup semi-final at Old Trafford, before taking on Everton again at Wembley in the final. Ian Rush, back from Italy, haunted the Blues once more with two goals in a 3-2 victory.

In the frenzy of the occasion, ticketless supporters tried every means of gaining illegal entry to the final (so much for taking care) and fans of both teams invaded the fence-free Wembley pitch. But there was no violence. Removing pitchside fences and converting terraces at major stadiums to seating areas were the key structural outcomes of the official inquiry into Hillsborough. But at least as important were the new ways established for dealing with spectators inside grounds. Clubs would now be in charge of managing fans, while police dealt only with matters of hooliganism. A new rhetoric slowly began to emerge around football stadiums in England: the job of stadium managers, stewards and senior police officers was to ensure, above all else, the *safety* of their customers. It was a new direction for the national game at last. Meanwhile, the various Hillsborough family supporter groups in the city would be frustrated by their attempts to make fully accountable those who were at fault in Sheffield. A private prosecution brought against senior police officers involved was abandoned when it was decided that the chief superintendent in charge on the day, David Duckenfield, was unfit to face charges.

Over more than 30 years, Liverpool supporters have ingested the disaster, the public response to it and the campaigns that have followed, as part of the identity of the club itself. No match at Anfield was complete without some sort of reference to 'the 96', and on 6 January 2007, for the first six minutes of the televised FA Cup tie against Arsenal, the Kop displayed a mosaic demanding 'The Truth', with Reds fans repeatedly chanting 'Justice for the 96'. On the 20th anniversary in 2009, an extraordinary and unprecedented 28,000 people turned up (including the author) to hear the annual Anfield service and to heckle Labour government minister Andy Burnham (an Evertonian). He got the message. The government finally agreed in July of that year that thousands of secret files pertaining to the events of 1989 should be released for public scrutiny under the auspices of a new Hillsborough Independent Panel. The panel finally produced its findings in 2012, squarely focusing on what everyone in Liverpool knew to be the case: the failings were from the police on the day rather than any alleged 'drunken, ticketless' fans. People's lives might have been saved with a more coordinated emergency response. A new inquest found in April 2016 that the fans had been unlawfully killed, but in November 2019 David Duckenfield was finally found not guilty of gross negligence manslaughter, charges pressed more than 30 years after he had commanded the police at Hillsborough. It had taken 27 years to publicly establish the real truth but nobody was ever held responsible, and to many people in Liverpool it still felt as if the only real winners in the case had inevitably been the British establishment.

They think it's all over

Back inside Anfield, on the evening of 26 May 1989, a committed Arsenal stole the league title at the last by winning 2-0, with future Liverpool man Michael Thomas scoring the decisive and dramatic last-minute goal. It divided the clubs only on goals scored. In the directors' box, even as the winning shot was ballooning into the net behind Bruce Grobbelaar, the Liverpool club secretary Peter Robinson rang down to the Anfield kitchen to get the post-match champagne redirected into the visitors' dressing room. The Kop was still a standing terrace that night – this would eventually disappear in 1994 – and thousands of us stayed on to sit on its great steps to applaud the new champions and watch the Arsenal celebrations. The outcome at least avoided the dilemma of knowing quite how to react to a Reds title win after such a catastrophic season. We Liverpool fans were left to reflect soberly, instead, on the enormity of what the football club, its players, staff and fans, had been through over the previous six weeks, and indeed over the past four years. These terrible experiences for the families involved had strengthened, rather than loosened, local bonds.

Indeed, there was time here to reflect that it had often been an emotionally draining journey since Bill Shankly arrived at Anfield back in 1959, many wonderful highs on the pitch, but punctuated by unimaginably desperate lows off it. In 1989 the world itself was changing. Just a few months after Hillsborough, the Berlin Wall was breached and communism went the same way as Liverpool's dominance of European club football. Writers, such as Jason Cowley in *The Last Game*, suggested that Hillsborough and this deciding match at Anfield was *the* defining moment that signified the move of English football from its local roots, traditional stadiums and its partisan masculine rituals, all of which had given the game its historic cultural traction, but had also deeply scarred it in the hooligan era. There may be something to this view. After all, Nick Hornby's memoir manifesto for new football, *Fever Pitch*, published in 1992, reaches a climax with Arsenal's title win, before sketching out a new, more civilised and inclusive future for the English game. Certainly, the media coverage of those who had tragically died at Hillsborough – the sons, daughters, husbands and friends – meant that football supporters in England would now be more likely to be seen publicly through the prism of the family rather than the usual hooligan lens.

And there was still time in this period of despair, loss and rapid transition for one more Liverpool league title – its 18th – to be collected in 1989/90. By now the stylish, but vulnerable, Swedish international Glenn Hysén and the impulsive West Midlander, David Burrows, were in the Liverpool defence.

The still irresistible John Barnes was free-scoring; 22 goals in 34 league appearances. John Aldridge, 60 goals scored in his last two Liverpool seasons, inexplicably made not a single start, replaced by the returning Ian Rush. Nevertheless, the cracks were also finally starting to open up in Liverpool FC's previously near invulnerable make-up.

Liverpool FC: League Champions, 1989/90

Grobbelaar
Nicol (Venison) Hysén Hansen Burrows (Staunton)
Houghton McMahon Whelan Barnes
Beardsley Rush

Kenny Dalglish reported later on the enormous stress involved for him in the club's early return to a 'creepy' Hillsborough to play a league match in November 1989: Liverpool lost 2-0. Few in the visiting party wanted to dwell on the result, or too long in Sheffield. Crystal Palace were thrashed 9-0 by Liverpool in the league at Anfield in September 1989 and Swansea City were later thumped 8-0 in the FA Cup, so this Reds team, with Barnes usually directing matters, could still turn it on and destroy weak opposition. But in an FA Cup semi-final at Villa Park in April 1990 – and this was perhaps the real turning point for the entire post-Shankly Liverpool project – a rapid but inexperienced Crystal Palace attack for once made Liverpool's defending look threadbare and inept. This shock 4-3 defeat was a sign of future struggles to come. Alan Hansen was now clearly at the end of his epic Anfield career and Kenny Dalglish was looking increasingly strained and drawn in the manager's seat. God knows, he had been through more than any club representative should be forced to endure.

The era of the great historic Scottish influence at Liverpool that had started way back in 1892 was now at its close. Indeed, Liverpool's great period of dominance of English football was effectively over. Even as the Reds thrashed Coventry City 6-1 in the last match of the 1989/90 league season, with John Barnes and the newly arrived, erratic Israeli striker Ronnie Rosenthal in full flow, there was already a sense that this magnificent extended run – 11 league titles and six second-place finishes in 18 seasons since 1972/73, plus numerous major cups won at home and abroad – could not go on. This remarkable league and cup record for one club was now at the end of its supernatural cycle and English football was about to change radically to try to escape from its recent nightmares.

Chapter 7

The Return of the Boot Room

Negotiating the Premier League future through the past

*Kenny bows out and Graeme Souness takes over at
Anfield – and makes some serious mistakes in the
new FA Premier League era. Modernisation at
Liverpool FC proves to be an elusive and painful
process. Although an FA Cup win delays the
inevitable, Anfield is barely ready for the global
game and the Champions League successfully
launches without it. Roy Evans follows in the
Liverpool managerial hot seat and inherits some
outstanding Scouse talent. But eventually Roy is
involved in sinking his own ship. The boot room is
finally out of time.*

Liverpool's great decline – call Graeme Souness

Kenny Dalglish said later that he had wanted to resign as manager
of Liverpool in the summer of 1990. Unsurprisingly, he was worn
out by the events of the past five years but especially those of the
previous 12 months. He also wanted to buy shares in the club he
loved. But he was able to do neither; the Liverpool board insisted
that he continue as manager and said that no shares were available,
not even for King Kenny. But by Christmas 1990 the huge strain

of what had gone before was obvious and the Liverpool boss was clearly ill and having trouble making decisions, the crucial terrain of any football manager's job. His signings for Liverpool had started to lose their early assurance and quality. Players such as Nigel Spackman, Ronnie Rosenthal, Jimmy Carter, David Speedie and Barry Venison simply could not match the men who had made the club so dominant in the previous two decades. His scouts, a lack of cash, and his own judgement were all letting him down. Also, the rising English giants at Arsenal, and especially Manchester United under Alex Ferguson, had finally got their act together, meaning there would be no more Liverpool cakewalks in the new Premier League era.

A crazy 4-4 fifth round FA Cup replay at Everton in 1991, where the manager dithered over making changes as the match see-sawed in front of him, was the moment Dalglish chose to make his announcement to resign. Rather like Bill Shankly before him, the Scot hinted later that had Liverpool waited over the summer of 1991, while he rested and got his mind straight, he might even have returned, refreshed and ready to continue in the job. But there is seldom time for reflection in football and – again like in 1974 – Liverpool FC felt that they had continuity assured in a more-than-adequate replacement for the departing Kenny. The former midfield enforcer and organiser at Anfield, Graeme Souness, now stepped forward.

Souness had been a successful, if controversial, managerial figure at Glasgow Rangers, so the Liverpool hierarchy thought that he could bring back to Anfield some of the old reassurance and swagger of the 1980s. But the game in England had moved on. For his part, Kenny Dalglish eventually re-emerged at cash-rich Blackburn Rovers, later claiming a Premier League title there as manager in 1995 in a confusing last-match losing finish at Anfield, when some Kopites even wore Blackburn shirts. Meanwhile, Liverpool under Souness and then under old boy, Roy Evans, continued to struggle. Crucially, all this emotional upheaval, disruption and uncertainty at Anfield happened at a critical moment in the development of the modern English game. The old British-style boot room competitive advantage would no longer work in this more technical and global age. The aftermath of Hillsborough had produced an agenda for stadium modernisation in Britain but it was also a moment when the game itself was being completely reconstructed and repackaged. This came with the birth of the brassy new FA Premier League in 1992, the rise of satellite TV as a major new funder for English football, merchandising and booming players' wages, and the globalisation of the elite levels of the English game. All was made possible, of course, by new technology and new marketing and communication techniques.

Despite rising crowds, 'new' football also had its doubters. As fans found their voice, so Liverpool's excellent local fanzine *Through the Wind and Rain* routinely poured scorn on the sport's commercial excesses, celebrity obsessions and its empty new promises. After all, Liverpool Football Club had been efficiently and very cleverly run by T.V. Williams and later by John Smith and Peter Robinson in football's 'old times'. Smith could famously get an AGM done and dusted in 20 minutes, while Peter Robinson was reluctant even to embrace new computer software in the club's finance offices. All this meant that Liverpool FC were hardly best placed – or especially motivated – to ride this new commercial and communications wave, especially as they had been immersed for years in the consequences of dealing with two terrible spectator tragedies and were focused on *avoiding* change rather than embracing it. Liverpool had also lost key guiding figures and some of the crucial domestic advantages they had enjoyed over their close rivals via continuous involvement in European club football. They only returned to European action in the UEFA Cup in 1991/92. Just as Liverpool FC had once lost momentum back in the 1930s and had then choked on their penny-pinching post-war conservatism in the 1950s, now they were falling behind again as the game's marketing, communication and commercial arms were undergoing a period of rapid and radical revolution in the 1990s.

On the playing side of things, the men at Melwood, understandably, had stressed continuity and stability in the golden years, rather than the sort of transformational and dynamic processes of adaptation in player management, coaching and marketing that seemed increasingly necessary in the new future for the game. One further sign of this general inertia at Anfield was that, regularly thwarted by the local residents and neighbours in its ground redevelopment plans, the Liverpool hierarchy was only able to open its very first executive boxes in August 1992 when a second tier of seats was finally added to the existing Kemlyn Road stand at a cost of £8.5m. The new Centenary Stand was officially opened on 1 September 1992 – 100 years to the day after Liverpool's first match played at Anfield. Suddenly, for things to stay the same, in terms of maintaining Liverpool's playing dominance at home and abroad, it seemed that everything else would have to change.

A new beginning?

To be fair, Graeme Souness was much less of a continuity candidate than he might have first appeared. For example, he lacked the loyalty and the communitarian values of the Shankly/Paisley dynasty; he had left Liverpool in 1984 for adventure and rewards in Italy, so in some ways he was built for the moneyed new Premier League era. Souness was no simple Liverpool disciple either, a man who was respected, rather than loved at Anfield, while Dalglish was adored. But Souness returned, supposedly, with a winner's mentality. He rightly realised that the club's traditions urgently required modernisation – no more fish, chips and lager on the away return bus. He recognised, too, that there was a danger of ossifying by resting on past glories when the football world was changing so fast. He thought that some of the club's older, high-earning stars – John Barnes and Ian Rush among them – were now past their best and were obstructing necessary change. Souness altered the Liverpool training regime to finally break with some boot room traditions – players would no longer change at Anfield and travel by coach to Melwood – and he stood accused by some Liverpool supporters and players of trying to alter too much, too soon.

In 2018, reflecting on his past managerial mistakes, Souness admitted he had changed too much and also that agreeing to sort out the players' contracts had proved to be a 'monster mistake'. He had been warned by Peter Robinson that the club was in trouble: 'The ability wasn't there and the attitude was bad.' The truth was that Souness took over at probably the most difficult time in the club's recent history, although Kenny Dalglish, for one, may argue differently. Any new manager might have had real difficulty turning Liverpool around at this precise moment but Graeme Souness hardly helped himself with his abrasive style of management and his chosen personnel. In fact, Souness the manager turned out to be a surprisingly weak judge of players. Looking to replace some of the 'real men' he had played with in the 1980s, some of his key signings – Dean Saunders, Paul Stewart, Torben Piechnik, Neil Ruddock and the West Ham skinhead, Julian Dicks – were flawed or simply not up to past Liverpool standards. Ruddock seemed to be perpetually struggling with his weight and the cartoonish Dicks liked to drink two cans of Coca-Cola before playing matches. He had regular run-ins with Ronnie Moran during training, while youth coach Steve Heighway simply refused even to talk to him. When Dicks was later dropped to the club's reserve team, the depressed defender got drunk in local pubs in the afternoon before matches.

In the past, the drinking cliques at Anfield were there for team bonding and they had seldom obstructed the professional responsibilities of the players. Now attitudes and values were changing. As Ronnie Whelan put it, in the 1980s senior Liverpool players had asserted their authority by asking young players to 'show me your medals'. Now some of the younger guys in the Premier League cash boom were asking Liverpool veterans to 'show me your money'. Souness claimed that he realised his men were not the right characters when Wimbledon's Vinnie Jones scrawled 'bothered' below the treasured 'This is Anfield' players' tunnel sign and no Liverpool player reacted. Because of this rising tide of unprofessionalism among a group of overpaid bad buys, Souness also risked squandering the talents of a rising group of excellent youngsters – the Dalglish signing Jamie Redknapp, and two irrepressible and brilliant Scousers, lung-bursting winger Steve McManaman and young left-side striker Robbie Fowler, among them – as he tried to reshape the club for the new era. An FA Cup Final win in 1992 over Second Division Sunderland briefly stayed local protests. As an ill George Kay had done in 1950, a pale and drawn Souness attended at Wembley after enduring a serious heart problem and undergoing emergency hospital treatment. He also faced fan criticism for crassly selling the story about his illness to the locally hated *Sun* newspaper. Another weak sixth-place finish for Liverpool in the newly minted FA Premier League in 1993 – some 25 points behind winners Manchester United – caused further rumblings.

Qualification for Europe in the new Champions League competition would become increasingly important now because the round robin group format guaranteed TV cash and increased international exposure. It offered protection against those early knockout European Cup exits suffered under both Shankly and Paisley. These new pressures and potential rewards, allied to poor performances, meant that in the summer of 1993 most Liverpool supporters confidently expected (and probably hoped) that Graeme Souness would be sacked. But with the Liverpool board dithering and divided under the new Liverpool chairman David Moores (a personal friend of the manager and of many of the senior players), Souness managed to hang on. It was a stay of execution only. After a brighter start to the 1993/94 league season, but with Liverpool soon out of Europe once more, things predictably began to deteriorate, producing a slide down the league table and out of Champions League contention. Early in 1994 the critical loss occurred, an inept home defeat to Bristol City in a January FA Cup replay. Even the hard man Souness realised that he could not survive this latest lapse and he resigned before he was sacked.

The return of the boot room

Souness was replaced, perhaps reluctantly, by the last of the boot room products. Roy Evans was a man who could claim 20 highly productive years' service on the Liverpool coaching staff, so the club's board was returning again to what they knew best. Evans was a calmer, much more reflective influence than Souness had been and vowed to bring the traditions of the 'Liverpool Way' right up to date for the demands of the new Premier League era of higher wages, celebrity players and global recruitment. His personal lineage at the club reached back, reassuringly, to Bill Shankly and he relied on advice from old Anfield servants, including Tom Saunders, the man who had spotted and raised young talent for the club for many years. Evans played 11 times for Liverpool's first team before being kindly advised to take up coaching instead. These traditional boot room reference points delighted many older Liverpool fans but again it looked, possibly, like a return to the past when the future seemed to be a very different place for English football. And did the rather kindly and reserved Evans really have the necessary ruthlessness of a Shankly, Paisley or Fagan to keep players in line, make tough decisions and drive Liverpool on in this new commercial era, in front of the all-seated, more pacified Kop? It seemed like a tall order, even for a more experienced candidate than Evans.

Unlike Paisley and Fagan, Roy Evans actually liked talking to his players and enjoyed hearing about their gripes. He also made step changes by appointing Liverpool's first goalkeeping coach, Joe Corrigan, and a full-time qualified physiotherapist, Mark Leather. These were important modernising moves but there were still doubts. With ex-Reds players Sammy Lee and Doug Livermore now joining Ronnie Moran on the coaching side, and on the field a rejuvenated midfield version of John Barnes promising a new model of the traditional Anfield brains trust, Roy Evans initially constructed a novel and attractive 3-5-2 playing system that, briefly, even threatened to win Liverpool the league title in the mid-1990s. The flashy and inconsistent David James replaced Bruce Grobbelaar in goal and a flexible and mobile back three was recruited, made up of the Souness signing Mark Wright, allied to the cerebral John Scales from Wimbledon and the pacey Phil Babb from Coventry City. With flying wing-backs, Jason McAteer and Rob Jones, Barnes now cleverly directed matters from a more withdrawn and protected midfield position. Jamie Redknapp and Michael Thomas (forgiven for that 1989 dagger) provided some midfield finesse, Steve McManaman offered stamina and brilliant wing play – but in a mazy new channel *across* the pitch – and the urchin Toxteth genius, Robbie Fowler, scored goals – seemingly hundreds of them.

This new Liverpool team under Evans passed and kept the ball superbly, albeit sometimes at the expense of penetrating weaker opposition and killing off matches. But behind the scenes things had not really moved on. John Scales later claimed that Liverpool's training and preparation were 'stuck in the 1960s', with little technical or tactical analysis and no discussion about diet or the mental side of the game. Ronnie Moran and Evans were raised never to praise players, but that general approach seemed out of date now, in terms of modern man-management and preparation techniques, as young players moved in new, more lucrative and more distracting circles. Unlike Liverpool, Manchester United were already offering media training to their young academy stars of 1992. Consistency was certainly a problem, too, but Fowler's goals and a McManaman-inspired League Cup Final win against Bolton Wanderers in 1995 offered future promise about returning more valuable silverware to Anfield. Perhaps this return to the diluted boot room ethos was going to work out after all?

Liverpool finished in the top four, if a distance behind champions Blackburn Rovers in 1995. But Evans had at his disposal the brightest local talent seen in a generation and he had devised a completely new and pleasing playing style. All seemed set fair, at least in a 'wheels might come off at any moment' kind of way. As Jason McAteer later confessed, this more attractive version of Liverpool 'just didn't deal with the shitty side of the game'. It preferred, instead, ball retention and attacking to any core belief in organised defence. Evans was also faced with the galling fact that, despite Liverpool's rush of young local talent, Alex Ferguson at nearby Old Trafford had just inherited a game-changing group of *six* top-class footballers from that club's youth academy. Unsurprisingly, United would dominate English football for much of the 1990s.

To add to his problems, on the back of this early promise, Roy Evans probably helped murder his own dream. Arguably, he made a major recruitment mistake, the sort that Bill Shankly or Bob Paisley seldom, if ever, made. If they did – Tony Hateley back in the 1960s, for example – it was soon and decisively corrected. These earlier Liverpool bosses checked, above all, with their scouts and informants on the *character* of their prospective recruits, as much as they did their football talent. This matter was becoming increasingly important as player wealth and off-field distractions grew exponentially in the 1990s and top footballers in England were fast moving from hero to celebrity status, often a dangerous route. Evans probably failed to remember this basic but crucial lesson about character because he signed, for a then record Liverpool fee of £8.5m, a player whose main focus was not the Anfield dressing room, winning league titles or the future of Liverpool FC. Evans's new recruit was troubled and fated to think only about himself.

The hugely talented but ultimately corrosive Stan Collymore joined Liverpool from Nottingham Forest in June 1995. Here was the missing piece of the puzzle, surely the man to challenge the United of Alex Ferguson and his batch of talented 'kids' and return the title to Anfield. This was the theory. Roy Evans even compared Collymore to the outstanding Brazilian forward, Ronaldo. And, although he often played with his head down and insisted on living with his mum in distant Cannock, Collymore really did have talent to burn. He had both strength and pace, plus a vital scoring habit. His Liverpool highlights include the winning goal in the fabled first 4-3 victory over Newcastle United at Anfield in April 1996, still considered by many good judges to be the best-ever Premier League match (it was exhausting even to watch). But Stan would have far too many lowlights for all this to matter that much. Depending upon who you believed, Collymore was either a football manager's dream who just needed some careful but stern steering, or else he was likely to be his worst nightmare. Most pundits eventually went with the latter. With more powerful senior players around him to haul Stan in, deal with his excesses and distractions, things may even have worked out. But such voices had long gone from the Anfield dressing room and Roy Evans lacked the gravitas and personal authority to enforce proper discipline and responsibility from his star forward.

White suits, no bollocks

Stan Collymore also had far too many personal demons in play at this moment, something that only fully came to light after he retired as a player. He could be brilliant or truly awful, and he often combined these two opposing traits in the same match. But, more importantly, like an invisible virus, he was guaranteed eventually to destroy the collective unity in any football dressing room he inhabited. He was the antithesis, in fact, of what a 'typical' Liverpool team player had been known to be in those recent decades of playing success. According to Robbie Fowler, Stan was 'fucking hopeless' in terms of his attitude to other footballers and to building the necessary collective ethos required of a successful football collective. He seemed aloof, a cut above, and self-obsessed on the pitch. Stan scored 35 goals in 81 appearances for Liverpool, a more than tidy return, but his performance in almost every really significant match he played for the club was poor, sometimes irresponsibly so. Moreover, he eventually alienated both Fowler and McManaman, his key forward partners, and had fist-fights with Liverpool squad players. In an era when players' wages and their power soared, Collymore wilfully challenged the authority of his caring and much-abused manager. 'Attitude was part of our problem,' Collymore said later. 'Our lads knew they could get away with too much.' He was talking about his own failings here.

Nevertheless, with Collymore in tow and with entertainers such as Robbie Williams mystifyingly sometimes allowed to travel on the Liverpool team coach to away matches, this team somehow briefly threatened again in the league in 1995/96, before finally falling away. But the Reds powered to the FA Cup Final in 1996, fuelled by two outstanding Robbie Fowler goals in a 3-0 semi-final win against high-flying Aston Villa at Old Trafford. The attendance at the match was halved because of a fan boycott and a dispute over ticket prices. In the final, Liverpool met the league champions Manchester United. By now, the Anfield club was haunted by press tales of WAGS, popstars, player excesses and a lack of discipline in the dressing room – the Liverpool Spice Boys. This was a little unfair on Roy Evans and the stories were often exaggerated, but it was also clear that the current squad was short of clear-eyed pitch leaders, was sloppy in attitude and lacked the professional focus of earlier Liverpool regimes. This was the infamous 'white suits' final, of course, where the Liverpool players looked both ridiculous and disrespectful in their pre-cup final outfits, masterminded by fashion guru David James. The 'suits' then simply failed to perform in an insipid contest.

It was a 'shit final' for Jamie Redknapp (and for all of us fans who forked out to attend), as Liverpool subsided to Eric Cantona's late goal. Evans's signature signing, Stan Collymore, was predictably substituted at Wembley, as he would be at half-time in a spineless Reds performance when Liverpool collapsed 3-0 in the UEFA Cup-Winners' Cup semi-final against Paris Saint-Germain (PSG) in April 1997. He was pretty much always absent at the scene of the crime. After the FA Cup Final defeat, John Scales called out both Collymore and the club's coaching staff on just how 'unprofessional' this famous Liverpool club had become. Under Paisley or Joe Fagan, the coaches may have locked the players alone in the dressing room to sort matters out among themselves. Not anymore. This team had some of the talent, perhaps, but not the mental toughness, dedication or leadership to win serious trophies. The group lacked bollocks – and managerial ruthlessness. The talented Scales left the club soon after, frustrated and disillusioned.

The most damaging part of Stan Collymore's brief and complex Liverpool career was now effectively over, a footballing enigma mired in a narcissistic, psychological trauma. Roy Evans had to stick with the forward for a while, given that hefty price tag, but Stan was soon consigned to the reserves. Not that Collymore accepted the demotion: he simply refused to play. Even now he continued to deride the manager who had so mistakenly trusted him. A rising new star, the much more committed and focused national icon, Michael Owen, was about to burst on to the Liverpool football scene to wash away memories of unreliable Stan. Sadly, Roy Evans's entertaining, and sporadically very promising, time as sole manager of Liverpool FC was coming towards its inevitable end. A decent man, he had one more trial to face, because in pursuing an entirely new direction the Liverpool board would finally turn to Continental Europe to try to revive its reputation and its fading league title dreams. The problem was they could not face sacking Roy Evans.

Going Continental, with Robbie and Michael

Towards the end of the 1990s, 'modernisation' in English football increasingly meant globalisation – looking towards the Continent and beyond for inspiration, science, creativity and discipline. These sorts of themes had come and gone in the English game in one way or another, at least since the Hungarians' defeat of England back in 1953. English football had few problems dispensing with the past: while working with the FA in the 1990s I was cast to a distant table at Wembley hospitality following a minor England international match. Sat alongside me in the outer limits was a certain Sir Alf Ramsey. But now the new money in

English football from satellite TV and the Champions League, the impending Bosman ruling on player transfer freedom in 1995 and a partial relaxation of the 'British-are-best' mentality, as physique gave way to brains, meant that club directors in England were increasingly willing to sign up their key managerial men from abroad. The previously unknown Arsène Wenger's coaching successes at Arsenal from 1996 seemed like a signal for the future direction of almost every top English club – except, of course, at Old Trafford. Wenger tamed Arsenal's fierce British drinking culture and combined discipline with tactical acumen, sports science and flair. He probably saved Tony Adams's life.

Roy Evans and his staff at Liverpool knew best the British route but the Bootle-born man had also started recruiting foreign players of his own – Berger, Kvarme, Bjørnebye – with mixed results. Lacking Wenger's global knowledge and experience about men from abroad, Liverpool's foreign buys were not always a success and the club was still best known for its decidedly domestic traditions and values. But some of these traits were now dying. Post-match drinking for Reds players had seemed fine in the 1980s when Liverpool were dominant and the press and the supporters were compliant but, now with Wenger on the scene, a session on 'the bevvy' was appearing outdated and self-indulgent. There was increasing talk in the game about high-protein diets, computer analyses of body fat and statistics on player performance. The club's supporters and local journalists were also starting to ask searching questions about the alleged lack of focus at Anfield, where some younger players seemed to be allowed just too much leeway.

Evans's latest major signings in the summer of 1996 to address some of these failings included £3.25m for Borussia Dortmund's Patrik Berger, a left-sided goalscoring Czech midfielder who had impressed during Euro '96 in England, a tournament that had also done Steve McManaman's international brand no harm at all. Berger was brought in by Evans as cover for the England man and made a flying start, even getting his distinctive own 'Speedy

Gonzales' Kop song. But soon the Czech found himself out of the team and unhappy. Local boy Dominic Matteo – a gambling problem in waiting – had also replaced John Scales in a completely revamped return to a back four, which included both Kvarme and Bjørnebye. But it was the exceptional youthful talent of Robbie Fowler that was effectively keeping Roy Evans's boat afloat, with another 31 goals in 44 matches in all competitions in 1996/97, including four against Middlesbrough at Anfield in December in a 5-1 victory.

Indeed, Liverpool and Fowler were challenging Manchester United for much of the season and even had a chance of topping the table on 6 April, at home against relegation-threatened Coventry City. The match was lopsided but the home forwards could not take their chances and David James contributed one of those last-minute mistakes that would come to characterise his game. Liverpool lost 2-1 and this was also the week they were humiliated in Europe by PSG. A home loss against Manchester United on 19 April confirmed the late-season slide but there was still one powerful note to sound for the future. Away at Plough Lane, Wimbledon, and 2-0 down after 56 minutes, a slip of a kid, a schoolboy star, came on to try to rescue Liverpool's fading Champions League hopes. Michael Owen scored his first Liverpool goal in a 2-1 defeat. In the away end that night, hope, at last, had returned.

John Barnes had now run his race – a great Liverpool career, one often played out in difficult circumstances – so Roy Evans decided to bolster his midfield by bringing in the hard-working Øyvind Leonhardsen from Wimbledon and the bolshy, experienced England international midfielder Paul Ince from Inter Milan. Evans also picked up the European Cup-winning German forward Karl-Heinz Riedle in the summer of 1997. The manager had finally lost faith in his 3-5-2 team shape and identity, with the ex-Manchester United man, Ince, supposedly adding the missing steel for a reversion to a 4-3-3 or 4-4-2 formation. Emerging too in 1997 was Jamie Carragher, a young Bootle-born midfielder or defender, a man who had both desire and leadership qualities. If only he had been around and mature in 1994 he might even have rescued the entire Roy Evans project.

The teenage wasp, Michael Owen, every mother's dream, was more than helping out with goals and adding to the general annoyance of all hulking defenders he faced. But could a club be just *too* blessed by having two young world-class strikers develop at almost exactly the same moment? Robbie Fowler was still only just 22 years old when Owen burst into the Liverpool first team, but it almost felt as if the brilliant Toxteth man's time was somehow already up at Anfield. Owen seemed so explosive and so demanding of that central striker's role, and it would only get worse for Robbie. In February 1998 he suffered a serious knee injury in the derby match at Anfield, which meant that it would be the electric Michael Owen, not Fowler, who would star for England in the summer World Cup finals in France, becoming a global product and a national treasure overnight.

This is pretty much how relations between the two forwards and Liverpool fans would now play out: Fowler as the beloved and flawed local hero, the wayward urchin striker; Owen as the clean-living, high-achieving, respected national icon. The tension was a difficult one to resolve. But there was a bigger problem for Roy Evans to address: was his new pragmatism really radical enough to turn things around at Anfield? Owen scored 18 league goals in his first full season, to injury-hit Fowler's nine, but Liverpool could do no better than third place in the Premier League in 1998. The club seemed to be treading water, even with all this great young talent coming through, playing in a very ordinary 4-4-2 format. Where had all the brio and attacking verve of 1994–1996 disappeared to? Moreover, Evans was losing his transfer judgement. A £2m punt on a trundling South African forward Sean Dundee, an Everton fan, looked like (and was) money instantly wasted. Perhaps more of a European influence at coaching or managerial level really could help get Liverpool back on track, and also aid Evans to develop his management skills? Maybe a partnership of the old boot room savvy and the new Continental science could finally do the trick? It might also rid the Liverpool dressing room of some of its bad habits acquired under Souness and not dealt with effectively by Evans. The Liverpool board, and Peter Robinson in particular, scanned the Continent and came up with just the man for a unique job-share.

Chapter 8

Allez les Rouges

The new Continental technocrats

Liverpool goes half-Continental but joint managers are built-in to fail. An affectionate Gérard Houllier plots a new direction. Robbie Fowler is aggrieved and Macca and Michael soon join the Galácticos in Spain. An extraordinary treble is won in 2001 as Liverpool re-join the elite European table. Illness again strikes a Liverpool manager and decline is imminent. The much-praised Rafa Benitez takes charge and starts a new rivalry with Chelsea. He first loses – then wins – the greatest-ever Champions League Final. Steven Gerrard feels unloved but is eventually persuaded to stay. He wins the FA Cup for his home club. Anfield's leaders promise no 'prostituting' of the Liverpool brand but the club rebuilds with new concerns brewing about the departure of trusted local custodians.

'We tell ourselves stories in order to live.' Joan Didion

Welcome, Brigadier Gérard

Into the modern Liverpool story now stepped the architect of the French Youth Academy, disciplinarian and confirmed Liverpool FC admirer, Gérard Houllier. Bringing Houllier into Anfield might have seemed to the club executive like some nifty problem-solving but it was actually a very risky strategy. At the very top level of the game the Frenchman's record was pretty patchy, including a last-minute failure to take a very capable French national team to the 1994 World Cup finals. And going for *joint* football managers – one an Englishman steeped in the Liverpool tradition, the other an internationally known Frenchman best regarded for developing youth players for the French Football Federation – was never likely to work at Anfield, or anywhere else in England. Roy Evans explicitly did not want it, and he later regretted that he had not insisted that Houllier become Liverpool's first director of football in a new management structure. But at least the joint role avoided the unpleasantness of sacking a decent man and a great club servant. Liverpool had rarely fired managers; it was simply bad form, not the Liverpool Way.

The argument here was that co-management could strengthen, not weaken, the Liverpool set-up. It would give Houllier a heads-up inside an English club before the inevitable (if unspoken) outcome of him taking over the first team on his own. At least Houllier had studied and lived in the city as a trainee teacher, and he admired the traditions and cultures around the club. He liked its working-class ethos and the way the terraced houses of Anfield folded around the stadium. The bond between the supporters and the team he likened to the importance of the pass on the pitch, in what he called the 'Liverpool imaginary'. Houllier lacked the forceful masculine credentials of some recent Liverpool incumbents, of course, but he was something of a boot room man in French clothing. Or so it was argued.

Gérard Houllier's appointment closely corresponded with the opening of the new Liverpool Youth Academy in Kirkby and the arrival at the club of Liverpool fan Rick Parry, one of the main proponents of the cash cow Premier League. Parry, an accountant by trade, was a chief executive in waiting while the veteran Peter Robinson picked his moment to leave the club. Parry had been a restless advocate of riding change in the game and he knew that Liverpool had suffered in comparison with the recent commercial developments at Manchester United and Arsenal. He also argued that eventually the Anfield club would have to finance a new stadium to keep up with its competitors. But Parry was also very wary of the real dangers for Liverpool of going down an ultra-commercialised route, because of the history and values of the club and its cultural importance in the city. In 2002 he said, 'The brand values that we have developed for Liverpool, well the key word for us is respect. In the '70s and '80s we were not loved by everybody but there was always a respect for Liverpool, and that's a value I think is very important.'

Parry favoured Gérard Houllier as co-manager with Roy Evans because he liked Evans, but also saw the future in the scientific approach, attention to detail and the urbanity and strong principles of the Frenchman. Houllier clearly also understood key aspects of the English game, pointing to the physicality needed to survive – he favoured good, big players over high-quality small ones. Parry trusted that Houllier was no simple foreign technocrat, that the Frenchman understood the cultural significance of the club and of the Liverpool Way. Houllier, for his part, thought that Parry was exactly the kind of ethical moderniser he could work with. Both men were determined to revolutionise the general approach to the organisation and discipline inside the club, and to develop tactics and player preparation at Melwood. And there was much work to do on all these fronts.

The appliance of science

It is fair to say that Gérard Houllier did not like what he saw inside Anfield when he arrived as joint-manager in the summer of 1998. There was too much drinking and lax ill-discipline, too little training that was intense and tailored to match situations, a training ground that needed rebuilding and modernising, and too little emphasis on scientific preparation in terms of diet, the use of computer technology and specialised coaching. Liverpool had fallen behind their global competitors. He also thought that Roy Evans was too close, too friendly, with the Liverpool players, some of whom had far too much to say about training regimes and tactics. A manager with authority needed to maintain his distance from his team to properly exercise his will. In contrast to the great Liverpool dynasties of the recent past, Houllier tended to interpret players who spoke out of turn as showing a loss of respect rather than demonstrating leadership. Many said later that this new Continental presence at Liverpool may have lacked something in personal security but nothing in terms of ego.

Gradually, Houllier asserted himself and his new approach during the shaky start to the 1998/99 season but by November 1998 Roy Evans already realised that this embryonic attempt at joint authority could never work in British club football. His players needed to know exactly who the boss was. For example, one of these joint Liverpool managers favoured rotating his players, the other sticking to a winning team in the Shankly and Paisley tradition. What exactly *was* the Liverpool policy? After an embarrassing dressing room bust-up for the co-managers over shirt-swapping following a European tie in Valencia, like the honourable man he is, Roy Evans took the hint and resigned. 'It would be easy to stay, but to give Gérard and his team a chance you have to walk away,' said an emotional Evans at the press conference held to announce his departure. 'I didn't want to end as a ghost on the wall.' It was an evocative phrase, harking back to Bill Shankly's messy departure and used later as the title of Evans's autobiography.

Liverpool had finished in the top four in each of Evans's four seasons in sole charge (but out of the Champions League places), had won one trophy and played (very badly) in one other major final. Briefly he had built an exhilarating team but he had also faced a Manchester United juggernaut. With Gérard Houllier in lone charge for much of the 1998/99 campaign, Liverpool slumped to seventh place. Worse, noisy neighbours United under Alex Ferguson completed the Premier League, FA Cup and Champions League treble. Houllier was already facing a stiff challenge to back up his Continental credentials.

Now the Frenchman acted decisively. He brought in ex-Red Phil Thompson to add some local knowledge and backroom steel and he started to clear out the players who were too old, those he could not work with, or those who openly challenged his authority. These included Ince, the error-prone David James and the defenders McAteer, Wright and Babb. Out, too, went the moderate foreigners Bjørnebye, Kvarme and Leonhardsen. In a much more costly loss under the new Bosman ruling, local man Steve McManaman turned down Liverpool contract offers and opted to join Real Madrid on a free transfer, the first example in England. This was a critical blow but the Scouser made it clear that the move was not financially motivated; Liverpool had offered him a good deal to stay. 'At that time, I had never played in the Champions League, which was a huge thing,' he said. 'I was playing really good football and I needed to test myself. I felt that I needed to go.' The urbane McManaman wanted to experience life abroad but he also yearned to be at a more focused club where the onus was not always on his shoulders to be the main creative force. Real Madrid had half-a-dozen men who could do that, including the great Frenchman Zinedine Zidane. McManaman would win two European Cups with Real, becoming a feted English workhorse of the highest quality, an authentic Madrid hero. Gérard Houllier and Liverpool had to move on.

Although his relations with Liverpool academy head Steve Heighway were not always cordial, the new Liverpool manager now began building his team around an emerging local core of top young talent from the area that he could mould. Included here was the forward prodigy Owen, the young defender-convert Jamie Carragher, the clever Chester-born midfielder Danny Murphy and eventually a brilliant youth team starlet who was beginning to make local waves, a quiet and still fragile Liverpool-born boy called Steven Gerrard. Local hero Robbie Fowler seemed much less trusted by the Frenchman; Robbie became truculent and increasingly unconvinced by the schoolmaster's approach of his new manager, and he eventually ended up a much more marginal figure.

From abroad, for 1999/2000, Houllier's first season in sole charge, in came defender Rigobert Song, the club's first black African player, and the Frenchman Djimi Traore. But the key signings here were central-defenders Sami Hyypiä and Stéphane Henchoz, Dutch goalkeeper Sander Westerveld, a slight but skilful Czech forward, Vladimir Smicer, and the excellent German international defensive midfield player, Dietmar Hamman. An elusive but limited Guinea forward, Titi Camara, and a mysterious young Croat midfielder, Igor Biscan, added a further touch of the unpredictable and exotic to this otherwise solid group. It was a mass internationalisation of the Liverpool Football Club playing staff to match those changes made way back in the 1920s, perhaps just as the club's current board had hoped and anticipated it would need to be. Houllier had actually wanted to buy the Englishman Rio Ferdinand but was priced out of the deal. Instead, the stylish Finland centre-back Hyypiä and the German enforcer, Hamann, were the standout figures here, powerful and reliable and technically excellent. They would provide much of the Liverpool defensive backbone – the bollocks – needed for the coming campaigns.

This new Liverpool in the early Houllier period proved to be highly functional rather than exciting, with the emphasis on a rather prosaic brand of counter-attacking football that was solid enough but had little of the romance or style of the early Roy Evans era. It was more like Bob Paisley but without the star quality and the inexhaustible will to win. It was sporadically effective but it could also be incredibly dull. The new manager and his sports scientists also insisted much more on the tactical rotation of his squad. It was the end, therefore, of the tradition that a reliable sign of a Liverpool title team was six or seven players who played almost every league and major cup match. Liverpool's rather regimented play also contrasted wildly with much of the more sophisticated and breathtaking football now played by Houllier's supposed role model, Arsène Wenger at Arsenal. With Robbie Fowler and Michael Owen both struggling for form and fitness, and even with the teenage Steven Gerrard just starting to become established in the Liverpool ranks, Houllier's early teams lacked badly for goals: only 17 scored away from home in the league in 1999/2000. Losing 1-0 at Anfield to Everton also dismayed the locals – until 2021 it was the last time Everton had won across the park.

But at least this Liverpool team was broadly competitive, and the signing of the brawny young England forward Emile Heskey for £11m from Leicester City in March 2000 was supposed to add missing goals and confirm the club's inevitable passage into the Champions League places for the first time. But the chunky, rather hesitant Heskey had problems settling and scoring, and his early presence and lack of confidence seemed to disturb, rather than inspire, his new team. With Robbie Fowler now deeply at odds with his manager, the Reds suffered a late-season goal drought and collapse, five winless and scoreless league matches in a row. Needing to beat relegation-threatened Bradford City in the closing fixture in May 2000, an emotionally empty Liverpool stumbled to a 1-0 defeat. So, it would be the UEFA Cup again into the new century after all. And what an unlikely bonus this last-minute demotion would turn out to be.

2001, and all that

Landing the highly experienced German international full-back Marcus Babbel on a free transfer in the summer of 2000 was excellent business by Houllier, and bringing in the versatile forward Nick Barmby from Everton for £6m kept the local sports scribes happy. Barmby was the first direct Liverpool signing from Everton since Dave Hickson back in the 1950s and there have been none since. Houllier reacted like he could care less about such local niceties. Christian Ziege, a left-sided German defender, arrived for £5.5m from Middlesbrough but never quite made the grade. A much less heralded arrival, but by far the most important Liverpool capture for 2000/01 in a flurry of transfer activity, actually turned out to be a veteran Scottish international who arrived on a free. Gary McAllister looked like an impending retirement case, a man recruited by Houllier mainly to advise, coach and cajole at Melwood. Not even his own fans at Coventry City thought Gary Mac, at 36, had anything much left to offer on the pitch.

When I interviewed him in 2002, McAllister remembered the 'negative vibes' about him in the Liverpool camp as soon as he arrived, but the Scot actually became a key player in an incredible treble-winning season. He gave the previously stodgy Liverpool team more leadership, cleverness, flow and direction from the centre of the pitch, all crucial ingredients. He also exemplified the 'best players are the hardest workers' ethos in training and offered an ideal role model and guide for the fast-emerging Steven Gerrard. McAllister would achieve special status among all Reds followers for scoring a ridiculous 44-yard last-gasp winning free kick for ten-man Liverpool at Goodison Park in a vital 3-2 league win during the packed Easter period of 2001. It is called cementing your relationship with the fans.

This new Liverpool began the season slowly, stuck in fifth place until Christmas and already the victim of a four-goal Mark Viduka league blitz at Leeds United. By the time the League Cup tie at Stoke City arrived in late November 2000, this could already have been a tripwire, but a Robbie Fowler hat-trick was the centrepiece of an extravagant 8-0 Liverpool win. Then, in back-to-back matches leading up to the winter festivities, first Manchester United were beaten 1-0 at Old Trafford and then Wenger's Arsenal were eviscerated 4-0 at Anfield. The embryonic Steven Gerrard had dominated Roy Keane and Patrick Vieira in consecutive matches and Liverpool were now playing with much more belief and freedom. Something was definitely happening here. Revenge at Leeds in the FA Cup followed in January in front of a massive away turnout, and then a two-leg defeat of Crystal Palace in the semi-final of the League Cup had cult figure Igor Biscan resplendent in a 5-0 second leg Anfield drubbing.

All this meant that Liverpool were still alive in all four of their entered competitions – if you count contending for a top-four league finish. They had already seen off Rapid Bucharest, Slovan Liberic and Olympiacos in the UEFA Cup without too much difficulty, before Michael Owen revived those memories of playing abroad for England in 1998 by scoring both goals in Liverpool's historic defeat of AS Roma in the Stadio Olimpico.. 'Michael barely touched the ball,' Gary Mac said later, 'but his two finishes were just world-class and that's what separated Michael from other strikers.' Porto would follow, also eliminated.

It was now becoming difficult for fans to keep track of these different competitions, so we can dispose of the League Cup right here. Wembley was being modernised, a lengthy job, so there was something different on offer for the finalists in 2001: a first English cup final staged in Wales, in the Millennium Stadium in Cardiff. Most Reds fans saw this venue and location as an improvement on the original, given that *this* national stadium was compact and in the middle of the city, surrounded by places to stay and with accommodation, beer and food prices half of those in the English capital. I spent pre-match hospitality from the Football League lunching on Welsh lamb with Ronnie Moran, a coaching masterclass. Michael Owen was controversially left out of the final side – 'an abundance of attacking riches', according to Houllier – while Robbie Fowler scored a stunning goal. But it still took extra time and penalties to see off the Football League outfit Birmingham City in a scruffy performance, with Jamie Carragher later confirming that he was 'shitting meself' before netting a screamer in the penalty shoot-out. Later, in the post-match buffet, one of our Welsh mates confronted his hero Ian Rush with a small figurine of Rushie that he carried everywhere.

'Would Rushie like to touch Little Rushie?' The real Ian Rush, fearing a mad stalker, quickly made his excuses and left.

Next up came a ruthlessly defensive UEFA Cup semi-final display by Liverpool in the first leg in the Camp Nou against FC Barcelona. This anticipated 'showpiece' fixture, observed by we travelling Reds fans from a vantage point way up in the Spanish gods, produced instead a dire, but invaluable, 0-0 draw, Houllier using a highly conservative 4-5-1 formation. This was also a first taste of front-foot Spanish policing for some Scouse travellers. For the players, 'We told them to play in one half of the field,' said coach Alex Miller later. 'Play it up into the corners, so they [Barça] had a long distance to attack from.' It was not rocket science, nor a strategy designed to entertain. Few Liverpool fans had ever seen their defenders instructed simply to clear the ball into Row Z at every opportunity. The then Barça midfield guru, Pep Guardiola, had nearly the whole pitch on which to construct his best plans, but it was to no avail. The sheer bloody-minded negativity of this display saw the Reds accused by some of the European football cognoscenti (including Johan Cruyff himself) of 'murdering' the game. Houllier offered no apologies. No one from the Liverpool 4 district complained, either, when Gary McAllister scored the only goal from the penalty spot in the second leg to take Liverpool through to the final in Dortmund.

In the FA Cup, meanwhile, Liverpool ended up with sixth round and semi-final contests against Tranmere Rovers and Wycombe Wanderers, respectively, so it was one of those years when one's name might just be on the trophy. Except that, after having a peculiarly leisurely route to the later stages, Houllier's opponents in the final were Arsenal, again in Cardiff. The Frenchman was realistic in his assessment of the opposition, despite that 4-0 league victory in December:

> I said to the boys that I think Arsenal are probably better than us, more experienced and mature when you look at some of their players, probably with more ability in some areas. But what's going to make the difference

between the two teams today is the mental strength, the capacity to deal with negative events in a game. I said, if you've got the moral courage not to let your head down for more than one minute, you'll be strong. And on some occasions, the will to win is more important than the skill to win.

If he actually *did* say this to his players, then it was a brilliant summary of how the contest would unfold and it pretty much matched the words used by Jürgen Klopp before Liverpool overturned Barcelona in a Champion's League epic at Anfield in 2019. A much superior Arsenal team threatened to overwhelm Liverpool in 2001, constantly prodding at their defence until it finally gave way on 72 minutes with a Ljungberg goal. It was the least the Londoners deserved. But Liverpool, playing in ecru (or beige), stayed mentally strong as Houllier had insisted. Then Michael Owen bent this grand occasion to his will in the Welsh sunshine, scoring an emphatic equalising goal in a crowded penalty area with just seven minutes left. Where had this come from? A shocked Arsenal suddenly looked open and vulnerable; Owen said later that he could see his opponents were shot but wondered did he have enough time to score again? And is this not the perverse beauty of football, that complete dominance can be undone in a few seconds? Owen's second goal will live long in the memory of all those in Red who saw it. As the clock ticked towards extra time, substitute Patrik Berger floated a long ball down Arsenal's right side, Owen brushed past England man Lee Dixon, and with his weaker *left* foot bent a gentle low shot across the advancing David Seaman into the only place it could possibly go to register a score. Owen now did a daft little somersault in front of delirious fans, because everybody knew that Liverpool (in fact, this irrepressible little teenager, virtually on his own) had positively *stolen* the 2001 FA Cup by 2-1 from under the nose of Arsène Wenger.

Coming back in the dying minutes to win a major final like this has a special satisfaction not often experienced at this level.

Marcus Babbel was particularly moved: he had been in the Bayern Munich team similarly robbed by Manchester United in the 1999 Champions League Final. Against Houllier's wishes, Robbie Fowler instructed the injured club captain Jamie Redknapp to lift the FA Cup with Sami Hyypiä, the end of a near perfect day. Another cup, and a return to winning ways at last. A triumph for the insight, discipline and hard work of the Liverpool board and for Gérard Houllier and his staff. But especially for Michael Owen. And after all the lean Liverpool years it was now difficult to take all this in. In this extraordinary season, the club had won two domestic cups already, were still on course to qualify for the Champions League and were in their first major European final for 16 years – an opportunity to atone, at last, for all those terrible memories of 1985.

And this was definitively *Houllier's* team, an international combination rapidly rebuilt, but one with a youthful local heartbeat – Murphy, Carragher, Gerrard, occasionally Fowler – a couple of young England forwards in Heskey and Michael Owen, and a venerable new Scottish professor, Gary McAllister, as its moral guide and brains. Danny Murphy admitted later how difficult it had been to replace these sorts of Liverpool glory days in retirement, as he lapsed into bouts of depression, heavy drinking, drug use and gambling. You can see what he means. What an occasion the 2001 UEFA Cup Final was. Fresh from snaffling the FA Cup from within Arsenal's grasp, Liverpool now faced the little-known Basques from Alavés in Spain. Oh, what a night!

Liverpool FC: FA Cup, League Cup & UEFA Cup winners, 2000/01

Westerveld

Babbel   Henchoz   Hyypiä   Carragher

Hamann

Gerrard McAllister (Berger) Murphy (Barmby)

Owen (Fowler) Heskey

On paper, this European final might have looked like easy meat, and Liverpool were clear favourites. But the Spanish team had dismantled Kaiserslautern 9-2 on aggregate in the semi-finals, so tough competition and goals were on the menu (although Johan Cruyff, remembering Liverpool's aching banality in Barcelona, predicted it was going to be one of the most boring nil-nil finals ever). Tens of thousands of we Liverpool supporters made the trip to Dortmund on a damp Ruhr evening, a new generation of European football explorers. The flags and songs we witnessed there made it seem just like old times, but the trip also lacked some of the crazy off-field excesses and the aggression of the 1980s – perhaps some harsh lessons had been learned. Alavés fans, in their first European final, were charming and hopeful, while Liverpool supporters were, well, just glad to be back on the big stage once more.

The city of Dortmund perhaps owed Liverpool a victory after the 1966 UEFA Cup-Winners' Cup fiasco, and it eventually delivered. But *what* a struggle it was! It did not look that challenging after 16 minutes when the Reds were already two goals to the good, scored by Babbel and Gerrard. Alavés looked nervous and lost but they came back almost immediately with a goal of their own, from Alonso. Game on: enough to stir Michael Owen to win a penalty, converted by a nerveless Gary McAllister. At 3-1 at half-time, it ought to have been enough to see Liverpool through but Sander Westerveld showed the arrogance and sloppiness which would soon cost him his Liverpool career. Danger man, Moreno, scored twice for the Spaniards to level things at 3-3. When a frustrated Robbie Fowler finally came off the bench, for Emile Heskey, after 65 minutes and scored with a sublime right-foot shot, most Liverpool supporters would have settled for this romantic ending. But instead Alavés replied again, with their third headed goal, this time from Jordi Cruyff. Liverpool had four beanstalks at the back, so this latest incision was just insulting. The final ended 4-4 after 90 minutes.

A contest that began as exciting and adventurous was now in danger of looking simply defensively naïve, and the slightly ridiculous mechanism of the extra time 'golden goal' would decide the 2001 UEFA Cup Final. Both teams were tired and adjusting for penalties but, three minutes from the end of extra time, as the TV companies were gleefully preparing for the shoot-out, a headed own goal by Geli after a McAllister free kick finally settled matters. The author celebrated by dancing a jig in the stadium with a pork-pie hatted Elvis Costello, who was seated just in front. Not that many Liverpool players knew the rules; they took their signal for celebrations from the Liverpool bench and the crowd's delirious response. The reborn McAllister was voted man of the match in the final (he was man of the season for Liverpool), and there was still time for the Reds to win their Champions League spot by thumping Charlton Athletic 4-0 away in the final league fixture, delayed in the congestion.

Three trophies and back in Europe's top bin. It had been an amazing final week for Liverpool supporters and an unprecedented return on all four fronts. Gérard Houllier had confounded his critics, who had worried away at his management style, conservative tactics and rigid formations. He deserved huge credit in the face of some vocal opposition. But not everyone inside Liverpool FC – even now – was convinced. Robbie Fowler was the pivot for this group of dissenters. The Scouser clearly hated the new regimentation of it all; he said he was 'sick to death' of rotation, the lack of enjoyment in training and on the field, and the fact that pretty much no banter or play-acting was allowed in the camp anymore.

The Liverpool greats of the past would certainly have missed these vital ingredients. Robbie had his sympathisers: Johan Cruyff, the guest of honour at the UEFA Cup Final was no lover of Houllier or Liverpool's supposed negativity. He whispered conspiratorially to the striker at his medal presentation, 'Don't let him get you down, you're too good.' Fowler also despised the way his new manager treated his players like schoolchildren and he was depressed by the dullness of some of the foreign recruits. 'I want the players to be nice,' said Houllier, 'to be good people, to have respect for each other but also respect for the girls in the canteen or the kit manager. I think if you are a nice man, you are a nice player.' Again, Jürgen Klopp would make almost the same speech around 20 years later. This kind of thing was probably a necessary riposte to the era of Dicks, Ruddock and Collymore, but for some local men it also offered a picture of a rather sanitised and authoritarian culture inside the Liverpool dressing room. A low point was reached for Fowler when the young French full-back Grégory Vignal was found sobbing by players in the car park when illness had frustrated his chances of a first-team debut. This was the last straw for these traditionalists: a first-team Liverpool player *crying* in front of his team-mates? Things had gone too far and Robbie Fowler, for one, was bemused and disillusioned by it all. He knew that this phase of his Liverpool career was now over.

A Liverpool managerial curse?

Emboldened by his successes and lauded by the Liverpool board and most of the club's fans, Gérard Houllier prepared for the new campaign by signing the Polish international goalkeeper Jerzy Dudek to replace Sander Westerveld. In fact, he bought *two* goalkeepers by accident, Chris Kirkland also arriving in a unique modern transfer confusion. The new BRIX software, now in use at Liverpool for player valuations, was clearly of no value here. The veteran Finnish forward, Jari Litmanen, long fancied by the club's coaches but now late in his career, and a young fitness fanatic, Norwegian left-back John Arne Riise, had also been signed. They would train at a new Melwood, an impressive £4m revamp completed under Houllier's guidance and with the manager's quarters suitably prominent for surveillance.

Liverpool's first match back in the Champions League, after 16 long years away from the elite, turned out to be a tepid 1-1 draw against Boavista of Portugal in a muted Anfield. But this was not the night's big story, not even close. The match took place in an eerie Anfield atmosphere on the evening of 11 September 2001, while Europe looked westwards to the United States, where the Twin Towers still smouldered in New York City. No one quite knew what might lay in wait for a world that was seemingly under attack. Would sports grounds next come under fire? Uncertainty and dread seemed everywhere.

A very different kind of fate lay in wait for the Liverpool manager, who was near the top of his game. It would change the whole trajectory of his project at Anfield, as well as his own life. His physical vulnerability echoed that of Liverpool management men before him, including Matt McQueen in the 1920s, George Kay in the 1950s and Graeme Souness in the 1990s. They were all victims of serious illness or accidents during their Anfield managerial tenures. Was this a manager's Anfield curse? Gérard Houllier would now have to be added to this list. The Frenchman suffered a damaged aorta, revealed during a league match against Leeds United at Anfield in October 2001, and spent much of the 2001/02 campaign in hospital, recovering from major heart surgery.

Nevertheless, the Liverpool first team, now under the control of Phil Thompson and with Gerrard, Hamman, Hyypiä and Carragher all offering on-field leadership, hovered around the top placings in the league, eventually finishing second to Arsenal. Houllier received a hero's welcome back at Anfield for the Champions League win against AS Roma in March 2002 and Liverpool reached the quarter-finals, to be beaten finally by Bayer Leverkusen. Testament to Phil Thompson's leadership, Liverpool collected 80 points in the league, including a double over Manchester United and a glorious 6-0 away trouncing of Ipswich Town. Mid-season loan signing Nicolas Anelka played a starring role by opening up defences and providing chances and space for Michael Owen.

Robbie Fowler was still not making the Liverpool first team and, feeling frustrated and unloved, he left in November 2001, bound for Leeds United. He was never Houllier's man and he had also started rowing with Phil Thompson, so the end was clear. There was only one winner in that contest. But Michael Owen *was* in favour and he came close to full throttle with 28 goals in all competitions. Most of Houllier's players seemed devoted to their recovering leader and, with a little more careful investment, surely the ultimate success in the league and Europe would come to this novel mix of a domestic and foreign-infused Liverpool squad. That was the plan.

Now back in harness, in the summer of 2002 Gérard Houllier made a critical decision, another game changer. He ignored the impressive Anelka and looked instead to Africa to complete what seemed like a coup. He recruited the much-coveted Senegalese pair of El-Hadji Diouf and Salif Diao for a combined fee of close to £15m. Both players had impressed in the World Cup finals that summer as Senegal defeated the holders, France. Here is how an elite manager must gamble: by putting his faith in players he little knows, men who are coming to a new country and into a new culture and who must succeed in it instantly. Plenty can go wrong here. In, too, came a lightweight French midfield man, Bruno Cheyrou, who joined from Lille with glowing references, and also a heads-down, youthful Czech international forward, Milan Baros. So far, so promising. Houllier liked to give his players pieces of paper in training before the season started to ask them to write down their ambitions. Some saw it as cod psychology, a joke, but in August 2002 Steven Gerrard wrote 'win the title' on his sheet. But when he saw these new signings perform in training, he realised immediately that this new team had little hope. Liverpool finished a distant fifth. Crucially, for the future of their French manager, all of these recently recruited players ultimately failed the test at Anfield. In fact, for his on-field insults and general attitude, El-Hadji Diouf would become one of the least popular players ever to play for the club.

Liverpool began with a fine 12-match unbeaten league start but then slid down the table and made little progress in the Champions League. The manager fiddled relentlessly with the team to try to find a winning blend. 'Asking Houllier to do nowt,' said keen Reds observer James Lawton in *The Independent* on 16 December 2002, 'to let a group of players grow organically rather than by constant Dr Frankenstein surgery, seems to be too tall a requirement of a passionate, hyperactive man.' He had a point. Liverpool were eliminated at the group stage in the Champions League after a chaotic 3-3 draw in Basle, but the Reds still managed to scramble another trip to Cardiff, to defeat Manchester United 2-0 in the League Cup Final, some reward in a difficult season.

The campaign had started to raise new doubts about whether this post-illness version of Houllier could ever really secure the very biggest prizes for his supporters and players. Since his medical problems the Frenchman had seemed much less decisive and far too thin-skinned, showing ever-darkening concern about negative media comment, especially from ex-Liverpool players. Rick Parry, certainly, thought that the manager had become more obsessive, had changed in character, since his heart issue. Being an elite football manager in England was no place for a man harbouring doubts about his own fitness – or his sanity.

The Australian winger Harry Kewell now joined Liverpool from Leeds United in July 2003 but something much more consequential for English football happened elsewhere, another new arrival. A Russian petro-billionaire Roman Abramovich bought Chelsea FC in the same month, thus changing the financial landscape of the English game forever and making management more testing, not least by paving the way for the introduction to England of one Jose Mourinho. This also meant that the proposed transfer of John Terry to Liverpool – a potential saviour for the entire Houllier plan – was fast aborted. By now the Liverpool manager increasingly seemed to put his store, instead, in recruiting young French players at 'bargain' prices. Florent Sinama-Pongolle and Anthony Le Tallec immediately appeared ill-suited to the physicality and pace of the English game, but time would tell. By November 2003, after a run of draws and defeats, Houllier's young captain Steven Gerrard was admitting to the press and in TV interviews that, after just 13 matches, it was already clear that Liverpool could not win the 2003/04 Premier League title. It was a humiliating public confession for a proud local man. Liverpool eventually finished 30 points behind champions Arsenal.

A pall of paranoia had suddenly settled over Anfield, the manager stalking its corridors like a character plagued by demons. I had interviewed a sparkling Houllier in 1999 and again in 2002 – the change was palpable. The Frenchman seemed increasingly lost and befuddled in a fog of statistics, which he now spewed out at every press conference. Journalists had begun to see past his urbanity and were questioning his managerial capacity – even his mental state. Another Champions League place won in 2003/04 could not disguise the fact that many of the club's supporters were also losing faith in their manager. Suddenly, this grand French march on the club's key opponents seemed to be heading nowhere, and Gérard Houllier knew it. After brief discussions with the Liverpool board, in May 2004 the Frenchman left the club. He said this in his parting interview:

> I think the club has improved a lot, both on the field
> and off the field. I mean, there was no Liverpool
> website six years ago! I think now the club has to keep
> developing and progressing. It's the most fantastic club
> in the world. It's now important the club manages to
> keep a balance between the economic and political
> needs, and I think they've done well on that front.
> The club also needs to remember its roots and also to
> understand that you cannot always have a quick fix.

It was a thoughtful and a wise way to end an exciting but also frustrating six-year period in charge. The promise of those early days and of 2001 had never quite been fulfilled and Houllier's public persona had become disturbed as his transfer policy became muddled and suspect. He ended up dividing his own players –

some loved and respected him, others felt disrespected and were too soon discarded. His devoted young captain, a world-class talent, was starting to have his own grave doubts. But Liverpool had made their first foreign managerial excursion and there was no going back now to the old days of the boot room or – so it seemed at the time – to British football managers.

The men from the Continent (2)

On the surface, the new Liverpool manager, the Spaniard Rafa Benitez, seemed to have plenty in common with the departing Gérard Houllier. He was a Continental technocrat, a coach with no great playing record, and a man who laid great store on preparation, tactics and team discipline. Benitez favoured the scientific assessments of players, and defence more than attack; he also liked to keep a rather cold distance between himself and his squad. He favoured squad rotation, to keep its members fresh. Unlike Houllier, however, Benitez had enjoyed some club management success in one of the toughest leagues in Europe, twice winning the Spanish title, and in 2004 also taking the UEFA Cup with a Valencia team that he had largely inherited. Despite these successes, Benitez was available because he had fallen out with his employers, who insisted that the director of football should recruit players who the coach (in this case Benitez) should then work into a team. Benitez much preferred the control offered by the English model, where the *manager* chooses his own players and then moulds them into a winning unit. 'Don't buy me a lamp when I ask for a table,' summed up well his frustrations with the management structure at the Mestalla. He was glad to leave Spain.

Aware of the growing tensions at Valencia, Liverpool chief executive Rick Parry had rushed to sign up Benitez, just a matter of days after Gérard Houllier had departed. The new man had barely been to Liverpool but he liked what he heard from Parry and his chairman David Moores. He would have the freedom – and the funds – to build his own team, with no board interference.

He could also bring in his Spanish coaching staff. Make no mistake, this managerial signing was a major coup. Benitez was arguably the most prized elite coach in Europe at the time but he knew little about managing in England, where Wenger was established and a provocative new young Portuguese coach was already making huge surfer's waves at moneyed Chelsea. But Benitez was no Wenger or Mourinho, and winning the Premier League crown would be more difficult than ever, especially given the west London club's new focus and financial power. Benitez immediately faced the qualifying rounds of the Champions League (a context in which he excelled), the hard yards of the Premier League (of which he had no experience at all), domestic cup football in England (which he seemed to dismiss), and threats from the club's star player and local symbol, Steven Gerrard, that the young Scouser was leaving, right away, for rivals Chelsea. Clearly it would not all be plain sailing for the new Liverpool boss.

The distracted Steven Gerrard eventually agreed to stay on at Anfield, although this was just a dress rehearsal for an even more disruptive version of this near-crisis in 2005. However, Michael Owen *did* leave – for Real Madrid. Owen said later that he loved Liverpool and that he had cried all the way to the airport. But he also said, 'I had to go and sample it – the Galácticos, that white kit, where everyone prances about like an angel. That amazing stadium, a different culture.' After a struggle in Spain, when Michael sought a fast return to England in 2005, he only wanted to come back to Liverpool, but the board – or the new Liverpool manager – refused to find the £16m fee required. Instead, Owen signed for Newcastle United and a couple of years of injury trauma. He had probably played too much football too soon to retain his fitness and preserve his incredible pace. When he lost that weapon, Michael struggled to get back to the very top of his game.

The unknown Antonio Núñez had joined Liverpool from Madrid as a right-sided forward to smooth the Owen sale. It was a difficult start for him – a serious knee injury in his first training session – which never really got easier. Benitez recruited in Owen's place Luis Garcia, a very talented, if lightweight, forward from Barcelona's reserves, for £6m. Garcia could light up a match but he could not quite replace Owen's electric pace, energy or goals. Who could? Arguably, in the early 2000s, Liverpool FC had been able to boast the two top young English strikers of their generation, but within three years they had neither.

Rafa Benitez now spent £10m on the quite exceptional 22-year-old midfielder Xabi Alonso, from Real Sociedad. Alonso was a quality passer, a game organiser not unlike Jan Mølby, but a man with much more mobility and tackling verve than the Dane ever had. He would be crucial to all his manager's best work at Liverpool. Josemi was also recruited, from Málaga in Spain, to play right-back but never convinced and was soon replaced by a late-Houllier signing, the solid and consistent Irish international defender Steve Finnan. Sami Hyypiä called him Liverpool's most underrated player. Benitez was also stuck with Djibril Cisse, a French forward who the departing Houllier had inexplicably been allowed to recruit from Auxerre for a then club record fee of £14m. Cisse was flaky and temperamental, the kind of forward who probably had the look of a powerful and daunting adversary in the French league but who could be bullied and clobbered by most of the British centre-halves he faced here. This agreement effectively tied the new manager's hands – and robbed him of transfer cash. Benitez tried to loosen the binds in January 2005 by bringing in Fernando Morientes, a great striker in Spain but half a yard and some courage short for the game in England. Morientes enjoyed, rather too much, the company of Melwood's physiotherapists.

Initially, Rafa Benitez struggled to make much sense of the English Premier League: he tried to rotate his squad in places it should not (and could not) be rotated, underestimating the capacity of any Premier League team playing at home to mug Liverpool, especially if his own team was stuffed full of still half-baked foreign recruits. It was a lesson Rafa found difficult to learn, especially as Arsenal, Manchester United and Chelsea were all now authentic candidates to win the Premier League title. In his first season Liverpool finished fifth, a punishing 37 points behind champions Chelsea. Benitez would also underestimate the symbolic importance to Liverpool fans of the FA Cup. He fielded a very weak team (David Raven, anyone?) at freezing Second Division Burnley in the televised third round tie in January 2005 and the Reds crumbled to a 1-0 reverse, his young French novice Traore scoring a comical back-heeled own goal. There was a near-hysterical reaction in the city to this humiliation and even early calls for the manager's head. Better progress came in the League Cup, where Liverpool eventually made it to the final in 2005, before losing out 3-2 to Mourinho's Chelsea. This rivalry was stoking up nicely: the flamboyant Portuguese versus the unflappable Spaniard. It had a few miles to run yet.

In contrast to his early domestic travails, Benitez excelled in the European arena, where he had more time to prepare and where he was less likely to come up against the sort of bludgeoning approach he was routinely encountering in the English game. In England, physical intensity could still smash up well-laid tactical plans. In Europe, tactics could better win out, but Rafa ended up, nevertheless, at the rear of the Champions League group stages in 2004. Liverpool needed to beat Olympiacos by two clear goals at Anfield in the last match to be certain of qualifying for the knockout stages. Actually, the Greeks had rarely secured a decent European result away from home in their entire history, but the Brazilian genius Rivaldo curled home a first-half free kick, meaning Liverpool now needed to score three unanswered goals in 45 minutes with a team full of inexperienced younger players. They got them, Steven Gerrard completing a famous second-half comeback with a late rocket past the stranded Nikopolidis in the Greek goal. Maybe something *was* happening here under the inscrutable Benitez?

Next up in Europe, Liverpool eased past the Germans from Bayer Leverkusen, before an emotional couple of meetings loomed with Juventus, the first time the two clubs had met since the terrible events back in 1985. Liverpool and their supporters tried to make public apologies to the Italians at Anfield with a mosaic – which was not well received by the travelling Italian fans – before squeezing out a 2-1 lead, courtesy of Hyypiä and Luis Garcia, to take to Turin. In Italy, it was much hotter for travelling fans off the pitch than it was for the team on it, with the Reds comfortably holding on for a near risk-free 0-0 draw. Returning from injury, Xavi Alonso was outstanding in organising Liverpool's defensive resistance, a Benitez masterclass.

It was much the same story at Stamford Bridge in the first leg of what would prove to be a volcanic semi-final versus Chelsea, which pitted Benitez against the self-proclaimed new 'Special One' of football management in England. Liverpool played for – and got – a cagey scoreless draw in London. This kind of disciplined shutout was clearly one of the Spaniard's specialties. He was hoping that the Anfield crowd might subdue a star-studded Chelsea back in the district of Liverpool 4. This night confirmed a significant tactical victory for the Liverpool manager over the two legs, little Garcia scoring the famous early 'ghost goal' at the Kop end, with the entire Liverpool crowd screaming catatonically from then on until the final whistle sounded. It eventually did. There had been many, many wonderful football occasions to celebrate at Anfield in the previous 113 years but there was little quite like this night so far. Nothing quite like the noise and the celebrations and the pinch-yourself-is-it-really-happening, drinking-pubs-dry exchanges, which followed around the city (it would be rivalled and arguably surpassed only in 2019).

Twenty years on from the disgrace of Brussels, the wild outsiders of Liverpool FC were back in *the* elite European football final. They were the lowest-ranked club, domestically, ever to have reached this stage of the competition, so Liverpool would deservedly be considered no-hopers in Istanbul. No matter. Because, for its counter-intuitive drama and its quite outlandish central narrative, there would never be another major European football final quite like this one.

The Miracle of Istanbul

Of course, every Liverpool supporter who was there has their own story to tell about Istanbul 2005: where I saw it; how I got there; what we did afterwards in the middle of the night; about how we had all given hope up at half-time. Everyone who was there will also remember the chaotic organisation at a stadium built, quite literally, in the middle of nowhere. How walking through open fields, travelling past goatherds and shoeless urchins was required just to reach the venue. How the stadium ran out of food and drink. But forget all this. This epic contest against AC Milan was simply the greatest-ever European final, possibly the greatest-ever major football final, one that straddled Asia and Europe. It kicked off on one day and finished on another and had just about everything in between. There have even been half-decent books written about this single match. It was a match that also raised all the difficult and controversial questions that had already been simmering around the Liverpool manager, their feted defensive Spanish coach. Should he be considered a tactical genius for turning around a three-goal half-time deficit against one of the best club teams in Europe? Or did he make a huge selection blunder, one from which he was eventually rescued only by the heart and unwillingness to accept defeat shown by the Liverpool fans and his players? The debate continues today – but the result always remains the same.

There is not much doubt that the Liverpool manager made a pretty big mistake by leaving out of Liverpool's starting line-up for the 2005 Champions League Final his most experienced midfield defensive player, Didi Hamann. This single move was so unexpected that when Hamann, distractedly, heard Benitez announce the team, he wondered why Xabi Alonso had been left out; his mind had blanked the fact that it was *his* name that was missing from the Liverpool team sheet. This match had seemed enough of an unfair contest right from the start, because Milan were stuffed with seasoned international stars – Cafu, Seedorf, Shevchenko, Pirlo, Maldini, Crespo, Gattuso, Kaká, Stam –

while Liverpool were naïve *arrivistes* by comparison. And now Liverpool would start without Hamman, their defensive anchor and a 2002 World Cup finalist. What sort of trick was being played here?

Liverpool FC: Champions League winners, 25 May 2005, Istanbul (vs AC Milan)

Dudek

Finnan (Hamann 46) Carragher Hyypiä Traore

Alonso Gerrard Riise

Garcia Baros (Cisse 85) Kewell (Smicer 23)

The usually cautious Benitez had seemingly tried to outwit his rival, Ancelotti, who was expecting a dour Liverpool performance, focused on counter-attacking. Instead, the Spaniard dispensed with his world-class midfield shield and played the fragile Australian winger Harry Kewell, a man who had only just returned from injury. This tactical ploy failed on all fronts. Kewell broke down in the first half but Benitez stubbornly stuck to his favoured pattern by bringing on the attacking Czech international Vladimir Smicer, rather than his German midfielder. This second mistake simply compounded the earlier selectorial blunder. Without the experienced Hamann, Liverpool had no means of coping with the advanced movement of the exceptional young Brazilian, Kaká, in a match that was far too open for this Liverpool line-up to control. Milan scored in the first minute, through Maldini, and then ripped through the Reds for a 3-0 half-time lead with two goals from Crespo, fashioned by Kaká. It could have been many more. This looked like potential humiliation, a possible record scoreline in a major European final. This was what some of the key Liverpool players (and fans) were now thinking: how could they face their mates and fellow professionals back home after this shameful show?

What exactly happened at half-time remains contentious even today. Did the Milan players celebrate prematurely, so provoking a murderous response from Liverpool? Did the defiant singing by the Liverpool fans raise the Reds players' spirits to launch an irresistible second-half assault? (few players remember hearing it). Did Rafa Benitez inspire his men to a recovery of Lazarus-like proportions with a splash of tactical genius and some motivational magic? Or did all – or none – of these things really happen? Did the Liverpool players simply decide to have a go at Milan in a typical piece of British-style football bloody-mindedness, just to see what might happen when they had nothing left to lose?

Initially, at least, the Liverpool dressing room appeared both devastated and chaotic. The players were in shock. The manager's first plan was to bring on Djibril Cisse for the outclassed Traore to try to attack his way back into this contest. The young French full-back was already heading for the showers when it became clear that the right-back Steve Finnan was injured, so Traore was reinstated. He played a very solid second half. Then Benitez decided to bring on *both* Hamman and Cisse, until it was pointed out that Liverpool now had 12 players in their new system. Some much-needed clarity now struck home. Cisse would stay on the bench after all, and Hamann *would* come on; Jamie Carragher would move to the right of what was effectively now a back three, with Smicer supporting in defence when needed. Steven Gerrard would push further forward to support his attackers. At least this looked like a tenable plan, one to offer some scintilla of hope in an otherwise hopeless situation. Nobody in the wider Liverpool camp really believed it could work – except, perhaps, the great unwashed, the resilient Liverpool army of spectators.

Initially, the restoration of Hamman at the interval looked too late; Milan continued to attack and it seemed likely they might grab more goals. In truth, they had half-expected Liverpool to respectfully submit – as an Italian side might – in order to avoid a thrashing. Instead, Benitez had essentially asked his players to try to score first and then see what happened. So much for scientific, Continental tactics. Liverpool needed some old-fashioned British grit to unnerve their opponents and get back into this uneven contest. They also depended upon the fantastic support of the Liverpool fans who swamped this arena and just refused to give this up. Captain Steven Gerrard, inevitably, led the charge. You all know the rest. Liverpool scored three times – Gerrard, Smicer and Alonso – in six, astounding second-half minutes. 'Six minutes' carries major symbolic importance for the Liverpool club, of course. Now the phrase would have a more joyous meaning for a new generation of Liverpool supporters.

Visibly rattled – amazed, in fact – Milan, for all their international experience, could not reply to this unexpected onslaught. Dudek, the Liverpool goalkeeper, a modest Catholic man from Polish mining stock, somehow saved point blank from Shevchenko near the end of normal time and said later that some divine intervention must have aided his impossible resistance. Perhaps it also helped him deal with the mental torment of the penalty kicks that followed. He did not need much help. The Milan players were drained, agog at the Liverpool response. They missed three penalties, Liverpool only one, and it was the usually deadly Shevchenko who meekly fouled up the vital kick. Liverpool had come back from the dead to win their fifth European Cup – their first under a foreign manager and with a largely foreign team. It was, surely, a miracle aided from above – some wags claimed, by the watching Anfield Holy Trinity of Shankly, Paisley and Joe Fagan. But without their two current Scouse rocks, Jamie Carragher and Steven Gerrard, and without the club's extraordinary supporters, none of this would have been even remotely possible. Which left one key question: did Liverpool win the 2005 Champions League despite or because of the actions of their acclaimed manager? In football, as they say, history is written by the winners.

Still chasing a dream

What could possibly follow this mighty comeback? Implausibly, it was another severe bout of 'Gerrard is going' anxiety in the summer of 2005, as well as new ambitions for winning the Premier

League title. The emotionally complex Gerrard, an outstanding Liverpool player, technically gifted, fearless and a goalscorer, was highly valued elsewhere and he wanted some valedictory love from his Spanish boss. Rafa Benitez simply seemed unable to supply it. This was not complicated. Gerrard clearly loved the club and he had played in at least three different positions in the epic in Istanbul. He had led the fightback with courage and great skill, so he believed he deserved some visible public affection from his manager. Instead, Benitez seemed inert, wrapped up in his technocrat's armour. So now Gerrard was publicly torn between staying, or leaving for Chelsea, where the emotional Mourinho was a big fan and a very different character to the rather repressed Benitez. The Spaniard seemed quite bemused by the public soap opera that was being played out here; he was unable to respond. If Gerrard left, then Rafa would simply find someone else to replace him. When all this division and uncertainty came out, fans started publicly burning Gerrard shirts and it took Rick Parry's calming intervention to talk some sense into the two parties. It was resolved that Steven Gerrard would stay and that Rafa would need to loosen up a little, show his men a little more arm-round-the-shoulder compassion. How long would this last?

The Liverpool manager might have been nominated by some to join the Liverpool greats simply because of what had happened in Istanbul but he would never be fully accepted into the inner sanctum until he had conquered the significant domestic peaks. He climbed another one in 2006. A small mountain, Peter Crouch, was brought in to help him, an unlikely stretched-out target man who could not score at all at the start of his Liverpool career. 'Bolo' Zenden also arrived, an experienced Dutch midfielder whom the manager vainly tried to sell to the Liverpool crowd by describing him as 'Middlesbrough's best player'. 'Momo' Sissoko was also signed up, a destructive Malian midfield player who Benitez had worked with in Spain and who achieved some brief cult status in Liverpool 4. But his poor technique was a vital flaw and injury clouded his brief Liverpool stay. Arriving, too, was a highly promising and cool young Danish central-defender Daniel Munthe Agger, from Brøndby, although injury also blighted his start with the club. Finally, there was even an unlikely, romantic return to Liverpool for a local folk hero who had been summarily dispatched by Houllier to Leeds in December 2001 for an inflated £12m fee. Perhaps to try to make up for his Steven Gerrard mismanagement, Rafa Benitez now publicly embraced Robbie Fowler as a veteran forward option, a local totem and a man with impeccable Liverpool credentials. All these incomers had some quality. Some made an impact; some were too late in their careers; and others simply struggled to match expectations at Liverpool. A mixed bag, but Robbie's return was at least treasured by fans.

As European champions, Liverpool contested FIFA's invented Club World Championship tournament in December 2005 in Japan. They had lost twice in the old version (in 1981 and 1984) and had barely taken the matter seriously. In 1981 Bob Paisley had even warned his players to avoid bookings because of much more important league matches to come back home. Things had changed in 20 years. Benitez showed his deep commitment to the club and the event by staying with his team in Japan, even after news of his father's death in Spain. This tournament also intruded badly into the Premier League season and was palpably more important for marketing purposes than having any serious football worth. In the event, having comfortably beaten CONCACAF champions Deportivo Saprissa in the semi-final, a strong Liverpool line-up lost 1-0 in a final they dominated (with three disallowed goals) in Yokohama to the South Americans from São Paulo.

Back in the real football world, meanwhile, the Reds eventually finished third behind Chelsea and Manchester United in the Premier League, scoring a paltry 57 goals in the process, despite their new strikers. But there were compensations. The Liverpool manager out-thought Jose Mourinho again, in an FA Cup semi-final victory at Old Trafford on 22 April 2006, a win immaculately sculptured by Luis Garcia. This led, in turn, to another Steven Gerrard-inspired dramatic final win in Wales, this time on penalties, after a pulsating 3-3 draw with luckless West Ham United.

By now, captain fantastic Gerrard was sorting out his gremlins and was assuming the mantle of one of the club's all-time greats, routinely dredging his team out of seemingly impossible situations, carrying inadequate colleagues and scoring vital goals. He had every quality – power, technique, vision and coolness in front of goal – even if, as a shy man, he sometimes seemed to lack self-belief. By his on-field heroics, Gerrard was also helping his manager stave off potentially difficult press interviews. Saving the crucial penalty kicks in Wales in 2006 was a new Liverpool goalkeeper, the Spanish son of a custodian, Pepe Reina, who had replaced the appreciated but occasionally slipshod Jerzy Dudek.

Indeed, Istanbul was the swansong for a group of players recruited under Houllier who had all played vital roles in the final. Smicer, Baros and Dudek had all left the club immediately, and Hamann and Traore were reduced to only minor roles. In the summer of 2006, Rafa Benitez had funds for transfers, if not (as he liked to point out) the vast sums afforded to those in charge at the two clubs that had just bettered his team in the Premier League title race. In came Craig Bellamy, a talented, unruly and unpredictable Welsh forward; Fabio Aurelio, a brittle Brazilian full-back who Benitez knew well from Spain; Mark Gonzales, a Chilean international winger who Benitez had chased for two years, but who proved quite unsuitable for the English game; Dirk Kuyt, a hard-working, underrated striker from the Netherlands; and – a quite startling signing this – the inconsistent and wayward right-sided forward, Jermaine Pennant, from Birmingham City. The much superior Argentina international and water carrier, Javier Mascherano, joined later in the campaign, on loan from West Ham, to add energy and first-class defensive solidity to the Liverpool cause. He would eventually cost a bargain £17m to keep. Collectively, these players added strength towards building a potential title-winning team, but Liverpool finished third again in the Premier League in 2007, distant from Chelsea and trailing repeat title winners, Manchester United.

Working closely with his coach and friend Pako Ayestarán, Benitez's counter to criticism about his Premier League failures was again in Europe, where the Reds comfortably saw off PSV Eindhoven, Bordeaux and Galatasaray in the Champions League group stages, won sensationally in Barcelona after Bellamy and Riise had publicly fallen out before the match using a golf club as a preferred weapon, and then thumped PSV again later in the knockout phase to set up yet another meeting with Chelsea in the semi-finals. Remarkably, Rafa Benitez outsmarted Jose Mourinho for a third consecutive occasion, with Liverpool winning 4-1 on penalties, after 1-0 victories for both teams in their home legs. Pepe Reina in Liverpool's goal was beginning to show all the class and assurance his manager had identified in him and he was a devil to beat in penalty shoot-outs.

But, alas, there would be no happy ending here. Under new American owners, and in a near chaotic setting in Athens, pitched against AC Milan, those old enemies from 2005, Liverpool lost the final 2-1. The Milan team of 2007 was older and definitely weaker than it had been in 2005, which suggested, therefore, that the same might also be true of Liverpool. But a more ambitious approach from Benitez might have brought another European trophy win, despite the flaws in his 2007 Liverpool squad. The perpetually under-performing Pennant got into great positions but failed to deliver, and leaving Peter Crouch on the bench for 78 minutes, by which time Milan had established a winning two-goal advantage, was certainly not the Liverpool manager's finest hour. Crouch's late goal was rendered meaningless.

The reputation of Liverpool's support was also later dragged through the mud by UEFA because of ticketless intrusions into another very poorly organised venue. An allocation of 17,000 tickets fell far short of the 40,000 Liverpool supporters who were present in Athens. We were funnelled through abject security checks, with some fans flashing cigarette packs and even photocopied press passes in lieu of match tickets. Police later gassed and baton-charged supporters who *did* have tickets, but for whom there was no longer room in the stadium. In short, it was business as usual in parts of the Liverpool fan base, but especially among the highest echelons of UEFA, European football's inept governing body. At Anfield, two Champions League final appearances in three years, one win and one FA Cup was some compensation for Benitez and his relative failings in the Premier League. But by now things happening *off* the field at Anfield had begun to cloud the Liverpool manager's vision of his rightful place at the club. In fact, these developments in the Liverpool boardroom and across the Atlantic suddenly seemed to threaten the entire future of Liverpool Football Club.

Chapter 9

American Pie

The Liverpool ownership crisis 2007–2010

*Liverpool FC are in search of a new stadium and
new owners. Local finance evacuates, as Middle
Eastern promise gives way to American bluster.
Rafa Benitez and Fernando Torres almost land
the Premier League title but both end up leaving.
Supporters unite in protest as the club is taken
to the very financial brink. Liverpool FC land
up in court – and come out the other side. FSG
take charge and have to sack a floundering Roy
Hodgson. Torres downs tools and Kenny Dalglish
has to pick up the pieces. Meanwhile, a toothy-
looking Uruguayan mini-earthquake now lurks
in the wings.*

Red Men go Yankee

Liverpool FC now had an ambitious and settled international manager who seemed well suited for Europe, if rather less certain at home. But the economics at the club still lagged behind these positive developments on the field, and the ailing remnants of the Littlewoods empire could no longer provide the sort of cash needed to build a new stadium and fund an elite-level squad in the global era. Abramovich's dirty billions had changed the game. In their search for investors to finance a new ground on nearby Stanley Park, club chairman David Moores and chief executive Rick Parry were keen to try to conserve as much as possible of the cultural heritage and the traditional family ethos of the Liverpool club. Ideally, the Liverpool Way, built patiently over many generations of essentially conservative (and often Conservative) club stewardship, might somehow remain intact and relatively unsullied in the new corporate era.

But despite this ambition and Liverpool's complex mix of parochialism and historical 'openness' as a city, the realisation that investment was now being sought from all corners of the globe made some fans – especially locally based Liverpool supporters – understandably uneasy. Back in May 2004, the billionaire prime minister of Thailand, Thaksin Shinawatra, had offered a £65m investment for a 30 per cent stake in Liverpool FC, while a hostile counter-offer of a reported £73m had been placed on the table from local building magnate, Steve Morgan, to buy outright control of the club. Both were eventually rejected, Shinawatra's possibly because of rising public unease about his alleged corruption and human rights abuses in Thailand. Morgan's bid was at least made up of more local capital but the Liverpool board argued that it severely undervalued the club. In hindsight, they were dead right. Even within five years, such offers would look risible. Morgan also, undoubtedly, posed a threat to the future at Liverpool FC of both Moores and Rick Parry.

In light of the obvious difficulties involved, other commercial avenues were now tentatively explored by Liverpool's executives, ones that much more clearly stressed the local affinities of the club. There had even been discussions about a shared stadium with neighbours and eternal rivals, Everton FC, for example. The Goodison Park club was also eyeing several potential sites for relocation (including the vacant King's Dock on the city's waterfront). Predictably, some fans viewed the sharing proposal as little short of sacrilegious and the idea quickly died. But more than two years of searching later, Liverpool still had no new investment capital.

Then a consortium representing Dubai International Capital (DIC), an arm of the Dubai government and ruling family, reportedly offered a total of £156m for the purchase of all existing Liverpool shares, plus funds to cover debts and the building of a new stadium. The total package was said to be worth around £450m. This was more like it. The Liverpool board seemed keen, despite further human rights concerns. However, just two months later, in February 2007, two American sports and property tycoons, Tom Hicks and George Gillett Jr, men who had never worked seriously together in business or sport, raised the offer for the club to £5,000 a share, or £172m, plus promised funds for a new stadium. The DIC group had earlier sneered that the 'soccer-phobic' Gillett would not know Liverpool FC from 'a hole in the ground', and it was now publicly furious at the sudden swerve in negotiations, describing the Liverpool board as 'dishonourable' and the club as 'a shambles'. On reflection, they may have had a point.

Parry and Moores now had to weigh up the pros and cons of the American and Middle Eastern options. They eventually decided to take the plunge and Moores agreed to sell his controlling stake to the US entrepreneurs. Rick Parry soothed: 'Be assured, the only thing David Moores is concerned about is the club being in the right hands for the future. You can be certain he has done his homework carefully and will make a decision in the best interests of the club.' Moores, himself, was clear: 'When you have a decision to make like this and you are so desperate to see the club go into the right hands,' he told journalists, 'then you have to be comfortable with whatever you decide.' Moores would certainly be 'comfortable' as he stood to raise his own cut of the club buyout by some £8m, to a reported £89.6m. He was also installed by the Americans as honorary life president in recognition of his decade-and-a-half service, and was charged by the new owners to act as something of a nominal boardroom delegate to represent the views of Liverpool fans.

To be fair, Moores may well have favoured the Americans for reasons other than profit. After all, these were two identifiable benefactors from across the Atlantic, men who seemed to understand the sports business and who appeared to have 'clean' money to invest. They claimed to have the best interests of the club at heart. Hicks and Gillett may also have looked a better bet for a city with strong business and cultural links to the USA, than a faceless and rather 'alien' corporate government body from the Middle East. It was a business deal typical of the new age of global liberalisation, but one that also risked traducing the core tenets of the Liverpool Way. Funding for elite Premier League clubs had now moved inexorably into the orbit of global billionaires. Liverpool were simply the next club on the rank. As it turned out, this deal was unlikely to endear David Moores to any Liverpool fans in the period between 2007 and 2010, even those who had approved, initially at least, the American investment over that offered by the shadowy men from Dubai.

Fistfuls of dollars

These two American billionaires, Tom Hicks, owner of the Texas Rangers baseball franchise and the (US) National Hockey League's Dallas Stars, and George Gillett Jr, owner of the Montreal Canadiens and formerly of the Miami Dolphins, cobbled together in just two months an unlikely alliance. They secured a reported £470m funding package via a loan from the Royal Bank of Scotland (RBS) to buy Liverpool FC and to allocate some £215m to begin work on a new stadium. Hicks, a Texas acolyte and former Republican business partner of President George W. Bush, had made his fortune from raising private equity to fund multimillion-dollar corporate takeovers. Liverpool were suddenly in the hands of the sort of global sports capitalists who made no secret of their financial motives, their ignorance of 'soccer', or of their ambitions to model this highly atypical English football club along the commercial lines of an NFL franchise. They openly highlighted the attractions of English football's booming TV international markets, the growing internet income streams available for the English game, expanding opportunities for the Liverpool club in South-East Asia and in South America, the possibility of selling stadium naming rights and even their plans for introducing American-style 'bunker suites' into the proposed new Liverpool ground. These were underground 'living rooms' where corporate elites could dine in plush splendour and watch banks of TV sets before taking an elevator ride to their match seats. This seemed like sport in corporate America writ large.

And yet local resistance on Merseyside to this US takeover was surprisingly muted, to say the least. This was mainly for four reasons. First, there was a realist resignation among most Liverpool supporters that global financing was inevitable for any English club with serious pretentions to be competitive for titles at home and in Europe. More knowledgeable (and, perhaps, more cynical) Liverpool fans could even make the appropriate historical connections here about the very origins of the club under John Houlding and the commercial hard-headedness of its great leaders of the past.

Second, this cosmopolitan 'city of the sea' was no stranger to global cultural exchanges and American commercial investment. Indeed, for much of its history the city of Liverpool had looked more to the United States than it had to British locations for its cultural and commercial connections. Historically, Americans had been widely envied and admired in Liverpool for their supposed modernity and stylishness. This maritime connection from the past – the 'Cunard Yanks' – also fed directly into on-street idioms and language, nightlife and music, with this 'most American of English cities' acting as a site of feverish transatlantic cultural exchange. It was the sort of interplay that had allowed the city of Liverpool to take the world lead in pop music during the early 1960s. In short, Merseyside already had ingrained American sensibilities and sympathies, well before Tom Hicks and George

Gillett strode into Anfield early in 2007 with their 'good old boy' homilies about 'tradition' and 'heritage' and their promises to make Liverpool FC the most successful football club in the world. The possibility of transatlantic investment and exchange in football probably did not strike most Liverpool fans as an especially alien, or threatening, intrusion.

Third, the new Liverpool co-owners were experts in selling themselves to Liverpool supporters in the set-piece press conferences that followed. They showed little of the public arrogance of the Glazer family at Manchester United, for example, who seemed to believe that money was its own explanation for their actions. With the Merseyside press acting as enthusiastic cheerleaders, the general assumption here was that the Liverpool buyout would *not* involve the kind of leveraged deal that had loaded Glazer debt on to the Manchester club. Indeed, in the offer document the Americans made it very clear that any loans taken out to secure the deal would be personally guaranteed and that payment of any interest 'will not depend to any significant extent on the business of Liverpool'. The new owners also cleverly, and rather humbly in this charm offensive, played back to the club's supporters some of the familiar and comforting rhetoric about the past. 'We are custodians not owners of the franchise,' Gillett said, thus combining the Victorian Britain of John Houlding with the language of contemporary American sport, in a way that was both reassuring and alarming at the same time. It was left to David Moores to admit that 'I don't think we have maximised our world brand and hopefully they [Gillett and Hicks] will help us get into these areas where we have fantastic fan bases.' George Gillett coyly told the same group of journalists on 6 February 2007 that:

> I don't think it's appropriate for Tom or I to try to convince the fans today that we understand the history, the support or the legacy anywhere as well as they do. What we would try to say to the fans is that we have respect. Respect is the way we feel about the history and the legacy of this franchise [sic] ... I am still learning

about the club but I will get it into my blood in every
way I can.

Finally, another familiar device, skilfully employed by the
Americans to mask some of the bleak economics of the deal, was
the concept of the Liverpool 'family'. The Martindale, Cartwright
and Moores family boardroom dynasties would now be seamlessly
replaced by their transatlantic equivalent. This message about
'respect' and 'family values' was strongly reinforced in words
and images in a commemorative booklet issued by Liverpool
FC, carrying pictures of the American buyers and their adult
sons at Anfield. It was almost as if the club had been acquired
through marriage by some august royal family from a superior but
supportive foreign power. Gillett's son, Foster, would come over to
work inside the club on a day-to-day basis and at an executive level
with Rick Parry, while Tom Hicks Jr would join the club board.
This arrangement seemed potentially full of tensions and conflict
and, by the end of the 2006/07 season, there were already reports
that Rafa Benitez had started to bypass Rick Parry by talking
directly to Foster Gillett in order to expedite transfers and other
matters. Parry was now the self-appointed guardian of continuity
and the main defender of the Liverpool Way inside the club but
he would soon start to look disturbingly isolated in the emerging
new Liverpool ownership structure.

The men from Weetabix

So, this was the mercantile background against which, in May
2007, Liverpool reached the Champions League Final for the
second time in three years. By the autumn of 2007 it became clear
that the club's American owners would have to renegotiate a new
financial package worth £350m with RBS and the American
investment bank Wachovia in order to pay off their original
loans and raise the cash needed to begin work on the proposed
new Liverpool stadium. Revised plans for the new ground had
considerably increased its price, so proposals to raise a further
£300m in funding would now have to wait until 2009.

Worse, despite their initial denials, the Liverpool owners now, reportedly, *did* want to load some of the original acquisition debt of £298m on to the club's balance sheet, thus replicating core aspects of the Glazer deal at Manchester United. Gone was the earlier American talk about the 'special heritage' of the Liverpool club. Instead, Hicks chose to compare the purchase of Liverpool FC to that of a breakfast cereal company: 'We bought Weetabix and we leveraged it up to make our return. You could say that anyone who was eating Weetabix was paying for our purchase of Weetabix. It was just business. It is the same for Liverpool: revenues come in from whatever source, and if there is money left over it is profit.'

The first element of the refinancing package was finally agreed in January 2008, with £105m of the debt saddled on Liverpool and £185m secured by a holding company, Kop Investment LLC, held in the tax havens off the Cayman Islands and in the US state of Delaware. Here were the routine machinations of global capitalism in full flow. The Americans increased their personal guarantees, mainly in the form of credit notes, to around a reported £55m. This suddenly looked like very deep financial water and not the sort of deal that Liverpool fans – or Moores and Parry – had anticipated at all. Added to this, in November 2007, a very public row between manager Rafa Benitez and Tom Hicks over the availability of transfer funds mobilised Liverpool spectators squarely behind the manager and against the new owners, sparking organised fan protests.

By January 2008 any debates there might still to be had about these American owners at Anfield had been replaced by a stark pragmatism. Broadsheet newspapers carried pictures of Kopites holding up a large home-made banner reading 'Yanks out, Dubai in. In Rafa we Love.' This fan position hardened still further when it was revealed that Parry, Hicks and Gillett had secretly met with ex-Germany national coach, Jürgen Klinsmann, to discuss the managerial position at Liverpool should Benitez's position at the club become untenable. Finally, despite repeated promises given by the new owners – and this was the main reason, after all, why the club had sought new investors – no visible progress had yet been made on building the proposed new Liverpool stadium.

As rumours began to circulate early in 2008 that DIC were considering making a new £500m offer for the club, it was clear that Hicks and Gillett were no longer in direct communication with each other, nor could they agree on the future of Liverpool FC. Gillett looked as if he might be willing to sell his shares, possibly to DIC, while Hicks publicly demanded the resignation of the 'failing' Rick Parry. Both Americans' businesses were struggling in the face of global economic downturn. The bemused Parry would soon leave Anfield as the club's commercial and leadership uncertainty started to make it look like a public laughing stock. David Moores pronounced himself 'disgusted' at Parry's treatment and he retired from the Liverpool board in June 2009, saying that he was 'heartbroken' at how the new owners were treating the club. At the same time, Merseyside MPs called for the UK Government to resist an application from the Americans for the loan of £350m from the majority government-owned RBS. Liverpool Football Club, once a model of conservative and unobtrusive stability in the English game, suddenly seemed to be impossibly split, rudderless and constantly in the public eye for all the wrong reasons. Public protests organised by the Spirit of Shankly fans group continued in the city into the 2009/10 league season, as the increasingly desperate Liverpool FC owners were reputed to be looking for new Middle Eastern investors in the club. Make it up, you could not.

In Torres, we trust

Despite all this hugely distracting background noise and a lack of focus and direction *off* the field, Rafa Benitez had soldiered on and had continued to strengthen his team and his squad by bringing in several new signings in the summer of 2007. The Israeli Yossi Benayoun was among them, a forward with some ability, speed, mental strength and loads of energy – and he could also score goals. Arguably, he was the signing Liverpool should have made when Benitez had brought in Jermaine Pennant. The new man might even have helped secure a second Champions League for Rafa in 2007. The much-hyped Brazilian midfield man Lucas Leiva joined from Gremio in Brazil, having won the coveted *Bola de Ouro* (Golden Ball) for being the best young player in the 2006 Brazilian championship. He would take time to settle but eventually became a fans' favourite. Ryan Babel, another highly rated young star, joined from Ajax for £11.5m, a man who, when focused, could score extraordinary goals. But the forward seemed destined to be better known for his DJ ambitions and reported 'romps' with serial Liverpool WAG, Danielle Lloyd, than he would be as a key figure in the Benitez project (not that Rafa went out of his way to offer warmth, support or encouragement to Babel, the Dutchman claimed later).

However, the signature signing was the £20m capture in July 2007 of the Atlético Madrid centre-forward Fernando Torres, on a six-year deal, with Luis Garcia joining the Madrid club in return. Here was a young man who pretty much guaranteed front-end goals. Torres was already a major football figure in Madrid, the Atlético captain at 19, so he had some maturity and sense of responsibility as well as the necessary selfishness and quality of an authentic front man. He also had power and threatening pace and, when confident, he was a brilliant finisher. He had turned down a move to Chelsea in 2006 and the only question mark here was how he would stand up to the sheer physicality of the English game. Torres showed some early signs at home that he could be consistently lethal, but away from home he could also lose enthusiasm and belief if defenders were allowed to buffet him and Liverpool came under the cosh. His presence would grow at Anfield.

Playing in concert with a supporting Steven Gerrard, Torres soon showed exactly why the Liverpool manager had signed him. He scored 24 goals in 33 league matches, the first Reds striker since Robbie Fowler to score 20 or more in the league, and a record for a debut season for a foreign striker in England. In February and March 2008, he became the first Liverpool player since Jackie Balmer in 1946 to score consecutive Anfield league hat-tricks (vs Middlesbrough and West Ham). When he scored the winner against Manchester City on 4 May 2008, Torres equalled Roger Hunt's club record of scoring in eight consecutive league matches at home. The Madrid man ended up scoring 33 goals in 46 matches in all competitions in his first full season and was now already shoved into the post-war shortlist of great Liverpool goalscorers, among Liddell, Hunt, Dalglish, Rush, Fowler and Owen. This was all good news, of course, even if the fitness of Torres and his away match reticence could seem like a trying problem.

Nevertheless, wider doubts persisted about Benitez and his general approach. The manager was now at odds, for example, with the club's youth policy and academy director Steve Heighway, who had managed to produce occasional first-team graduates and *two* recent FA Youth Cup-winning teams out of his Liverpool youngsters. These two men clearly cared little for each other and had very different views about youth-team football. Heighway wanted to develop mainly local talent in a caring and supportive environment and he thought that some of his young stars should be getting more opportunities in the Liverpool senior squad. Benitez wanted to recruit more globally and thought the academy was producing substandard products, players ill-prepared for the intensity of the Premier League. He was probably right. Heighway soon left the club, muttering about the loss of important Liverpool FC values.

Another low point – and these doubts never fully went away – came in February 2008 when a rotated Liverpool team, excluding Torres and other senior players, abjectly lost 2-1 at home in the FA Cup to modest Championship club, Barnsley. This kind of submission – an invitation to defeat in a competition that the club had spent decades trying to win – was a trial for those Liverpool supporters hungry for more success at home. Benitez seemed to care too little for the domestic cups, and his raft of expensively recruited international stars were often vulnerable or inconsistent. Later, however, in a generally fretful season, the invaluable Fernando Torres almost got Liverpool to another Champions League final with an equalising goal late at Stamford Bridge (where else?) in the semi-final second leg in 2008. But, at last it was the turn of Chelsea to slide past the Reds in extra time, only to be defeated in an all-English affair in Moscow by Manchester United. Tough cheese.

The trials of Rafa Benitez

Against the background of increasingly disruptive boardroom uncertainty, the Liverpool manager had now assembled his talented Hispanic spine – a more than capable goalscorer, a sophisticated midfield organiser, a quality defensive shield and a world-class goalkeeper. Also, his key English midfielder, Steven Gerrard, now seemed truly settled again and his other Scouse leader, Jamie Carragher, was still solid and vocal at the back. Benitez had signed defensive cover in the shape of Martin Škrtel from Zenit Saint Petersburg in January 2008 for £6.5m, and was given more money to invest in the summer of that year. This was looking like a real title-challenging squad in the making. Some judicious recruitment now and Liverpool would surely run their rivals very close.

But some of Rafa's transfer work in 2008 was mystifying. The chase for model professional, Gareth Barry, from Aston Villa would eventually have a corrosive impact on his entire Liverpool project. Barry was highly rated and left-sided, so he covered a current weakness at Liverpool. Benitez reasoned that he would probably need to sell the pivotal Xabi Alonso to raise funds to bring in the Villa man. It looked like a risky decision, then made worse because all this rationalisation became public and took place long *before* Barry was a confirmed Liverpool capture –the England international eventually decided to stay in the West Midlands. Predictably, the excellent Alonso decided he would leave Liverpool when the next chance came – which would be to Real Madrid in the summer of 2009 for £30m. Steven Gerrard, for one, said later that he was 'devasted' by Alonso's departure, a view shared by the vast majority of Liverpool fans.

Benitez then agreed to the signing, for an inflated £20m fee, of Robbie Keane from Spurs to replace the struggling Peter Crouch. But Rafa immediately seemed puzzled at how to fit the Irishman into his Liverpool team. He appeared unimpressed by what he had bought and started to play Keane wide or to leave him out altogether, even after decent performances. Stripped of any confidence, the striker returned to White Hart Lane soon after, for a hefty loss. This left a Liverpool squad with little experienced forward cover for Torres in the second half of the season. Left-winger Albert Riera joined his Spanish international mates at Anfield but he had already tried – and failed – to make it in England, at Manchester City. Riera lacked pace and a little heart, deficits not recommended in the Premier League. Finally, Liverpool's first-ever Italian signing, international left-back Andrea Dossena, joined from Udinese for around £7m in July 2008, a direct replacement for John Arne Riise. On paper this looked potentially good business; the top Italians are usually very good defenders, men with a cynical edge. But Dossena lacked positional acumen and tackling ability. When Glen Johnson arrived at Anfield in the summer of 2009, the England international picked up Dossena's No. 2 shirt and the Italian was allocated the pretty marginal No. 38. Already, he had an uncertain present – and no future – at Liverpool FC.

Despite all these off-stage issues, it was actually very nearly a great Liverpool season in 2008/09, the Premier League title almost won at last. Benitez still struggled in the domestic cup competitions – falling to Everton in the FA Cup – but in the Champions League there were two famous wins, home and away, against a tepid Real Madrid, including a 4-0 mauling at Anfield, before Liverpool fell, again to Chelsea, 7-5 on aggregate, despite a wild 4-4 second leg quarter-final draw at Stamford Bridge. Only two Premier League matches were lost by the Reds all season, unluckily at Tottenham and mystifyingly at eventually relegated Middlesbrough, where Rafa Benitez fielded an unbalanced line-up for such an important fixture, including a debut for a soon discarded young French-born Moroccan forward, Nabil El Zhar. Against the other top four teams Liverpool remained unbeaten, defeating both Chelsea and Manchester United home and away, with the latter crushed 4-1 at Old Trafford. This sort of away resilience in difficult locations was a major improvement on early Benitez seasons. However, injuries to Torres and an inability to break down the defences of moderate opposition at Anfield cost Liverpool dear. Another remarkable 4-4 draw, this time at home in the league to Arsenal in April with Andrey Arshavin scoring all four goals for the visitors, effectively ended the title race for Liverpool. Worse still, Manchester United – by four points the champions – were now level with Liverpool on 18 league titles won.

After five full seasons at Anfield, assessments of Rafa Benitez still varied on Merseyside. For many people, his tactical awareness and his achievements between 2005 and 2009 in Europe put the manager almost beyond criticism. The duplicity and instability of the new Liverpool owners, it was argued, had put him in an impossible position; it certainly deflected criticism that, on occasions, might otherwise have been aimed at the Liverpool boss. For others, Benitez remained just too cautious and too uneven in his judgement of line-ups, players and transfers to ever forge a title-winning squad at Anfield. His substitutions and player selection still confounded, despite the European successes and the title near miss in 2009. In 2009/10 Benitez seemed to have a first XI capable of beating anyone in the Premier League but Liverpool lacked the sort of depth and squad balance that was now necessary to be truly competitive across numerous fronts. The back-up forwards he recruited later, including the Ukrainian Andriy Voronin, did little to excite Liverpool fans or suggest that the Spaniard still had what was required to win the domestic title. The ownership situation was a severe handicap, for sure, and the new economics of English football also meant that, by 2009/10, clubs such as Manchester City and even Tottenham could also be challenging more strongly in the future for top four places. Things were getting more difficult in England, not less.

The claim from the Benitez camp was that the Liverpool manager had simply been outspent by all the other top clubs since 2004. But these contentions were challenged by the facts. Abramovich's Chelsea were the only major club in England to outspend Liverpool over the Benitez era, by £186m to £122m. Benitez had spent an average of £20m over income for each season he had been in charge at Anfield. Manchester United's net *total* spend over the same six-season period was just £27m and Arsène Wenger at Arsenal had actually made a net *profit* on deals during this period of around £27m. What was also different about the Benitez regime was his signing of 23 players who had each cost a fee of £3m or less. Hardly any of them succeeded. Perhaps his hands were tied by his board to sign only younger men who had an eventual sell-on value, but this attempt at shrewd investment mostly ended up being money (and time) wasted. Liverpool, at one stage, were reported to have as many as 62 professional players on their books. Bob Paisley would have shuddered at the duplication and waste.

Boardroom unrest and lack of finance, combined with a lack of judgement, were key problems at Anfield as, in the early part of 2009/10, Rafa Benitez's depleted team slid into a string of league and European defeats. Clearly, the lack of direction, leadership and commitment from Liverpool's divided American ownership was a crippling issue and the manager's fate looked uncertain once more. In fact, it was difficult to predict then what the future might hold for Rafa Benitez, or for his expensively assembled squad. Or, indeed, if there was a future at all for the famous club he still managed.

Meet the new boss …

Let's get it right, the very idea of Liverpool Football Club as a kind of social glue, a binding historic and contemporary pact struck between local working people in the city and this treasured local sporting institution was seriously threatened in the terrible months between January 2008 and October 2010. The spirit of the great Reds manager of the 1960s, Bill Shankly, no less, had to be routinely called upon by supporters in symbolic defence of what the club meant to local people in these trying times. Marches, protests, blogs and organised campaigns rained down on Hicks and Gillett. The relationship between the club and its fans survived, as we knew it would, but Liverpool FC could even have gone under at various moments in this chaotic period. Football fans learned more during this spell than they knew (or possibly cared) about the crazy economics of global capitalism, which insists that enormous debt can best be lumped on to profitable businesses in order to purchase and 'grow' them.

For those already deeply anxious about the Anfield club's future, the sheer scale of the global financial crisis that hit from 2008 was truly terrifying. The sub-prime mortgage fiasco would claim in its wake many bigger fish than a mere Premier League football club, no matter its great history, cultural significance and community rootedness. In the end, the crash proved to be both a warning and a saviour, at a moment when Liverpool FC seemed under most threat. Notwithstanding their corporate flannel and the 'spade in the ground in 60 days' early day promises about a brand-new Anfield, Tom Hicks and George Gillett had made a grave yet simple mistake back in 2007. They had underestimated, or perhaps misunderstood, just how intensely ordinary working people in Liverpool and in a thousand other places around the world actually cared about their football club. These supporters saw the attempted commercial exploitation of the club, its fans and its traditions, as a violation; at best an act of injustice, at worst an attempted mutilation – a *murder*. Exhausted and frustrated by it all, Rafa Benitez finally left Liverpool on 3 June 2010 after European failure, a seasonal total of 19 matches lost and a hugely disappointing seventh-place league finish. Benitez had his faults and he had made some misjudgements, but he was also a

Champions League and FA Cup winner and a world-class coach, a man who had been working for some time in near-impossible circumstances.

Fan protest marches against the owners now accelerated as supporters responded as they might do to a potentially fatal external threat to any member of their own family – with a mixture of anger, passion, cunning and eventually desperation that this gross malfeasance should not be allowed to continue. The fans, alone, did not heroically win their battle with these hated Americans who had set out to try to destroy what the club had meant, and for mere profit. In reality, it was the crippling impact of the world financial crisis that finally did for Hicks and Gillett; it affected their loans from RBS and Wachovia and forced their hand to concede, spitting and screaming, to a sale in the British courts. By this stage RBS had loaned the pair around £300m and the bankers wanted their money back.

Liverpool fans around the world had used their on-line savvy to make the lives of these Yank carpetbaggers increasingly intolerable by making ownership of Liverpool FC toxic in the Americans' own commercial backyard. Ironically, it was the emotional and communal depth of feeling for the club – those things that are valued most of all by fans and are often (mis)reported as 'brand value' by owners – that finally eroded the worth of the club to Hicks and Gillet. We all live in an era in which elite team sport is increasingly colonised by global markets, transforming its organisation, production and consumption. Elite football will never return to its local origins, to a less complicated format, no matter how profound our wishes are that one day it might. Instead, as the courts ousted Liverpool's first American owners, so new ones from the same neck of the woods waited patiently in the wings.

It seemed briefly possible in 2008 that the global crisis might make a new world order in sport and culture possible. The UK tabloid press was getting a public kicking for phone tapping. A UK parliamentary select committee was soon critically examining the governance of the English game. UEFA's new 'financial fair play' proposals for clubs playing in European competitions were aimed at reducing wild spending and debt. These plans were scrutinised and critiqued but UEFA at least acknowledged the risk that global capital might ultimately destroy the sport. Of course, it was unlikely that top European competitions would *really* proceed in the future without some of the game's giants (and their TV audiences) if they fell foul of these new times. But how to finance elite football was a legitimate concern.

It was on 6 October 2010 that Liverpool FC was finally sold for a knock-down price of £300m. The sale was organised by Liverpool's acting chairman, Sir Martin Broughton, who had been appointed by the club's creditors in April 2010 with an urgent remit to sell. The main buyer was John W. Henry, son of an Illinois soybean farmer, a partner in the New England Sports Ventures, soon to be FSG. Henry had made his money in hedge funds and futures markets, the new face of global finance. Tom Hicks had hoped for a £600m buyout and described the deal as 'illegal', but a last-ditch Texas court's blocking order was ruled invalid in the UK. Unlike the Hicks and Gillett deal, this new transaction was forensically scrutinised by fans and officials alike. Liverpool's induced debts would now be erased by their new proprietors. Henry and his backers soon established reasonable links with Liverpool supporter groups by meeting with them soon after the buyout. FSG confirmed that John Henry and others would (occasionally) attend Liverpool matches, and they committed to investing heavily in the transfer market in the summer of 2011. Henry and his colleagues even began talking about modernising the historic Anfield stadium in preference to moving to a new arena on Stanley Park, although finances would surely dictate here. There were no signs at all that making the new men accountable to fans' interests was on the agenda. We remained powerless, in the hands of whatever these distant billionaires planned for us next.

But, as current owners in the USA of the Boston Red Sox baseball franchise, FSG were able to demonstrate considerable strategic financial and sporting acumen. Under their watch, the Red Sox had become the second-most valuable franchise in US baseball, trailing only the New York Yankees in that department. More importantly, Henry and his advisors had returned the Sox to World Series triumphs in 2004 and 2007 after an 86-year absence and had demonstrated their care and management of the *cultural* heritage of this venerable American sports club. The historic Fenway Park was modernised and improved, for example, rather than demolished. 'We were surprised how beautiful Anfield was,' said Henry later (not even all Liverpool supporters thought *that*).

All this seemed like good news, relatively speaking, and most Liverpool fans accepted that global billionaires were now probably required to make the club competitive again at home and in Europe, even if replacement American proprietors were not to the taste of all supporters. How did FSG plan to make their money if their main emphasis was on improvement and investment? Henry pointed, predictably, to reducing the club's huge salary base and increasing matchday revenues and commercial income. More tellingly, he revealed, 'Someday [hopefully a long time from now] these clubs and businesses will probably be worth more than we paid for them, but only if we do the right things, day-to-day, for the long term.' He *sounded* like someone who was in it for the long haul, even if profit inevitably came at the end of this rainbow. He also seemed hard-headed and focused, as he told the club's fans, 'We will have to be bold, thoughtful and aggressive in order to do the right thing for the community, for the supporters and for the club long-term.' Liverpool fans would have cause later to remember this claim.

On 3 November 2010, days after the latest international purchase of Liverpool FC had been completed, *The Guardian* carried a telling photograph of John Henry at the Liverpool training ground at Melwood. The new owner, wearing a casual open-necked shirt and owlish dark glasses, was captured walking past the famous bust of Bill Shankly. Behind him, enlarged and clearly visible on the wall, sat a famous quotation from the old Reds manager:

> Above all, I would like to be remembered as a man who was selfless, who strove and worried so that others could share the glory, and who built up a family of people who could hold their heads up high and say: WE ARE LIVERPOOL.

Perhaps the late, great Bill Shankly can be allowed this brief moment of hubris here; not even his greatest supporters, I am sure, would describe the wonderful Scot as *entirely* selfless. But these sentiments were sound and clear enough and they were squarely aimed here at the club's newest corporate owners, after what had been a quite desperate struggle for Anfield survival. These words imply, of course, that one can destroy a facade, dismantle a building, even sell the best assets of a sports business; one can also try to treat a football club as callously and coldly as one might any other commercial venture. But it is much more difficult to kill familial togetherness and the bonds of collective memories around football clubs. Harder still to extinguish an ideology or a way of being, something that seamlessly links generations of working people. In short, and despite all the invidious ambitions of investors who were now operating in elite-level football and elsewhere in sport, it is difficult to slaughter a credo. For these reasons, and despite everything it had been through, the Liverpool Way remained badly bruised but still alive and kicking in 2010. If anything, it may even have been strengthened and reaffirmed by recent events. But could the club's new manager and its owners reverse the slump of 2009/10 and challenge for the league title once more? Good question.

Roy Hodgson's brief fling

Rafa Benitez's last season at Anfield, in 2009/10, had been a hugely difficult one. For much of it, the Liverpool club was effectively up for sale and it seemed an unhappy place to be, one on a downward trajectory with an uncertain future and a reluctant, departing coach. Not a place for top players with ambition, even though Liverpool reached the semi-final of the Europa League. It was in this gloomy climate, under the ownership of Hicks and Gillett that the veteran Englishman, Roy Hodgson, briefly took charge as the new Liverpool boss in June 2010. In part, this made some sense. The well-travelled Hodgson was no simple British meat-and-two-veg merchant; he spoke five languages, had European experience and was a wise, affable old head, if a rather uninspiring one. He had managed in eight countries, including the Swiss national team, and had routinely served as a member on UEFA technical study groups (Bill Shankly would have been suspicious from the start).

Hodgson was clearly an able and respected coach, an experienced British technocrat, and he had even managed to haul modest Fulham to the Europa Cup Final in 2010, probably why Liverpool's new managing director, Christian Purslow, negotiated the appointment. Along, of course, with the fact that Hodgson was unlikely to challenge publicly the policies or practices of his American bosses. His essence was as a deferential and defensive leader and organiser, so he had something in common with the much more capable and more charismatic Rafa Benitez. But, unlike Rafa, Hodgson's record as a proven winner in the more difficult European leagues was questionable, to say the least. All this confirmed that a considerable downgrade was in play – as did Hodgson's early signings. So, too, did his melancholic media style, especially given that a positive public profile was an increasingly required feature of Premier League football club management. Benitez was no genius at it but Hodgson, frankly, was pretty terrible in front of the cameras.

Liverpool fans probably thought, unfairly or not, about their new man as Winston Churchill once did about Clement Atlee. To paraphrase: 'An empty taxi drew up, and Roy Hodgson got out.' But his arrival at Anfield was lauded by a broadsheet national press clearly in thrall to the Fulham man for his urbane decency and as an intellectual English coach with international experience. It was, as *The Guardian* journalist Paul Hayward put it, 'the first step out of the darkness' and a release from the 'creeping joylessness and mechanical pragmatism' that, he argued, was increasingly practised at Anfield under late Benitez. 'High on Hodgson's to-do list,' reasoned Hayward, 'will be to perform expert surgery on a bloated squad.' The British sports media had certainly bought into the Hodgson managerial shtick, and this last point about a necessary clear-out was a reasonable one. Towards the end, Benitez, under the yoke of Hicks and Gillett, *had* seemed obsessed with chancy bargain buys. But could Roy Hodgson do any better? 'From boardroom chaos,' concluded Hayward, 'miraculously, comes an appointment straight out of the old Liverpool school of wisdom.' How crazy this assumption seemed at the time, and how utterly wrongheaded it turned out to be.

Joe Cole, from Chelsea, was perhaps the most intriguing of the new arrivals under Hodgson. Cole was available on a free transfer and, at 28, a four-year deal at £90k a week for a recent England international with some creative skill might have looked plausible, especially given a following wind. Cole also fitted the Hodgson modus operandi of hiring experienced players who needed a refit. But could Joe stay injury-free? (or even *on* the pitch?). Cole got his Anfield career off to an ill-judged start by being red-carded on his Premier League home debut, versus Arsenal. Dogged by injury and poor form thereafter, he made just seven league starts for Hodgson. Cole later blamed FSG for ending his Liverpool options and he was eventually farmed out to French club Lille on loan, his Anfield stay already over.

The Portuguese international midfielder Raul Meireles would slip conveniently into the No. 4 shirt soon to be vacated by another failed late Benitez signing, the high maintenance, overpriced and lightweight midfielder, Alberto Aquilani. The Italian claimed later that managerial changes and injury problems had dogged his Premier League chances. Meireles had some physicality, stamina and a little class and might even have made a decent Liverpool player to help his ailing coach if he had managed to find his goal threat *before* Hodgson left the club. A run of goals in three consecutive Premier League matches in February 2011 – including the winner at Stamford Bridge – signalled these possibilities. But, complaining about unspecified 'broken promises', in September 2011 Meireles moved on to Chelsea and imminent Champions League success.

The journeyman English defender Paul Konchesky followed Hodgson to Anfield from Fulham for a modest fee. Another Londoner, he later complained that Merseyside was 'too small' and was 'controlled' by fans. Konchesky was error-prone and he never convinced as a top-level full-back. Seen as a conduit for his hapless manager, he was soon jeered off by his own supporters in a telling home defeat to Wolves. The Danish midfielder Christian Poulson may once have been able to handle the pace of the English Premier League but palpably not at this advanced stage of his career. Poulson's embarrassing struggles fed bubbling local gossip in pubs and in the stands on Merseyside that the new Liverpool coach was simply not up to the job. The arriving Serbian striker Milan Jovanović at least offered some surface attraction – a free transfer and his record of 52 goals in 116 matches for Standard Liège may have looked impressive on paper but he was hardly still developing his game (he was 29). There were also very good reasons why Jovanović was still plying his trade in Belgium. He barely started a match for his new club. Midfielder Jonjo Shelvey had arrived from Charlton Athletic under Benitez in May 2010 for £1.7m, a talented young prospect and a good passer. But Shelvey was also inconsistent, a young man with a limited football intelligence and a fragile temperament. He was generally ill-equipped, therefore, to learn from his new manager or from the England player he had been brought in to shadow and eventually replace, the hard-to-impress Steve Gerrard.

There seemed no obvious strategy or policy inference in the early Hodgson purchases. Some were cheap panic buys – stopgaps

– players brought in towards the end of their careers as a means of bridging the club through a difficult phase. Perhaps Hodgson thought the approach he had used at Fulham to revitalise dying careers – Hughes, Murphy, Duff and Baird – could work similar magic at Anfield? But the manager soon seemed out of his depth and, of course, he had not been FSG's choice. His general approach seemed at odds with John Henry's stated intentions to build for the longer term while trying to provide the club's fans with a more progressive, forward-thinking style of play. Henry had individual conversations with members of the Liverpool squad in November 2010, saying:

> I've met with a number of our players and had private discussions with some of them. I've been greatly impressed by them, personally. They are all exceptionally bright and they all want to be here. The question they have had, rightfully so, is whether or not the club is going to go in the right direction.

John Henry seemed to find European footballers more interesting than US baseball players, but this question of moving 'in the right direction' was a critical one. Hodgson's first Liverpool selection under Hicks and Gillett in July 2010 had been for the Europa League qualifiers against the mysterious FK Rabotnički from North Macedonia. The fixture was treated like a training-ground run-out, with the selected Liverpool team looking more like a rag-bag of global journeymen and young trialists than it did even a convincing back-up XI from a top-flight Premier League squad: Cavalieri; Kelly, Škrtel, Kyrgiakos, Agger; Aquilani, Lucas, Spearing; Amoo, N'Gog, Jovanović. To be fair, this menagerie was mainly what Hodgson had inherited from Benitez. Save for Škrtel, Agger, Lucas and perhaps local boy Martin Kelly, even committed Liverpool diehards today would probably have trouble ranking many of these guys.

Hodgson also faced Premier League trouble right from the very start. Before the 3-0 trouncing by Manchester City on 23

August, Javier Mascherano, one of the few truly world-class players remaining at the club, delivered a transfer request to escape this rapidly sinking ship. FC Barcelona had been in touch and that was enough. Without the Argentine, from 19 September to 21 October this depleted Liverpool won none of their seven fixtures, against largely unimpressive opponents. By now the rangy, 6ft 3in French striker David N'Gog, signed from France in the scattergun, parsimonious transfer period under Benitez, had started to figure, a precursor to the much superior Divock Origi. N'Gog was a young man with similarly wasteful flaws but without the exceptional goal tally of the Belgian. Sound the alarm: Liverpool briefly languished at 19th in the Premier League table, with a possible relegation struggle not yet off the table.

The FSG takeover now promised to relieve some of this rising pressure, but the club's first match under Hodgson after the sale had been ominous: Everton at Goodison Park, on 17 October 2010. Liverpool supporters hoping for early signs of a new dawn were rudely disturbed by a 2-0 defeat, with the Blues comfortable and quite unruffled. John Henry attended, checking up on his £300m Limey investment. As he left the Goodison directors' box, journalists reported hearing shouts from well-wishing Evertonians of 'I hope you've kept your receipt' (it was never like this at the Red Sox). But worse was immediately to follow. In the post-match press conference at Goodison, Roy Hodgson implied that the possibility of winning under his watch on the rival patch across Stanley Park existed only in his wildest imagination. 'That was as good as we've played all season,' he started out, avidly on the front foot. 'I have no qualms about the performance, whatsoever. To get a result here would have been utopia. But I can only analyse the performance: there is no point in trying to analyse dreams.' There were audible gasps from local journalists at this aside. Here was a Liverpool manager happily eulogising over a derby-day *defeat*. Hodgson might get by in selecting strange formations, in not recognising members of his own staff, or even in bluffing his way through media briefings. But this casual acceptance of a derby-day loss was quite beyond the pale. It was probably the moment when most Liverpool supporters – and the men at FSG – knew that this latest manager would have to go.

The last vestiges of public support for Hodgson from the Kop had seeped away after his 15th match in charge. Several Liverpool fan websites joined forces to publish an on-line November poll of 4,000 supporters, which showed that 95 per cent would like to see the manager removed – immediately. These were the sort of polling figures usually reserved for the return of one-party state politicians. As if this was not enough, the club was fast heading into the sort of psychodrama last seen when Steven Gerrard had been struggling with his own demons and insecurities back in 2005. This time it was Liverpool's erstwhile attacking jewel, Fernando Torres, who had seen enough.

The leaving of Liverpool's No. 9

By now Fernando Torres had become an iconic figure for the club's supporters, a man with his own distinctive song, which even featured in Spanish Nike commercials. But things had changed fast at Anfield. His friends and world-class players – Alonso and Mascherano – had moved to Spain, and his mentor Rafa Benitez was no longer in charge. Some key Hispanic links had been severed and the club was seemingly in a tailspin, despite its ambitious new American owners. Later, Torres told author Simon Hughes, 'By the time I left Liverpool, when everybody was leaving, I did not have the feeling that I was going to win there. It was hard because I had been so happy. I'd never felt happier than during my time at Liverpool. But then I felt betrayed. That's the truth.' Torres said he was reluctantly departing a rudderless ship, a now 'selling' club with absolutely no title pretensions, little prospect of winning trophies or even challenging for those so vital Champions League places.

Torres clearly did not respect the new coach or the club's vision, whatever that now was. Once on the pitch, few professional players refuse to run or chase, compete or try to aid the cause, but Torres increasingly looked entitled and confused, showing no appetite at all for the battle. 'What am I doing here?' his whole on-pitch demeanour screamed. He was clearly disillusioned and he wanted people outside – including potential suitors – to know his feelings. Moreover, he claimed that none of the senior figures at the club could guarantee that Liverpool would soon rise again. Torres was hugely ambitious and he lacked the rooting place ties that had bound Steven Gerrard to Liverpool in 2005 and again in 2009. But Torres also wanted to appease those Liverpool supporters who feared his likely departure. He resented the way the club fed stories to the press that it was the striker who had demanded a transfer and who was set on leaving, even though, broadly speaking, this seemed increasingly to be true. Kenny Dalglish would have to deal with this growing shit-storm when Roy Hodgson was finally dismissed in January 2011. The problem for the incoming Dalglish would be how to 'sell' a Torres transfer to the club's fans. If the adored Spaniard left, who could he possibly get in, at minimal notice, to soften the blow and replace his top striker? Who, indeed?

FSG usually called Roy Hodgson to wish him luck before the club's matches but, as results began to slide late in 2010, even this contact began to wane. Mindful that the manager's unpopularity might soil their own brand, FSG decided to keep their distance and wait until Christmas to make the break, still hopeful that there may be an uplift in Liverpool's form in the meantime. There was, as yet, no chief executive in place at the club to buffer local relationships and FSG risked looking like the inept regime of the previous owners if Hodgson was allowed to bumble on, with Liverpool now locked around 12th place in the league standings and with no coordinating presence in the boardroom.

Roy Hodgson had enough problems on his plate without an authentic local hero, Kenny Dalglish, waiting poised in the wings to take over if things went belly-up. As indeed they royally did. The press release announcing Hodgson's departure said it was by 'mutual consent' and this may well have been true, but a serious pay-off was also in order. Club chairman, FSG's Tom Werner, took time to reflect on a dismal season so far, featuring home defeats to Northampton Town in the League Cup and to lowly Blackpool and Wolves in the Premier League. This was not what the owners had in mind when investing their cash back in October, but action had now been forced upon them. The appointment of Kenny Dalglish as interim manager was a reluctant move. That seemed clear enough: 'Kenny will bring considerable experience to the position and provide management and leadership for the rest of the season,' Werner said through clenched teeth. He was implying, of course, that we had seen little of either in the six months of Roy Hodgson's tenancy.

The ex-Fulham man claimed that Liverpool fans had never been fully behind him, and this may also have been true. But results and performances told their own story. At least Hodgson was spared an embarrassing third round FA Cup defeat at Manchester United – Dalglish would have to field that latest disappointment. Another loss followed immediately in the league, at soon-to-be-relegated Blackpool, an unlikely league double over Liverpool for the Tangerines. But Dalglish was happy to take over; he looked energised and fit, although he had been out of club management for more than a decade since a brief caretaker stint at Celtic. So, it was asking a lot, even for Kenny, to turn this listing tanker around. He brought in ex-Chelsea coach Steve Clarke as his assistant, knowing that FSG were not totally sold on his new appointment but that they needed a quick fix. A new manager's bounce – an eight-match unbeaten run – ensued, including an impressive 3-0 victory at Wolves on 22 January, with two goals from an apparently rejuvenated Fernando Torres. Perhaps the Spaniard already knew what was about to happen next?

Chapter 10

King Kenny to the Rescue (Once Again)

Or what FSG learned about running a top-flight English club

Following the FSG takeover, the new men extend their 'soccer' knowledge and gingerly flex their ownership muscles. There is new talk about the worldwide monetisation of the Liverpool brand. Under interim manager Kenny Dalglish, 'Wor Andy' tries hard and almost rescues the FA Cup. Luis Suárez stars but ends up in racism trouble, a matter very badly handled by the club's manager and board. A trophy is won but King Kenny is soon on the slide, despite his cup success. It is Liverpool's worst top-level league showing, points-wise, since the relegation season of 1953/54. This ain't going to last.

Cleaning out the garbage, bringing in the new

January transfer windows are generally known in the football trade for offering a potential lifeline for clubs in trouble, or poor value for those shopping at the higher end of the market. Who, willingly, sells their best performers in the middle of the season? So, the last-gasp sale by Liverpool of Fernando Torres to Chelsea for a British record £50m fee in January 2011 caused a huge media splash, but it was no real surprise for the people around the Anfield club or to its more perceptive fans. Kenny Dalglish reacted with a terse and pointed statement about how 'movement is part and parcel of football', and that 'the most important people at Liverpool football club are the ones who want to be here'. Ouch.

Anticipating a huge backlash from the supporters as the end of the deadline approached, Liverpool announced not one, but *two*, new signings to replace Torres. One was Luis Suárez, a long-pursued tough and unorthodox Uruguayan forward, currently ruffling defensive feathers and the disciplinary authorities in the Netherlands. The other was the more familiar figure to English eyes of Newcastle United's Andy Carroll, a tall and combative target-man-style centre-forward. This 22-year-old was strong in the air, with underrated quality on his left side on the floor, and Liverpool were desperate to make a statement signing, if only to offset the negative public impact of selling Torres. Price was no object. So, Newcastle squeezed a club record £35m fee out of Anfield for a novice, a young buck with fragility problems who had played just 18 Premier League matches. It felt like (and was) extortion. Neither of these signings actually seemed to be a complete replacement for Torres but each offered something different. Suárez immediately caught the eye for his aggression, work rate and finishing, performing well in tandem with Gerrard, Dirk Kuyt and the Argentine Maxi Rodriguez. Carroll provided different options and a change of playing style, if he was ever to hold his place. Injuries always permitting.

Sod's law meant that Chelsea vs Liverpool followed soon enough after the window had closed. Torres was lured into the usual PR pre-match trap of saying that Chelsea FC were 'on a different level' to Liverpool, and that London offered a 'better lifestyle' than Merseyside. This was too much salt tipped into still open wounds. Ritually enraged, some Liverpool supporters took their kids' No. 9 Torres shirts to Stamford Bridge to burn them or to chuck them at the now rejected ex-Liverpool striker. Effigies had already been torched back on Merseyside. Torres, whose recent Liverpool form had been patchy at best, looked unnerved at facing his recent colleagues and by the hostile reception from those who had so recently loved him. He was substituted before Meireles scored the winning goal for the visitors. It was sweet revenge – of sorts.

On 11 April 2011, a 3-0 Liverpool home win against a rapidly rising Manchester City offered even more promise for the future. Andy Carroll, over his latest injury scare, scored with a conclusive header and a thunderous left-footed drive, all faculties in full working order. It was part of a late flurry of new hope at FSG's Liverpool: smart new owners; a flood of goals and wins; a trusted, familiar manager; exciting new strikers; and an almost respectable sixth-place finish. Mediocrity had been rescued from potential catastrophe in one of the most extraordinary periods of the club's entire history. What lay next in this period of remarkable and convulsive change at Anfield was, as always, an interesting question. The explosive Luis Suárez, a powerful and controversial new presence from Uruguay, promised to have at least some of the answers. And he posed plenty of questions.

The 2011/12 season was Liverpool FC's 50th consecutive in the top flight – and a new beginning. There was a detectable 'can-do' feeling of positivity in and around Anfield once more, with people working for the club reporting a 'friendlier' atmosphere, as well as more direction and greater drive from the top. New Liverpool managing director Ian Ayre insisted that the mere presence of the great Kenny Dalglish in the hot seat once more had instantly lifted the mood, even with no European football. The Scot embodied for Liverpool fans the spirit of Bill Shankly that had been so threatened by the Hicks and Gillett chicanery, and by Roy Hodgson's rather gloomy persona. This sense of moving forward was confirmed when the failing signings brought in by Hodgson – Cole, Konchesky, Poulson and Jovanović among them – all left, along with Greek defender Sotirios Kyrgiakos, forward David N'Gog, and chunky Argentine left-back, Emiliano Insua, who had briefly become a fixture under Rafa Benitez in 2009/10. It signalled something of a cleansing of the stables, with younger, mainly British talent coming in the opposite direction.

The new men included Jordan Henderson, a raw but enthusiastic 20-year-old attacking midfielder from Sunderland, and there was a pre-season first look at a precocious 18-year-old academy defensive midfielder, Conor Coady, his name erroneously inked in for a post-Steven Gerrard Anfield future. Henderson may have been a US-inspired moneyball signing: rely on the analytics, buy players who are young and ambitious, embed and increase their sell-on value. He lacked experience and finesse but Henderson was reliable and durable, featuring in 48 out of 51 Liverpool matches in 2011/12, more than any other player. Local lad, Jon Flanagan, had also begun forcing his way into the argument about the first-team right-back slot held by Benitez signing Glen Johnson, but more for his defensive bite than any obvious creativity or skill. Left-footed wide England attacker Stewart Downing was signed from Aston Villa for £20m to provide the aerial ammunition 'wor Andy' would need to survive as Liverpool's new target man. Club historians had the usual warning here: Liverpool's last true forward bruiser, Tony Hateley, scored 27 goals in 1967/68 but he was ruining the Liverpool style of play. He lasted one season.

Continuity was provided by a core of familiar and trusted faces: Pepe Reina, Jamie Carragher, Daniel Agger, Lucas Leiva, Dirk Kuyt and Steven Gerrard all remained. But the left-footed, one-paced Scot, Charlie Adam, was signed from relegated Blackpool, ostensibly to provide creativity on the Liverpool left side to complement Henderson's running and enthusiasm on the right. This 4-4-2 version of Liverpool, with the untried partnership of Suárez and Carroll up front, generally looked as if it might be short on pace and limited in width and hard yards. This was despite the arrival of an erratic but game left-back from

Newcastle United, the Spaniard Jose Enrique, and the late return of veteran winger Craig Bellamy as a free agent. The Liverpool squad certainly lacked the gas that was being shown by a Jamaican-born London teenage kid, who had been signed from QPR by the academy director Frank McParland in February 2010 for an initial fee of £450,000. This would soon look like giveaway money because this tough little flying machine was already ripping it up for the youth team in Kirkby. But in August 2011 Raheem Sterling was still a little way off the Liverpool first-team squad.

Steven Gerrard was missing, too, nursing a groin injury since April, but most of this new intake played in a troubling 1-1 opening home league draw with Sunderland – only four players had survived from Roy Hodgson's starting line-up just a year earlier. Had there ever been a more rapid turnover at Anfield? Nevertheless, few problems seem to have been solved by these extensive changes. Suárez excited and he scored goals, but his pairing with Carroll looked both forced and awkward. The season began with a curious mixture of victories and defeats: a promising 2-0 win at Arsenal, Suárez scoring again, was soon followed by a 4-0 trouncing at Spurs, with two Liverpool players, the ponderous Adam and makeshift right-back Martin Škrtel, sent off. Another red card, at Goodison, this time a harsh one for Everton's Jack Rodwell in a 2-0 Liverpool win, made the rather erratic early season form of Dalglish's teams difficult to read. Other statistics were perhaps more telling: in Liverpool's first 100 years of existence, 38 players had been dismissed; in the 19 years since, 58 had gone the same way. The game and its officials had changed.

John Henry in charge

The very concept of red and yellow cards was probably a mystery to John Henry and his colleagues from FSG, who had watched the Reds' limp capitulation at Spurs on TV in a Boston hotel room with sports journalist David Conn from *The Guardian*. Although the FSG men were impressed by exactly how *far* this big lump

Carroll could head a football, Henry acknowledged that, as a 60-year-old lifelong fan of American sports, he knew 'virtually nothing' about Liverpool Football Club or the Premier League before buying into the English game. His real love was baseball. He had grown up with an ill father on an isolated Arkansas farm, where listening to St Louis Cardinals' games on the radio provided romance, solace and escape. Later, Henry played in rock bands and even experimented for a time as a professional gambler in Las Vegas. He was not afraid of risk or making big decisions.

His interest in Liverpool FC had been kindled by an email about the club's dire condition but strong commercial prospects, from an FSG employee and Liverpool fan, Joe Januszewski. This simple connection prompted a meeting with Inner Circle, a US merchant bank that had brokered previous investment deals in European sport, including in the Premier League. There were positive vibes. The fact that Premier League clubs kept their own income from sponsorships and other sources immediately appealed to FSG – in USA sport a central cash store is often generated before being divided between competing sporting franchises.

Fenway executives also got excited when they reflected that the audience outside the USA for the bore-fest NFL Superbowl spectacular was around 50 million; Liverpool vs Manchester United alone attracted more. The Premier League claimed a cumulative worldwide audience of some three billion. Henry was astute in his early interviews in talking about Liverpool FC's global reach and the club's 'incredible' fan base. He clearly recognised the importance of getting supporters onside after the torturous relations of the past few years (he may have forgotten his own lesson in 2021). Henry also admitted that he thought it a gamble to bring back Kenny Dalglish after his extended period out of management. Inexplicably, FSG had wanted to continue with Roy Hodgson but had then been swayed by the sheer negativity of Liverpool supporters and the vocal support for their Scottish hero. One sensed already that Kenny would not get long to prove his worth. It was also clear that buying into English football made sound business sense, even for American investors who were pretty clueless about what the sport meant to the people who watched it. Ed Weiss, Fenway's in-house lawyer, for example, explained the core of Liverpool FC's appeal to the FSG group in typical international business-speak:

> So much internet clutter competes for mindshare now. Big sports clubs are one of the few things which can cut through and capture mindshare. The Liverpool numbers blew us away. We believe there is a significant amount of monetisation we can do, on a worldwide basis, which is not occurring now.

Talk about global 'mindshare' and the value of 'monetisation' may not have impressed Liverpool fans still trying to come to terms with Kenny Dalglish's new playing strategies (would this kind of discussion make Andy Carroll look any less immobile?). But the seductions of 'soccer', with its global markets and with UEFA's new Financial Fair Play regulations now in place, had been made very clear to the 19 FSG partners. Talk was already afoot, too, about stadium redevelopment, but the Americans felt hemmed in by the English urban landscape, not least the residential communities clasped tightly around Anfield. The new owners seemed pretty clear that a potential stadium share with Everton was now out of the question, which also meant the costs of building an entirely new ground on Stanley Park would prove prohibitive. The successful FSG regeneration of the historic Fenway Park in Boston was a useful guide to the future: the redevelopment of Anfield, with more seats aimed at cash-rich hospitality clients, rather than relocation, was now the likeliest outcome.

Swimming against the tide

'The very serious function of racism is distraction. It keeps you from doing your work.' Toni Morrison

Defeating Everton at Goodison in October 2011 came near the start of a Liverpool run of one loss in 17 matches in all competitions, but six draws (four at home) and a struggle to score goals clouded any notion of a convincing recovery for Dalglish. The run ended with a comprehensive 3-0 defeat at Manchester City, as Yaya Touré and Sergio Agüero dismantled their visitors. Much more of this lay ahead for Liverpool at the Etihad. But a bigger story was brewing here, involving new man Luis Suárez. He had been player of the tournament at the 2011 Copa América, so it looked as if Liverpool had made a stellar signing at a relatively knock-down (reported £22.8m) price from Ajax. But the effervescent Uruguayan was struggling to find his best form and to curb his temperament in England. Tiredness may have been an issue. Suárez had been a free-scoring force in the Netherlands but one with serious disciplinary issues, collecting sheaves of yellow cards and the occasional red. He was also accused by rivals in the Netherlands of being a master simulator – a diver. His greatest asset was as an irrepressible dribbler and provocateur, the ball often bobbling off opponents, invariably back into his path. He was a smart finisher and a man never to be discouraged or bounced off the ball by a bigger defender. In a stronger, front-footed team with real quality and pace alongside him, it was clear that Suárez could be a major force.

But this was not yet *that* Liverpool team. His volatility first emerged at home to Manchester United on 15 October 2011, in a 1-1 draw. Awaiting a corner, Suárez was involved in an aggressive verbal exchange with United's French full-back Patrice Evra directly in front of the Kop. It looked inconsequential but the affair ended up with accusations of racism levelled against the Uruguayan. The FA was (quite rightly) on high alert for racist abuse – England captain John Terry would soon be in the dock – so the Suárez incident was investigated with unusually forensic intensity, eventually producing a 117-page report. Included here was work by specialists on cultural differences in the use of language in South America – *negro/negrita/negrito* – to describe people of different ethnic origins. Suárez protested his innocence on the grounds of cultural difference and he may have been used as a convenient example – an overseas scapegoat – but he was found guilty in the inquiry that followed. The FA imposed a £40,000 fine and a weighty eight-match ban. This might have been the end of the matter, a serious but not fatal blow for a player moving towards his best work in a rather ordinary Liverpool team. However, the Liverpool players had worn pro-Suárez T-shirts while warming up before an away fixture at Wigan Athletic in December. It became a front-page story. To pour further petrol on the fire, the squad now issued a corroborating statement:

> We totally support Luis, and we want the world to know that. We know he is not racist. We have lived, trained and played with Luis for almost 12 months and we don't recognise the way he has been portrayed. We will continue to support Luis through this difficult period, and, as a popular and respected friend of all his team-mates, he will not walk alone.

The last clause was a nice Liverpool touch from whoever in the Anfield media offices had produced this red rag. The sophistry about whether Suárez was a racist, or unintentionally guilty of a racist act, would play out for some time to come, but this story was now back in the headlines. Ex-Red John Barnes sagely suggested to *Channel 4 News* that pragmatism would win out in the end: 'Even if Suárez is 100 per cent guilty, and Suárez scores 50 goals this season and they win the league and they win the cup, that's showbusiness. So, ultimately, that is all that matters.' Later, Kenny Dalglish foolishly told talkSPORT radio that 'truth' had been mangled in the case and that he would probably withhold his cooperation in future inquiries. 'It might have been misguided and not have been right,' he said about the T-shirts, 'but it was not me who decided it.' It was a weak and ill-judged defence from a highly respected, experienced and much-loved club icon.

Kenny was out of his depth on this particular issue but there was some mitigation. First, the lack of effective executive leadership at Anfield, given its absent American owners; second, misplaced loyalty to a valuable team-mate on behalf of the players under attack from outsiders; third, ill-informed misjudgement from a coach protecting a prime asset; and, finally, the routine underplaying of racism as a poisonous issue in the British game. It was probably a combination of all these things. You can, arguably, add another associated element: the expressed views of many Liverpool fans that Suárez had indeed been set up and that he should be defended at all costs by the club against a specious, unprovable charge.

Liverpool supporter websites soon proclaimed that Luis Suárez was the subject of a witch hunt mired in some 'he said, she said' uncertainties. Some Liverpool fans even blamed United and Patrice Evra for the whole sorry affair. Meanwhile, the episode continued to seriously damage Liverpool morally and in PR terms. When the clubs next met, Suárez practised some naïve adolescent handshake avoidance with Evra in the pre-match rituals. Despite Ian Ayre's later grudging acceptance that Liverpool should have handled things differently, from the key people in the USA there came precisely … silence. When he was eventually sacked in May 2012, Kenny Dalglish was forced to deny that his inept handling of the racism row had helped cost him his job. Who knows the truth of this? He certainly looked out of step with the times – his club was, too – but what was also clear was that the Scot had been allowed to make some serious mistakes in a volatile climate and that he had received little guidance or support from his employers from across the pond.

Cup compensations

Luis Suárez was now benched for a thrilling Liverpool 2-0 win at Chelsea in the League Cup in November, and then missed both legs of the semi-final clash in the new year with league leaders Manchester City after another suspension. Liverpool defended positively and in strength at the Etihad for a 1-0 win, a Steven Gerrard penalty. At home, with neither Carroll nor the banished Suárez in the team and twice behind, with Joe Hart in outstanding form, it was Kuyt and Bellamy who provided much-needed fluidity and pace up front. The latter scored the decisive equalising goal for a well-deserved (and victorious) 2-2 draw. Three days later, on 28 January, Manchester United were satisfyingly put to the sword at Anfield in the FA Cup fourth round. A restored Andy Carroll headed on to pave the way for Dirk Kuyt's late winner. This was how it was supposed to be: the Big Man firing, an early cup final sorted and despised regional rivals sent packing.

In the stands, meanwhile, Luis Suárez celebrated this United defeat wildly, like any other Liverpool fan might. It had been a difficult period for the leaders in the Liverpool dressing room but this was Kenny Dalglish's best work on the pitch in his latest bout of Anfield management. It looked like a potential repeat of Liverpool's early 2000s cup successes in Cardiff under Gérard Houllier. A decade on, the club had eyes on possibly *two* domestic cup finals and Liverpool were back at Wembley Stadium for the first time since that doomed white suit affair of 1996. Things, at last, were looking up. Indeed, if the main function of any football club is to challenge for trophies, then Kenny Dalglish could rightly claim to be active in two of the three competitions the club had available back in August 2011. The third and the most important – the Premier League – was proving much more taxing.

The League Cup Final at the end of February 2012, pitting Liverpool against First Division (Championship) Cardiff City, was a chance to demonstrate Kenny Dalglish's management skills, but instead it became a trial. Liverpool won only after falling behind, going ahead, conceding an equaliser in extra time and then missing the first two kicks in the resulting penalty shoot-out. It was a coruscating, draining experience for any Reds fan present. A welcome trophy, perhaps, but one won without honour. It also came in the middle of a wider playing slump, because between 11 February and 1 April 2012 Liverpool lost six out of seven Premier League fixtures, beating Everton in the other. The final tally in the Premier League would show a ruinously average season: won 14, drawn 10, lost 14. A finish of eighth, behind Everton and level on 52 points with Roy Hodgson's old club, Fulham. It was Liverpool's worst top-level league showing, points-wise, since the relegation season of 1953/54, and an unforgiving 37 points behind the emerging petro-cash-fuelled champions, Manchester City.

But in the FA Cup in 2012 there was a very different narrative in play. Liverpool saw off Oldham Athletic, Manchester United, Brighton and Stoke City, all at home, before facing a semi-final against Everton, at Wembley. A derby *semi*-final at Wembley was still a novelty to everyone on Merseyside, the price paid by fans everywhere for the costly reconfiguration of the national stadium. It was a rousing affair in an impressive setting, decided, after an early Everton lead, by Sylvain Distin's loss of concentration snaffled up by Luis Suárez, and Andy Carroll's irresistible late header. These two slightly ill-fitting replacements for Fernando Torres – who was still struggling at Chelsea – had delivered on the big stage.

The final against Chelsea was a very different, frustrating affair. Played disrespectfully on a Saturday evening after Premier League matches had already been staged, Kuyt and Carroll were left on the bench, with academy product Jay Spearing brought in to shore up the Liverpool midfield. It looked like a timid defensive Liverpool formation, while Torres was again out of the Chelsea squad. Mistakes by Spearing and Reina gave a dominant Chelsea a one-goal early lead, backed up, inevitably it seemed, by a second from Drogba early in the second half. Liverpool made little impression until Carroll, on as substitute, scored and then had a brutal late header miraculously saved by Petr Cech – it may even have been over the goal line. But it was all too little, too late. Liverpool's record in FA Cup finals now read an unimpressive played 14, won seven. Poor team selection, or a predictable loss to a stronger outfit? Take your pick, probably a combination of the two. More symbolic hurt was to follow when, improbably, Chelsea won the Champions League crown in Munich in the most unlikely of circumstances, with Fernando Torres claiming his second major medal – from the bench.

It was tough, of course, for FSG in the summer of 2012 to dispense with the services of one of the club's greatest-ever servants, particularly after two cup final appearances. After all, Kenny Dalglish had been placed in an impossible position in January by the Fernando Torres affair and his team had recovered well in some respects, even if its new forward formations seemed forced and improbable. But whatever the Wembley outcome had been, Dalglish's fate was probably already sealed by his rather traditional British approach to football management in the era of science and data analysis, and especially by his failure to even hint at qualifying for the Champions League places, on the back of just six home league wins.

Liverpool's director of football, Damien Comolli, had left the club in April, later bizarrely blaming his own sacking on the £16m signing of Jordan Henderson. The departing Dalglish spoke honestly as a football man – and a fan – when he confessed, 'I am disappointed with results in the league, but I would not have swapped the Carling Cup win for anything.' However, one thing was clear: his bosses FSG sure knew now where the money and the futures market lay in the English game, and it was not in winning the domestic League Cup.

Chapter 11

'Lucho' and the Man with the Silver Shovel

How Luis Suárez and Brendan Rodgers almost wowed the Kop

Brendan Rodgers takes over and reluctantly stars on American TV. He also tries very hard to give Jordan Henderson away. A January transfer window sets up a plausible title challenge, but can Luis just keep his biting habit in check? Liverpool score at will but concede freely, too. Cruelly, THAT slip, and Mourinho's black arts, steal away the 2014 title in sight of the line. An undeserved but irrelevant outcome ensues at the Palace. A new Main Stand is proudly on show at Anfield but Mario Balotelli fails to stir the savvy patrons. Liverpool's triple-S frontline also goes missing. Steven Gerrard's stellar Liverpool career has an inglorious end in the Potteries. Brendan Rodgers's Anfield project has run its course.

The man with the silver shovel

As the London Olympics and the football Euros loomed in the summer of 2012, journalist Andy Hunter from *The Guardian* fielded on-line questions from Liverpool fans about a potential successor to Kenny Dalglish. Guardiola, Capello, Benitez, Villas-Boas and Roberto Martinez of Wigan Athletic were all in the frame according to the press and to his inquisitors. 'What about Dortmund's Jürgen Klopp?' one contributor asked. Hunter paused and then replied, 'Klopp would be one to captivate Liverpool and would show the ambition and the attraction of the club remains, what its supporters expect.' But he also warned about the problem of extracting Klopp from Germany. Hunter agreed that FSG must recruit a modern, younger coach and put an entirely new management structure in place, one that could serve the club for the long term by filling all the positions that FSG had made vacant in recent weeks. Ian Cotton, director of communications for 16 years and Peter Brukner, head of sports medicine and sports science, had been recent departures. It felt like an administrative and football clear-out and the real beginning of FSG's reign at Anfield. The Americans now appointed Jen Chang as Anfield director of communications, who was then a senior editor at *Sports Illustrated* and a man who covered US soccer for ESPN.com. It looked like a left-field choice of convenience. Chang lasted barely a few months, sacked following a public spat with a spoof fan blogger who claimed to have inside information about the club's transfer dealings. It was an inept and embarrassing start to FSG's reconstruction.

Managing director, Ian Ayre, claimed that the selection of Dalglish's successor was 'the most critical decision in the club's recent history'. All managerial appointments are 'critical', of course, but here Ayre perhaps had a point. The director of football role was to be fragmented in a new structure, although the new manager would continue to have a major influence on transfers. Liverpool faced a third season outside the Champions League and UEFA's Financial Fair Play rules were due to kick in during

2013/14, meaning the Anfield club simply had to get back into the European game's elite group. It could not risk falling further behind the new powerhouses of the English game.

For a while, Roberto Martinez (Wigan Athletic, 15th in the Premier League) looked set for the job; he had reportedly met in the USA with John Henry, and his chairman Dave Whelan even told Sky Sports that Martinez had been offered the post. Untrue. Instead, Liverpool revealed the Northern Irishman Brendan Rodgers (Swansea City, 11th in the Premier League) as their new boss and the club's 18th manager. Rodgers had no big-club experience but he was widely praised as a gifted young British coach. Swansea had embarrassed, outplayed and outpassed Dalglish's Liverpool at Anfield earlier in the season, the elfin-like Joe Allen running the game from midfield. The visitors were applauded off by the Kop for their 0-0 draw and the impression had lingered. Rodgers played hard to get by resisting being part of a group of prospective coaches who were formally interviewed by Liverpool. Instead, he waited for an offer – and eventually one came.

As a player at Reading, Rodgers had been injured out of the professional game at 20, so he had moved early into non-league play and coaching, eventually becoming the academy director at the Berkshire club. He travelled around Spain to improve his languages and coaching knowledge. Steve Clarke, then coaching at Chelsea, convinced Jose Mourinho in 2004 to invite Rodgers to come on board as head youth coach. He duly impressed and was promoted two years later to youth team manager, but then left Chelsea in 2008 to join Watford in the Championship as manager. After a difficult start, Rodgers stabilised and remodelled Watford and got them playing, but he was soon lured back to Reading to take the manager's job there. It was a move fraught with anger and charges of deceit by Watford officials and fans, to the extent that Rodgers hired bodyguards for when the two clubs next met. Maybe it was just bad karma, but he failed at Reading and was duly sacked in December 2009. Supporters later complained about

Rodgers's 'death by boredom' philosophy of a possession-based style of play, as Royals players 'tippy-tappied' the ball around before losing it. 'The only excitement,' one supporter recalled later, 'was the fear caused by the inevitable opposition attacks and goals.' Rodgers admitted that he had tried to impose a short-passing playing style on a group of players who were unsuited to reproducing it, a useful lesson.

At Swansea City in 2010, Rodgers found a very positive connection with the club chairman, Huw Jenkins, and a better tactical fit with the superior players he had in South Wales. He built his success around the defensive solidity of Welsh international Ashley Williams, but more emphatically on his midfield trio of ex-West Ham man Leon Britton, the 'Welsh Pirlo' Joe Allen, and the on-loan Icelandic international Gylfi Sigurdsson, who Rodgers had worked with at Reading. All three were comfortable on the ball and had excellent technique, movement and passing ability. They were at their collective best when 'playing through' the opposition. This approach, although easy on the eye, did not necessarily produce a harvest of goals – 44 from 38 league matches – but given the presence of Luis Suárez and the resources to attract other top-level strikers, it might show dividends at Liverpool. Few people in and around the club, in any case, were likely to be complaining about the quality of the build-up play under their new coach and his assistant manager Colin Pascoe.

Tom Werner, at the modest press conference called on 1 June 2012 to announce the new man's arrival, said that Rodgers was a motivator and technician, someone who was intelligent and would bring 'attacking, relentless football' back to Anfield. It would certainly be a sophisticated, possession-based brand of the game. Werner also name-checked Rodgers's (limited) European experiences and that the new man spoke Spanish and had been recruited as a coach at Chelsea under Mourinho, currently the English game's new gold standard. Rodgers was turned out for the conference in a club suit and tie, like a junior clerk, but he batted away questions about his young age for the job – 39 – by pointing to Kenny Dalglish's success as a player-manager at Liverpool at just 34. He also emphasised his 20 years of coaching experience in the professional game, including four at Chelsea. He was young in age but not, he insisted, in the necessary football heft to take on this formidable task. He recognised Liverpool's 'frustration' about the present – more than 20 years now without a league title – as both a challenge and an attraction.

Rodgers spoke well, if rather conservatively, and the whole event was a decidedly low-key affair for such a major job at a club of this stature. Rodgers spoke to journalists later of his social class credentials for the Liverpool post; his father had been a painter-decorator in the seaside village of Carnlough. Rodgers said that he had been born with a silver shovel in his hand for hard work, not a silver spoon in his mouth. It was a nice touch and a decent line for the press boys. Rodgers defined his new club by its 'offensive, attractive football, but with tactical discipline'. A coach's way of saying get forward when you can but do not leave yourself open at the back. Good advice. We would have to wait to see whether he could follow it in the hothouse of Anfield.

Being Liverpool

Another Liverpool clear-out was in order in the summer of 2012, the price of recruiting three managers in quick succession, all with different philosophies, all wielding chequebooks. Dirk Kuyt left after six years of excellent service, and so too did Aurelio, Maxi Rodriguez and Craig Bellamy, the latter after a brief but entertaining career reprise. Charlie Adam was quickly discarded for half his purchase price, as was the unfortunate Andy Carroll, who had ricocheted from record Liverpool signing to on-loan outcast at West Ham in the space of just 18 months. In came Fabio Borini, a more mobile young striker from Roma, and the 22-year-old Joe Allen, the new coach's comfort blanket from Swansea City. Gylfi Sigurdsson might have arrived, too, had a deal been possible with his owner club, Hoffenheim. As Carroll left, Rodgers needed to add to the club's forward options and he decided, very late in the day, that Fulham's experienced journeyman American striker, Clint Dempsey, was the best available buy in a weak market. But FSG, perhaps mindful of the wastage of last season's transfer expenditure, baulked at a £6m fee for a 29-year-old with no sell-on value. The Americans wanted Rodgers to sign Manchester City's under-exposed Daniel Sturridge instead.

Desperate, and on the last day of trading, Rodgers panicked and offered Liverpool's recent signing Jordan Henderson to Fulham as part of a trade for Dempsey. Henderson got the news while preparing for a match and cried in his hotel room; he felt written off, devalued and in danger of being cast aside for the sake of a quick fix. But he refused to go, telling Rodgers that he wanted to stay to fight for his place. His decision and bravery may well have saved the rookie manager his job and Henderson an outstanding club and international career. But without a forward replacement, Liverpool would now be reliant for back-up on the injury-prone, untried Italian forward Borini.

Rodgers had the added burden in his first Liverpool season of an 'insider' TV documentary *Being Liverpool* being made with full support from FSG about the forthcoming campaign, for Fox Soccer TV. Woodenly narrated by actor and Liverpool fan, Clive Owen, and featuring supporter-poet Dave Kirby and a cast of other Scousers as a Greek chorus, it was obviously aimed by the new owners at achieving some kind of exposure and commercial synergy with the American market. For US viewers, Liverpool's playing kit was their 'uniform', Melwood was described as Liverpool's 'practice headquarters' and a new Disney-lite club mascot, Mighty Red, got a first (largely unwelcome) outing. The series started with some toe-curling intrusions into the home lives of the manager and some of his key players, including the South Americans. They had recently been boosted by the arrival of young Uruguayan centre-back, Sebastian Coates, from Luis Suárez's old club Nacional, a possible long-term candidate to replace Jamie Carragher, now coming to the end of his 660-plus game, one-club Liverpool career. Coates's current job was much simpler: to make sure that hot property Luis Suárez and his family felt at home on Merseyside.

Being Liverpool's early focus was also on Brendan Rodgers as a new, young hands-on coach, someone working hard, pre-season, with younger players in a familiarisation project about the mental side of the game. This included a rather humiliating and very public lecture in a USA training camp about 'attitude' and discipline for the emerging 17-year-old prospect Raheem Sterling, an episode that would come back later to challenge Rodgers and the Liverpool hierarchy. Back in the UK, and in a weird piece of reverse-psychology hokum during an evening's tactical briefing before the season's opener proper at West Bromwich Albion, Rodgers was also shown on camera holding up three envelopes, which, he claimed, contained the names of three players who would let the Anfield group down this season because 'they fight everything'. As it turned out, *any* three Liverpool players could have been chosen for those envelopes from the West Brom performance. The new Rodgers era started very badly indeed.

Liverpool, playing a possession-based 4-2-3-1 system, conceded a first-half wonder goal from the Hungarian Zoltán Gera and also two penalties, with Daniel Agger sent off in a chastening 3-0 defeat. Albion would go on to do the league double over Rodgers's embryonic new project. Filmed in the dressing room later, the manager was very controlled and low key in his message to the players. He talked about 'unwarranted' penalties and an 'unjustified' red card, and ended with a slightly chilling 'everyone is out to kill us' message. A 2-2 home draw with champions Manchester City – which should have been a Liverpool win – was much more encouraging, but early home defeats to Arsenal and Manchester United hardly lifted the local mood.

Nevertheless, Liverpool *were* playing differently, showing more invention, control and a better attacking shape than under Dalglish. A first real sign of what might still be possible came at Norwich City in late September with Luis Suárez, at his impish best, pickpocketing defenders and finishing clinically in a 5-2 win. Those canary yellow shirts seemed to irritate the Uruguayan; two hat-tricks, 12 goals in six meetings. Another early irritant was the Everton manager David Moyes. In a 2-2 draw at Goodison in October, Suárez's goal celebration included a very public illustrative response to accusations from Moyes that the Uruguayan was a diver. More headlines followed. With Suárez around, this period would never be dull. Rodgers's first season – like Suárez's intervention here – proved entertaining but inconclusive. However, two January signings would end up changing the entire complexion of his Liverpool adventure.

Birmingham-born Daniel Sturridge had been noted at the Manchester City youth set-up as a future star and at 16 years of age he featured against Liverpool in a losing 2006 FA Youth Cup Final, scoring two goals. Those of us present that night could see that he was a top prospect, a much-talked-about future full international. After a handful of first-team appearances, this uber-ambitious 19-year-old left City for Chelsea in 2009 on a tribunal fee after the Manchester club conceded that they were 'staggered' at his £55,000 per week wage demands. At Chelsea, Sturridge played rarely for the first team. The word in coaching circles was that he had talent but was ill-disciplined and lazy, a poor defender from the front. He also wanted to play as a central striker at the Bridge, a position where Didier Drogba was the Chelsea king. Ironically, the signing of Fernando Torres from Liverpool probably confirmed Sturridge's fate in west London. But he at least made the bench for the 2012 FA Cup and Champions League finals, although he never got on the pitch.

Frustrated at the lack of first-team opportunities, Sturridge now looked to one of his old coaches at Chelsea, Brendan Rodgers, to rescue him from what appeared to be a potential downward spiral. Rodgers had actually known Sturridge from 12 years of age at Coventry. He thought the striker had been in wrong places at wrong times and that he required trust and nurturing to show his true quality. In an interview with *GQ* magazine soon after, Sturridge said that he modelled his game on 'foreign' players and on the influence gained from playing informally with mates. 'Guys that don't make it,' he said, 'are probably more technical than ones that do make it. I learned most of my skills from playing on the streets.' He certainly had not been over-coached, because Sturridge could find space and score goals at ease, especially on his left side, and from almost any angle. But he was now 23 years old with few suitors and little first-team experience. Still uncertain, Rodgers told Sturridge that this was his last chance to succeed at the highest level. It looked like a £12m punt.

By the age of 20, the Brazilian Philippe Coutinho had already played under two top European coaches who would make their name mainly in England: Claudio Ranieri at Inter Milan, and on loan with a young Mauricio Pochettino at Espanyol. Shortly after he was sacked by Inter in December 2010, another respected coach, Rafa Benitez, had phoned Frank McPartland, head of Liverpool's academy, to catch up. Benitez raved about Coutinho and told McPartland that Inter did not see the youngster's real potential. By 2012 Andrea Stramaccioni had taken over from Ranieri as coach at Inter and the Milan-based club needed to raise funds to sign Mateo Kovačić from Real Madrid. The new coach could find no place in his team for this lightweight Brazilian. Was he a midfielder or a wide player? Coutinho showed up well in training in Italy but he had problems with the pressure of first-team play.

The young attacker certainly fitted Brendan Rodgers's plans – he was similar in playing style to Nathan Dyer, a key man for the coach at Swansea City – and he also suited FSG's new transfer policy of targeting, wherever possible, players aged 20 or under who cost less than €10m. Southampton, now managed by Pochettino, had an offer of £10.2m in instalments accepted by Inter but, knowing the player favoured the higher wages at Anfield, Liverpool's muscle memory produced a cash bid of £8m upfront – and they waited. Coutinho finally signed for £8.5m in a transfer described by Inter Milan's sporting director, Piero Ausilio, as 'the greatest regret' in his 20 years' experience in the game.

But could Coutinho cope with the greater pressure and physicality of first-team football in England? He had quick feet and a good finish, sure, but he struggled initially at Anfield, overwhelmed by the sheer relentlessness and pace of England compared to what he had known in Brazil, Italy and Spain. He was very young but he could go one of two ways: either ape the overpowered Italian, Aquilani, and disappear; or else he might adapt and possibly make a Liverpool name for himself, as Suárez seemed to be doing. In fact, Coutinho became a key figure in Brendan Rodgers's bold attempt at winning a Premier League title.

Liverpool certainly needed a boost right now, because Rodgers experienced his first semi-serious crisis as Liverpool manager in late January 2013, when a strong team (one containing Suárez as captain and Gerrard from the bench) went down 3-2 at lowly League One outfit Oldham Athletic in the FA Cup fourth round. For we travelling fans, the Neanderthal policing and shambolic state of Boundary Park was a stark reminder of pre-Premier League days. On the pitch, it was a lifeless and spineless show by Liverpool, one worthy of the Roy Hodgson era; a real leadership void and a loud wake-up call. There had been some promise shown elsewhere but this was still an immature, incomplete Liverpool squad. However, things would improve now in the league, only one defeat in 12, from 17 February until the end of the season, although it was also a run littered with frustrating draws. In the Europa League, meanwhile, after stumbling through qualifying rounds, the Reds scraped through the group stage before succumbing 2-0 to Zenit in the first leg of the last 32 in a freezing St Petersburg. Those of us among the 800 Reds fans who travelled to Russia were greeted by hostile natives and 2,000 police, only to see Luis Suárez inexplicably squander a litany of chances. A dominant 3-1 second leg win at Anfield was just not enough to retrieve the tie.

313

As the season meandered to a close, Liverpool's battling 2-2 home draw with Chelsea on 21 April was broadly indicative of Rodgers's squad and his thinking towards the end of his first season in charge: Reina in goal; Johnson, Carragher, Agger and Enrique (although Škrtel increasingly, and also Flanagan and Martin Kelly, pushing for places) in defence; Gerrard, Lucas and Henderson (with Jonjo Shelvey and Allen also involved) in midfield; Coutinho, Suárez and Downing (but with Sterling, Sturridge and Borini – when fit – increasingly figuring) up front. The favoured system was either 4-3-3 or 4-2-3-1. It looked, and felt, more fluid and more attack-minded than the teams under Dalglish, and much stronger and pacier in wider areas than those under Hodgson. There were still problems, of course: Pepe Reina had started to leak goals low down at his near post; both Agger and Carragher were close to the end of their Anfield careers; Sterling routinely gave the ball away but he was also powerful and elusive – and still *so* young. Coutinho and Sturridge had started very raw but now they were finding their feet and showing some real quality. Jordan Henderson was also coming on strong in midfield. One week after the Chelsea home draw, a similar Liverpool team casually put six goals, with no reply, on Newcastle United – *away* from home. It was a stunning display. For all this collective promise, however, it was also becoming crystal clear that Liverpool's game plan under Brendan Rodgers, the reason why they might even be placed to launch a title bid at last, revolved mainly around the tenacity and brilliance of one man, Luis Suárez. He was frightening every defender he faced with his dogged, aggressive persistence and sheer will to win. It was Suárez who had scored Liverpool's very late equaliser against Chelsea. But that goal was not what people would remember most from Luis Suárez vs Chelsea in April 2013. Not for one second.

The wild man of Uruguay

Uruguay's great football heritage was built on the back of waves of migration from Brazil, Italy and Spain between the mid-19th century and 1920 and, historically, the sport remained available for all social classes and ethnicities, a way of defining and producing this emerging multiracial nation. Its football history and small population size today (3.5m people) still feeds the 'warrior' sensibilities of Uruguay's elite footballers, the legend of the *garra charrua*, the native Charruan fighting spirit. This David vs Goliath mythology and patriotism runs through Uruguayan male culture. As 1950 World Cup-winning captain Obdulio Varela put it, 'With Uruguay in our hearts we are at least twice the men we normally are.'

Like most Uruguayan boys, in his home town of Salto Luis Suárez had played 'baby' football in mini-teams for four- to six-year-olds, but when he was seven his impoverished military family moved to Montevideo. His father left the army to work in a biscuit factory, his mother was a cleaner. When his parents divorced in 1996, life for Luis and his brothers became harder still. But at 12, little Luis was recruited by his local club Nacional, where his early coaches could not decide whether he was clumsy, lucky or simply inspired, as he stumbled through challenges to score goals. They had no doubt that he wanted to win. As his biographer Luca Caoili later recalled, at 15 and playing in an important match for Nacional, Suárez got so frustrated at a refereeing decision that he head-butted the official. Even now it was clear that Suárez, or 'Lucho', had both talent and demons. In Nacional's youth teams, his sheer desire to win made him snatch at easy chances, a problem that persisted into the first team, where his own fans sometimes jeered his panicky early efforts to score. But as he settled, he did score goals and he learned well the other necessities of how to survive as a striker in elite football in Uruguay; by showing skill and courage, but also by diving, faking injuries, protesting and goading both referees and opponents.

In 2006 FC Groningen of the Netherlands scouted Suárez and eventually agreed on a £1m fee to bring the 19-year-old to Europe. His new team-mates were initially unimpressed: Lucho was overweight, technically poor and a complainer in training.

But then they saw him play: ten goals in 29 matches, a determined and brave young hustler. A year later, in one of those 'network' stories that connect clubs to specific players in a chain, Ajax sold Ryan Babel to Liverpool for £11.5m and then identified Suárez as his superior replacement. Initially, Groningen refused to sell but the deal was bulldozed through at a bargain price for Ajax of £7.5m. Were the Liverpool scouts watching?

At Ajax, Suárez was soon made captain, simply because of his overwhelmingly aggressive leadership and desire. But his goal tally was also fantastic: 35 league goals in 33 appearances in 2009/10, rivalling even Lionel Messi at Barcelona. He was adored by fans for his fighter's persona in Amsterdam, although his coach, Marco van Basten, also deplored the new man's fouling and occasional fakery. At the 2010 World Cup in South Africa, Lucho was vilified once more for being red-carded after punching off the line what would have been an historic winning last-eight goal for Ghana in time added on, and then celebrating wildly on the sidelines as the resulting spot kick was missed. Uruguay won the ensuing penalty shoot-out (Suárez received a hero's welcome back in Montevideo). On 20 November 2010, in a melee during a heated Ajax vs PSV encounter, Suárez leaned into his direct opponent Otman Bakkal ... and casually *bit* him on the neck. *De Telegraaf* called him 'The Cannibal of Ajax', and a seven-match ban resulted. Suitors had been warned.

Fast forward to Anfield on 21 April 2013 and Luis Suárez was aiming for a full house of match contributions for Liverpool against Chelsea: a typically exquisite assist for Daniel Sturridge's opener; a penalty conceded by him for handball; a sly bicep bite delivered in a penalty area tussle in front of the Kop with astonished defender, Branislav Ivanović; and, of course, a 96th-minute equalising goal for his club. All on national television. The Sky Sports TV presenters went ballistic. The bite was a child's nursery offence but also a serious wrongdoing committed in front of millions. Prime Minister David Cameron, on some specious morality agenda, even waded in, condemning in the House the 'savagery' of the Liverpool man. It took the FA only three days this time to deliver its verdict: a ten-match ban. Liverpool officials described the sentence as 'harsh' but there was no appeal. Is a playful bite worse than a leg-breaking tackle, even if it is an affront to good taste and English masculinity? Lucho might need psychiatric help was the British press verdict, a man perched uneasily between rationality and madness. Rodgers and Liverpool, heading for seventh spot and out of Europe, would now end the season without their talisman and would start the first five league matches, in what turned out to be a 2013/14 title challenge, shorn of the club's inspiration, its wildest – and best – footballer.

LFC Women to the fore – and then to the floor

Notwithstanding Lucho's difficulties, the men's team at Liverpool was now clearly recovering under Brendan Rodgers from the trauma of the 2010 ownership crisis and Roy Hodgson's calamitous reign. Meanwhile, the formation in England of the semi-professional WSL in 2011 had signalled a new direction for *women's* football in England, which had long been dominated domestically by Arsenal. The Gunners were one of the few professional men's clubs in Britain to have had the foresight to support the female game with any real energy and financial commitment, and their reward was a European title and nine straight women's league triumphs in England. Liverpool Ladies had finally come into the fold at Anfield back in 1994, reaching two WFA Cup finals in the 1990s. But it was in 2013 that Liverpool broke the Arsenal spell in the women's game in England by taking the new WSL crown and then repeating the trick in 2014.

After all the historic tribulations and barriers faced by women's football on Merseyside, this finally looked like a breakthrough moment. The vision and the initial investment by FSG had turned things around, bringing women's football properly in-house and transforming a bottom-of-the-table team to title-winning material in just one season. In the USA, women's football has both status and financial support, and Liverpool's new owners initially seemed to see the promotion of women's football as part of a broader plan for their newly purchased football club. The Liverpool Women's squad now included world-class talent, including England internationals Lucy Bronze, Becky Easton and Fara Williams, and the German stars Nicole Rosler and Corina Schröder. All seemed set fair for a period of growth and continued success for the female game on Merseyside. But then things began to fall apart.

The Liverpool Women's team was finally modernised and rebranded as Liverpool Football Club Women in July 2018, but by this stage Manchester United, Chelsea and Manchester City, among others, had all upped their game in support of women's football, just as Liverpool FC Women were allowed to deteriorate and to haemorrhage their best players to these competing outfits. All this was happening just as the women's game was also building its international and media profile, with potential marketing and commercial returns sure to follow. Ironically, at the very moment the Liverpool men's team finally won the club's first Premier League title, in 2020, so Liverpool FC Women were relegated from the WSL, with several players voicing their concern about the recent lack of support from FSG. Criticism of the club's owners also revolved around the new £50m Liverpool training complex at Kirkby – a 9,200m² facility built to house the men's first team and youth players but with no apparent room for the women's team. 'Just a lack of care' was how one of the Liverpool Women club stalwarts described it. It was difficult to disagree with the myopia on show and with the general frustration expressed at the lack of continuing support from FSG for developing the game for women and girls in the city in a way that might yet build anew on those unique successes of 2013 and 2014.

Within a slip

The truth about the Liverpool men's brave, but eventually Devon Loch-like, attempt to match the Liverpool Women by winning the 2014 Premier League title was that its failure had little to do with the misdemeanours of Luis Suárez. Despite missing the season's opening fixtures, the Uruguayan finished as the league's top scorer with 31 goals in 33 starts, and he won the Premier League Golden Boot, as well as the PFA Players' Player of the Year and the Football Writers' award. Daniel Sturridge was the league's second-highest scorer with 21 goals. Frankly, this was a remarkable story of personal redemption for Suárez. He was simply irrepressible, his every sinew straining each week for the points and this elusive 19th Liverpool title.

But because it was Lucho, there also had to be histrionics, some scene-setting drama. In May 2013 the Uruguayan had said that he 'loved' the Liverpool club and its people, sure, but that now might be exactly the right time to leave. He had never felt at ease in England, he told the South American press: 'They never say anything good about me.' He wanted a move to Spain but neither Barça nor Real Madrid were in a position to buy. Confusion reigned over a supposed £40m buyout clause in his contract and when Arsène Wenger at Arsenal cheekily offered that sum, plus a pound, Suárez seemed quite keen on a move to London. A man experienced in such matters, Steven Gerrard, pleaded with him to stay. The extended FA match ban on Suárez actually aided Liverpool at this point, because it provided the space needed to calm the situation. Rodgers confined Lucho to some cleansing, low-key training with the Liverpool kids, so the Uruguayan (and his agent) could have time to get his head straight. The whole affair left a bad taste but Luis Suárez would not be leaving Liverpool Football Club. At least not right now.

With no European distractions to concern him (one of Suárez's key complaints) Brendan Rodgers had somehow nurtured his team into authentic domestic title contenders by showing ruthlessness when it was required. Pepe Reina was replaced in goal by the Belgian, Simon Mignolet from Sunderland. Out, too, went Borini (on loan), Shelvey and Stewart Downing. In came two young Spaniards, Luis Alberto and Iago Aspas, and an incoming loan deal for Victor Moses from Chelsea. Mamadou

Sakho eventually signed from PSG as a direct £15m replacement for the retired Jamie Carragher, but Kolo Touré was also recruited on a free from Manchester City to offer experience, leadership and defensive cover. With Glen Johnson nailing down the right-back position, young Jon Flanagan would now do some surprisingly good and uncompromising work on the left. The Liverpool midfield promised balance and depth, with three out of Coutinho, Lucas, Allen, Gerrard and Henderson typically favoured.

But the real strength here was in the forwards. If Aspas could contribute anything at all and Suárez, Sturridge and Sterling could gel, stay injury-free and show some consistency, then Liverpool would surely score goals. That was the aim. And it all began solidly enough, with Sturridge in early scoring form. But it was when Luis Suárez returned from his FA ban to face Sunderland on 29 September 2013, after a jarring Reds home defeat to Southampton, that sparks began to fly. Two Suárez goals, both laid on by Sturridge, the last a counter-attacking blur, signalled that something was brewing up in L4 on Merseyside. A defeat at Arsenal in November checked the flow, but by now Liverpool were averaging close to three goals a match. An inexplicable 3-1 defeat to eventually relegated Hull City on 1 December preceded a run of 17 goals in four wins, including a 5-0 rout away at Spurs and a 4-0 romp against the Londoners at home. Liverpool would be top before facing Manchester City at the Etihad on Boxing Day. A narrow defeat here and then away to Chelsea three days later, both without a hamstrung Steven Gerrard, saw Rodgers's team fall to fifth at the season's halfway point, below Everton and six points behind leaders Arsenal. There were bumps on this title-chasing road.

But now things really took off again, a goal-soaked 16-match unbeaten run, including 14 wins. Suárez, particularly, was often unplayable in this period, but Sterling and Coutinho were also sparkling. Perhaps this was one reason why Rodgers, reportedly, turned down the possibility of signing a certain Mohamed Salah in January 2014, a player he was lukewarm about and thought was

Take three great Scots. The cornerstone of Bob Paisley's Liverpool, European champions again in 1981

Ronnie Moran, Kenny Dalglish and Roy Evans, the post-Heysel managerial Brains Trust at Anfield

*John Barnes, the new face of
Liverpool FC*

*Hillsborough memorial, Haymarket,
Liverpool*

Graeme Souness's Liverpool win the 1992 FA Cup

Rush and Fowler, goals galore

Roy Evans and Gerard Houllier, never quite seeing eye to eye

A brilliant steal: Michael Owen's winning goal in the 2001 FA Cup Final against Arsenal

Gathering cups in May. Gerard Houllier's health failed him after the triumphant 2000/01 season

New leaders are born: Steven Gerrard loots silverware for Rafa Benitez in Istanbul in 2005

Always penalties? Another winning shootout, 2006 FA Cup Final against West Ham United

Liverpool fan protests against US owners Hicks and Gillett reached fever pitch in 2010

New owner FSG's John Henry and wife Linda fit right in

Brendan Rodgers works it out

And it all so nearly happened in 2014: Sturridge and the mercurial Luis Suarez fell just short

Jürgen Klopp and Mo Salah. Their secret soon powered Liverpool to glory

Cult figure Divock Origi celebrates his goal with friends in the Champions League Final in Madrid in 2019

League champions under Klopp (and Covid) in 2020, after 30 long years of frustration

Dual domestic cup winners in 2022 – but no quadruple

overpriced. Merseyside-born journalist Tony Evans reported later that Rodgers had said at a press conference that missing out on the Egyptian was 'hard to take'. Asked why the winger ended up at Chelsea, he replied, 'That's for the money guys to say.' It was a politician's defence. Meanwhile, a 4-0 home defeat of Everton in late January conclusively answered the question about top dogs in the city, but it was the manner of the 5-1 lunchtime beating of league leaders Arsenal in February that made supporters and the rest of the Premier League take note.

Liverpool played with the sort of freedom, incisiveness and pace that Arsenal simply could not match. Mesut Özil and Jack Wilshire in the visitors' midfield were outfought and over-run, a potentially career-ending outing for both. Martin Škrtel contributed two first-half headers and Raheem Sterling added two more goals. This crushing win had set the standard. In three matches in March 2014 Liverpool saw off Southampton, Manchester United and Cardiff City in consecutive away matches to the aggregate tune of 12 goals to three. This team looked unstoppable going forward, if invariably leaky in defence – 50 goals would be conceded in the season – but Manchester City just refused to go away.

In close-run title races like this, one match often defines the season, and on 5 April 2014 Manchester City came to Anfield, with the two clubs locked on 74 points at the top of the Premier League table. City were ahead by nine on goal difference but the two outfits were level on goals scored (90). For once, the contest matched the occasion. Raheem Sterling sat down both Vincent Kompany and Joe Hart in front of a foaming Kop before stroking in the opening goal in a 3-2 Liverpool win, completed by a brilliant Coutinho finish. A late sending-off for Jordan Henderson seemed like mere detail at the time, as Steven Gerrard gathered his troops in a post-match on-field huddle. TV cameras poked their noses inside as he told his team-mates, 'We go again.' On the Kop we were convinced this was the Rubicon crossed: the waiting looked to be over at last. Rodgers's team, its confidence soaring and in the middle of a long winning streak, now needed just seven points from the remaining three matches to be sure of the title. The only problem was that it was Chelsea and Jose Mourinho who lay immediately ahead. The Chilean international Carlos Caszely had once spoken about 'greedy' football: low risk, defensive play, designed to live off opponents' mistakes. 'It's the tactic of the bat,' he said. 'All 11 players hang from the crossbar.' Jose Mourinho was currently King of the Bats in England.

Chelsea and Mourinho were more focused on later Champions League action than league matters, so there was no Hazard, Čech or John Terry present at Anfield, and some unfamiliar names – Mo Salah, Tomáš Kalas and Andreas Christensen – started the match. But the visitors also dug in, put their bodies on the line and wasted time as if their very lives depended on it. Later, Rodgers was blamed for Liverpool's supposed naivety in defeat. Critics said that his team should have played for a draw here, trusting themselves to win the final two matches, against Crystal Palace and Newcastle United, and thus claim the title via that more strategic route. But this made absolutely no sense: this was Anfield, and Liverpool were on a roll against weakened, distracted visitors.

With hindsight, Steven Gerrard later spoke of his concerns: 'I've never been able to say this in public before,' he wrote in his autobiography, 'but I sensed an over-confidence in Brendan's team talks. We played into Chelsea's hands. I feared it then, and I know it now.' Post-facto rationalisation? First-half Liverpool pressure on the Chelsea goal was persistent but unproductive – why was Sturridge left on the home bench? It was proving difficult to build up a head of steam. As Gerrard admitted, 'I think we sort of underestimated the power of Mourinho. He came and he spoilt the game. He ruined it.'

On the Kop we began to show our collective anxiety. Approaching half-time, Liverpool still looked a safe bet at 0-0 – and then *that* slip happened to Gerrard, the club's most loyal servant, to arguably the best all-round player ever to have played for Liverpool Football Club. And to the local man who wanted more than anything to win this league title for himself, his club and for its imploring fans. Striker Demba Ba pounced on the Liverpool captain's fatal stumble, ran 20 yards and scored in front of the Kop. Rodgers's men now panicked, resorting to trying shots from all angles and distances, the crowd wild with dread, as Chelsea remained resolute. The late second away goal for Willian mattered only because of the Fernando Torres assist involved: 0-2. Devastation.

Liverpool FC: Premier League runners-up, 2013/14

Mignolet

Johnson Škrtel Sakho Flanagan

Henderson (Lucas) Gerrard Coutinho (Allen)

Sturridge Suárez Sterling

That single moment would haunt Steven Gerrard – and millions of Liverpool fans – until the club finally won the Premier League title in 2020. Much newsprint and discussion has been spent since on psychoanalysing Liverpool's later capitulation at Crystal Palace from 3-0 strollers after 78 minutes, to a 3-3 surrender, as if *this* was the moment that the 2014 Premier League title was finally handed to Manchester City. Brendan Rogers conceded that at Selhurst Park: 'We thought we could play Roy of the Rovers football and make the goal difference up, but tonight was about winning the game.' It was a fair point, but had Liverpool not been playing just this kind of attacking stuff all season? In any case, after the Chelsea defeat none of this really mattered anymore, because everyone at Anfield knew that Manchester City would not allow a slip of their own. And they did not.

But make no mistake, this was one of the outstanding seasons in Liverpool's history and it included some of the club's very best football. But the images that would define it all were of a captain's wretched slip and a young Hispanic man sobbing uncontrollably into his white Liverpool shirt on a football pitch on a damp spring evening in deepest south London. Luis Suárez was the one player that the Liverpool club was compelled to retain in order to build on – even improve upon – this magnificent league campaign. But Lucho from Uruguay had already been planning what to do next, and it did not involve another rain-drenched ten months battling behemoth defenders and his own demons in the north-west of England. His Merseyside employers had promised him a way out and he was going to take it.

Life without Lucho

'Luis sent us a lovely text this morning, wishing us all the best, which was a great gesture.' This is Brendan Rodgers after a very functional Liverpool opening-day victory over Southampton at Anfield on 17 August 2014. 'He is a friend now of Liverpool. He's a great boy, but he is gone.' Wise words, uttered through gritted teeth. Lucho was now happy again – at FC Barcelona. But it was difficult to counter the feeling that, with Suárez focused and at his irresistible best, Steven Gerrard in his last great flowering, and Sterling, Coutinho, Sturridge and Jordan Henderson all excelling, Liverpool might just have missed their great chance to win the Premier League title under this management team. Recovering to 'go again' after such a disappointment was likely to be a mammoth task, and it proved just beyond the man from Carnlough.

Not that transfer activity diminished at Anfield for the new season – far from it. Some of this work seemed plausible and thoughtful, some of it downright surreal. None of it seemed especially coherent, and the big risk here was that the identity of the Liverpool team, which had been so painstakingly built by Rodgers in 2013/14, would now be carelessly dismantled. It was certainly an unfortunate quirk – or a serious character flaw – of Luis Suárez's short time at Liverpool that he did not miss a single match due to injury, yet spent a total of 19 matches absent, suspended. Luis had great desire and he was an impressively mobile physical presence, but he also had a very fragile mental make-up. His new club in Spain would soon have to fall into step with the demands of Lucho's confused world. Playing for Uruguay, and after seeing off the challenge of England in the 2014 FIFA World Cup finals, Lucho bit Italy's Georgia Chiellini. Another four-month worldwide ban followed. Those impressive front teeth were an apparently uncontrollable, brutal weapon. Suárez was an authentic talent, no doubt about that, but he was also a deeply flawed performer, a man who 'explained' that his often execrable behaviour on the pitch was the outcome of unresolved frustration. He just wanted to win too badly.

But Luis Suárez was no longer Liverpool's potential saviour, or their problem. Brendan Rodgers had initially managed to see off FSG's preferred structure of a coach with limited powers who worked under a sporting director (Louis van Gaal was criminally mentioned), but the compromise solution was a transfer committee at Liverpool, led by Ian Ayre and head of performance and analysis, Michael Edwards, plus scouts and recruitment specialists, Barry Hunter and Dave Fallows. So, player recruitment might be the uneasy result of compromise and trade-offs, although the manager probably needed the back-up. Rodgers could seem arrogant, a small man struggling to impose himself in a tough business. But he was also still a very young and inexperienced leader, someone who was suddenly coaching some seasoned internationals – Steven Gerrard was only a few years his junior. Maintaining one's authority while recruiting, managing and coaching a global squad in the English Premier League is a huge challenge, even for the most experienced and imposing of operators. Few players complained that the coaching at Liverpool was not of the highest quality. However, title expectations were raised again at Melwood, so the challenges would only get bigger for the Liverpool manager.

Rodgers was looking bruised and was made uncertain by the final events of 2013/14. Who wouldn't be? But at least one matter was resolved: Liverpool FC would be staying at its historic Anfield home. Despite some local opposition, enabling work for the redevelopment of the Main Stand began in June 2014, when the demolition of nearby houses was launched. By December 2014 the site would be cleared and foundation works started. In March 2015 the very first steel prefabs would be installed and from there progress was expected to be rapid towards a delivery date of July 2016. The newly enlarged Main Stand would hold over 20,000 people, an increase of around 8,500 from the starting point. With fans spread across three tiers (9,300/3,100/7,900), the new seats would also provide extensive (and expensive) new facilities for corporate clients, crucial in recovering for FSG the investment cost of some £75m. Anfield would eventually hold just over 54,000 fans, so potentially we were back to home attendances last seen in the early 1970s. It was impressive work aimed at accommodating more fans and draining the corporate market – although the most expensive seats would often remain empty on matchdays. Of course, no new infrastructural transport or parking arrangements for fans were included as part of the plan. But, like it or not, the Premier League had been a huge commercial and popular success story, and FSG wanted a bigger slice of it.

On the pitch, meanwhile, Adam Lallana was an intelligent but unlikely replacement for Lucho, both ability and temperament-wise, but he came in from Southampton anyway, alongside a Scouse striker cast-off, centre-forward Rickie Lambert. A much feistier defensive colleague followed from St Mary's to replace Daniel Agger, the Croat Dejan Lovren. Saints fans complained loudly about this multi-player drain northwards. The combined cost of this trio left about one-third of the reported £75m Suárez transfer income, the bulk of which Rodgers and his advisors now squandered on a young Serbian international winger, Lazar Marković, a mystifying forward who would spend most of his time at Anfield in the shadows or on loan elsewhere. In, too, came a diminutive 22-year-old left-back from Seville, Alberto Moreno, a favourite with some team-mates and his Liverpool coaches but rather less loved by the Liverpool crowd. A fee of

£12m seemed an inordinately high price to pay for quite this level of defensive insecurity and lack of basic footballing intelligence. Moreno was noted as a positive dressing room personality but he never convinced Liverpool fans on the field. The much talked-about and imposing young Bayer Leverkusen defensive midfielder Emre Can looked better value at £9.75m, and the 19-year-old forward Divock Origi was certainly an interesting arrival for £10m from Lille.

Origi had impressed for Belgium during the 2014 World Cup finals, both for his strength and his pace, and the Liverpool coaching staff insisted that they had been tracking their man back from Under-15s football. 'They knew about my qualities,' Origi said later, 'and when I saw the values of the club – passing, pressing, fast players – I was like: "This is the place I want to go."' He certainly talked a good game for a young prospect, but could he immediately come up with the goods his manager needed? This list of arrivals lacked experience, consistent quality and convincing evidence of strategy. When pressed, Rodgers often quietly blamed the owners for lacking ambition, for not producing the funds for truly top-level talent. FSG responded badly to this message, with journalist Tony Evans reporting later that one angry internal missive from the USA stated, 'I'm fighting the urge to call and tear him [Rodgers] a new asshole.'

In Super Mario's world

As the end of the 2014 summer transfer window approached, Brendan Rodgers made it known that Liverpool were still in the market for a 'top-class striker' a man to fully replace Luis Suárez. We were back in Clint Dempsey territory. However, his options on this score were increasingly limited and those mentioned hardly complied with the FSG transfer model of buy them young and sell on for profit. Last week's favoured solution was soon substituted in the sports press by a new one. Meanwhile, the Liverpool transfer caucus was running out of time. No name for the role of new international forward recruit at Anfield was quite so unexpected as that which eventually emerged under blue Merseyside skies tied to a £16m price tag. Or, so ill-advised.

Mario Balotelli is the son of Ghanaian immigrants who were forced to give him up at an early age for adoption to white Italian foster parents. His African heritage meant that Balotelli routinely came up against rejection and racism in life and in Italian football, which may well help to explain some of his behavioural idiosyncrasies later. He had faced some awful abuse. Balotelli had played in England for title-winning Manchester City in 2011/12, where he became something of an eccentric cult hero. But his obvious talent was often overshadowed by training ground bust-ups, lapses of concentration and stories of his routinely bizarre off-the-field adventures. They included indoor fireworks and the incredible philanthropy of handing out cash to homeless people in Manchester city centre. Eventually shunted out of City, Balotelli returned to Italy in 2013 to play for AC Milan, but his form and the repeat experience of racism there forced him to look back to England. He had impressed for Italy against England in the 2014 World Cup finals, so his quality was clear enough – *if* Mario could just add consistency and deal with his various demons.

Brendan Rodgers initially laughed off media suggestions that Liverpool might actually buy this ill-fitting, troubled import but he may also have been tempted to take on the challenge of getting the best out of the wayward Italian. After all, Luis Suárez had thrived at Liverpool, despite his many character flaws. It was never entirely clear whether it was Rodgers or the Liverpool transfer committee who finally decided the purchase was a good idea. In time, both would deny responsibility. But Super Mario duly arrived at Melwood to a muted trumpet roll, an arrival symptomatic of the confusion and many misdirections at Liverpool Football Club in that crucial summer of 2014.

Just when the club had been so close to achieving its main goal it now seemed to be setting off on a different path entirely, hurtling towards a dead-end. The Balotelli signing split Liverpool fans – and its players. Some saw him as an authentic star, a maligned, cut-price maverick asset, a man who might even replace in their affections the lamented, lost Uruguayan. Others regarded him as the first indicator that Rodgers had released his grip on reality. There were some early signs of the latter. In training, for example, if things did not go his way, the Italian could simply ruin the session, petulantly and childishly kicking the ball out of match practice, or scoring own goals. Steven Gerrard was not amused. Early results on the field were little guide to what lay ahead; a predictable defeat at Manchester City (Moreno's first match, his first crucial error), but then a 3-0 Liverpool away win at Spurs, with Moreno on the scoresheet and Balotelli contributing. Maybe this could work after all? But poor form in the league followed, with a stuttering frontline failing to produce after the thrilling and free-scoring performances of just a few months ago. Four wins in the first 12 league matches sounded the alarm, then in nine Premier League fixtures between 13 September and 23 November, Liverpool scored a miserly ten goals, while losing to Aston Villa, West Ham United, Newcastle United and Crystal Palace in the process. Daniel Sturridge was a long-term absentee with 'muscle injuries', while Balotelli looked unwilling to work and was often impotent and lost, the pace of the game increasingly passing him by. Rickie Lambert looked even worse than the Italian, Sunday league-pedestrian. Eventually, Mario was left out of Liverpool squads altogether, Brendan Rodgers explaining that he was 'failing to sufficiently impress in training for selection'. This judgement was a piece of sophistry that hid a multitude of sins. Balotelli later claimed that joining Liverpool was 'the worst decision of my life', and he had already made some pretty bad ones.

Group stage elimination from the Champions League now added to the general sense of Anfield anomie. Steven Gerrard was controversially 'rested' by Rodgers for the glamorous away tie at Real Madrid, thus virtually conceding the points and accepting the club's fate. Stories now began to leak out about interest in the Liverpool captain from Major League Soccer (MLS) clubs in the

USA, a sure sign of a listing vessel that had been struck below the waterline.

FSG, for their part, were reportedly frustrated by the manager's reluctance to play some of his new signings. Under pressure from FSG's president Mike Gordon to change matters, Rodgers moved from his favoured 4-3-3 to a new 3-4-3 formation and things improved. A run of one defeat in 17 league matches ensued, some decent performances but others that simply did not merit Rodgers's often gushing interviews and his rhetoric about this 'outstanding' Liverpool team. In the middle of this improving spell, Rodgers gave an off-the-record interview with a group of journalists. According to Tony Evans, he talked about his long, sleepless nights when he weighed up complex tactical issues and how he arrived at a 'eureka' moment to get better performances out of his squad and individual players. He talked at length about his CORE philosophy – Commitment, Ownership, Responsibilities, Excellence – and explained how to apply each point. This sort of hokum read a little like a middle-ranking sales manager who had finally overestimated his powers of persuasion. As one member of his audience unkindly put it later, given the way that Liverpool had actually ended the previous season and started this new one: 'All that was left was the lingering smell of bullshit.'

This sequence of more positive Liverpool results was finally ended by defeat to Manchester United at Anfield in March. In more managerial 'creativity', Steven Gerrard started on the bench for this A-list fixture and, boiling with frustration, he was brought on by Rodgers at half-time. The Huyton man lasted precisely 38 seconds, sent off for a frustrated lunge on Ander Herrera. Basic man-management seemed to be distinctly lacking here. Gerrard commented later that he had thought about having it out with his manager there and then. It might even have been entertaining viewing. But perhaps the FA Cup could yet save Liverpool's sliding season and maybe Brendan Rodgers his job? After a series of easy cup draws made difficult by poor performances, Liverpool eased into a Wembley semi-final against relegation-threatened Aston Villa. Here was an obvious chance, a free hit, to try to rescue a season otherwise blighted by poor recruitment, unfulfilled promises and disappointments. If only, that is, Liverpool had bothered to turn up at all. Starting with Emre Can at right-back and the frequently absent Marković in front of him, Rodgers's selection looked unbalanced and weak from the start. Nevertheless, Liverpool stole the lead through another Coutinho goal, but were then comfortably outplayed by a Villa led by the youthfully precocious Jack Grealish in a quite ruinous 2-1 defeat. Replacing the hapless Marković with Balotelli at half-time felt like a cruel joke delivered by the manager with a punchline nobody in red could quite understand.

The Liverpool dressing room no longer seemed behind its increasingly self-regarding, under-pressure coach. None of this was even remotely funny anymore, as the rest of the season now crumbled away into so much dust. Steven Gerrard's last home match at Anfield (his family on the pitch for the after-match goodbyes) proved to be a despairing 3-1 defeat to Crystal Palace, but worse, much worse, was to come. A demoralised Liverpool squad travelled to Stoke City for the season's (and Gerrard's) last Liverpool fixture, with nothing but pride at stake. Playing in funereal black, with three at the back and the witless Moreno in wide midfield, Liverpool looked punch-drunk and vulnerable whenever their opponents attacked – which was often. The 5-0 lead Stoke established in 45 first-half minutes did not flatter the home team, with Mignolet exposed and found wanting time and time again. LA Galaxy-bound Steven Gerrard at least notched his final Liverpool goal in the second half, his 191st in 748 emotion-packed Liverpool appearances, but this was little consolation in what was a terrible 6-1 submission. It was certainly no way to call time on one of the club's greatest and most loyal footballers. 'I think about it [the slip] most days,' remarked Steven Gerrard in the insightful 2018 Amazon Prime film, *Make Us Dream*. 'Football is not about turning up and playing. It is about dealing with everything that comes with it.' He had coped with his fair share.

How had all this happened – and so quickly? Some 17 defeats in all competitions, a very ordinary sixth-place finish on just 62 points, only 52 league goals scored and some 25 points behind champions Chelsea. In short, in one season Liverpool had managed, somehow, to shed 49 goals and 22 points under the same coaching team. Luis Suárez was an exceptional footballer but surely nobody was quite *that* good. Perhaps the obvious thing to do now – the kindest thing – was to sack Brendan Rodgers. Did FSG have any alternative? Had a new manager already been lined up but could not take over right now? Coaches were dismissed and highly rated Liverpool academy coach, Pep Lijnders, took on the role of first-team development in another new management structure. Matters darkened when Raheem Sterling's agent negotiated a painful and protracted departure for his client to Manchester City in the summer of 2015 for an eye-opening £49m fee (he would prove to be worth every penny of it). For all the Liverpool fan talk now about Sterling and Rodgers on that USA tour, and Sterling's alleged 'greed', the real message here was that this ambitious young English forward had lost faith in his manager's capacity to help him win medals and trophies at Liverpool.

Playing for Liverpool was still a step up in class – and pay – for Christian Benteke, who arrived in the summer of 2015 for a record £32.5m fee on the back of performances that had previously distressed the men he was now joining. But Benteke never managed at Anfield what he seemed to attain so easily at Aston Villa. Lacking a big-club mentality may have been an issue, but superior technique and desire were also absent. The charge could not so easily be levelled at Roberto Firmino, a Brazilian forward recruited from Hoffenheim for an initial £21.3m fee. Firmino had considerable football intelligence and talent, but where would he fit into Rodgers's system (or systems)? He was no reliable goalscorer and rumours soon spread that he may not even be the manager's signing. How long would Brendan Rodgers be in post for the Brazilian to find out?

Just three wins in Liverpool's first eight league matches in 2015/16 provided the answer. A quite shameful 3-0 home defeat to West Ham at the end of August – the Londoners' first win at Anfield since the 1960s – sounded the final death knell. Defenders Joe Gomez and Nathaniel Clyne and, crucially, James Milner on a free, had all arrived, but Brendan Rodgers was suddenly gone. Here was a Liverpool manager who had spent inconsistently on players, had briefly produced one of the best Liverpool teams ever seen at the club, but who left in October 2015 struggling for respect and with no trophies to his name. Weirdly, he seemed to be carelessly disparaged by some Liverpool fans. Suddenly, there was a new sheriff in town, and life for the club's fans and players alike would never be quite the same again.

Chapter 12

The Age of the *Gegenpress*

The time of Jürgen Klopp

*'Kloppo' takes charge and charms the British press.
He also starts to imprint his personality on the club,
the city and its people. Mo Salah brings his scoring
boots to the north-west of England. Liverpool fans
soon learn that a football team is like an orchestra.
Cup disappointments follow, before intense
Champions League Final frustration in Kiev.
Liverpool need (and find) a reliable goalkeeper.
A new defensive shield, a Dutch master of
vertikalspiel, also arrives. Nothing will ever seem
quite this good at the back again. But 97 points for
Liverpool is still not enough to win a first Premier
League title. Nor is a 3-0 lead enough for Lionel
Messi and FC Barcelona to protect at a jubilant
Anfield. Onwards to Madrid.*

'Knowing is not enough; we must apply.
Willing is not enough; we must do.' Goethe

'Kloppo'

In 2005, as manager at Mainz 05, Jürgen Klopp, strangely agreed to a lie detector test for an interview with the German football magazine *RUND*. When asked what his biggest career meltdown was, Klopp answered immediately that it was head-butting his teammate, Sando Schwarz, who had twice fooled him and put Klopp on the floor in a training session. This German was no shrinking violet. In 2008 *Stern* asked the new coach at Borussia Dortmund what counted most in life. Klopp replied, 'That wherever you were, you made it a little better. That you gave it all you could. That you loved, were loved, and didn't take yourself too seriously.' Okay, there was some idealistic flannel here, but Klopp also sounded like a pretty decent human being. In 2013 a Dortmund fan recalled how fortunate his club had been to recruit 'Kloppo', a man who seemed to reflect the aspirations and values of this communal working-class city and football club so perfectly. 'We say in Dortmund,' the fan confided, 'he fits like an arse in a bucket.' A colourful, down-to-earth image for the ages. Liverpool might have settled for that after all its recent near misses and traumas.

Jürgen Klopp spent his childhood in a small south-western German village called Glatten, near Stuttgart, captaining the local junior club, before moving to TuS Ergenzingen u19s, where a coach recalled that his new man could barely manage even three keepy-uppies. An early report pithily summed up Klopp's performance as 'completely useless: did not win a single tackle'. If not hugely talented, Klopp was a tall, adaptable player who could play attack or defence. His chief attribute seemed to be in his versatility and captain's leadership qualities, rather than any great technical merit as a striker, midfield workhorse or defender. He bounced around in lower league German football before being recruited by Mainz 05 in the German second division, where he played all of his professional career between 1990 and 2001, logging up 352 appearances and 52 goals.

As Raphael Honigstein recalls in *Klopp: Bring the Noise*, it was as a player at Mainz that Klopp was first introduced by his 'football professor' coach, Wolfgang Frank, to the very non-German tactic of high-pressing the opposition. Frank was an intense football man, an obsessive who lacked Klopp's humour and his hinterland beyond sport. Frank's son said that he doubted whether his father knew even the price of a bread roll, so wrapped up was he in the challenges and technicalities of the game. Frank rejected the deep-lying sweeper and the man-marking systems then popular throughout Germany. He wanted zonal marking and a flat back four pushed high up the pitch to help sustain a press aimed at regaining possession in the opponents' half, an approach long championed by the great AC Milan coach Arrigo Sacchi. Frank later reported that it took him 150 hours of theoretical work, on the pitch without a ball and in video analysis, before his ideas took root.

Mainz team meetings could go on for hours. It was serious, exhausting work but it produced a style of play that made a deep impression on the all-action Klopp, a man who reviled the 'turf chess' that, he argued, now dominated the elite, sterile European game. His later assistant and video analyst, Peter Krawietz, said that the best way of describing Klopp's football was 'chess, but with dice'. A mixture of structure and intense spontaneity and risk. Above all, the high press option taught Klopp a huge managerial lesson: that a team with better players can be beaten by using a reliable system and superior tactics. He would refine the press and live by it throughout his own coaching career.

To local media ridicule, in February 2001 Mainz appointed the raw 33-year-old Klopp as their new coach to fight the threat of relegation from the German second division. He had no experience of coaching – or even the right qualifications – but he completed the job, relying on chutzpah, the high press and some unusual motivational techniques. He urged his players to become like rugby union's New Zealand All Blacks – proud and unbeatable. He played the haka on the team bus for inspiration. Once, on a return trip from Ulm, Klopp told the coach driver to pull into a service station and he instructed his players to wear disguising sunglasses so that they could enjoy a post-match beer in peace. It was pure Brian Clough from the 1970s.

Based on a collective belief in aggressive pressing, 'Kloppo' next steered his club into promotion contention, but twice they missed out at the last gasp, once causing Klopp to burst into tears before an interview with the German national TV broadcaster ZDF. His emotional commitment and honesty, his playing philosophy and the collective trust he generated from his players all meant that Klopp eventually got the club promoted into the Bundesliga for the first time in Mainz's history. Remarkably, they lasted three seasons there. Klopp stayed on after relegation and when, in 2007/08, he failed to achieve promotion again, he decided his 18-year spell at Mainz as a player and coach was over. He would be missed. An estimated 30,000 people gathered in the central Gutenburgplatz to say their goodbyes, offer their thanks and their manly tears. Seldom could failure have ever received such communal acclaim. Typically, Klopp told his people between sobs and in a decidedly candid and Shankly-esque moment, 'All that I am, all I am capable of, you all made that possible for me – everything.'

Klopp was now a rising young coach in Germany but not all elite clubs favoured his intense playing style or his personal unconventionality. His casual dress sense – unshaven, no tie, usually jeans – and his smoking put off a few suitors (he was later caught lighting up on camera at Melwood and at Kirkby, Joe Fagan reborn). His surprisingly high salary at Mainz discouraged others. Klopp perhaps best resembled the great Chicago Bulls basketball coach of the 1990s, Phil Jackson, for his likeable hippyish, left-field leadership style and the primacy of the team ethic over star players, Michael Jordan notwithstanding. Borussia Dortmund – not long out of a financial crisis themselves – initially hesitated but then took the plunge and appointed Klopp in July 2008. Soon his face appeared on giant hoardings around the city, anticipating his transformative arrival. He started winning hearts and minds right away by attending staff quizzes and sports days, personally phoning corporate fans who were thinking of giving up their season tickets, and meeting with local ultras to answer their concerns. He attended lengthy social events for past Dortmund players and members, and he even met with officials' elderly parents to celebrate their birthdays. Again, like Shankly, he energetically imprinted his personality on the club, the city and its people.

Season ticket sales boomed. It took two years to get there but, working in concert with chairman Hans-Joachim Watzke and sporting director Michael Zorc, two league titles, one German cup and a Champions League final (lost narrowly to Bayern) followed in quick succession. Klopp won the Bundesliga title in 2011, playing 4-2-3-1 with one of the youngest teams ever to do so, initially built around a pair of precocious 19-year-old centre-backs, Mats Hummels from the Dortmund academy and Neven Subotic, who had followed Klopp from Mainz. A mesmeric young forward Mario Götze, also from the Dortmund youth system, was joined later by a then-unknown Polish centre-forward, Robert Lewandowski, and a hard-running, goalscoring Japanese midfielder, Shinji Kagawi, both brought in for small fees. The whole was electric, a wonderful blend of audacious local talent, meticulous recruitment, team spirit, hard work and inspiring leadership. Subotic argued later that Klopp's main on-pitch strategy for Dortmund – his famous *gegenpressing* – was really a simple proposition: 'To run the opponents into the ground.'

The British journalist and author Michael Cox has argued that the work of Klopp and his coaches at Dortmund – with Krawietz and the Bosnian master tactician, Željko Buvač – was rather more complex and different from the pressing successfully used, for example, by Pep Guardiola at FC Barcelona. For Guardiola, intense pressing high up the pitch was a means of re-establishing possession and rebuilding for another attack, thus slowly generating pressure. For Klopp, *gegenpressing*, or 'counter-pressing', was in itself an attacking opportunity. By channelling opponents into defensive cul-de-sacs and overwhelming them, one was potentially only a simple pass away from creating a good goalscoring opportunity. No playmaker in the world could be as useful or as effective as *gegenpressing*, because the opposition are caught deep, out of their shape and unprepared. This was Klopp's answer later to those who despaired about an alleged lack of creativity in the Liverpool midfield. Better to regain the ball high and strike by collective pressing through chaos, than asking any midfield man to work out how to cut through a well-set deep block.

This, at least, was what he had learned through his experience at underdogs Mainz. It was not infallible and Dortmund's defeat to Bayern Munich in the 2013 Champions League Final hit Klopp hard, as did the later sale of both Götze and Lewandowski to Bayern. The Munich club was now reasserting its familiar dominant position and commercial power. All this added to uncertainty at Dortmund in 2013/14 and Klopp struggled in the dugout, too, attacking officials a little too feverishly in both the Bundesliga and the Champions League. Touchline bans followed. Was he losing his grip? Dortmund finished a distant second to Bayern but things got much worse in 2014/15 when injuries, bad luck, opponents negating the *gegenpress* and also a growing reluctance on the part of some of his Dortmund stalwarts to keep on delivering body-wrenching performances, combined to put Klopp's team in the relegation zone. Stability eventually returned but he had seen enough to realise that, with Bayern strong and without the Champions League cash needed to rebuild his squad again, it was time to move on. He needed some rest but most of all he needed another challenge. He wanted to find another Dortmund, but this time in the English Premier League.

The 'Normal One' takes charge

If the arrival of Brendan Rodgers at Anfield in 2012 had been a low-key, muted affair, perhaps partly out of respect to the departing Kenny Dalglish, the arrival of Jürgen Klopp at Liverpool in October 2015 was anything but. It was more like a jubilant carnival, the coming of a new Messiah. The German had received the phone call while on holiday in Lisbon. The excited faces of his two sons simply confirmed his future path. Whereas the inexperienced Rodgers had looked diminished, formal and stiff, Jürgen Klopp was physically imposing, relaxed and open. He was fit and tanned, dressed in black casual – a suit and shirt, the last time we would see this for a while – and he exuded confidence and good humour. Klopp had previously had talks at Manchester United but rightly dismissed Old Trafford as a media circus. He was even unhappy when some Reds fans followed him with cameras in Hope Street in Liverpool. At Anfield, he described himself as a 'lucky guy' to be taking over this 'special' club. Klopp reiterated his commitment to the team ethic rather than eulogising about individual players: 'I'm not a dream man,' he said. 'I don't want to have Cristiano [Ronaldo] or Lionel [Messi] and all these players in one team. I want these guys [the Liverpool squad]. Now we start working.'

Signed initially on a three-year deal, Klopp skilfully batted away questions about possible targets and the Liverpool transfer committee, before moving off into a charming, clearly unrehearsed soliloquy about his 'normal' Black Forest background and the pride of his mother, who was watching all this play out at home on TV. Talking of Jose Mourinho's claims to be the 'Special One', Klopp said that he was comfortable enough in his own skin to be known only as the 'Normal One'. This room, crammed with crusty tabloid journalists and hangers-on, dissolved into laughter. He asked for time and patience (although knew he would get neither) and also reported, with a sly grin, of the warnings he had received in Germany about the scheming British sporting press: 'So it's up to you guys,' he told his audience, 'to show me that they are all liars!' More laughter. He already had them.

Managing in England in this bloated era was no easy task. In Germany, Klopp could at least focus only on besting Bayern, but here he had Arab and Russian sports-washing billions to counter, not to mention the global corporation nearby at Old

Trafford and also local rivals Everton. The big football question, of course, was whether Klopp and his assistants, Krawietz and Buvač, could bring their 'heavy metal' full-throttle style of play to the higher-tempo English Premier League, which, as yet, had no recuperative mid-season break.

We soon had the answer. Klopp was satisfied with tenth-placed Liverpool's first-up 'wild' 0-0 away draw at Tottenham (his team ran a record 116k) and with a victory over Jose at struggling Chelsea, but less so when his new team lost 2-1 at home to Crystal Palace. His annoyance was part-directed at those Liverpool fans who gave up the fight and started leaving the match early to avoid the traffic. He openly chastised the part-timers behind him in the Main Stand for their lack of trust, for leaving him and his team alone at such a difficult moment. Soon after, when Liverpool snatched an injury time 2-2 home draw against West Bromwich Albion in December, Klopp celebrated wildly and got the players to salute the remaining crowd from the field to show how fans' patience and support could help retrieve a valuable point. It seemed overblown to be so enthusiastic about a limp home draw against weak opponents, but the wider message was clear: stick with us and together we can get out of any hole.

However, the first real sight of authentic Kloppo's Liverpool came in a dazzling 4-1 away win against league leaders Manchester City in November. Playing a 4-2-3-1 system, with a front-roving Firmino backed up by Lallana, Coutinho and Milner, this version of *gegenpressing* strangled the air out of City. The two Brazilians were quite emphatic in their forward movement and understanding. Klopp had been an enthusiastic supporter of Firmino in Germany – perhaps he had played a role in signing him for Liverpool – but this performance revealed an added dimension, something little noticed under Brendan Rodgers. A 6-1 League Cup dismembering at St Mary's of a strong Southampton team including Vigil van Dijk followed, with Joe Allen pressing feverishly and Daniel Sturridge and Divock Origi now parading their finishing skills. This was all after a certain Sadio Mané for the hosts had caught Moreno napping after just 41 seconds. His work was duly noted.

But in these early months not everything was plain sailing: a frustrating 2-0 league defeat at relegation-threatened Newcastle in early December hurt, with Gini Wijnaldum powering the length of the field to score the hosts' late second goal. The Liverpool staff again stored this memory. Nevertheless, scraping past Stoke City in the League Cup semi-final meant that Klopp's first Liverpool final came within five months of his arrival on Merseyside. A tight Wembley contest against Manchester City on 28 February 2016 could only be decided on penalties – in favour of Pep Guardiola. A downbeat Klopp looked distinctly uncomfortable in the official press conference, dressed in a tie, grey V-necked sweater and jacket. He said that it had been a 'perfect' day – except for the final penalty. He added subversively to journalists' sniggers: 'If I was allowed to say shit, I would say shit, but that is not allowed.' He had them again. Three days later Liverpool dumped Manchester City 3-0 at Anfield in the league, with Adam Lallana irresistible. It did not wipe out the Wembley hurt but for we fans present at both it certainly helped.

A general pattern seemed to be emerging from these early months under the new coach: if Liverpool could get ahead early, then they were capable of catching any of their opponents in transition, overwhelming them physically and scoring a hatful of goals. Five came at Norwich, four against Everton and Stoke, six without reply away at Aston Villa. But inconsistency and conceding goals – another 50 shipped in the league alone in 2015/16 – remained a serious problem, the main reasons for Liverpool finishing in an underwhelming eighth place on 60 points, 21 behind the 5,000/1 champions, Leicester City. It was actually a worse league showing than in Brendan Rodgers's last full season but the promise and future direction was now becoming clear.

The core issue to be addressed seemed to be shielding the defence, but also improving the quality of Liverpool's full-backs and correcting the judgement of goalkeeper Simon Mignolet on both crosses and shot-stopping. Bruce Grobbelaar weighed in by saying of the Belgian keeper, 'I would make him move his feet a little bit more, and his starting positions are not where I would have it.' Plenty to work on, then. However, Liverpool had made progress into the knockout stages of the Europa League, eliminating a Manchester United team increasingly aimless under Louis van Gaal, and eventually setting up a 'dream' quarter-final tie with Klopp's old buddies at Borussia Dortmund. A highly professional 1-1 draw in Germany prefaced the deciding second leg. Two early goals from a superior Dortmund at a fizzing Anfield put Liverpool on the back foot and effectively out of the tie by half-time. An early Origi goal after the break was almost immediately rubbed out by Marco Reus, to Klopp's visible despair. But replies from Coutinho – how often he had delivered – and Sakho at the Kop end set up what TV folk like to call a 'grandstand' finish. This is Anfield in Europe under the lights, right, so we all know what happens next. Deep into injury time, a free kick: Sturridge to Milner wide right; the Dortmund defence turns off as the back post is overloaded in red; a knee slide and a dinked cross on to Dejan Lovren's head – and in. The place is now in complete meltdown – 4-3. Only Jürgen Klopp, circling near the Liverpool bench, was unsure whether Lovren's header had actually crept inside the post. Perhaps he did not want to celebrate too soon, or too much, his old club's fate? At half-time, Klopp had been calm and focused, reminding his players about Steven Gerrard and Istanbul in 2005, but now he was euphoric, not least because of how his nascent group was able to 'drag down' a better team through sheer will. 'No game is over, not with this Liverpool team,' he said. 'Something was happening in this stadium; you could smell it.' It was that scent of expectation and fear he had long hoped Anfield could produce.

The semi-final against Villarreal was a dull stroll by comparison, a 3-1 aggregate win. So, it would be two cup finals for Liverpool in this truncated first season under Klopp, and the first for the club in Europe since 2007, a decent return by any measure. Could it get better? Well, not right now. At 1-0 up against Sevilla – a sumptuous Daniel Sturridge outside-of-the-left-foot drive just before half-time at a Scouse-infested St Jakob-Park in Basle – all seemed fine. The Spaniards, playing a defensive long-ball game, looked on the ropes, a beaten team. *After* half-time the story was instantly reversed. Aiming for a run of three consecutive Europa League titles, Sevilla scored almost directly from the kick-off (two bad errors from Moreno) and the momentum completely shifted as a result. This was a nothing goal, conceded even before the real play had started and the corporate guests had reached their seats, but it visibly lifted these well-tried men from Spain. Was it tiredness or inexperience that now kicked in for Liverpool? Or a lack of confidence on a big occasion? Or was it simply the timing of the second-half concession that so shattered Klopp's men, because they faded very badly indeed, eventually losing 3-1.

For Klopp, the impact of the instant second-half goal had been crucial, not only for the momentum shift but also in revealing the work that still needed to be done to instil belief in his players about the system they were now playing. 'It changed: we lost in a second everything, our faith in our style of play,' he said. 'We couldn't reach our level. I take responsibility, but we will use this experience. We will be back stronger, one hundred per cent.' It was a serious blow and another major final defeat for a coach increasingly used to the experience. But Klopp also impressed Jordan Henderson with his upbeat approach by pulling the squad together in the hotel bar later to assure the players that this was no time for regrets, it was just the beginning. As always, it seemed, the German saw this defeat as an important marker, another step forward. He was determined to find an answer to how to convert these admirable journeys into trophies.

Life, God and the good world

New managers arriving part-way through a campaign can mean an anxious time for professional players, an opportunity for those left on the margins in a previous regime but a potential threat to others trying to hold on to a first-team spot. Am I staying or packing my stuff? French defender Mamadou Sakho was definitely not loved by Jürgen Klopp. He had failed a drugs test, thus missing the Europa League Final, although later his UEFA ban was lifted. Klopp was unamused, nevertheless. Under this already existing cloud, the centre-back was sent home from the 2016 pre-season tour of the USA after missing meetings and showing a 'lack of respect' for the group. For all the arm-round-round-the-shoulders hugging and 'cool' vibes emanating from his chilled manager, the respect issue was a capital offence in the Klopp firmament. Sakho never played for the club again. Klopp and his coaches now had a chance to remake this squad into something closer to their own image, importing new blood to add to the rhythmic and complementary strengths his core group already offered. Soon after arriving at Anfield, he said:

> A football team is like an orchestra, and if one new guy comes in, he can't just play the violin, or whatever, because that's what he wants. He has to wait to see what the rest of the group needs and how he fits in and you do everything as one in harmony. This is what we have worked on together. We are really a team.

The analogy was a good one for developing a group of players the Jürgen Klopp way. James Milner, for example, for close on 15 years had been a right-footed, right-sided forward or midfielder by trade, but he now found that the particular football orchestra Klopp was currently assembling in the north-west of England required an emergency, dependable left-back for 2016/17 – and he was it. Dealing with defensive weakness was now a priority, which is why the utterly reliable Milner needed urgent retraining.

'What do we do when the other lot have got the ball?' was the first question Klopp asked in every pre-season at every club he managed. Accordingly, two new German-based centre-backs arrived at Anfield: the Cameroonian, Joël Matip from Schalke

04, and the Estonia international Ragnar Klavan from FC Augsburg, for a combined cost of £4.2m. A physically imposing young goalkeeper for the future, Loris Karius, a man recently voted second-best in the Bundesliga, was recruited from Klopp's old club Mainz 05 for what looked like a bargain price of £4.7m. Here was forward planning and a complete defensive revamp from Germany, all for under £10m – if it worked.

More eye-catching, perhaps, were the signings of Georginio Wijnaldum from Newcastle United for an initial £23m, and Sadio Mané from Southampton for £30m. This duo was experienced in England but still young, a couple of offensive-minded Premier League players who could go straight into any Liverpool starting XI (Klopp had actually turned down the chance to buy Mané for Dortmund because he did not like the African's 'rapper's' baseball cap). Klopp recouped this cash – and more – by dispatching Benteke, Balotelli, the unlucky Joe Allen, veteran servant Martin Škrtel, a hesitant young forward, Jordon Ibe, and a group of lesser-known squad players, all for close to £77m. It looked like very smart work on a budget, the precise model demanded by FSG's accounting staff. When Manchester United forked out record cash for celebrity man Paul Pogba in August 2016 Klopp said:

> The day that this is football, I'm not in a job anymore, because the game is about playing together. That is how everybody in football understands it. You always want to have the best, but building the group is necessary to be successful. Other clubs can go out and spend more money and collect top players. I want to do it differently. I would even do it differently if I could spend that money.

Klopp was once asked by a German TV company what he talked about to those players he was recruiting. If the professional diligence was already completed, the German said he relied on his Christian principles to judge character. 'We don't talk at all about football,' he confided. 'We talk about life, God and the good world.' It really could be Shankly again. But could Klopp use his faith (Shankly's was socialism) and his clever transfer work to address the inconsistency and leakage that had dogged his first iteration of what was potentially an exciting new Liverpool team? 'Liverpool, we know, can attack if the opposition push up and leave space behind them,' argued journalist and tactical analyst, Jonathon Wilson. 'They can impose themselves physically on teams not keen on the battle. But can they defend? Can they break down sides who play a narrow back four and sit deep? And can they really turn Jordan Henderson into Sergio Busquets?'

These were all good questions, not totally answered in Klopp's first full *gegenpress* season. Henderson, for example, struggled to hold down a place with Emre Can around, but Wijnaldum and Mané added new energy and penetration, while Joël Matip slowly found his feet and the ever-willing Milner successfully battened down the troublesome left side of Liverpool's defence. The boys from Brazil, Coutinho and Firmino, generally excelled, but with Daniel Sturridge fading from the picture and Origi still troubled by a serious injury incurred back in April, no Liverpool forward offered a consistent enough goal threat for the club to mount a serious title challenge as we moved towards 2017. For the spanking new 54,074 capacity Anfield, Klopp wanted more *vertikalspiel*: getting the ball forward quickly and accurately from a structured base. The young Matt Hummels had been a master of this at Dortmund, pinging diagonals into dangerous positions. Keeping possession was no good for its own sake.

A 4-3 loss to Bournemouth in mid-December 2016 flagged up some of the early strengths and weaknesses of his emerging new Klopp team. With Liverpool 3-1 up and Mané and Emre Can seemingly in total control, Bournemouth launched an unlikely late comeback, stoked by an early gift from what would become Loris Karius's formidable mistake locker. The players worried that their Christmas party would be cancelled as a result of such feebleness but Klopp insisted it went ahead for team-building. He had no love for punishing his footballers. However, after a strong seasonal start, by the traditional January–February winter 'dig-in' period in England, Klopp's Liverpool seemed to hit a wall: one win in seven league matches and early elimination from both domestic cup competitions, neither of which the Liverpool coach seemed to take especially seriously. The home FA Cup tie versus Plymouth Argyle in January 2017 produced a 0-0 draw played out by Liverpool's youngest-ever first team. The last time a tier four team had forced a draw at Anfield in the competition was 42 years previously. Predictably, Klopp railed instead about the lack of a mid-season break in England. One played even *more* matches in the winter months in the English Premier League, he complained, rather than recuperate, as the rest of Europe sensibly did. How did England ever expect to win international tournaments?

But was it the intensity of Klopp's style of play that was actually leading to this mid-season exhaustion at Liverpool? He tried rotation but he needed reinforcements, and towards the end of the season he got some useful game time into the legs of Trent Alexander-Arnold, a raw West Derby teenage full-back convert from the Liverpool academy. This scrawny Liverpool kid had loads of promise but he played more like a threatening right-winger than a defensive back. Some opponents spotted his early vulnerability. But with Conor Coady long sold on to make hay elsewhere and enjoy an international career, at least Kirkby was starting to produce again some prospects for the Liverpool first team, to follow Owen, Carragher and Gerrard back in the 1990s.

Without Europe or domestic cups as a distraction, the best Klopp's new squad could do was a fourth-place finish in 2017, enough for the qualifying round of the Champions League and to still any potentially uncomfortable questions from his American bosses. In truth, it had been several encouraging steps forward: 'We fought for each yard,' said the beaming coach, enthusiastic at the progress made. After the home win against Middlesbrough to clinch fourth place he told TV interviewer Des Kelly that the communal team ethic had been the key: 'You need to be sure at your back that somebody saves your life.' It was a short phrase that, nevertheless, might sum up the German's football and life philosophy.

By now Liverpool-born Peter Moore had taken over as CEO at Liverpool, having been COO at the global games company Electronic Arts. Moore had spent some of his early years as a PE teacher in Llangollen, North Wales, so he was suitably grounded in work in local communities in Britain, as well as in the corporate leisure culture of the USA. Moore reported directly to FSG, a conduit between the coach and the owners, and he seemed like a good fit. He admired Jürgen Klopp's 'left side of the brain' analytical approach to football but he also praised the manager's humanity and sociability. 'He's a liberal, left-winger in the right side of his brain,' he said of Klopp in 2020, 'where everybody gets a hug, everybody gets a pat on the back of the head, everybody gets a whisper. He's incredibly tactile and incredibly gregarious.'

A *New York Times* perspective on the Liverpool FC 'revolution' under Klopp highlighted the depth and scale of the wider changes at Anfield by focusing on the impact on individual players of the diets prepared by new nutritionist, Mona Nemmer, recently captured from Bayern Munich. 'Slowly, almost imperceptibly,' the story began, 'Nemmer has changed habits. Instead of a candy pick-me-up at half-time, Lallana, Milner and Jordan Henderson now have a slug of apple juice laced with caffeine.' Nice kitchen work and science in cooperative action here. Nemmer would publish a book on sports diets in 2021. Bayern's head of fitness and conditioning, Andreas Kornmayer, had also followed Nemmer to Anfield. From now on, those Liverpool FC bodies would get the best possible care: a still hobbling Tommy Smith might have shown a wry smile at the very prospect.

Like Gérard Houllier before him, Klopp wanted his players to respect and understand the importance of these key workers and the general staff around the club and at Melwood. At the sharp end of club affairs, the head coach was invested, of course, in diet, sports science, player preparation and detail. He supported pre-season lactate acid tests, for example, using small blood samples taken from the ear lobe to assess players' stamina capacities. This item soon featured on podcasts from Melwood for ordinary fans to enjoy. Klopp wanted his players to train in short spells, matching kick-off times with the intensity he demanded on matchdays, but he was also concerned that players of his own generation had been made to train far too hard, often to the point of physical sickness. Nevertheless, Jordan Henderson reported later that his manager spent much of his time being playfully angry at training, upping the intensity and demanding more. Fitness was a key to success but tired players could not compete effectively, given the intense matchday physical demands of *gegenpressing*.

'Kloppo' now had a whole division of staff to compile statistics on diets, training profiles, player activity and potential transfers, all increasingly prominent features of the modern game. 'The Brain', his assistant manager Željko Buvač, a man of few words but all of them significant, was now the most reliable source of high-end tactical insight at Anfield. Live video clips from Peter Krawietz were also an essential feature of training and matchday half-time debriefings. Searching for greater passing speed, Klopp even raised concern about the alleged dryness of the Anfield pitch, complaints that had the club's senior manager of grounds, Dave Roberts, busy applying zeolite to the offending surface, a volcanic ash that acts as a magnet to hold moisture in the root zone. All bases were covered, all details observed. But, like the great elite coaches, Klopp ultimately preferred to rely on his own observations and instincts to judge tactics, pace and player performance. 'After all,' he remarked drily, 'I've got nothing else to do but train a team and deal with football, day in day out.'

In search of goals and *vertikalspiel*

But how to resolve the Liverpool goalscoring conundrum for 2017/18? Klopp enjoyed the movement and flexibility of his front players but he needed more forward intensity and pay-off. An unlikely target was Mohamed Salah, that Egyptian left-footed, right-sided attacker who had started for Chelsea at Anfield in the match that had ended Gerrard's title dreams and Brendan Rodgers's Liverpool career back in 2014. Jose Mourinho had signed Salah from Basel in 2013 as a promising 21-year-old but, typically, the Portuguese had trouble fitting Mo into his experienced Chelsea team. 'He was just a lost kid in London,' Mourinho moaned later. 'We wanted to work him to become better and better and better. But he was more of the idea of wanting to play, and not wait.' The impatient Salah was sold to AS Roma where, in 2016/17, he claimed a combined total of 28 goals and assists.

This Egyptian was on his radar, but Klopp credited the Liverpool scouts and his sports analytics team for being constantly in his ear about Salah. The aim was to sign a flexible and versatile player, neither striker nor midfielder, but an offensive all-rounder, a reliable hard-working, goalscoring team player. No pressure, then. The Egyptian actually fitted the bill perfectly. 'We knew what we were getting,' said Klopp later, 'a very offensive-minded midfielder who plays a lot of games as a striker, but also has the ability to make goals, to set up goals.' The complete package, a typical Klopp trait. For a fee rising to £43.9m this seemed like a challenging agenda, but Salah far surpassed it. Like the reaction many older Liverpudlians had when they first heard 'She Loves You' by the Beatles, when they first saw Mo Salah play at top speed, they knew the world had changed forever.

Two other key players arrived at Anfield in the summer of 2017: Andy Robertson, a tough, hard-running Scottish left-back from Hull City for £8m, and another all-round offensive player, Alex Oxlade-Chamberlain from Arsenal for a fee eventually reaching £40m. Robertson had looked efficient and reliable at his relegated club but he had to wait his chance at Liverpool behind Milner and Moreno while his attacking game was developed in training. He would become close to world-class. 'The Ox', long-admired by Klopp for his energy and quality, appeared to have lost his way under Arsène Wenger, so he was looking for a new challenge up north. He would certainly get it.

A long-term injury to Nathaniel Clyne meant that Alexander-Arnold briefly held down the Liverpool right full-back slot in 2017/18 rather earlier than his manager had anticipated. With Mignolet back starting in goal, Matip, Lovren, Klavan and the young Joe Gomez, signed earlier from Charlton, mainly vied for the centre-back positions, with Gomez also acting as right-back cover. Moreno was back, once more, to haunt the left side of Liverpool's defence while Robertson got up to speed. But in front of this reconfigured Liverpool back line a new problem was brewing. Chief creative, Phillipe Coutinho, reported a mystery pre-season 'back problem', amid dark rumours that the Brazilian was actually bound for FC Barcelona. When he emailed in a transfer request, even as the new season began, the top brass at Liverpool simply glared with an 'over our dead body' response. Klopp was distressed but realistic; he understood the draw of the Spanish giants for his Hispanic players. Nor was it easy for his club officials to claim the moral high ground here. Because, in June, Liverpool had been forced into a humiliating climbdown in their own illegal pursuit of Southampton defender Virgil van Dijk, having to issue a public apology as a result. Barcelona had now performed the same trick.

Without the suddenly 'indisposed' Coutinho, the Liverpool front six, in a conventional 4-3-3 formation, now seemed fairly fixed: Wijnaldum, Can and Henderson in midfield; the Holy Trinity of Mané, Firmino and Salah up front. Oxlade-Chamberlain offered a very palatable bench option and Adam Lallana now waited eagerly on the fringes. It looked a compact, strong and reliable (if very small) group. Philippe Coutinho finally got his move to Spain in the January 2018 transfer window for a fee that could rise to an implausible £142m. Liverpool invested just over half of the cash wisely and immediately, on the same Virgil van Dijk they had chased in June. The club's summer antics had cost a £25m price hike for the defender but here was Liverpool's new defensive shield and a Dutch master of *vertikalspiel*. The elegant and imposing Van Dijk could dominate opponents and spray passes 60 yards and more. Even at £75m, taken overall this was excellent recruitment work.

And the 2017/18 domestic league season did have its many high points: Liverpool scored four or more goals 11 times, managed 84 goals overall, conceded a reduced 38 times, and were unbeaten at home – but with seven punishing draws. Here is where a possible league title challenge sank, plus an early 5-0 rout at the Etihad (Mané sent off) and an embarrassing 4-1 capitulation away to Spurs (Lovren in a very public mental breakdown). It was a league performance good enough for another fourth-place finish, so guaranteeing Champions League football. However, for all Klopp's talk about 'the collective' and a team ethic, this league campaign belonged to one player, Mo Salah, with a record 32 goals in 36 league appearances, and an astonishing 44 goals in all competitions. On many occasions, high-stepping and straight-backed with hair flowing like a sporting Charlie Chaplin, dipping inside on to his powerful left foot, little Mo, the man rejected by Mourinho, seemed brutally strong, deadly on his left side and he was often virtually unplayable. Defences beware.

The road to Kiev

Ejected early, once more, from the domestic cups, the main Liverpool focus after Christmas 2017 was on the Champions League knockout phase. In the group stage Liverpool were unforgiving, twice delivering 7-0 beatings, and they were record scorers, so nobody in Europe would be overjoyed to face 'Kloppo's' men over two legs. A 5-0 aggregate last-16 demolition of FC Porto underlined the point but it left Liverpool facing a daunting quarter-final meeting in April 2018 against Guardiola and Manchester City. With the home leg first, Liverpool fans massed around Anfield and some pelted the City bus with rubbish en route to the stadium. But it was on the pitch that Pep's real problems lay. Not unreasonably, Guardiola was reluctant to accept that any opposition plan could undo his brilliant City team, so he came to Anfield prepared to play. Which was perhaps the biggest mistake of his coaching life, because this was the most ruthless demonstration of defensive resolve and dynamic *gegenpressing* we had seen so far, squeezing the life out of opponents and then striking clinically in transition.

The coordinated pace and energy and the collective closing down in Liverpool's system, driven on by a hysterical crowd, meant that City's great stars – Silva, De Bruyne, Sané, Jesus – had little time to settle on the ball. Breaking at bursting speed, first-half goals from Salah and Mané sandwiched a blinding strike from broken play by Oxlade-Chamberlain, who by now had seamlessly settled into Coutinho's berth. Guardiola shrugged helplessly on the visiting bench. He already looked beaten. As thrilling as this blistering 45-minute 3-0 show had been, Liverpool's second-half defensive calmness under Trent and Robertson marshalled by the unflappable Van Dijk to preserve their lead was almost more impressive. City were simply never in this contest – no shots on target.

At the Etihad, the Mancunians briefly threatened after an early goal and a wrongly disallowed second, but Klopp pushed his centre-backs further forward at half-time and goals from Salah and Firmino extinguished City's faint hopes. In truth, it had been a pitiless Liverpool demonstration against England's great league champions. A flummoxed AS Roma were similarly dismantled at Anfield (5-2) in the semi-final first leg, but at a high cost: a serious knee injury to the Ox. After seeing out matters in Rome for a slightly bizarre and misleading 7-6 aggregate scoreline, and with the suddenly departed Željko Buvač mysteriously missing from the away bench, Liverpool were back in a Champions League final after more than a decade away.

Kiev is a beautiful, calm city in late spring, and we Liverpool supporters filled its streets, bars and parks with drunken song in the last few days of May 2018. We came from all points and via all routes. I spent a chilly night sleeping at Warsaw airport and then on someone's floor, but many fans were welcomed wonderfully into the houses of local people to dodge scammers and inflated hotel prices, before heading eventually for the central NSC Olimpiyskiy Stadium. We fans were expectant but also uneasy. For all its vibrant invention and management brio, this was a young and very inexperienced Liverpool squad at this level and now a much depleted one, too. Alex Oxlade-Chamberlain was out, and a soon out-of-contract Emre Can was half-fit, making it only on to the bench. A failing Divock Origi was still out on loan in Germany, so the only viable forward-looking replacement for Liverpool was Adam Lallana, a man who had started precisely one Premier League match all season. None of this tiny Liverpool squad had played in a Champions League final before. In that sense it felt like 2005 all over again.

Opposing them were Real Madrid, trying for three consecutive European titles – Ramos, Marcelo, Varane, Bale, Benzema, Ronaldo, Kroos, Modrić – the established elite of European football. Before the final, Klopp had told a reporter that 'in the end it will be a test of whose desire is bigger'. But that is not how things worked out at all. Liverpool supporters turned the occasion into Anfield on the Dnieper, loudly driving their team on, but it was chicanery and another injury that ultimately shaped the contest. With Liverpool confident and on top, Sergio Ramos, targeting Mo Salah, dragged him to the turf on 30 minutes, leaving the Egyptian – the one player Madrid truly feared – stricken with an injured shoulder.

'It was not the best script for us tonight,' Klopp mused later before the world's press, understated for once. It was clear what he was referring to. Psychologically, Liverpool had been visibly broken by the Salah incident, their talisman soon wrecked and on the sidelines. But it was still a fairly even contest – Mané even equalised Madrid's opener – until another disaster occurred. Goalkeepers are terribly exposed in a team game, expected to make saves, pilloried for their costly mistakes. On the game's biggest stage, Klopp's young goalkeeping protégé, Loris Karius, now killed his team's chances and effectively ended his Liverpool career. Two catastrophic breakdowns in concentration allowed first Benzema and then substitute Gareth Bale to plunder two quite shocking goals out of nothing. That Mané equaliser and a quite outstanding Bale overhead kick felt almost incidental, mere window dressing by comparison. Bad luck, poor selection – or fate? Whatever: Real Madrid 3, Liverpool 1.

In recovery

An Egyptian lawyer Bassem Wahba later threatened Sergio Ramos with a \$1bn lawsuit if Mo Salah missed the approaching World Cup finals in Russia, and more than half-a-million people signed an on-line petition demanding that the Madrid man be punished for his Kiev misdemeanours. UEFA was unmoved. Loris Karius, shamefully, receive death threats. A young foreign journalist thanked Jürgen Klopp at the official post-match press conference for an 'epic' season and called him 'a rock and roller who plays against big money in football'. A track-suited Klopp, one of his fingers mysteriously bandaged, demurred but the point was clear: he was no typical coach. He really did look and feel like an anti-corporate outsider. He was certainly not a man who saw spending big money as a satisfying route to playing success. Klopp described the Salah incident as 'wrestling' and the Madrid goals as 'strange'. A journalist offered that 'everything tonight went wrong, really, really wrong'. The Liverpool coach agreed and looked close to tears. An admiring female correspondent then told him he was 'a fantastic manager who makes football better'. Klopp now smiled through the pain and replied, 'We wanted everything, but got nothing – or minus nothing.' He looked wrung-out, a man on the rag-end of misfortune and another major final defeat. Who could blame him for that? But as preparations for the 2018 FIFA World Cup finals now consumed the global football public, the immediate task for the Liverpool manager was to take stock, seek some rest and then find a goalkeeper to replace his shell-shocked German youngster. There was no way back at Liverpool for Karius.

There is an idiom in football about developing elite squads from positions of strength, and Klopp made his point forcefully to

FSG in the summer of 2018 – the same issue would come up again in 2021. Klopp had successfully piloted a young, if shallow, group to the Champions League Final, but to stay at this level, and then improve again, Liverpool would have to spend wisely – and invest for the future. Divock Origi was back from his unimpressive loan to Wolfsburg with things to prove at Anfield. Agreement had already been reached with RB Leipzig for the purchase of the creative Guinea midfielder Naby Keïta for £52.75m, and the goalkeeping problem was comprehensibly solved by paying some of that Coutinho money out as a record fee for Alisson Becker, from AS Roma, for an initial £56m. Another Brazilian, the versatile defensive midfielder Fabinho, arrived almost immediately from Monaco for £40m, anticipating Emre Can's departure to Juventus. The experienced Swiss international, Xherdan Shaqiri, seemed simply too good a bargain to pass up at £13.5m from relegated Stoke City. Was Shaqiri even Klopp's kind of player, and how he might fit into Liverpool's preferred systems of play? There were no obvious answers here.

Coming back from a disappointment so acute and in such circumstances is not always easy; a dip in form was to be expected. But this was a young Liverpool team at the beginning, rather than the end of its journey, now boosted by an infusion of expensive new talent. Pep Lijnders, a big talker and very popular with the players, now stepped up to replace Željko Buvač as Klopp's assistant, and the German manager Klopp actually seemed lifted by the new arrangement after 17 years working productively, but quietly, with the monosyllabic Bosnian. So, new energy was in place in the backroom and, with renewed faith in Van Dijk, more defensive strength from Fabinho and with Alisson imposing in goal, the Liverpool staff quietly believed that they finally had a squad fit and balanced enough to compete to win the Premier League title and even to avenge this Champions League defeat.

The new season proved outstanding and frustrating, almost in equal measure. Astonishingly, Liverpool lost just one league match – by an 11 millimetres goal-line decision, away to Manchester

City, of course – but such was the latter's consistency that even 97 points was good enough only for second place for Klopp's team. In two seasons, City had now harvested a sensational 198 points. A spate of four Liverpool draws in a six-match period after Christmas proved critical, as City ploughed on. Klopp's system involved his talented full-backs pushing high up the field as auxiliary attackers, Mané and Salah threatening inside, with Fabinho dropping deep to augment the defence, while Firmino as a false nine cleverly linked midfield with attack. Sadio Mané stepped up to match Mo Salah in the goalscoring department – not even the magical Egyptian could keep up last season's exploits. The remarkable Van Dijk reigned supreme behind, not only in marshalling Liverpool's defences but in practising *vertikalspiel*. He made more accurate, long passes than any player in the league. Injuries were also kept at bay, although Oxlade-Chamberlain missed almost the entire campaign. But all this was simply not enough, not given City's unrelenting league excellence.

In Europe, Liverpool narrowly escaped from a qualifying group containing both PSG and Napoli, losing all three away matches, and the price paid for a second-place group finish was a tough-looking last-16 draw against Klopp's old foe, Bayern Munich. A hard-fought 0-0 at Anfield suggested the worst, but a quite brilliant show by Sadio Mané in particular ('His first goal I will watch 1,000 times,' said Klopp later) produced a hugely satisfying 3-1 victory in the Allianz Arena. FC Porto were again easily dispatched, thus lining up a written-in-the-stars semi-final meeting with Coutinho, Suárez and Lionel Messi at FC Barcelona. Liverpool had a decent record in the Camp Nou, and their first-leg performance was by no means disappointing, although the result certainly was, a crushing 3-0 defeat. Opportunities for a vital away goal were royally spurned. 'Yes, there is no party in the dressing room, that's true,' said Klopp icily afterwards.

Liverpool created and missed chances but the difference, of course, was Messi. After the familiar menace of Luis Suárez had opened things up with a wildly celebrated goal, it was the Argentine master who scored the vital second and then the normally conclusive third, a wonderful, unsavable, free kick. It was – take this in – his *600th* goal for his one professional club. Messi should even have claimed an assist for a fourth, late on, but Ousmane Dembélé missed a clear penalty-area opening from Messi's perfectly weighted pass. The Argentine's reaction was significant: he was furious at the young Frenchman's wastefulness. Was the masterful Leo really so worried that even a three-goal lead may not prove enough for his club to survive at Anfield? We would see.

Mentality monsters

The Barcelona coach, Ernesto Valverde, may have had similar thoughts to Messi's, because he rested every single first-team player for his club's 2-0 La Liga defeat by Celta Vigo before the second leg at Anfield. By contrast, Klopp lost both Firmino and Salah through injury for the Anfield return, the first time since their arrival that he had been without both forwards for any Champions League or Premier League match. Shaqiri and Origi came in. A turnaround looked improbable, at best. Klopp had even told his wife Ulla not to arrange the usual after-match party, fearing a deflating anticlimax. But he said something in the team's Hope Street Hotel on the morning of the contest that clearly inspired his squad, a comment for the club's annals to rival anything said by its greatest leaders of the past: 'What we do tonight, I would say, is impossible,' he began. 'But, because it is you, there is a chance.'

Adam Lallana later recalled that the Liverpool players completely believed in Klopp's knowledge of the European game and how he had recounted that his Dortmund team had once been 3-0 down to Real Madrid, made seven or eight changes and winged the second leg 2-0, when a 5-0 scoreline would not have been flattering. 'I have told the players that story,' Klopp said. 'It doesn't mean that it will happen again, but it is enough for me to believe.' What followed was, arguably, the greatest single night at Anfield in the club's entire 127-year history so far. Which was why, speaking live on BT Sport immediately after the match, a euphoric Klopp dispensed with all usual protocol: 'The boys are fucking giants,' he gushed. He looked out of his mind with happiness. So, this is the story of that evening. Even now it is hard to believe.

If everything went wrong for Klopp in Kiev on that sultry May evening in 2018 – and it had – then pretty much all things went right here at Anfield on 7 May 2019. Looking for the single goal that would change everything, Barcelona attacked from the off, Coutinho and Messi weaving elusive patterns, but these artists continually made wrong decisions and Liverpool defended with both organisation and resilience, Alisson and Van Dijk unmoved. The Reds also pressed hard, stopping the Spaniards playing out comfortably from the back, and then scored early on through Origi after a mistake by Jordi Alba. A precious 1-0 half-time lead left Anfield cocooned in hope. We could all calm down for 15 minutes. Andy Robertson had earlier Scottish-cuffed a grounded and outraged Lionel Messi, but the Scot was now injured, so James Milner moved into the left-back slot, his new specialist position. The unplanned second-half midfield replacement for Milner, Gini Wijnaldum, then took charge, scoring two quick goals by making third-man support runs behind Liverpool's attackers, receiving crosses from both left and right. The emotional Dutchman said later that he was angry and 'charged up' that his coach had left him out of the home starting XI. He channelled his anger well, so even this crazy selection decision had worked in Liverpool and Klopp's favour.

Three-all on aggregate now: it said as much on the red electronic scoreboard high up to our right, so it must be true. Anfield was still wild with expectation. George Sephton, the Liverpool match announcer, wrote later that his glass room above the Kop to our right started vibrating alarmingly from the noise generated below. The Catalan TV commentator present also knew what was coming: 'It's the eternal nightmare,' he shrieked. 'Each and every one of the ghosts are reappearing!' He was right. The fourth and clinching Liverpool goal was barely imaginable, born out of the super-smart supply for a Reds' corner of Anfield's itinerant ball boys – Oakley Cannonier, the kid concerned, signed his first professional playing contract with Liverpool in July 2021. It may even have been because of this moment. With the ball instantly in the quadrant, Trent Alexander-Arnold (who else?) took a half-step away from the corner flag before returning, like some drunken Irish dancer, to instantly strike a low ball, an afterthought, which Divock Origi (the only player half-watching) then calmly swept home with his right foot. Complete bedlam broke out. There was a ball in Barça's net but half the Kop (and Klopp himself) had missed the play completely and would only catch it later on TV. Had this really happened? No Barcelona player, those highly trained and extravagantly rewarded football thoroughbreds, had so much as *moved* for this prematurely taken corner kick. It was an act worth millions, but delivered as if among a group of kids in a scratch match on Everton Park.

Now the Catalans were publicly embarrassed, completely undone, swallowed up by waves of noise that were surely shimmering even over the distant Albert Dock. There was no way back for them; Anfield was juddering, the Kop bewildered with joy. And at the final whistle Milner and Wijnaldum, together, in the pitch corner where the Kop meets the Kenny Dalglish Stand, caressed the match ball before launching it on to the Kop, and then fell hunched on their knees and in tears. Grown working men in the seats around us were also weeping. Others were simply dazed, dumbfounded, hands clamped to heads, eyes popping. Only football does this, crashes one's emotions in this way, makes you speechless and out of control with that collective and sheer blissful 'thank god I was there' psychosis of it all. It is all returning to me now, even as I write this through wetted eyes. Later, the entire Liverpool squad and staff – 'mentality monsters' Klopp called them – celebrated together on the pitch what had been a quite staggering evening in a surging, full-throated, finale in front of the dazed and exhausted Liverpool Kop.

Typically, when he had finally calmed down, Jürgen Klopp was keen to stress to journalists the combination of factors that had driven his team home on this glorious night: 'We know this club is the mix of atmosphere, emotion, desire and football quality,' he said. 'Cut off one, and it doesn't work.' The emotionality and togetherness of the Liverpool collective, as always, had to come through, the irreducible bond between the stands and the pitch. Let me ask, right here, in what other part of one's over-controlled and hyper-managed existence today is it even remotely possible to experience this sort of ecstatic joy with complete strangers, with people who are all, nevertheless, somehow known to us, who are our deepest comrades, our next-of-sporting-kin? And, be in no doubt, this memorable and frenetic evening was right up there with all those quite fantastic and historic Liverpool European occasions of the past: Inter Milan in 1965, Saint-Étienne 1977, Barcelona 2001, Olympiacos 2004, Chelsea 2005, Real Madrid 2008, Dortmund 2017, and Manchester City 2018. Many experienced Liverpool fans – including the author – would argue that it was actually *better* than all of them. And now Liverpool FC, under this laid-back, charismatic, but also driven German coach, had yet another European trophy to chase. And who could argue, after what had happened just a year ago in Kiev, and now on this famous night in Anfield, that it was anything other than fate that had brought us here?

Chapter 13

Oh, Happy Days

Madrid 2019 and the Premier League title, at last

*Spurs offer a welcome early leg-up in Madrid.
The new football world arrives, according to VAR.
Liverpool almost forget how to lose in the Premier
League. Kloppo's head is blown off over mad
fixture congestion. Liverpool's youth teams take on
both domestic cup competitions and Everton are
humiliated in the FA Cup. In Qatar, the 2020 Club
World Champions have a familiar look. Adrián
and Atlético together, somehow, derail the World
Champions in Europe, as Covid looms. It is the last
football crowd we will see for some time. Lockdown
short-circuits the entire season but Liverpool return
to an empty Anfield to claim the easiest of their 19
league titles, after a 30-year wait.*

Madrid 2019

It is some kind of heresy, of course it is, to say that a Champions League Final, the biggest club fixture in world football – in global sport – can ever feel like an afterthought, an expensive chore one has to attend to and curate, as any dutiful fan must. This is especially true when three-quarters-of-a-million souls will turn up later on the streets of Liverpool just to see the cup brought home. But the truth is that following that epic Anfield occasion against Barcelona – the ritual humiliation of the world's best footballer and the club he calls home while overturning a three-goal deficit – for some Liverpool supporters this was probably how the 2019 Champions League Final felt. Do we *still* have to do this, even after seeing off Messi and Barça? Were we not here in this final just last year?

But Liverpool fans did indeed have to step up again, not least because their leader Jürgen Klopp was on a losing streak of six finals, a run he simply had to break. *We* had to help him do it. Nevertheless, the €180 final ticket for this rather sterile new Stadio Metropolitano venue on the outskirts of Madrid offered expensive access to an event that lacked much of the essential drama and the colour of a truly great European football night, even in the lovely central Spain early evening sunshine. Okay, there were the tens of thousands of Anfield pilgrims lapping it up in Retiro Park; we had the usual madcap Liverpool banners and the inevitable Jamie Webster songs; the bizarre UEFA dancers, plus the Imagine Dragons still doing their pre-match thing, even as the teams were taking the field. And the drink, there was always the drink. Buckets of it. But was this not just going through the motions a little bit here?

The people of Liverpool were here in their droves, of course, but on-street relations with their rivals were peculiarly courteous and familiar. This was because the opposition was English and also inexperienced. Spurs had completed a run to their first Champions League Final that was almost as unlikely as Liverpool's. They were here, well, because they were here. They had *stolen* their place in this festival at the last, via VAR at the Etihad and larceny at Ajax of Amsterdam. Tottenham, with a quarter-fit Harry Kane on the bus and in the team, had no realistic plans to actually take home the Champions League trophy to north London and that stellar new ground of theirs.

Deep down, they knew they were really sightseeing, experience-gathering. Part of the landscape.

This was Liverpool's first major all-English European final in 55 years of studied avoidance, and it was not much welcomed. The whole experience of a European football adventure had changed beyond recognition since that first Liverpool Icelandic escapade abroad in 1964 and the club's first European Cup Final in Rome back in 1977. For that occasion, people travelled with neither knowledge nor fear, an endurance test to southern Italy, no overnight stops.

Now a trip like this could bite into a month's salary, a whole week away in a posh hotel or a swish apartment for some; a proper football holiday. But another reason why this particular final would pale against everything that had gone before it was that rather than always working hard for their rewards, as Jürgen Klopp insisted they must, Liverpool were gifted a very early advantage in this showpiece. A ticket to ride. Sadio Mané gently lifted a ball on to Moussa Sissoko's innocently outstretched arm in his team's first attack. Back in 1977 (or even in 2007) this is no penalty, never even a shout. But today? Today, VAR confirms the unfortunate sentence for Spurs. So, a bashful Mo Salah has his early chance to make up for last season's personal injustice, which he thrashes in from the spot.

From this moment on, right up until substitute Divock Origi's late second-half goal (his only positive, but wonderful, contribution), it was pretty much a case of Liverpool fans watching the stadium digital clock grind slowly down, quietly praying and seeing out time. Spurs pressed, but with Trent and Robertson in defensive mode, it was more out of hope than expectation. Alisson Becker offered complete solidity in the Liverpool net, the kind of presence that simply highlighted the enormity of the vacuum and the transgressions of poor Loris Karius just 12 months before (his belief in Karius and perhaps his loyalty to Moreno were the only two major charges that we could reasonably level against Jürgen Klopp so far).

Which all meant that this final was, to be perfectly frank, a rather poor-quality contest with few surprises and an obvious outcome. At the final whistle, the Liverpool players flopped to the floor in ecstatic joy, of course they did – had they not expected to win? Even as Origi scored Liverpool's second goal, Virgil van Dijk was slumping flat to the turf, already contemplating the enormity of it all. Cue at the final whistle the building of the on-field stage and the clunky, essentially phony, UEFA presentation ceremony, all daft flames and sponsors' confetti. And then the lap of honour and the usual media 'human interest' stories began to flood out: about Milner's dream, Hendo's poorly dad and Trent's mates in the crowd. But for all the tears, bear hugs and singing, and the taking home of some serious silverware at last for that 750,000-strong crowd back home to goggle at, everyone in red knew that this meeting was actually no more than a (very) fancy dessert after the main course. That meal had been served up at Anfield so spectacularly a month before. But Liverpool fans will take it, every time – European Cup number *six*. Got that, Manchester? Have one, Arsenal? See this, Chelsea? *This* is what European history looks like.

Winning made easy

This Liverpool manager had performed some remarkable, restorative surgery on his team to get them to this place in fewer than four years of reconstruction: major finalists, champions of Europe, convincing Premier League title challengers, FIFA Club World Cup contenders. That key quintet from 2014 – Sturridge, Suárez, Coutinho, Sterling and Gerrard – were all gone now, but in truth they had barely been missed. Alisson, Van Dijk, Mané, Fabinho and Salah, all world-class signings, five top-quality performers, had been recruited by the Liverpool transfer committee right there, on the spin. The conversion of Jordan Henderson into an authentic leader, captain and hero, the new expanded role for Firmino and the moulding of the Liverpool full-backs into a pair of world-class marauding predators, was also all Klopp's work. So, too, was developing Wijnaldum's discipline and all-round excellence. This signified the very highest level of motivational coaching and recruitment expertise.

But none of it was especially done on the cheap: Liverpool's total wage bill in 2018/19 was £310m, only a margin below Manchester City's. However, it was also only 58 per cent of the club's total turnover – compared to 85 per cent, for example, at neighbours Everton. Liverpool's commercial staff were busy churning out the product, pulling in new global partners. After seeing off New Balance in the courts, the club's new official kit manufacturers, Nike, were soon reported to be willing to cough up at least £75m a year for the privilege of marking those precious red shirts with a white swoosh from 2020. Why not? Liverpool FC have fans all over the world and a coach that personified the Nike global brand image of an uber-successful, off-beat slacker. The new Liverpool corporate sections at Anfield were also bringing home the bacon, even if some of those hyped £400 hospitality seats, linked with hotels and restaurants around the city, were still conspicuously empty for some very big Anfield occasions. Main Stand fakers below them were now, annoyingly, stumbling back to their seats, often ten minutes after half-time, carrying *pizzas*.

These hapless consumers and part-timers would also have plenty more time for in-game snacks this coming season because the dreaded VAR system finally came to the Premier League, with a promise of 'maximum benefit, minimum interference' – who actually believed this? VAR *could* have been used sensibly enough to wipe out 'clear and obvious' mistakes by match officials. But, instead, in the English Premier League the Professional Games Match Officials Limited, under the hapless Mike Riley, decreed that every goal, every part of every human body, be mapped against geometric lines, examined in some distant bunker with forensic scrutiny. It felt like death by exactitude, designed only for the distracted amusement of armchair fans. VAR was not even used effectively to challenge referees' errors if the VAR man – another referee of course – could see how the mistake had been reasonably made. In-ground goal celebrations were now on regular hold. It was video assistance designed by Franz Kafka and applied by a hopeless drunk. Nevertheless, the Liverpool defence coaches saw VAR as a potential ally. Playing a high line well could only work in the past if the officials were on their game. VAR took away that uncertainty; Van Dijk and his men could now become kings of the offside trap.

There were still problems to solve at Anfield, naturally. Or at least some not yet overwhelming playing successes. Naby Keïta, for one, remained largely unimpressive and injury-plagued, expensively struggling to hold down a first-team place and to manage his own bodily malfunctions. The Karius problem had been shelved with a loan out to Beşiktaş, and Simon Mignolet was sold back to Belgium for £6.4m in the summer of 2019, which meant a new back-up goalkeeper was needed. Adrián, an experienced shot-stopper and a self-proclaimed 'character' from West Ham United, a man also known for making the occasional howler, apparently fitted the bill. He was familiar with the English game, dangerously over-confident but, crucially, happy to sit out most of the season on the Liverpool bench. After all, reserve goalkeepers were seldom seen, right?

In fact, Alisson Becker crocked himself in the Premier League's 2019/20 seasonal opener, a Friday night league home fixture against newly promoted Norwich City, so the buoyant Adrián was immediately required. He played nine league matches in sequence, as well as in the European Super Cup, a glorified cash-raising friendly with a trophy in Istanbul, where he did his job in the penalty shoot-out against Chelsea. Historic footnote here: this was Liverpool's first-ever senior match controlled by a team of *female* officials, French referee Stephanie Frappart, with Manuela Nicolosi of France and Michelle O'Neal from the Republic of Ireland, as her assistants. It only took 127 years of waiting and, guess what, the sky did not cave in. The downside here in terms of gender politics in football was that relegation of

Liverpool FC Women from the WSL in 2020. But we are already getting ahead of ourselves …

By the time the men's team goalkeeper Alisson Becker stepped out again, at Old Trafford on 9 October 2019, his understudy had successfully defended a remarkable Liverpool run in the Premier League of nine consecutive victories. The draw at United broke the spell, but no matter. Liverpool immediately set off on *another* run of 18 consecutive Premier League victories, thus equalling a record of Manchester City. Some 35 wins and one draw or, to put it another way, 65 consecutive Premier League matches with only one defeat, and that by the finest of margins at the Etihad way back in January 2019. The numbers here were mind-boggling and the levels of consistency and mental strength required in a league of this quality almost unimaginable.

In a run of this magnitude there would have to be some narrow squeaks, and there were: a home goalkeeper howler at Sheffield United in September; a 95th-minute Milner penalty to see off Leicester City at home in October; two goals in the closing minutes to chisel out a thrilling win at Aston Villa in November. In pre-season, Klopp had invited the German extreme sport surfer, Sebastian Steudtner, to talk to the Liverpool squad about how to deal with high-pressure situations using breathing techniques. Here was the reward. And the league victories in England kept coming, including a 3-1 home comfort against Guardiola and Manchester City in November. But so, too, did the fixtures. Relentlessly so.

Jürgen Klopp had already started to boil his top in October over fixture scheduling, saying that leagues everywhere needed to 'think about their players and not about their wallets', as if these two features of the sport were not, in any way, connected. The FIFA Club World Cup in Qatar in December, which Liverpool would have to contest, meant 10, or even 11, first-team fixtures in the month leading up to and around Christmas. After seeing off Milton Keynes Dons in the League Cup, Klopp tried to manage the impact of this impending logjam by fielding a low-strength team for the home tie against Arsenal at the end of October. But the Liverpool kids, marshalled by an off-message Adam Lallana, were defiant in fighting out a chaotic 5-5 draw and then producing a win on penalties. A super-confident, languid young Scouser, Curtis Jones, who had been at the club from nine years of age, made a TV name for himself by scoring the winning kick.

Despite losing again in the Champions League in Naples, Liverpool managed to survive the group stages once more, by defeating a troublesome RB Salzburg in Austria (some floppy-haired kid called Haaland scored at Anfield. Whatever happened to him?). This European run produced two important casualties – the dogged Fabinho, out for several months, and Jürgen Klopp's usual calm exterior. Because now there really *was* an authentic scheduling problem and it seemed, for a time, that Liverpool may have to withdraw from the League Cup because of the ensuing fixture snarl-up. Klopp was definitely unhappy, angry even, but he was not anarchic. He wanted to solve the conundrum, he said, while respecting the domestic cups, which, to be honest, he had not always seemed to value too much in the past.

The agreed outcome just about touched all bases. A Liverpool team of sorts – basically a pre-season select youth XI – would play away to Aston Villa in the League Cup the day *after* the first-team squad had set off to Qatar. This mix of Under-19 and Under-23 staffers would be managed by Neil Critchley, the Liverpool U-23s coach, as Klopp and his first-team staff would already be in the Middle East. This was highly unorthodox but it was a solution of sorts. This Liverpool squad, the youngest ever to have contested a first-team match for the club, actually out-footballed a weakened Villa for half-an-hour, but they were also physically overpowered by their hosts, ending up 4-0 down at half-time. Klopp, watching in Qatar, texted an interval message to Critchley, which read, 'Don't change anything, carry on doing what you're doing. You've been brilliant.' Which could be read as real praise, or relief that Liverpool could finally wave goodbye to the competition lowest on its crowded list of priorities. Villa, respectfully, turned off the gas in the second half, so a final 5-0 scoreline in the circumstances could be regarded as a job well done for both clubs. Jürgen Klopp and his senior players could now turn their attention to rather more pressing matters out in the winter desert.

Top of the world

Historically, let's face it, Liverpool have had a difficult relationship with the FIFA Club World Cup competition in its various guises. Back in the late 1970s, Bob Paisley and chairman John Smith saw the Intercontinental Cup match-up between the European and South American champions as an often violent two-legged distraction, so Liverpool gave it a wide berth. When the competition became a one-off affair, against his better judgement Paisley agreed to take his team to Japan, but with minimal preparation, and they were duly gubbed 3-0 by the Zico-inspired Brazilian team Flamengo. Paisley could care less and the match had little commercial benefit and drew little media attention back in the UK. But now, during the Copa Libertadores in 2019, one song had been ringing out louder than any other among the Flamengo ultras: 'In December 1981,' they chanted, 'we ran rings around the English.' *They* had not forgotten.

In 1984 Liverpool lost again, this time 1-0 to the Argentines from Independiente. The South American teams (who really valued this event) won seven of the first ten finals played in Japan and, despite their period of dominance in Europe, no English club could manage even a goal in these final contests. From 2000 the event format had been expanded to include winners of all the confederations, with FIFA deciding that the victors could now rightfully call themselves Club World Champions. Which was probably an inopportune moment to take four years off, until a restart in 2005. Money, as is so often the case for FIFA, was obviously the problem. Its return was just in time to welcome new European champions, Liverpool under Rafa Benitez, but the revised format did not help the Reds. However, by 2019, global exposure, owner vanity, Asian commercial markets and simple trophy hunger had all upped the ante to actually win this trinket. For FSG, to be recognised as Club World Champions now would sell a pile of red jerseys in this and other parts of the world, especially with Nike soon to be on board. In short, Liverpool were expected to win this event.

Klopp, unlike Bob Paisley before him, also looked serious about Qatar. He had his entire first-team squad and back-ups there, with no concessions at all to the League Cup back in England. Moreover, he had just signed a new five-year contract with Liverpool until 2024, making it clear that this decision to stay was not just about progress on the pitch. 'I have seen the commitment from the ownership,' he said, 'through to every aspect and function of the club you can think of.' Klopp's assistants, Peter Krawietz and Pep Lijnders, also extended their deals, as did the apparently growing younger James Milner. In fact, many of the key actors at the club, both on and off the field, had now committed themselves to long-term service, so things looked remarkably stable, a veritably happy ship.

Made happier still, perhaps, by the announcement in December of the signing of Takumi Minamino from Red Bull Salzburg for a bargain release clause price of £7.25m. A few things were going on here. Minamino had impressed for Salzburg in an earlier 4-3 Champions League loss at Anfield and Liverpool had an obvious need for versatile forward cover, at cost price. Second, Klopp's success with the exceptional Shinji Kagawa at Dortmund had made him prize the skills and work ethic of the Japanese. And, third, probably the clincher, the club's commercial department was slavering over marketing Liverpool in Asia with an international player from the region in the squad. It all made perfect sense – *if* the new man could match the exacting standards of Premier League play. Initially, he struggled to make an impact.

But first Minamino would have to watch his new team-mates toil against the Mexicans from Monterrey in their World Club Cup meeting in Doha. Playing this event in Qatar was a way for FIFA to offer a gentle rehearsal for the World Cup due there in

2022, but none of the socio-political concerns about this location had disappeared in the meantime. Liverpool had backed calls by human rights groups for a probe into the deaths of foreign workers in Qatar and the club had also rejected a luxury hotel offered to its players after claims that its construction had breached labour laws. Chief executive Peter Moore had sought assurances that LGBTQ+ fans could safely attend these Club World Cup matches, and Paul Amaan from LGBTQ+ group Kop Outs did attend with his husband, and said, pointedly, 'Quite honestly, we felt as free in Qatar as we do in Liverpool, where equally we don't make public displays of affection or hold hands in public because of the shocking rise in hate crimes that we've experienced.' Some 6,000 Reds made the trip and they were allowed to drink weak beer in official fan zones. They may also have been worried about how long it took their heroes to finally subdue the CONCACAF champions in the semi-final, a late goal for substitute Roberto Firmino sealing a very patchy 2-1 victory.

Flamengo, like all the South American clubs, really did want to win this competition. The Brazilians had seen off their great Argentinian rivals River Plate 2-1 in the Copa Libertadores final on 23 November and they were crowned champions of their domestic league just 24 hours later – by 16 points. Flamengo enjoyed attacking, and their twin strikers, Gabriel Barbosa – on loan from Inter Milan – and Bruno Henrique, were their key men. After defeating Al-Halil in the other semi-final, they were certainly an authentic threat, but a more open approach might also suit their English opponents. Flamengo had brought 10,000 vociferous supporters with them to Doha, as well as drawing on plenty of local support. Nevertheless, the goalless 90 minutes was hardly the incisive, attacking treat FIFA had hoped for. But in extra time a combination of Mané (the season's Liverpool standout, so far) and Firmino produced a goal for the Brazilian, so making the trip more than a mid-season encumbrance, a distraction for a club aimed at winning its first domestic league title for 30 years. The outcome was, indeed, that Liverpool

FC, under Jürgen Klopp, could at last claim to be Club World Champions for 2019. It sounded right enough, and one might almost have heard the tills already kerchinging away in the club's diaspora of merchandise outlets. Now, about that *other* business …

Striking for home

When Liverpool returned from Qatar in 2019, immediately to visit Leicester City, it was a buoyant Foxes they faced, a team placed just behind them in the league standings and now managed by a resurgent Brendan Rodgers. One could see the headlines already being written. This was, in short, a Boxing night fixture bristling with negative intent, but at least it would be played out against a background of a gaping 13-point post-Christmas Premier League Liverpool lead. A defeat here would be damaging but not a catastrophe. Leicester's season had been constructed on the same sort of defensive solidity as Liverpool's; both clubs had conceded only 14 times in 18 league matches. But Rodgers's team would leak badly here. And let's be clear, winning 4-0 anywhere in the English Premier League is not easy, although Pep Guardiola could seemingly conjure up such landslides at will. But to win away like this, against one's nearest rival and after a mid-season haul across to the Middle East, was really exceptional.

Rodgers helped matters by starting James Maddison wide on Liverpool's left side, thus marginalising his midfielder's invention and allowing Trent to cause merry havoc down Liverpool's right flank. The full-back was imperious, offering assists as well as a flashing fourth goal. With ten minutes to go the home areas of the King Power Stadium, a furnace at the start, were silenced and already less than half full, bliss for we travelling supporters, now in full voice. These Liverpool victory chants had barely died down before, on the very next evening, ten-man Manchester City were brought down by Wolves at Molineux, thus taking Klopp's men 17 points clear of the only rival capable of sustaining the sort of extended winning run now required to catch the runaway leaders.

How had such a lead been manufactured? The general view was that Jürgen Klopp had sacrificed some of the cavalier work of the previous season in favour of a more solid shape, usually built around three hard-working midfielders, relying on the full-backs and the Liverpool front players to conjure up goal chances. Some of this was true, but crucial too was how Virgil van Dijk and Alisson Becker now spread serene assurance behind. Nobody caught these guys on the break – especially with VAR monitoring for offsides. Whatever else was going on, this new combination was working. Coaches and commentators also began to admit that, unlike Manchester City, this Liverpool team could win football matches in numerous different ways: by pressing and out-muscling opponents at difficult venues, as happened at Chelsea; by having the mentality and defensive strength required always to win closely fought contests, as at Villa Park; or they could simply outplay rivals at pace and ruin them, as at Leicester. And behind it all was rock-solid form at home at a seemingly impregnable Anfield. After seeing off a resilient Sheffield United at the beginning of January 2020 in a 2-0 home procession, the uncomplicated United manager, Chris Wilder, admitted that his team 'had not laid a glove' on the champions-elect. He offered later a brutally honest assessment of the quality, allied to old-fashioned values and sheer hard work, that the rest were now up against:

> They did all the things. You talk about Academy coaches and all this nonsense about technical and tactical stuff. So, they won every first ball, every second ball, dropped on every second ball. Ran forward and ran back. And they did all that stuff miles better than us. So, when Academy coaches and all this nonsense that comes out about coaching, just have a little peek at Liverpool tonight.

Wilder's point was that, even in an era of big transfers, sports science, tactical acumen and analytics, football remained a simple game built on organisation and hard graft and made difficult only by fools. The Sheffield man would have admired Liverpool successfully fighting it out in an epic struggle three weeks later on a damp evening in Wolverhampton, where Andy Robertson was royally undressed by the rapid Adama Traore. Nevertheless, Roberto Firmino scored another late winning goal in a hard-fought 2-1 Liverpool victory, a welcome recent habit. Among the vast away contingent, this felt like a crucial statement. 'We don't go for perfection,' admitted Jürgen Klopp, discussing the scrappy but urgent Liverpool response to the Wolves equaliser. 'We go for a perfect *reaction*. We try to fight back in difficult situations in games, which is what the boys did again. I'm really, really pleased.' He would have taken a draw in this difficult contest – we all would. Watching Liverpool away from the *side* of the pitch is a joy. Nineteen points clear of Manchester City, with only 14 matches to go. What could possibly go wrong in the league from here?

(Not) up the for cup

Truth is, Jürgen Klopp had never quite got his head around the fixture load in England, or the importance to locals of the FA Cup. The early stages of the cup were now treated by Liverpool and most Premier League (and some Championship) clubs as a testing ground for promising academy products, or else as a means of giving squad players a run-out for their ginormous salaries. The message here was that you probably wanted out of it as soon as possible – unless, of course, you could guarantee to go all the way. The financial importance of the Champions League, maintaining a place in the elite or cementing a possible promotion push had all long usurped the FA Cup competition's place in the football firmament, although this seemed illogical when club success was supposedly measured by winning trophies.

This was certainly true for most fans – and for Pep Guardiola. The FA was partly to blame, of course, for denigrating its own flagship competition by moving kick-off times around, selling out to whatever commercial and television sponsors demanded and playing even cup semi-finals at Wembley. FA Cup attendances had plummeted as the quality (and cost) of the Premier League product had soared. Klopp protested, always, that he wanted his players to win *every* match they played, but he had never quite worked out how to showcase his deep dismay when his team were routinely ejected in the early stages of domestic knockout tournaments. So, a third-round tie involving rising local rivals Everton at Anfield in January 2020, the Blues now under their own new stellar manager, Carlo Ancelotti, required some deep thought. Go strong, or go home? Or so it seemed to local Reds, if not, of course, to Jürgen Klopp.

Again, Lallana, plus Origi and Gomez and a soon-injured Milner were the first-team squad men enlisted to try to hold together a team of promising novices against a full-strength and confident Everton. All bets were off. How badly would home supporters take this inevitable derby-day cup clubbing and another early FA Cup submission? What sort of stick would the Liverpool manager endure for allowing it to happen in front of the Kop? Except, somehow, Liverpool took charge of this contest, with Pedro Chirivella, a neat Spanish midfielder from Valencia who had been loitering around Kirkby since 2013, totally running the show, again under Lallana's watchful eye. The match looked like it might meander towards a well-earned and perfectly honourable 0-0 draw, when that lanky Scouse kid, Curtis Jones, stepped up once more. This time he hit a wondrous bending and dipping right-foot shot high into the top left-hand corner of Jordan Pickford's net. And this goal, this thing of some beauty, was celebrated by Liverpool fans on the Kop at least as joyfully as that Origi winner against the mighty Barcelona in the Champions League had been only a few months before. Jones even cheekily told the BBC later that, *of course*, he should be playing in this world champion Liverpool team, playing full-time. 'He's not short of confidence,' said a smiling Klopp later. A priceless FA Cup debut: Liverpool kids 1, Everton 0.

The same group went to Shrewsbury Town for the next round, a late 2-2 draw, with a traditional televised FA Cup full-throated home pitch invasion thrown in for good measure. Interviewed live afterwards by the BBC, a clearly irked Klopp then dropped his guard and threw down his second grenade of the season. This replay was during the official Premier League season break, so he reasoned that the Liverpool kids would have to start in this match – like, the *real* Liverpool kids, the U13s – and that he would not be there to see it. He and his squad had better things to do. So, the BBC, the FA and their precious little cup could go hang. Neil Critchley would be doing Kloppo's job at Anfield once more, acting up as first-team Liverpool coach – with the kids.

National jaws slackened. Now, hold on here. This was a Liverpool manager taking paid holiday leave while his club was playing in the fourth round of the precious FA Cup, the world's oldest and best knockout football tournament? The same cup that the club had slogged for 73 years to win? For some long-servers, this was especially hard to take in. And there was to be no compromise here, no sneaking in a few first-team squad members on the sly, those men who actually could really *use* a game right now. *Verboten*. For Klopp, this was a matter of principle: he had stood up for a mid-season break and he thought it an act of deep hypocrisy now to abuse it, even by playing a few seasoned pros in the historic English FA Cup. It was also a message, of course, about the club's cast-iron European and Premier League focus. Which all meant that Curtis Jones's reward for his brilliant cup performances so far was to be made the 19-year-old captain of this Liverpool FA Cup XI that showed a record low average age of 19 years and 102 days. There were players involved here that even seasoned watchers of the Liverpool academy teams could barely recognise. In front of a packed, reduced-price crowd that was little older, on average, than the team they were watching, it was the apprentice Welsh right-back, Neco Williams who forced a second-half own goal from a tiring Shrewsbury Town defence to decide the contest. That a weakened Liverpool next played Chelsea in round five and lost 2-0 at Stamford Bridge (Adrián badly at fault, a warning) was merely a predictable footnote to what had been a heroic and bizarre FA Cup run ... for the Liverpool youth team.

Sunk, by Adrián and Wuhan

Any football club facing Atlético Madrid in the last 16 of the Champions League knows that this is a booby-trapped invitation for managers and coaches with serious European ambitions. Here were the cynical subverters of the beautiful game, a club coached by an Argentine arch tactician, Diego Simeone, a man you would not readily buy a watch or a car from. Simeone was a souped-up version of Helenio Herrera, whose Inter Milan had duped Bill Shankly way back in 1965. So, it was little surprise that when Liverpool duly returned to the Wanda Metropolitano, the scene of their most recent Champions League glory, they were mugged in the first leg of this tie, losing 1-0. It was a nothing goal, fortuitously scored from a fourth-minute corner, that settled this contest. Liverpool lacked ideas, as their hosts sat deep and wished the time away. As always, it was the Liverpool 'nil' that was the potential problem here; scoring two goals at Anfield with no reply against these experienced misers was no gimme.

But Liverpool had to park that immediate problem in order to continue their exceptional Premier League run, sneaking past West Ham at home, before moving on to Vicarage Road, Watford. Loose talk was starting up about Liverpool possibly 'equalling' the Arsenal Invincibles' unbeaten league record of 2003/04 – which was, frankly, preposterous. Those north London fakers had drawn 12 – *twelve*! – of their league fixtures. Here, Liverpool had reached 29 February 2020, round 28 of league matches unbeaten, and had drawn just *one*. Statues get erected for less. But although Watford were in relegation hardship, they had found some recent form under their savvy new English manager, Nigel Pearson, and these Hornets had created (and missed) a hatful of recent chances. Nevertheless, those learned folk at *The Anfield Wrap* podcast were predicting a three- or four- goal Liverpool win in a way that seemed both obtuse and asking for trouble. Which, of course, is precisely what Liverpool got. But this time there was to be no heroic recovery from falling three goals behind.

Watford were organised and determined, while Liverpool looked a little stale, *expecting* things to happen for once. The pressure of constantly having to win also seemed, finally, to have had its impact. The sheer scale of the defeat – 3-0, with the Liverpool back four constantly beaten by good movement and pace – was explained for critics by the performance of Dejan Lovren against the wily Troy Deeney. But young Trent at right-back also regally lost the plot here. 'Your form is not something you can take for granted,' said Klopp sourly in the post-match press conference, his voice almost drowned out by the singing coming from the home dressing room. 'We performed exactly as they wanted.' Watford's pacy Senegal international winger, Ismaïla Sarr, had proved impossible to handle. The magnificent Liverpool run was over; 44 league matches, all told, with no losses had been a remarkable feat of endurance, consistency and quality. Now Liverpool had to begin from scratch once more – but it was with a 22-point league cushion, enlarged to 25 points when our new friends at Old Trafford, unexpectedly, managed to see off their noisy neighbours from City.

While Liverpool had been securing the Club World title in Qatar and building an unassailable lead in the world's most difficult league, elsewhere in December 2019 a virus was emerging at the Wuhan live animal food market in China, from an interaction between an animal and a human. Scientists speculated that it had originated in bats but had transferred to humans via an intermediary animal in the same way that another coronavirus – the 2002 SARS outbreak – had moved from horseshoe bats to cat-like civets before infecting humans. The animal suspected this time was the pangolin, a scaly delicacy, the most illegally traded mammal in the world for their meat and the claimed medicinal properties of their scales. Who knew? The Chinese state was reluctant to reveal the details but people in China had started to die from the infection before Christmas 2019 and it had now moved across Europe into Italy and Spain. Britain had its first officially recorded cases on 29 January 2020. By early March, with the hapless UK Government fatally dawdling, we were already witnessing a pandemic, and deaths from the Covid-19 virus were reported to be 'surging' across Britain. On Wednesday, 11 March the new chancellor, Rishi Sunak, announced a £12bn package of emergency measures to help the nation cope with the expected onslaught from this coronavirus, which the World Health Organisation had officially declared a global crisis. Within a week, the UK Government's chief scientific adviser was warning that as many as 55,000 local people may now be infected and that it would be a 'good outcome' if the eventual UK death toll could be kept below 20,000 (it would not be, not even close).

It was actually on that same evening of 11 March, in the very eye of this developing storm across the world, that Liverpool played the second leg of the last-16 Champions League tie against Atlético Madrid in a packed Anfield containing some 3,000 Spanish fans. We mixed merrily together on the Anfield streets. Nobody here was practising social distancing – except marginally the players, instructed not to perform the pre-match handshake. Twelve days later, Britain would be in total lockdown. In hindsight, hosting this contest was a quite foolish mistake, the last major football match seen by a crowd anywhere in Europe for some time. The uncertainty around it actually had echoes of the Boavista Champions League match played at Anfield on that haunting evening of 11 September 2001. Medical experts estimated later that staging the match may have cost an additional 37 lives on Merseyside alone, but how exactly this was calculated is beyond mere mortals.

Quite how Liverpool lost this match – and therefore the tie and their holders' place in Europe – is even harder to explain. Except to say, as Jürgen Klopp did later, that Roberto Firmino scored Liverpool's second goal three minutes too late, early into extra time. But at 2-0, and completely dominant, Liverpool should still have closed out this contest, and then we could all have gone off into lockdown and waited for football and the world to resurface. But the other crucial element of what turned out to be a choking defeat was the role played by the respective goalkeepers: Oblak's general excellence, set against Alisson's injury absence and Adrián's horrible mistakes for Liverpool. The ex-West Ham man allowed Marcos Llorente to score an embarrassing equaliser. It comprehensively changed the match and the tie. Atlético, suddenly alive, eventually won the match 3-2 in a contest in which they had only really been competitive for 15 of the 120 minutes played. Klopp moaned later about the visitors' cynical, defensive approach, but that Liverpool had effectively snatched defeat from the jaws of victory was the real truth. Deep down, he knew it.

So, as we drifted home from Anfield, it was to the news that sport and much of the world would now close down, frozen as if in some kind of toxic science fiction movie. Gone was the 2020 Olympic Games, the Grand National and the Wimbledon tennis championships. The 2020 European Football Championships, with the final stages scheduled for England, were now moved to 2021, shunting the women's version back to 2022. In England, the WSL was foreclosed, confirming early demotion for the Liverpool Women. There was also a bit of a local wakener here about both the parlous economic state of the female game and the threat of Covid. The Liverpool captain, Sophie Bradley-Auckland, was unable to return to club training because of her increasingly fraught day job as a care home manager. Respect. For the men, the club's 30-year wait for a league title would be extended into the summer, just as that 1947 weather-affected championship season had ended a 25-year hiatus with matches then played well into June.

It seemed clear that the entire structure of the English game might need to be reset, given the financial problems that would now be faced by smaller clubs as lower league fixtures were abandoned or played behind closed doors (when Portsmouth FC completed play-off fixtures with no fans, top-hatted superfan 'Pompey John' missed his first match, home or away, for 41 years). There was even loose talk, mired in self-interest, of *voiding* the entire season for all professional football clubs in England, thus erasing the greatest and most consistent winning record in the modern history of top-flight English football. As usual, Klopp summed it up best, by honouring the NHS but also calling for a restart as soon as possible of 'the most important of the unimportant things'. Liverpool's supporters were left in some emotional pain, tongues lolling, stranded at the very water's edge. It would take another three months of waiting before they knew they could slake their thirst again – but only in a manner of speaking.

Champions – in lockdown

It was actually Bundesliga football that first returned to UK TV screens in front of empty grounds, but the Premier League finally re-emerged in England on 17 June, behind a wall of tests, protocols and safeguards and in yawning venues, denuded of all sound or colour beyond the suddenly audible yapping and cursing of players and coaches. All 92 outstanding league fixtures were to be completed and televised in a six-week period, a TV sporting bulimic's dream. All matches began with players taking the knee to honour the Black Lives Matter global campaign, as if the game had just discovered the racism in the world and in its own camp. As it turned out, Klopp's Liverpool would need only two matches in this surreal echo chamber to confirm the Premier League title. An away fixture at Everton recalled a similarly redemptive league restart after Hillsborough back in 1989. Both matches ended 0-0, with Everton defending deep in 2020 and Liverpool, without Robertson and Salah, lacking both the width and the guile needed to break them down. Klopp refused to be downhearted.

Manchester City, meanwhile, kept on crunching their opponents, meaning that a tiny hint of concern was in the air when Liverpool faced Crystal Palace on 24 June 2020 in an eerie Anfield. It was misplaced anxiety for an utterly dominant home show. With Firmino and Fabinho in complete control of the centre of the pitch, the home team racked up four goals without reply.

Palace, under Roy Hodgson of course, were unable to register even a single touch of the ball in the Liverpool penalty area, the first such case in the history of Opta statistics. Music was played in the stadium after the Liverpool goals, an act immediately condemned on Twitter and Facebook by Anfield traditionalists. Manchester City now played in the evening at ambitious Chelsea and had to win to delay matters further. It was beyond them, their eighth league defeat of the season. Liverpool had finally won the Premier League title, locked down in their Formby hotel, leading by 23 points and with a record seven matches to spare.

Liverpool FC: Champions League winners, 1 June 2019, Madrid (vs Tottenham Hotspur) & Premier League champions, 2019/20

Alisson
Alexander-Arnold (Gomez) Matip Van Dijk Robertson
Henderson Fabinho (Milner) Wijnaldum
Salah (Origi) Firmino Mané

As some wags pointed out, this was both the earliest (those seven remaining matches) and the latest end to a top-flight league season in the history of the English game. Covid meant that an Anfield communion and wild celebrations with fans were cruelly ruled out, but it did not stop some diehards turning out at Anfield with their banners, flares and supermarket ale. What else were they to do? A mass weekend celebration at the Pier Head produced more local public condemnation. Jürgen Klopp, for once, found it difficult to talk on television and he often left his interviews in tears, praising 'the boys' for their extraordinary effort. Past Liverpool greats, Souness, Dalglish and Carragher among them, were all unstinting in their admiration. None had ever played in a Liverpool team quite so dominant or so resilient; a 'brotherhood', Virgil van Dijk had called it.

At the moment the title was finally confirmed, remarkably Liverpool had dropped a seasonal total of just *seven* points. Further records were still eminently possible: winning every league home match; beating Manchester City's 100 points record of 2018 and their 198 points haul for two seasons combined, 2018 and 2019; beating the record number of league wins in a season, 32, again held by City. With the pressure off, none of these were achieved in the end – or really mattered. Klopp, himself, repeatedly shook his head when asking exactly what sort of team could finish quite this far ahead of a cash machine managed by this coaching genius Guardiola. It was a rhetorical enquiry of course. His point was just how *exceptional* his own team had been. 'Yeah, put an asterisk by our name,' he insisted, to disbelievers, 'one hundred per cent. For winning the title in the most difficult season in the history of English football.' He could be incredibly, occasionally annoyingly smart, this amazing German.

The astonishingly talented young Trent Alexander-Arnold had played all 38 league matches and had 3,664 touches of the ball, more than any other player in the Premier League. Virgil had repelled all comers, often with consummate ease. The magnificent Liverpool front three – Mané, Firmino and Salah – rivalled all those great Anfield forward formations from the 1960s, 70s and 80s. But none of this talk about all-time-greats or records changed anything right now, and who could really blame Jürgen Klopp and his staff as they proceeded to do what many past Liverpool title-winning teams had done – take the rest of the season off? With no fans, the remaining matches felt even more like training exhibitions, mere chores after the real business had long been completed. Losing 4-0 away to Manchester City in an empty Etihad in the first week of July was City's meaningless cup final. More importantly, after 30 years of trying, the job of getting Liverpool FC back on to their rightful perch was finally complete. Celebrating the feat on a platform erected on the Kop facing an empty Anfield was like some weird sort of performance art, but Klopp's men were European, Super Cup, World Club and Premier League champions. And no English club had ever been able to say that sentence. Of course not.

Chapter 14

The Season that Never Was

Stumbling into a pandemic and a crisis

*In which Aston Villa achieve the unthinkable.
Perfidious Everton help do the Liverpool season
in, and a gamble with defensive cover is cruelly
exploited. A mid-season crisis beckons – whatever
happened to home comforts? Stability goes entirely
missing with Virgil van Dijk, along with the
Anfield crowd, absent for a record six home
Liverpool defeats in a row. FSG refuses to respond
to a club emergency, as Naby Lad fails to rise to the
challenge in Spain. Even Alisson Becker eventually
loses his nerve. Meanwhile, secretly, Liverpool's
owners are preparing to go disastrously off the rails.*

'Only the noble of heart are called to difficulty.'

Søren Kierkegaard

After the goldrush

What do you even *do* after a season like this past one? How on
earth do you recover mentally when everything has already been
achieved and, because of Covid, stadiums remain vast ghost towns

hosting glorified training events in the middle of what feels like a ceaseless plague? How do you enjoy this greatest of triumphs and recover the air of invincibility that had informed it after so little time has been made available to reset? And how 'real' does it even feel without your own people to play for, to dance and celebrate among? Imagine the size of the crowds on the streets of Merseyside if this latest Liverpool victory parade had been allowed to happen in the summer of 2020. In short, Jürgen Klopp had built a highly emotional title-winning vehicle working at full throttle, but this machine was now stripped of much of its fuel.

This was, without doubt, the most bizarre aftermath of all of the 19 Liverpool league title successes, as the club set out as champions for the first time in three decades, but with no supporters for company. 'We want to attack it, not defend it,' a bullish Klopp had insisted to journalists in a virtual press conference later when discussing the newly condensed league season. But maybe he secretly knew, despite all the puffed-up talk, just how difficult this title retention was going to prove, a lonely slog acted out for who knew how long again, and in front of a silenced Kop. Klopp had a limited squad in terms of numbers, and a relatively weak back-up having sold Dejan Lovren. He generally shunned player rotation but the new campaign would surely demand it. Manchester City, by contrast, had a sizeable group of expensive conscripts all warming the bench and ready to serve. Klopp's key players had started pretty much every fixture in the 2019/20 season and they were now faced with another intensive trial. Where was the motivation, energy and drive going to come from to keep his exhausted Liverpool team moving forward in this eerie vacuum? And what if injuries finally hit?

To try to provide some answers, Klopp made two key signings in a brief close season, a planned injection of vim for an overcrowded fixture list. The experienced Spanish midfield international Thiago Alcantara was much talked about and fresh from a Bundesliga title and Champions League double with Bayern Munich. Few could doubt his pedigree and class.

Klopp then used the cash from the sale of Rhian Brewster to Sheffield United to help sign a forward off most people's radar. Portugal's Diogo Jota, a modest scorer only, had been quietly impressive for Wolves but really not much more than that. But the Liverpool analysts had spotted hard work and good movement, plus exceptional shot accuracy and impressive successful dribbling statistics at pace. Jota was also a great header of a football. At 24 and £45m, he was an investment gamble, but not an excessive one. Jürgen Klopp, after all, had a net spend of £12.3m on transfers in two seasons, so he perhaps deserved a little leeway here. Jota could also be expected to show some patience behind Liverpool's established attacking talent. Thus, simultaneously diminished and replenished, but at little overall cost, Liverpool were made favourites for the 2021 league title. It did not turn out that way.

The new headquarters of Scouse football

Following a mid-September start in depressingly empty venues, there were no early signs of alarm from Anfield. By the month's end, in fact, Liverpool had seen off Leeds, Chelsea, Arsenal and Lincoln City (in the League Cup), scoring 16 goals to six conceded in the process. But seven matches lay ahead in a savage October. To lessen the load, Jürgen Klopp fielded a scratch XI in the League Cup, losing on penalties to Arsenal, before taking his first-team champions to Aston Villa on 4 October, minus the injured Alisson and with an isolating Thiago already a Covid case. Klopp went for a front-foot threat by playing Naby Keïta in right midfield. The African offered neither attacking thrust nor defensive solidarity in front of Trent, and Jack Grealish ran riot. Ollie Watkins's pace and industry also seemed to unsettle Joe Gomez and a hazy Virgil van Dijk. Watkins had scored a first Premier League hat-trick by half-time, and Villa's industry and precise finishing continued to perplex stand-in keeper Adrián in the second period. It was difficult to keep count in the frenzy that followed, but most newspapers reported it as a remarkable 7-2 home win for Aston Villa. This result was widely interpreted as an outlier, a freak outcome in the strangest of circumstances. Even Klopp seemed to be smiling ruefully: the champions conceding *seven* goals has to be an accident, pure fluke, right? How else could it be understood? Not even Manchester City in season 1937/38, the only English league champions to be relegated straight after winning the title, had been beaten by such a huge margin. It was the worst defeat Liverpool had suffered since the 1950s. Write it off – move on.

But then a 2-2 draw at Everton on 17 October produced what every official, coach, player, fan and dinner lady at the club feared the most: a season-ending injury for the pivotal figure of Virgil van Dijk. Jason Pickford's wild assault on the Dutch defender went unpunished but his actions produced arguably the most damaging single injury in the Liverpool club's entire history. The returning Thiago was also crocked at Everton for a lengthy layoff of his own, so when Joe Gomez suffered a similarly serious knee injury to Van Dijk's in training in November and Joël Matip was crocked soon after, those casual pre-season murmurings about a possible lack of midfield and centre-back cover now began to haunt this campaign.

By this stage Liverpool had left Melwood, their training home for 70 years, to connect up all the men's football development activity in one location, at the extended £50m AXA Training Centre in Kirkby. Now the Liverpool tots and youths could breathe the same air as the stars they one day hoped to emulate. The new development included three full-size pitches and goalkeeping and warm-up areas, along with two gyms, an extended sports hall, pool, hydrotherapy complex and specialist sports rehabilitation suites. Jürgen Klopp even had his own clay tennis court built at what he pronounced to be 'the headquarters of Scouse football'. Perhaps the new location might even reduce Liverpool's mounting injury toll. The Liverpool transfer committee now knew that *both* of its first-choice centre-backs were out for the season, so it had the best part of two months to line up suitable replacements for when the transfer window reopened in early January. Liverpool were still playing well, so Jürgen Klopp would have to muddle through until then, with little in the way of reliable back-up if more injuries occurred. But the coach could wait.

As January's transfer window approached, FSG looked on, hands stuffed resolutely in pockets. Their English 'soccer' investment had begun to slip out of the top four and so beyond the crucial Champions League qualification places. Pallid draws with relegation candidates Newcastle United and West Bromwich Albion started the alarm bells ringing. FSG took stock and finally became (barely) alive only in late January when a cut-price and weak young Turkish defender, Ozan Kabak, was brought in on approval from Schalke 04, a relegation club that had leaked goals and points all season in the Bundesliga. The little-known Ben Davies followed from Preston North End for £1.6m, but he seemed injury-prone and unlikely ever to get a Premier League start. Was this good PR or sporting suicide?

Things would now get much, much worse: an unprecedented *six* home league defeats on the bounce between 21 January and 7 March at what had previously been, under Klopp, a near unbreachable Anfield. The pandemic had certainly undermined home field security across the entire Premier League but this was exceptional vulnerability by any measure. A couple of rookie centre-backs, Nat Phillips and Rhys Williams, were now variously experimented with by Klopp, but they could do little to stop the rot. In those few phases when they were both fit at the same time, Jordan Henderson and Fabinho made up an unlikely centre-back partnership, thinning the Liverpool midfield and simultaneously destabilising the front players. No solution appeared at hand.

Modest clubs visiting Anfield could suddenly plan on snatching a goal against a depleted press and uncertain rearguard, and then comfortably low-block against home forwards suddenly drained of all confidence. It produced results. On 7 February, visiting league leaders Manchester City took a very different route and shot huge holes through Liverpool's defences, with even star goalkeeper Alisson Becker reduced to little more than an error-strewn passenger in a 4-1 loss. Everton won for the first time at Anfield this century, while Liverpool strained to score any goals at all at home from open play. The previously devastating Sadio Mané was starting to look as if football was a completely foreign sport to him. During this period, Jürgen Klopp's press conferences were like listening to that small boy who had asked St Augustine how to empty the ocean using only a seashell. He seemed spent, defeated. And yet, even now, away victories claimed at both West Ham and Tottenham, with Mo Salah continuing to score even under this extreme duress, provided some much-needed sunlight.

When Alisson Becker met Big Sam

It is possible, of course, that director of recruitment Michael Edwards and even Jürgen Klopp himself, had counselled against reckless spending in January 2021 for defensive players who were not first-choice options. Finding top-class men capable of playing in a very high defensive line in the middle of the season is no easy task. In any case, this depleted version of Liverpool still seemed to be thriving *away* from Anfield and it had eased into the knockout phase of the Champions League, with Diogo Jota outstanding. But inexplicably Klopp risked the Portugal man in a dead rubber against FC Midtjylland in December and a long-term injury inevitably followed.

Although Manchester United dumped Liverpool out of the FA Cup in January 2021, RB Leipzig were easily dealt with in the last 16 in Europe, and Liverpool's form slowly began to return. The club's defensive problems, and an injury now to Jordan Henderson, meant that he and Fabinho – the fulcrum of the title-winning team – had started only one match together in midfield all season, that fateful 2-2 draw at Goodison back in October. No title holders could have had a worse time with injuries or, arguably, done so little in the transfer market to resolve them. Nevertheless, Kabak and Phillips (the 18th seasonal change so far to Liverpool's centre-back partnership) could survive against clubs offering little forward threat and there was even a last-minute home win against Aston Villa in April to end the Anfield losing curse. Perhaps the worst of it was now over.

But taking on Real Madrid in the Champions League last eight was to prove a different matter entirely. A listless Naby Keïta was dragged off even before half-time at the Bernabéu, with the home team already 2-0 to the good. Toni Kroos ran the show from deep, missing out the midfield with passes that rained into areas inadequately policed by Keïta, Nat Phillips and Alexander-Arnold. Trent's sudden loss of form would briefly become the lightning rod for wider discussions about Liverpool's dramatic decline, but the truth was that the whole team was spluttering. Mo Salah (who else) eventually clawed a goal back, before comical defending by Phillips and Alisson (again), this time directly from a throw-in, gifted Vinicius a second and Real's third. It was Real's night for a 3-1 win – but hardly Klopp's best work. Two goals behind in Europe was usually enough to sink most teams and Liverpool had not scored three goals at home against anyone since 6 December. For the return leg, local scallies decided to brick the Madrid coach just to try to turn up the heat a little and hint at threatening nostalgia. Liverpool dominated but they spurned chances in a flaccid 0-0 draw. Europe – without fans – for once under Jürgen Klopp was proving to be another country.

The Premier League season was now threatening to drain away with Liverpool, disastrously, in 8th place and, very possibly, failing to make even the top four. Except that a few wins and, at the very last moment, a delayed trip to Old Trafford in mid-May, involving decoy transport, mass policing and evading United fan protests, produced the sort of performance that echoed the recent title-winning Liverpool season, a coruscating 4-2 victory. It was orchestrated from the right flank by a back-to-form Trent, a typically high-wire display of audacious brilliance. It even featured two goals from Roberto Firmino. Where did this late revival come from? It meant that three more wins to end the season could still squeeze this frazzled Liverpool into the top four after all. And do you know what? Things just kept on getting bat-crazier from here, because after a dire showing at The Hawthorns against an already relegated West Bromwich Albion marshalled by Sam Allardyce, in the fifth minute of added time and up for a final corner, it was goalkeeper Alisson Becker who conclusively and absurdly headed Liverpool's winning goal. It was the first time in the club's 129-year history, and the first time in the entire English top flight, that a keeper had scored a goal to win a match. This whole season had been mad and here was the final proof of it.

Alisson had experienced a desperately emotional lockdown in 2021, losing his father to a drowning accident in Brazil in February, with no final goodbyes possible, and then fathering a son in May. No wonder his recent performances for Liverpool had been so uneven. Jürgen Klopp had lost his own, devoted mother in February. The German had looked increasingly distraught and angry in press conferences. It was easy to forget that coaches and players have lives away from the football bubble and the bull pit of the playing area, so this was a moment for some very special emotional bonding. A deeply Christian man, Alisson was in tears in the TV interviews after his goal, and was then embraced with love by his new 'father' figure, one Jürgen Klopp. Both men had used their faith to counter real grief in an incredibly difficult season. And it was interesting to reflect right now on the number of players in this Liverpool squad who – like its manager – had religious or spiritual leanings.

Galvanised by the momentum of this last-ditch win and by rivals' Leicester City's loss to Chelsea, Liverpool easily saw off Burnley, 3-0 at Turf Moor, the club's fledgling centre-backs, Phillips and Williams, standing firm. The former was rapidly becoming something of an uncomplicated cult hero among Reds fans. Here he admitted that a goal-line clearance had given him much more satisfaction than scoring Liverpool's first goal. As Jamie Carragher wryly observed, 'If a double-decker bus drove into the penalty area, Nat would head it clear.' Some fans were even back at Anfield on the last day for Crystal Palace and a routine win: third place had been achieved out of a desperate struggle. It was an unlikely run of eight wins and two draws in the last ten league matches that did it. Had FSG and Klopp secretly known about this ending all along? Just about anything could be believed right now.

FSG go off-piste

As English football and Liverpool FC stumbled towards the end of a season like no other, FSG's reluctance to spend hard cash on a top-ranked emergency defender when it was desperately needed suddenly came into much sharper focus. Advanced plans to form a midweek European Super League of top clubs, including Liverpool, Manchester City and four others from the Premier League, had finally been blurted out publicly on 18 April 2021. This was just as UEFA was about to go to press on a hairbrained scheme of its own to extend the Champions League competition to 36 clubs. It was no coincidence that this latest UEFA plan was designed to address the greed of Europe's elite clubs. Suddenly, FSG's frugal pandemic transfer policy in 2021 began to make much more sense: why waste cash on new Liverpool signings for a top-four finish when the club was to become a founding (and perpetual) member of an ESL from next season? *That* was their insider thinking. The future was already here, and it was good for business.

Allegations about the increasing weakness of domestic leagues underpinned this new venture. Real Madrid's club president Florentino Pérez, an old-stager, had been predicting a European league since the 1960s but, unlike previous plans, this latest venture was rooted in hard cash, a reported €3.25bn funding package from JP Morgan. Merchant banks were to be the new financiers of global football. The aim was to run two leagues of ten clubs each, made up of 15 founders and five annual qualifiers, followed by knockout stages. But why now? The ESL press release archly name-checked the 'instability' in the European game accentuated by the impact of Covid-19.

Co-conspirators (and financial basket-cases) FC Barcelona and Real Madrid each reportedly had largely self-inflicted debts of over £1bn. An initial £350m payment per club and a structural fund would smooth their support for this new venture. Pérez, the only willing public spokesperson for the ESL project, claimed that the world game was currently in 'freefall', that TV viewing figures and the value of rights were declining for elite clubs, which were 'on the edge of ruin'. He added, 'We don't want the rich to be richer and the poor poorer. We have to save football. Everything I do is for the good of football, which is in a critical moment.' Frankly, this kind of top-down altruism was unfamiliar to most keen students of elite European club football. Like seeing a dog talk, in fact.

If this high-end scam had legs, then it would pose an existential threat to the Champions League, some national leagues and to many smaller clubs. It would also undermine a central premise of the European game, something that had routinely puzzled US sports entrepreneurs: how sporting merit and jeopardy defined annual processes of qualification, promotion and relegation. This specific arrangement was suddenly very bad for business, explained Florentino Pérez, because football had four billion fans around the world and 'polls' (research?) suggested that 40 per cent of those people aged between 16 and 24 were no longer interested in the product on offer. They could barely watch a match all the way through. Pérez was talking here about global TV's 'future fans', not so-called 'legacy fans', those who bothered in their old-fashioned ways to actually *attend* matches in Europe. How to deal with this armchair disconnect? Remove financial risk and routinise the fixtures between the elite European clubs, that's how. Guarantee some weekly quality content, ensure regular top sporting entertainment. Apart from its five annual qualifiers, the new league would be sealed off from other competitions and other clubs. It would be a closed cash cow for a select few. The proposal was met with almost universal disapproval and resistance by the European football community.

No going back

What had actually happened here? The top Spanish clubs *were* in deep financial trouble and the Americans in charge at both Manchester United and Liverpool were quite at home to solving sport's financial problems by limiting risk for its owners. To them, it was a nonsense that financial planning was made tricky in European soccer because sporting caprice, or simply better opponents, threatened one's position in the most rewarding competitions. But what was perhaps most striking of all about this entire, miserable ESL 'launch' was just how unprofessional it looked – it had a laughable website – and how unprepared its proponents seemed to be to face the tsunami of opposition it predictably unleashed.

Even Jürgen Klopp, clearly embarrassed and out of the conspiratorial loop, faced searching media questions in a pre-match interview at Leeds United for which his employers had effectively thrown him off the boat. The usually loquacious coach stumbled for words or opinions: he looked downcast and all at sea. It later turned out that FSG had informed no LFC staff at all about their plans, a ploy smacking of paranoia, casual arrogance and possibly incompetence too. To put it bluntly: how does anyone un-fuck something quite as monumentally fucked up as this? After barely 48 hours of relentless negativity and implacable opposition to the proposed breakaway, the six English clubs involved were all forced to withdraw their support. FSG's John Henry finally emerged from behind the bushes with a robotic video message of personal regret, aimed for consumption by the club's sponsors, stakeholders, supporters and staff:

> I want to apologise to all the fans and supporters of Liverpool Football Club for the disruption I caused over the past 48 hours. It goes without saying, that the project put forward was never going to stand without the support of the fans. No one ever thought differently in England. Over these 48 hours you were very clear that it would not stand. We heard you. I heard you.

This was almost the most insulting thing of all. Tellingly, John Henry was unable even to cite the dead league in his statement, so toxic had it instantly become. His apology was only for the 'disruption' caused – like workers explaining a strike – rather than the threat to the heritage of a great sport, an historic football club and to its most loyal investors, the fans. This kind of post-facto faux contrition was unlikely to cut much ice with committed Liverpool followers – although it convinced some. People were angry and hurt about this latest cash-driven misadventure with no wider consultation. Even Klopp himself was soon talking about how the club he now loved had been 'trashed' by this proposed scheme. John Henry went on, presumably struggling to keep a straight face: 'It's important that the Liverpool football family remains intact, vital and committed to what we've seen from you globally, with local gestures of kindness and support. I can promise you I will do whatever I can to further that.' These were familiar themes, of course, ones drawn directly from the hated Hicks and Gillett era playbook of 2007: about common purpose, the ties that bind and the sanctity of the Liverpool 'family', etc. Perhaps this is what hurt the most: that the club's supporters had been deceived and unconsidered. It was almost as if this particular family's most reliable and faithful members had been locked out of their own home as other, more attractive but distant relatives were being shamelessly wooed.

Covid-19 had certainly hit European football hard – a final £120m income shortfall for Liverpool FC alone in 2020/21 – but FSG had also recently sold 10 per cent of its share value, some £538m, to RedBird Capital Partners, a private investment firm that had bought a controlling interest in Toulouse FC. Moreover, Liverpool FC was now valued by Forbes at around £3bn, almost double its valuation in 2019 and ten times the £300m initially paid out by FSG in 2010. Business was temporarily bad, sure, but FSG was hardly on its knees and its English soccer investment was thriving in terms of on-field success and accrued value. Nevertheless, the Americans wanted the club to 'wipe its own face' during the pandemic while the owners had secretly sought out new ways of reducing risk and securing on its investment. This was just the latest (but by far the biggest) in a series of commercially driven misreads that put FSG at odds with the club's fan base. Could trust ever really be restored? That now seemed to be in some serious doubt.

Supporters take hold

A 'cultural shift' in football was now urgently demanded by fans, commentators and even by the UK Government. It would need to involve greater regulation and that the supporters of elite clubs faced their own complicity in demanding global owners who might have no skin in the game but could offer a bottomless pit of cash to spend. We soon learned that fans of Manchester United were not going to hang around wondering anymore. They were primed to challenge their own apparent lack of agency. United fans had long been frustrated by the Glazer family, US carpetbaggers who had registered United in the Cayman Islands, loaded debt on to the club and routinely dipped into the Old Trafford treasure chest – some claimed to the tune of £1bn. For these fans, the ESL debacle was just about the last straw and desperate measures were called for. A few thousand United diehards (and others) organised to invade Old Trafford to prevent the flagship United vs Liverpool Premier League match of 2 May 2021 even kicking off. This was something we had not yet seen: Sky Sports and other media outlets and sponsors thrown into a blind panic by direct fan action. A largely peaceful pre-match pitch invasion in a poorly guarded stadium was an audacious move, a real signal of effective fan power that, at a stroke, took their grievances worldwide.

A fan-led government commission now creaked into delayed action and there was talk of a supporters' 'golden share', the 50+1 model of German ownership with fans on boards, and even the possibility of an external regulator. We would have to wait to see the outcome of all this 'after the stable door' good intention. Without obvious irony, Liverpool soon announced their own plans for a new supporters board, one designed to deliver 'meaningful' fan representation to the club's main arteries of power. But, frankly, no knowledgeable Anfield fan (or any supporter anywhere) was holding their breath right now, dreaming eternally of a better world, somewhere beyond the machinations of brutal oil states, greedy entrepreneurs and breakaway leagues. Even with its globally recruited millionaire stars, the game itself remained largely the same but its defining structures and power elites had become something quite different since Bill Shankly had first ushered his beloved Liverpool club into European competition some 57 years before. That moment of incredible promise and excitement, with fans its very heartbeat, suddenly seemed like a very long time ago indeed.

Fog (clearing) on the Tyne?

Just months after the ESL fiasco the Premier League, in its wisdom, agreed to allow struggling Newcastle United to be bought for £300m by Saudi Arabia's Public Investment Fund. And let me say right here, this fund was definitely *not* connected to the repressive, homophobic, brutal dictatorship in that country, oh no. There were even hints that this same UK Government, the one that so recently had committed to reforming club ownership practices in England, had leaned on the Premier League to usher in these unpleasant new proprietors. Britain PLC, after all, has invaluable business links with the Saudis. The deal was brokered by the familiar, black widow figure of Amanda Staveley of PCP Capital Partners (a 10 per cent stake), a company that acts via 'offshore private equity affiliates' as a vehicle for the investment of Middle Eastern money in sport and UK banks. Back in 2007 Staveley had tried to organise a similar Middle Eastern buyout of Liverpool FC. Now she was the new grand dame at St James' Park, claiming, ingenuously, that 'football is inclusive to all'. The truth here was that the 'bone-saw boys', as *The Guardian*'s Barney Ronay cruelly described the Saudis, were suddenly in the lavish Premier League house. Instantly, they had made this traditional north-east basket-case the richest football club in the world. Go figure.

Loyal Geordie fans were now ritually wheeled out by the press boys to admit that they were, of course, 'conflicted' by the purchase, but had they not endured 14 wasted years of misery under owner Mike Ashley and more than 60 seasons in a row without a major domestic trophy? And did they not now deserve some of the good life, even if their new owners were, ahem, perhaps just a little suspect on certain matters? (The wild public celebrations at the buyout on Tyneside hinted at none of these reservations, by the way.) And, surely, the club's new leader, Mohammed bin Salman, would now be funding public works around the city, including (grotesquely) a project to promote more *women's* football? Amnesty International and other interested bodies looked on wide-eyed.

This 'money conquers all' approach to refinancing some of England's major, historic football clubs meant threatening new competitors were likely to emerge to challenge the existing elite. Which also meant pressure building, once again, to reform the wider European game. After all, these money men from over the hills and far away were not investing their billions into the Geordie nation to risk merely sitting on the margins of the top events when important global influencing work was on the agenda. In short, there was more than just a stench of hypocrisy and morality-laundering to all of this. And the very bad smells that were emanating from the Anfield boardroom and elsewhere around the European club game were unlikely to go away anytime soon.

Chapter 15

On the Shoulders of Giants

Jürgen Klopp and his Liverpool legacy
How should we rank the players of the quadruple-
chasing 2021/22 Liverpool team and where does
Jürgen Klopp fit into that lengthy list of great
Liverpool managers and coaches?

The greatest ever?

'I think four of Klopp's side could get into our best-ever Liverpool team.' This is me driving home, provocative and bored, after Liverpool 4 Southampton 0 in the Premier League in late November 2021. Lacking originality, I go for Alisson, Virgil, Trent and Mo Salah as potential all-time Liverpool greats. Three of these men were recruited by Klopp and one has been carefully managed and curated by him into a unique conversion of the traditional right-back role. But my mate Steve is not having it: he wants Clemence over Alisson, every time, he says. Proven consistency. In the back seats, Riaz makes the case for the utterly reliable Phil Neal over the defensively suspect Trent, while Gazza insists that Andrew Robertson must be included: 'The best left-back I've seen at the club.' (We have not always been blessed in this position.) Fowler, Hunt, Rush, Torres and Suárez are all rightly mentioned for a forward role. The reflective Chris makes the tired but important point that it is difficult to compare players from different eras, but we are enjoying ourselves now and we have a meaty topic to discuss.

On WhatsApp later our larger fan group eventually settles on seven men who *must* be included in this 4-3-3 greatest modern Liverpool team, one made up of players many of us have seen. Which means that both Robbo and Trent can start (sorry, Phil Neal), Kenny is a false nine, and Mo has his spot up front on the right side, just about edging out Rush, Suárez and even the late, great Sir Roger. John Barnes is on the left – none of us saw Billy Liddell in his pomp. Van Dijk is our top defender, Gerrard our best all-rounder, and Dalglish the most complete forward link player. Who could argue? (You could!)

Liverpool FC's Greatest Modern XI?

Clemence

Alexander-Arnold Hansen Van Dijk Robertson

Gerrard Souness Hughes

Salah Dalglish Barnes

This is outrageous, of course. How can *four* players from the team we are currently watching under this German coach better nearly all those Liverpool stars who played in the 1960s, 70s and 80s under Shankly and Paisley, men who hoovered up trophies? Is this simply the curse of the now? Our own history man, JS, prefers the heroic Gerry Byrne at left-back, but he has no supporters old enough to know as much. We lack agreement on a left-sided midfielder and settle, controversially after some debate, on the power and enthusiasm of a young Emlyn Hughes over Ronnie Whelan. Even Ian Callaghan (among many others) does not make the final cut. Kevin Keegan said that you could play for 200 years and never meet another football man as good as Cally. 'How privileged we have been,' says JS later, 'to have seen so many great players at our club.' Nobody disagrees with that, or with the view that we are watching some authentic

Liverpool greats right now, men melded together by a truly exceptional manager.

On the radio later during the Southampton return trip, we hear of a referee at an FA Trophy tie that day who responded to a car numberplate announcement on the public address system by suspending proceedings for ten minutes in order to re-park. True story. We could, of course, debate the best *referee* we have ever seen, but no one is really interested in that outcome. Or has a viable candidate. The retiring Mike Dean reports that fans once threatened to petrol bomb his house, so feelings run high here. Nobody has recently seen a *black* ref with a chance to show us the way, although a novel based on the life of Uriah Rennie has just hit the newsstands. The recruitment of match officials is just one more pathway effectively off-limits in the English game to people of colour – or, apparently, to anyone with any reasonable judgement.

On the shoulders of giants

So now we have established Liverpool's greatest modern team, where exactly does this Jürgen Klopp guy figure in the pantheon of great Liverpool characters and leaders? With his politics and style, he fits this club like few others can. But how does he match up to those who have gone before him? The great Tom Watson all but invented the modern British football manager's role back in the early 1900s, producing two title-winning teams in 1901 and 1906 under the captaincy of the great Alex Raisbeck. Watson certainly deserves mentioning here, a pioneer and an original. Liverpool's management for the consecutive title years of 1922 and 1923 was something of a moveable feast under a powerful board of directors, before a pre-war slump followed under secretary George Patterson. After a lengthy period in the doldrums, it was left to the troubled George Kay to try to keep the 1947 Liverpool title-winning team on track for a period of dominance. Sadly, it proved impossible. The men who followed Kay found it hard to reason with the miserly Liverpool board in the difficult 1950s, even with Billy Liddell starring. Directors still selected the Liverpool team.

Which takes us to December 1959 and Bill Shankly, the man who insisted on his managerial independence in order to drag the Liverpool club from its long slumber and out of the Second Division. That Shankly invented the modern Liverpool is clear enough. Before him, the club had never really been a consistent force in the game. Shankly not only secured promotion but he won three league titles and two FA Cups. He also led Liverpool into Europe for the first time and won their first European trophy (the UEFA Cup) in 1973. Bill always claimed that he was cheated by scoundrels in not winning the European Cup in 1965. Shankly was a true charismatic, a force barely contained by the game and much more than just a football club manager. His personality, core principles and belief in the people of the city meant that he became both a national icon and a local liberator and leader. He revived the relationship between Liverpool fans and the club's players, a vital link from the 1920s onwards that had been allowed to fade away in the dismal and autocratic 1950s. Only on this foundation did any of what came later become even remotely possible. Shankly stands alone.

It was Bob Paisley's fate to reluctantly follow Shankly. Bob inherited great players and signed others who willingly shared leadership responsibilities, but Paisley was also inspirationally understated, a first-class judge of fitness, talent and character. He was a quite brilliant builder of systems of play. His lack of ego and the simplicity of his problem-solving often undid other managers, men who seemed to see football as unfeasibly complex. After Paisley, Joe Fagan had his one outstanding season in charge, a treble won in 1984, and then Kenny Dalglish responded, astonishingly, when the club was in full-blown crisis in the mid-1980s. It is difficult to overstate Dalglish's wider importance to Liverpool FC over four decades, initially as a great player and then in offering leadership and navigating the choppy waters of the late 1980s and early 1990s. His devotion almost cost him his health but Kenny was energetically back in the Anfield management seat in 2011 when he was once again needed.

By the mid-1990s the whole Liverpool enterprise required updating; it had fallen behind in commercial matters, player preparation, global recruitment and tactical acumen. Or else the rest of the football world had caught up. Graeme Souness tried, unsuccessfully, to modernise and Roy Evans was the last of the honourable boot room bosses (and one of the best), but he had Wenger and Ferguson to contend with. So, too, did the Frenchman, Gérard Houllier, who led Liverpool into the new digital era of data, diets and science and in 2001 piloted the club to one of its greatest-ever seasons. Had serious illness not struck him down, Houllier may even have become a true managerial great at the club. Instead, he paved the way for the Spaniard Rafa Benitez, another deep student of the game, if not of the emotional complexity of some of his own players. Rafa was an anti-Klopp in many respects, a highly talented coach more, perhaps, than a great man manager and leader. Nevertheless, he won major trophies before being hamstrung by the Liverpool leadership crisis of 2007–10, another modern Liverpool boss who was the victim of circumstance not of his own choosing. Brendan Rodgers briefly flickered brightly in 2014 but then lost all faith and direction.

And now there is this bear-like, smiling German, a man with a thousand hugs and a diploma in sports science from the Goethe University of Frankfurt. Like Shankly, Jürgen Klopp has quickly built his own version of Liverpool Football Club but, unlike Shanks, he would soon claim the greatest European prize, as well as the league title and World Club crowns. In 2022 he even started collecting domestic knockout cups. The German clearly has the emotional heft of a Shankly; arguably, he is the first Liverpool manager since the early 1970s to really understand and cultivate the deep well of affection that links the club, its players and local supporters. Kenny Dalglish and Bob Paisley largely managed their own connection with Liverpool fans by saying as little as possible to them, or to the national press. In a very different media age of 24-hour coverage and televised press conferences, Jürgen Klopp often seemed casually to be *playing* the press boys, even at the height of his own personal and professional despair in 2021. Like Shankly, too, Klopp has a hinterland beyond the game, a wisdom, humour and a socio-political outlook that most people of the city could easily identify with. He treated his players as complex human subjects more than just managerial assets. Indeed, both he and Shankly sometimes struggled to let their favourites go in order to rebuild another successful Liverpool family. Rafa Benitez, for one, saw his elite players as more like distant cousins, easily replaceable.

Bob Paisley was a serial winner, of course, the greatest accolade of all. But success could still be built then largely on domestic talent, and his Liverpool often had first choice of all the top British players. Crucially, too, Scottish professionals were still a force in the world game. Paisley briefly suffered domestically against the virtuosity of Brian Clough at Nottingham Forest, while Manchester United and the major London clubs struggled. A wide range of provincial also-rans finished league runners-up to Paisley's Liverpool at a time when losing seven or eight matches was no barrier to winning the league title. By contrast, arguably Jürgen Klopp has worked his tricks by underspending in a much more competitive global era, and at a time when United and rule-busting Manchester City and Chelsea all had superior resources and at least equal pulling power in terms of player recruitment.

The German can be stubborn, perhaps resisting change when it is needed. But what is definitely not in doubt is that Klopp is a great judge of a player and was generating, over 50 years later, the sort of love and mutual respect among the club's followers that only a Bill Shankly could once lay claim to as both manager and club figurehead. Kenny Dalglish and Bob Paisley never had to work that hard at being loved; in fact, Uncle Bob had little need or desire to develop an engaging public persona at all. Even his own players struggled to understand him.

The real question here was whether this avuncular, articulate and warm figure of Klopp in the 2020s could not only continue to foreground his emotional intelligence, his leadership skills and his public popularity to carry forward the legacy of Bill Shankly, but could he keep on winning titles and trophies against the odds in the uber-competitive, cash-rich 2020s, just as Bob Paisley had done on the more level playing fields of the 1970s and 1980s? That is, after all – and always will be – the acid test of true managerial greatness at Liverpool Football Club.

The bitter end?

If Jürgen Klopp does see out his newly agreed 11-year period as manager at Anfield – so beating Bob Paisley's stint and behind only Bill Shankly in managerial club service in the modern era – this incredible German will surely remain in the hearts of all Liverpool fans and in the mind of pretty much every player, employee and volunteer who has, in some way, come under his jurisdiction. Journalists will miss him too. Like Shankly himself, Klopp is without doubt an exceptional human being, as well as being a truly great football coach. (Ridiculously, in a recent international poll it is Cristiano Ronaldo who is said to be chasing Obama and Bill Gates for the title of the most admired man in the world. All sensible people know it really should be Klopp.)

The question we were left with, nevertheless, is one Liverpool fans dared not even talk about as this wonderfully crazy quadruple season was winding down painfully in the spring of 2022. It is the same question that the Liverpool club has faced at various moments throughout its history, often with little warning. It happened way back in 1914 with the death of Tom Watson, but also in 1974, in 1983 and again in 1991. This time it is: how are we ever going to replace the great smiling hugger, this powerful moral presence and driven team builder and strategist if he does leave us forever in 2026? Perhaps, if not knowing the answer is better than knowing a bad answer, then simply do not bother asking the question. COYR!

Sources

A'Court, A. *My Life in Football*. The Bluecoat Press, 2003.

Allt, N. (ed.) *Here We Go Gathering Cups in May*. Canongate, 2007.

Allt, N. *The Boys from the Mersey: The Story of the Annie Road End Crew*. Milo Books, 2004.

Baldursson, A. & Magnusson, G. *Liverpool: The Complete Record*. deCoubertin Books, 2011.

Bale, B. *The Shankly Legacy*. Breeden Books, 1996.

Belchem, J. 'Celebrating Liverpool', in J. Belchem (ed.) *Liverpool 800: Culture, Character and History*. Liverpool City Council & Liverpool University Press, 2006.

Belchem J. (ed.) *Liverpool 800: Culture, Character and History*. Liverpool City Council & Liverpool University Press, 2006.

Belchem J. & MacRaild, D. 'Cosmopolitan Liverpool', in J. Belchem (ed.) *Liverpool 800: Culture, Character and History*. Liverpool City Council & Liverpool University Press, 2006.

Bowler, D. *Shanks: The Authorised Biography of Bill Shankly*. Orion, 1996.

Callaghan, I. *Cally on the Ball*. Sport Media, 2010.

Carter, N. *The Football Manager: A History*. Routledge, 2006.

Chinn. C. *Better Betting with a Decent Feller: A Social History of Bookmaking*. Aurum Press, 2005.

Collins, T. *Rugby's Great Split: Class, Culture and the Origins of Rugby League Football*. Cass 1998.

Corbett, J. *Everton: The School of Science*. Macmillan, 2003.

Corbett, J. 'Shankly: Forgotten Man', *Observer Sports Monthly*, November 2009.

Cowley, J. *The Last Game: Love, Death and Football*. Simon and Schuster, 2009.

Dalglish, K. *Dalglish: My Autobiography*. Hodder & Stoughton, 1996.

Dicks, J. *Terminator: The Authorized Julian Dicks Story*. Polar Publishing, 1996.

Dohren, D. *The Ghost on the Wall: The Authorised Biography of Roy Evans*. Mainstream Publishing, 2004.

Doig, E. & Murphy, A. *The Essential History of Liverpool*. Headline, 2003.

Du Noyer, P. *Liverpool Wondrous Place: Music from the Cavern to the Coral*. Virgin Books, 2004.

Evans, T. *I Don't Know What it is but I Love It*. Viking, 2014.

Fishwick, N. *English Football and Society: 1910–1950*. Manchester University Press, 1989.

Foot, J. *Calcio: A History of Italian Football*. Fourth Estate, 2006.

Gerrard, S. *Gerrard: My Autobiography*. Bantam Books 2007.

Gill, K. *The Real Bill Shankly*. Trinity Mirror Sports Media, 2006.

Hale, S. & Ponting, I. *Liverpool in Europe*. Carlton Books, 1992.

Harding, J. *Football Wizard: The Story of Billy Meredith*. Breedon Books, 1985.

Hargreaves, I., Rogers, K. & George, R. *Liverpool: Club of the Century*. Liverpool Echo Publications, 1988.

Harvey, D. *Football: The First Hundred Years: The Untold Story*. Routledge, 2005.

Herbert, I. *Quiet Genius: Bob Paisley, British Football's Greatest Manager*. Bloomsbury Sport, 2017.

Hewison, D. *The Liverpool Boys Are in Town: The Birth of Terrace Culture*. The Bluecoat Press, 2008.

Hey, S. *Liverpool's Dream Team*. Mainstream Press, 1997.

Hill, J. 'Rite of spring', in J. Hill and J. Williams (eds.) *Sport and Identity in the North of England*. Keele University Press, 1996.

Holt, O. *If You Are Second You Are Nothing: Ferguson and Shankly*. McMillan, 2006.

Holt, R. *Sport and the British: A Modern History*. Oxford University Press, 1989.

Honigstein, R. *Klopp: Bring the Noise*. Yellow Jersey Press, 2017.

Hopcraft, A. *The Football Man*. Cox & Wyman, 1968.

Horton, S. *We Love You, Yeah, Yeah, Yeah*. Vertical Editions, 2014.

Huggins, M. & Williams, J., *Sport and the English: 1918–1939*. Routledge, 2006.

Hughes, S. *Secret Diary of a Liverpool Scout*. Sport Media, 2009.

Inglis S. *Engineering Archie: Archibald Leitch – Football Ground Designer*. English Heritage, 2005.

Inglis, S. *Football Grounds of Great Britain*. CollinsWillow, 1987.

Inglis, S. *League Football and the Men Who Made It*. Willow Books, 1988.

Inglis, S. *Played in Manchester: The Architectural Heritage of a City at Play*. English Heritage, 2004.

Inglis, S. *The Football Grounds of Great Britain*. CollinsWillow, 1985.

Jones, C. (ed.) *The Social Survey of Merseyside Vol. 3*. Liverpool Corporation, 1934.

Jones, S. *Sport, Politics and the Working-class*. Manchester University Press, 1988.

Joyce, M. *Football League Players' Records 1888 to 1939*. Soccer Data, 2004.

Keith, J. *Billy Liddell: The Legend Who Carried the Kop*. Robson Books, 2003.

Keith, J. *Bob Paisley: Manager of the Millennium*. Robson Books, 1999.

Keith, J. *Dixie Dean Uncut: The Last Interview*. Sport Media, 2005.

Keith, J. *Shanks for the Memory*. Robson Books, 1998.

Kelly, S. *Idle Hands, Clenched Fists: The Depression in a Shipyard Town*. Spokesman, 1987.

Kelly, S. *Rotation, Rotation, Rotation*. Heroes Publishing, 2008.

Kelly, S. *The Kop: The End of an Era*. Mandarin, 1993.

Kennedy, A. & Williams, J. *Kennedy's Way: Inside Bob Paisley's Liverpool*. Mainstream Press, 2004.

Kennedy, D. 'Class, ethnicity and civic governance: a social profile of football club directors on Merseyside in the late-nineteenth century', *The International Journal of the History of Sport*, Vol. 22 (5), 2005.

Kennedy, D. 'Locality and professional football club development: the demographics of football club support in late-Victorian Liverpool', *Soccer and Society*, Vol. 5 (3), 2004.

Kirby, D. 'Rome, 1977', in Allt, N. (ed.) *Here We Go Gathering Cups in May*. Canongate, 2007.

Lawson, H. *Elisha Scott's Diaries and Press Cuttings*, Go-Subsist, 2012.

Leigh, S. *The Cavern: The Most Famous Club in the World*. SAF Publishing, 2008.

Liddell, B. *My Soccer Story*. Stanley Paul, 1960.

Liversedge, S. *Liverpool: From the Inside*. Mainstream Press, 1995.

Liversedge, S. *Liverpool, We Love You!*. Soccer Books Limited, 1997.

Lloyd, L. *Hard Man: Hard Game*. John Blake Publishing, 2008.

Lowe, A. *The Man with the Keys of the Bank of Anfield*. Sport Media, 2012.

Lupson, P. *Across the Park: Everton FC & Liverpool FC Common Ground*. Sport Media, 2009.

Macilwee, M. *Tearaways: More Gangs of Liverpool 1890–1970*. Milo Books, 2008.

Macilwee, M. *The Gangs of Liverpool*. Milo Books, 2006.

Mason T. *Association Football and English Society 1863–1915*. Harvester 1980.

Mason, T. 'The Blues and the Reds: a history of the Liverpool and Everton football clubs', *The History Society of Lancashire and Cheshire*, No. 134, 1985.

Matthews, T. *Who's Who of Liverpool*. Mainstream Press, 2006.

McInnes, M. *Homo Passiens: Man the Footballer*. Swan & Horn, 2017.

Milne, G. 'Maritime Liverpool', in J. Belchem (ed.) *Liverpool 800: Culture, Character and History*. Liverpool City Council & Liverpool University Press, 2006.

Munck, R. (ed.) *Reinventing the City? Liverpool in Comparative Perspective*. Liverpool University Press, 2003.

Murden, J. 'City of change and challenge', in J. Belchem (ed.) *Liverpool 800: Culture, Character and History*. Liverpool City Council & Liverpool University Press, 2006.

Neveling, E. *Jürgen Klopp: The Biography*. Penguin, 2016.

Nicholls, A. *Scally: Confessions of a Category C Football Hooligan*. Milo Books, 2002.

Overy, R. *The Morbid Age: Britain Between the Wars*. Allen Lane, 2009.

Page, S. *Herbert Chapman: The First Great Manager*. Heroes Publishing, 2006.

Pead, B. *Liverpool: A Complete Record 1982–1990*. Breedon Books, 1990.

Ponting I. & Hale, S. *Sir Roger: The Life and Times of Roger Hunt*. Bluecoat Press, (undated).

Pooley, C. 'Living in Liverpool: the modern city', in J. Belchem (ed.) *Liverpool 800: Culture, Character and History*. Liverpool City Council & Liverpool University Press, 2006.

Powley, A. & Gillan, R. *Shankly's Village*. Pitch Publishing, 2015.

Quinn, A. *Klopp: My Liverpool Romance*. Faber & Faber 2020

Rollin, J. *Rothman's Book of Football Records*. Headline, 1998.

Rollin, J. *Soccer at War: 1939–45*. Headline, 2005.

Rous, S. *Football Worlds: A Lifetime in Sport*. Faber and Faber, 1978.

Russell, D. *Football and the English: A Social History of Association Football in England, 1863–1995*. Carnegie Publications, 1997.

Russell, D. *Looking North: Northern England and the National Imagination*. Manchester University Press, 2004.

St John, I. *The Saint: My Autobiography*. Hodder & Stoughton, 2005.

Sampson, K. 'Brussels, 1985', in Allt, N. (ed.) *Here We Go Gathering Cups in May*. Canongate, 2007.

Sanders, R. *Beastly Fury: The Strange Birth of English Football*. Bantam Press 2009.

Scraton, P. *Hillsborough: The Truth*. Mainstream Press, 1999.

Shankly, B. *Shankly*. Book Club Associates, 1977.

Smith, T. *Anfield Iron: The Autobiography*. Bantam Press, 2008.

Taw, T. *Football's War and Peace: The Tumultuous Season of 1946–7*. Desert Island Books, 2003.

Taylor, I. 'English football in the 1990s: taking Hillsborough seriously?', in J. Williams and S. Wagg (eds.) *British Football and Social Change*. Leicester University Press, 1991.

Taylor, M. *The Association Game: A History of British Football*. Pearson Longman, 2008.

Taylor, M. *The Leaguers: The Making of Professional Football in England, 1900–1939*. Liverpool University Press, 2005.

Taylor, R. & Ward, A. *Three Sides of the Mersey: An Oral History of Everton, Liverpool and Tranmere Rovers*. Robson Books, 1993.

Tischler, S. *Footballers and Businessmen: The Origins of Professional Football in England*. Holmes & Meier Publishing, 1981.

Ward A. & Williams, J. 'Bill Shankly and Liverpool', in J. Williams, *et al.* (eds.) *Passing Rhythms: Liverpool FC and the Transformation of Football*. Berg, 2001.

Ward A. & Williams, J. *Football Nation: Sixty Years of the Beautiful Game*. Bloomsbury, 2009.

Whannel, G. *Fields in Vision: Television Sport and Cultural Transformation*. Routledge, 1992.

Whelan, R. *Walk On: My Life in Red*. Simon & Schuster, 2011.

Williams G. *The Code War: English Football Under Historical Spotlight*. Yore Publications, 1994.

Williams, J. *Into the Red: Liverpool FC and the Changing Face of English Football*. Mainstream Press, 2001.

Williams, J. *The Liverpool Way: Houllier, Anfield and the New Global Game*. Mainstream Press, 2003.

Williams J. & Hopkins, S. *The Miracle of Istanbul*. Mainstream Press, 2005.

Williams, J. & Llopis, R. *Rafa: Rafa Benitez, Anfield and the New Spanish Fury*. Mainstream Press, 2007.

Williams, J. *et al.* (eds.) *Passing Rhythms: Liverpool FC and the Transformation of Football*. Berg, 2001.

Wilson, J. *Inverting the Pyramid: A History of Football Tactics*. Orion Books, 2008.

Wilson, J. *The Anatomy of Liverpool: A History in Ten Matches*. Orion Books, 2013.

Young, P. *Football on Merseyside*. Stanley Paul, 1963.

Index